MIXED
MESSAGES

A CENTURY FOUNDATION BOOK

MIXED MESSAGES

American Politics and International Organization 1919–1999

E DWARD C. LUCK

BROOKINGS INSTITUTION PRESS
Washington, D.C.

ABOUT BROOKINGS

The Brookings Institution is a private nonprofit organization devoted to research, education, and publication on important issues of domestic and foreign policy. Its principal purpose is to bring knowledge to bear on current and emerging policy problems. The Institution maintains a position of neutrality on issues of public policy. Interpretations or conclusions in publications of the Brookings Institution Press should be understood to be solely those of the authors.

Library of Congress Cataloging-in-Publication data

Luck, Edward C.
    Mixed messages : American politics and international organization 1919–1999 / Edward C. Luck.
    p. cm.
    "A Century Foundation Book."
    Includes bibliographical references (p.) and index.
    ISBN 0-8157-5308-x (alk. paper)
    ISBN 0-8157-5307-1 (pbk. : alk. paper)
    1. United States—Foreign relations–20th century. 2. United States—Politics and government—1945–1999. 3. United States—Politics and government—1999. 4. United Nations—History. 5. League of Nations—History. 6. United Nations—Public opinion. 7. League of Nations—Public opinion. 8. Public opinion—United States—History—20th century. 9. Political culture—United States—History—20th century. I. Title.
    E744 .L89 1999   99-6514
    341.23'73—dc21   CIP

9 8 7 6 5 4 3 2 1

The paper used in this publication meets minimum requirements of the American National Standard for Information Sciences—Permanence of Paper for Printed Library Materials: ANSI Z39.48-1984.

Typeset in Minion
Composition by R. Lynn Rivenbark
Macon, Georgia

Printed by R. R. Donnelley and Sons
Harrisonburg, Virginia

To my two beauties, Dana and Jessica

Contents

Foreword

FOR THE BETTER PART of a century, American foreign policy has had some of the qualities of Shakespearean historical drama. Presidents, secretaries of state, and a handful of others have played great roles on the world stage, meeting crises, raising life and death issues, and rallying public support for vast expansions of international responsibility. At the same time, comic relief has always been readily available—usually with members of Congress smoothly slipping into the roles of fools or knaves. During periods of both hot and cold war, of course, there has been a tendency, as Prince Hal found expedient, to set aside our Falstaffs and meet serious challenges with a stern and unified government. And, of course, the United States actually won the cold war—although just how remains a mystery.

In the real world of governing, even happy endings only mean new beginnings; for example, the demise of the Soviet Union initiated a new and unsettled stage in American foreign policy. There were and are fresh opportunities for statesmanship—and for mischief. Politicians and policymakers alike realized that they had to adapt quickly to new forms of international cooperation, a broader diversity of western opinion, and a complex and novel array of threats to peace and security. But the unforeseen and rapid end of the cold war left little time to reflect on the new world. Without the old certainties, policy seemed to be "made up as we go along."

While attempting to find their balance about their future role in the new Europe, Americans also have found themselves anything but surefooted about the implications of the emerging mix of communism and capitalism in China. Foreign policy scholars, of course, would love to help. But they, too, have been scrambling to find ways to digest the changed environment and offer clear principles to guide future foreign policy. Along the way, numerous groups—both official and informal—have looked at everything from the needs of the military to the restructuring of the CIA. Basic questions, for example, have been raised about the composition of future American embassies and even how many nations require an actual U.S. embassy presence.

International organizations, particularly those created in the wake of World War II, have come under special scrutiny. Is the United Nations ready for a new, more activist role? Are the World Bank and International Monetary Fund outdated? The lack of clear answers to these questions makes it harder to lead and provides new scripts for low comedy. This confusion has been especially apparent in America's unwillingness to meet its financial responsibilities as a member of organizations such as the United Nations. As of this writing, the United States is $1.6 billion in arrears—and there is no resolution to the problem in sight. This situation is partially the result of the American belief that there are serious shortcomings in the way major international organizations, including the United Nations, have operated. It also reflects an inevitable reassertion of isolationist tendencies and, apparently, some think that the refusal to pay represents good politics.

These problems should be no surprise. Xenophobia and isolationism aside, antigovernment politics has become a staple of U.S. electoral campaigns. Just a few years ago, it was considered smart, politically, to close down the federal government. Thus, there is little reason to expect that international organizations will be treated with any more fondness than the homegrown variety. The same paranoia that sees the FBI raid on the Branch Davidian compound in Waco, Texas, as a symbol of the threat posed by an all-powerful federal government also finds plausible the notion of a takeover by UN commandos in black helicopters.

Therefore, when Edward Luck, executive director of the Center for the Study of International Organization of the New York University School of Law and the Woodrow Wilson School of Princeton University, and former president and CEO of the United Nations Association of the USA, approached The Century Foundation about collaboration on this volume, we reacted with considerable enthusiasm. As the pages that follow demonstrate, Luck has an unusual mastery of his topic. He understands the history of American ambivalence about international organizations, and he has recent practical experience that reflects the current manifestation of that phenomenon. Luck makes especially clear, however, that merely labeling U.S. attitudes and politics as "ambivalent" in this area may do more to confound than to increase our comprehension. This problem emerges most sharply in the generalized and often oversimplified style of many press accounts on this topic. He reminds us, by reviewing the polling data, that many nations share much the same mixed feelings about and frustrations with the United Nations as are found in the United States. American exceptionalism, then, is found not in the nature of the nation's popular attitude toward the United Nations, but rather in the recalcitrance of its politics—especially when it comes to paying its bills. Of course, in a more fundamental sense, the exceptionalism explanation is quite powerful. We Americans see—and have evidence to back this perception—our place in the world as unique. All too often, we have no interest in multinationalism; to us, all relationships are bilateral in the sense that it is us and them—whether they be one or a hundred other nations.

The Century Foundation has a long history of supporting works that examine multinational organizations and America's role in them, including Jerome Levinson and Juan de Onis's *The Alliance That Lost Its Way;* David Calleo's *Beyond American Hegemony: The Future of the Western Alliance;* Patrick Low's *Trading Free: The GATT and U.S. Trade Policy;* Max Jacobson's *The United States in the 1990s; U.S. Policy and the Future of the United Nations,* edited by Roger Coate; and Rosemary Righter's *Utopia Lost: The United Nations and World Order.* This book continues that work. In it, Luck marshals overwhelming evidence of public support for the United Nations and international engagement through multinational organizations. Still, the increasing partisanship of U.S. politics generally is reflected in the sharpening of congressional struggles about U.S. participation in these organizations.

In this environment, fresh ideas about how to break the current political deadlock are especially desirable. And Luck offers them. Despite the deep roots of American ambivalence, he is convinced that opportunities exist for real progress. The road ahead will not be easy, he argues, but a sensible and practical route is available. His idea of a new "domestic compact," based on hardheaded analysis of the strengths and weaknesses of the United Nations, in particular, could provide a foundation for new policymaking. Moreover, his notion of a new "international compact" between the United States and other UN member states could serve as the centerpiece of foreign policy in the next decade.

Reform agendas, if they are ambitious, are never the easiest course. Procrastination and temporizing almost always have greater political appeal in the short run (and politicians must, perforce, live in the here and now).

But much is at stake. American exceptionalism encompasses not only ambivalence about international bodies, it expresses the indispensable quality of American world leadership. Our elected officials, therefore, would do well to heed Edward Luck's analysis of the current stalemate and his formula for progress. On behalf of The Century Foundation, I commend him for this important contribution to our understanding of one of the major foreign policy issues before the nation.

Richard C. Leone, *President*
The Century Foundation
June 1999

Preface

FOR AN EXERCISE that began as something of a personal and singular quest, this book project has benefited from the invaluable assistance of an impressive number of institutions and individuals. While the responsibility for the final product rests with the author alone, his silent partners did a great deal to improve the volume and ensure its timely completion.

The Century Foundation provided much more than the essential financial support for the enterprise. Under Dick Leone's leadership, the Foundation offered consistently sound advice on the shape, substance, production, and marketing of the volume, without attempting to steer its policy conclusions. At the inception of the project, David Callahan made sensible suggestions about the initial project outline. Mort Halperin and Dick Leone reviewed the first draft of the manuscript in late May 1998, offering a number of insightful comments that improved subsequent drafts greatly. Throughout the publishing and marketing process, Beverly Goldberg's experienced judgment proved to be a considerable asset.

The writing phase of the project coincided with the period that Michael Doyle, Tom Franck, and I were putting in place the cornerstones of a new joint venture: the Center for the Study of International Organization of the New York University School of Law and the Woodrow Wilson School of Princeton University. I owe my colleagues at these two schools a debt of gratitude for their forbearance, as well as for their encouragement. This is one of the first publications to emerge from the Center, which conducts policy research and international dialogue on ways of renovating existing global and regional institutions and of developing fresh means of cooperation among governments and civil society. In that context, it is a pleasure to acknowledge the extensive international organization holdings and the consistently helpful staff of the NYU libraries, and particularly of the law library.

During the initial phases of the research, focusing on the first two decades of this century, I was able to use the excellent collections of Columbia University. John Ruggie, then dean of the School of International and Public Affairs, facilitated my appointment as a visiting scholar at the school for the 1996–97 academic year. At that point, Edgar Chen of Princeton University did some helpful research on congressional attitudes during the UN's early years.

Between August 1996 and May 1997, I interviewed a number of the more articulate and experienced permanent representatives to the UN in order to get their personal views on US participation in the world body. None of the points made in this book, however, should be ascribed to any of them, since I thought it best to use their interviews solely for general background purposes. They included Celso Amorim of Brazil, Richard Butler of Australia, Robert Fowler of Canada, James Jonah of Sierra Leone, Colin Keating of New Zealand, Razali Ismail of Malaysia, Prakash Shah of India, Juan Somavía of Chile, and John Weston of the United Kingdom. I am most grateful for their cooperation and for their valuable insights.

I also owe a considerable debt to the detailed and thoughtful suggestions of a number of scholars who reviewed the manuscript for the Century Foundation or the Brookings Institution Press, including Brewster C. Denny, Richard Gardner, Ole Holsti, and Michael Mastanduno. Professor Gardner also generously granted permission for the use of and quotations from his personal white paper on the article 19 crisis. Everyone at the Brookings Institution Press was most helpful, but none more so than Martha Gottron, who proved to be a most agile and congenial editor.

Throughout this project, I have depended heavily on the skills, dedication, and consistent good humor of Marilyn Messer. She not only word processed innumerable drafts of each chapter, but also proved to be an unusually keen and persistent researcher, often finding sources that I had overlooked or misplaced. Quite literally, this work could not have been completed without her untiring efforts.

By example, my father, Professor David J. Luck, taught me the love of writing from an early age. For that, and for my family's encouragement and patience through this exercise, I will be eternally grateful.

List of Acronyms

Administrative Committee on Coordination (ACC)
Advisory Committee on Administrative and Budgetary Questions (ACABQ)
American Institute of Public Opinion (AIPO)
Economic and Social Council (ECOSOC)
Food and Agriculture Organization (FAO)
General Accounting Office (GAO)
General Agreement on Tariffs and Trade (GATT)
International Civil Service Commission (ICSC)
International Labor Organization (ILO)
International Monetary Fund (IMF)
International Trade Organization (ITO)
Multilateral Agreement on Investment (MAI)
National Rifle Association (NRA)
North Atlantic Treaty Organization (NATO)
Organization of American States (OAS)
Organization for Economic Cooperation and Development (OECD)
Program on International Policy Attitudes (PIPA)
United Nations Children's Fund (UNICEF)
United Nations Development Programme (UNDP)
United Nations Educational, Scientific, and Cultural Organization (UNESCO)
United Nations Emergency Force (UNEF I)
United Nations High Commissioner for Refugees (UNHCR)
United Nations Operation in the Congo (UNOC)
United Nations Relief and Rehabilitation Administration (UNRRA)
United Nations Special Commission (UNSCOM)
Work Projects Administration (WPA)
World Health Organization (WHO)
World Trade Organization (WTO)

CHAPTER ONE

The Price
of Uncertainty
and Division

LIKE PROUD PARENTS, Americans took great pride in the birth of the United Nations in 1945. Seen as the product of American leadership and vision, the UN's principles and procedures were said to reflect the nation's values and traditions. The United Nations was to be a cornerstone of the more peaceful world order sought so earnestly by the American people following the most destructive war in history. Yet half a century later relations between the world body and its most important member state are in a shambles, dominated by finger-pointing, recriminations, and mutual mistrust. The same, and worse, could be said of congressional-executive relations in the formulation of U.S. policies toward the UN. Unless steps to mend these deep rifts are taken soon, one of the first acts of the new millennium could well be the revocation of the U.S. vote in the General Assembly. Unless an unforeseen payment is made, by January 2000 the United States will be more than two years behind in its payments to the world body and subject to the article 19 penalty of loss of vote.

Although only a symptom of the underlying political malaise, financial issues serve as a barometer of the degree of American engagement. At the UN's founding, the United States shouldered almost half of the financial burden with hardly a complaint. In 1999 Congress balks at paying a quarter of the UN budget and refuses to settle U.S. arrears until the other member

1

states agree to lower its assessment and to accept a long list of unilateral demands. With $1.6 billion in arrears, the United States in 1999 owes about twice as much to the UN as all 184 other member states combined.[1] Spurred by a warning from the General Accounting Office, an arm of Congress, that the United States could lose its vote in the General Assembly by January 1999 for being two years in arrears, a divided Congress in late 1998 came up with just enough dues money to postpone the day of reckoning for another year.[2] Indignant, the other member states then added fuel to the fire by voting to keep the United States off of the General Assembly's chief budget oversight committee, on which it had customarily served as the body's top contributor,[3] and by threatening to break the informal no-growth rule in the 2000–2001 budget.[4]

As the world organization verges on bankruptcy and partisan bickering divides America, this volume seeks to take a serious and sober look at the roots of American ambivalence toward the UN and its predecessor, the League of Nations. It asks: what has happened to turn U.S.-UN relations on their head? What led to such a dramatic reversal, as America turned from being the greatest champion to the loudest detractor of the UN and other international organizations? Why have Americans again and again been the first to create international institutions and then the first to forsake them? Why, eight decades after the historic Senate debate over the League of Nations, are the core issues—regarding America's place in the world and the effects on its national sovereignty of participation in international bodies— still unresolved and as divisive in 1999 as they were in 1919? What is it about the American political culture that has permitted ever closer economic, social, technological, and political ties with the rest of the world even as the opposition to institutionalizing these relationships has hardened? Are there any prospects for healing these feuds and for forging a bipartisan consensus on policies and strategies for the twenty-first century? Or are we headed for another century of doubt, uncertainty, and inconsistency?

In seeking answers to these queries, this volume considers ambivalence to be a phenomenon that operates on two levels: on the personal level it is reflected in the attitudes of individual citizens; while on the collective level it is expressed in inconsistent, hot and cold, national policies toward international organizations. Because these two levels of doubt tend to feed off each other, the analysis addresses them as parts of a single phenomenon. It seeks to trace the roots of the growing doubts that appear to have sapped the enthusiasm of many individual supporters of the UN, and before them of the League. It also seeks to shed light on the persistent divisions within the

American body politic that have resulted in U.S. national policies that have seemed to others to reflect uncertain and at times self-defeating tactics and strategies. The United States has had, and continues to have, more than its share of both hard-core supporters and hard-core opponents of international organization. In between have been large numbers of people lacking either strong views or much information about the procedures and activities of these bodies. So America is both divided and ambivalent.

Given the predominantly negative tenor of much of the recent commentary in this country regarding the United Nations, it is easy to forget that over the course of this century, as well as during the nineteenth century, America has produced some of the world's most vigorous enthusiasts for international cooperation and most creative architects of international institutions.[5] At the close of the First World War, President Woodrow Wilson was the prime advocate of the League of Nations, and a generation later during the final stages of the Second World War, presidents Franklin D. Roosevelt and Harry S Truman were the prime movers behind the creation of the United Nations. Yet the U.S. Congress, with Republican majorities, rejected participation in the League and in recent years has brought the UN to the brink of insolvency. These seemingly intractable contradictions in American perspectives have resulted in an almost perpetual crisis in U.S. relations with the very bodies it has worked to establish. To borrow Yogi Berra's trenchant phrase, with each new round of recriminations, one gets a weary sense of déjà vu all over again. In recent years, the chronically thin ice on which the U.S.-UN relationship rests has worn thinner and thinner, as it approaches the point where it will simply give way altogether.

Persistent strains of idealism and cynicism, multilateralism and unilateralism, internationalism and isolationism have long coexisted across the spectrum of American thinking. The resulting ambivalence, the product of fundamentally contrary political impulses, is as alive and as destructive in 1999 as it was in 1919 when President Wilson and Senator Henry Cabot Lodge clashed over the soul and shape of America's place in the world. Their struggle has yet to be resolved either intellectually or politically, leaving Washington unable to abandon world organization or to give it full support. Again, a president and a chairman of the Senate Foreign Relations Committee have asserted contrasting views not only of America's global interests and obligations, but also of the relative roles of the executive and legislative branches in translating these impulses into the nation's foreign policy. Again, the president appears unlikely to prevail. The latest round—in which President Bill Clinton vetoed the bill to pay a portion of the UN arrears because of unrelated abortion language attached by Congress—served chiefly to perpetuate the congressional-executive stalemate, producing no winners either in Washington or at the UN.[6]

If this see-saw pattern is so well established, why then should it be of such urgent concern? What are the costs of ambivalence to U.S. national interests? First, in an era in which problem solving in field after field demands closer cooperation among sovereign nations, the effects of America's split personality are reaching far beyond the United Nations and its finances. Among the recent victims of American ambivalence has been the potential for consistency, vision, and leadership in U.S. policymaking. In those rare cases when strategies are actually formulated in Washington, the resources to carry them out are frequently lacking, for the refusal to pay UN dues has been mirrored in cutbacks in the funding of U.S. foreign relations across the board, including for peacekeeping, foreign aid, and the International Monetary Fund.

Over the long haul U.S. ambivalence has led to less tangible but more consequential casualties. These include the integrity of international law, the viability of the global financial system, the credibility of American commitments to international undertakings, and relationships with key allies, whose often self-righteous reactions have contributed to a downward spiral of recriminations and mistrust. In the process, the quest to make the UN a more efficient and effective instrument for achieving important interests that the United States shares with others has been undermined and could be jeopardized altogether. The United Nations, a flawed but unprecedented experiment in international cooperation, has been left in limbo, neither strengthened nor abandoned. Instead, it drifts like an over-aged adolescent, yet to achieve its potential, clueless about what the future holds. None of this serves U.S. national interests, for in the end the nation will have fewer viable tools with which to conduct foreign affairs and a lessened sense of national will and purpose in a world in which both opportunities and dangers are growing. A weakened UN means fewer options for U.S. foreign policy.

It would be far too simplistic to conclude that American idealism created the UN and that American skepticism is killing it, for many hands have played a part in both. But the hot and cold pattern is worrisome, especially in a nation of such power and dynamism that its leadership is a prerequisite for most successful multilateral undertakings. The costs have been high not only for America's reputation, but more generally for the prospects of organizing effective multilateral coalitions when needed to respond to crises that the United States cannot or will not handle unilaterally. A vicious cycle is at work here. American skepticism about the viability of international institutions undermines their performance, reinforcing the doubts even as they become self-fulfilling.

Paradoxically, the mutual crisis of confidence between the United States and the rest of the UN community is deepening at a point when the values and perspectives of the United States and those of other member states seem in some important respects to be converging as the scope of their mutual interests expands.[7] A once-in-a-generation opportunity to reinforce the mechanisms, reassert the values, and broaden the base for international cooperation could well be lost on the shoals of domestic as well as intergovernmental bickering. Such an outcome would be a major opportunity cost. To a worrisome extent, in the halls of both the UN and Congress, a mean and narrow contrariness appears to have replaced the high aspirations and community spirit that led to the creation of the world body.

For once, these negative trends cannot be traced to any cataclysmic or unusually foolish event at the UN, nor to a groundswell of public resentment. The precipitating trends—such as the end of the cold war consensus on American foreign policy, the rise of single-issue interest groups, and the sharpening of partisan divisions—took place within the American body politic, not within the world organization. In fact, as detailed in chapter 10, public opinion surveys suggest that growing numbers of Americans are reluctant to act unilaterally, are seeking partners to share the nation's international burdens, and are increasingly conscious of the transnational nature of many of the biggest challenges facing the United States. Appreciation of the links between "domestic" and "international" issues appears to be growing, even as faith in the adequacy of the established network of intergovernmental institutions—with the UN at its center—is wavering. The message of internationalism may well be taking hold, but its flip side is likely to be rising demands and expectations for truly effective implementation and for forms of international organization that not only sound good, but are up to the demanding tasks at hand. In the beginning American idealism was critical to getting the UN off the ground. Over time, the projection of ideals has inevitably given way to evaluations of performance, to assessments of whether the UN is equipped to begin to fulfill the dream. Questions of decisionmaking, management, and finance therefore have come to the fore.

The greatest irony, of course, is that Americans—from presidents to jurists, from educators to environmentalists, and from humanitarians to arms controllers—have been in the vanguard of the movement to build international norms, laws, and institutions at least since the mid-nineteenth century. By the early years of the twentieth century America had a well-established tradition of support for international adjudication and arbitration and for the convening of the Hague peace conferences to address arms limitations and humanitarian rules of warfare. Beginning with the League to Enforce Peace, a succession of high-profile private organizations have mobilized many of the nation's most prominent Republicans, Democrats, and independents to speak out in support of stronger and more effective global institutions.[8] Fed by the internationalist instincts of many of America's greatest philanthropists, far more extensive scholarship and policy analysis of these matters have been undertaken in the United States than anywhere else, and student interest and enthusiasm remain high. All-American notions of human rights, democratic government, and law and order have repeatedly been projected onto a global screen, gaining broad international acceptance over time.

Yet even while the participation of American private citizens, non-governmental groups, relief organizations, and scholars in UN conferences, studies, and programs appears to be expanding, official ties face debilitating political and resource constraints. From Eleanor Roosevelt onward, Americans have played leading roles in the codification of international conventions for the protection of human rights, only to have the Senate delay for years—sometimes indefinitely—its consent to ratification. During 1997 and 1998, for example, U.S.-based advocacy groups championed international agreements, on issues such as land mines and a wide-ranging International Criminal Court, that went beyond what even the Clinton administration could accept. The chairman of the Senate Foreign Relations Committee, meanwhile, had already declared that in terms of Senate consideration, the court would be "dead on arrival."[9] A similar pattern of dual voices has been followed in such varied fields as arms control, trade, and environmental protection, as American prophets of international order have found more receptive audiences abroad than at home.

American ambivalence, like an artichoke, is a many-layered phenomenon. Uncovering the heart of the matter entails peeling away layer after layer in an effort to understand how they interact and how each contributes to the overall pattern of dissonance. This book is the first to trace the evolution of American attitudes and policies toward the League of Nations and the United Nations. During the course of my research, it became increasingly evident that eight core themes in the domestic debate have been repeated generation after generation. They remain unresolved, defining an unending political struggle that will undoubtedly be one of the legacies of this century to the next. These themes are addressed in the following order, with the most fundamental and stubborn ones first: (1) the notion of American exceptionalism and the difficulty of reconciling national power with the decisionmaking processes of global bodies; (2) the preservation of national sovereignty in an increasingly interdependent world; (3) negative attitudes toward other countries, races, and social systems; (4) the minority status in which the United States frequently finds itself in international forums; (5) the dilemmas involved in putting military forces at the disposal of global organizations; (6) the extent to which national security interests and international commitments overlap; (7) persistent questions of UN reform and restructuring; and (8) recurrent squabbles over burden sharing and the financing of international organizations. On the surface, at least, much of the current policy debate revolves around the last four themes. These issues, however, would be far more manageable if progress could be made in addressing the more fundamental concerns encompassed in the first four themes relating to America's place and comfort level in global political bodies. Each of these concerns, it should be stressed, is made far more problematic by the peculiarities of the American political system, with its separation of powers, single-issue constituencies, partisan divisions, and domestic preoccupations.

The first of the eight themes is addressed in chapter 2, which speaks of some of those national characteristics that make America different, in its political culture, in terms of its substantive interests, and its preeminent power. The resulting sense of exceptionalism makes it hard to blend the United States smoothly into the ranks of the so-called community of nations and into the rules and procedure of intergovernmental decision-making processes. Surely Americans are not the only nationalistic people in the world, yet the nation's history, geography, power, and political culture do work to set it apart. Most Americans believe in international organization, but as a way of propagating American values, not of compromising them in order to get along with the majority. Confident in their nation's principles and bound by the demands of both geopolitics and domestic political forces, time and again U.S. representatives have seemingly relished playing in global forums the part of the lonely voice for national interests and values.

Yet, as chapter 3 relates, Americans, for all of their power and self-assurance, are also remarkably sensitive to any attempts to impose limits on individual liberties or on the nation's freedom of action. The United States, as a result, is as jealous of its national sovereignty as any small nation less able to protect its interests and prerogatives. This strain of sovereignty consciousness has tended to compound America's traditional wariness about government at all levels, particularly when it appears distant and unaccountable. If global government looks to some Americans as a panacea, to many others it looms more as a threat to their individuality and to their treasured way of life.

Chapter 4 introduces a third contrary element of the national political culture: the tendency to mistrust the motivations, values, and intentions of others who are thought to have designs on America's affluence and freedom. The Senate debate over the League of Nations, for instance, combined pervasive suspicion of European craftiness with sometimes virulent expressions of racism. Antipathy toward the United Nations was fueled initially by fears of communist influence inside and outside of the organization and in recent decades by caricatures about the nature and legitimacy of developing country governments. For some Americans these prejudices have been reinforced by concerns about immigration and the uneven domestic effects of the globalization of the economy, producing a volatile mix of national and global issues.

Taking this line of analysis a step further, chapter 5 considers the fourth theme—America's frequent minority status—through the lens of a series of cases in which the United States has found itself to be badly outnumbered on important questions within the "United" Nations. Quite prepared to go it alone if necessary, Americans nonetheless have at times questioned the value of the organization when the majority of member states appeared to hold divergent objectives from those of the nation that did so much to give it birth. By focusing on congressional reactions to a series of crises in U.S.-UN relations, the chapter seeks to shed some light both on the growing interplay between domestic and international agendas and on the evolution of the kinds of disputes that have triggered the most negative and sustained reactions on Capitol Hill. One of the worrisome conclusions is that domestic political forces are pushing U.S. policies in one direction, while the dynamics of interdependence and multilateral diplomacy are pushing them in another, sharpening the dissonance within the American body politic on issues of international law and organization.

Chapters 6 and 7 address two sets of themes that define a dilemma that has baffled international institutions throughout this century: how to organize sovereign nation states for the pursuit of common concerns for peace

and security. No other questions have had a greater impact on the motivations for creating, curbing, or abandoning global organization. As chapter 6
explicates, Americans have been persistently divided about what to seek or
expect from either the League or the UN in this regard. From Cambodia to
Kosovo, should peace or justice be given the higher priority, and can peace
be obtained through war? For all of their idealism about the need for collective action to discourage or punish aggression, the American people have
tended to want to have their cake and eat it too, to maintain both reliable
collective security mechanisms and national freedom of action. UN supporters have too often denigrated the need for a strong national defense,
while the advocates of a strong military have too often dismissed the utility
of effective forms of international cooperation. As a result, the symbiotic
relationship between these goals tends to get lost in the polarized debate
about U.S.-UN relations.

Perversely, since the end of the cold war, these sources of ambivalence
have been compounded by a pervasive national uncertainty about where
American interests lie and what price Americans are willing to pay to secure
them. These doubts have been compounded by nagging congressional-
executive disputes over their relative war powers. These questions are considered in chapter 7, along with two controversial matters—who should
command international forces, and who should pay for them—that were
never settled in the establishment of either the League or the UN. These
unresolved issues continue to plague U.S.-UN relations today, limiting the
world organization's capacity to carry out its primary founding mandate
and reducing public confidence in it.

Chapter 8 deals with a source of persistent criticism of international
organizations in general and of the UN in particular: their structures and
management. Calls for reform, it turns out, are as old as the organizations
themselves, and as American as apple pie. Supporters and skeptics, idealists
and realists are all quick to agree that the United Nations is in dire need of
a major overhaul, that its bureaucratic structures and antiquated personnel
system stand in the way of effective performance. The problem, of course, is
that, beyond a common perception that the UN does not work well, different constituencies have very different views concerning what should be
done about it. There is no common vision or agenda regarding what a
reformed UN should look like. Some advocate a stronger, more independent body and others a smaller, less ambitious, and tamer one. As with military matters, this fundamental divide in American thinking tends to get
translated into policies and attitudes that appear essentially ambivalent.

Addressing the final theme—another question that perennially has been a source of disagreement within the United States as well as between the United States and the other member states—chapter 9 examines issues of finance and burden sharing. Like reform, finance is a matter that has shadowed the world body since its earliest days and that remains an unresolved and controversial question. Over the years, congressional unhappiness with the terms of burden sharing within the organization has manifested itself in one legislative initiative after another to withhold dues payments, resulting in the current financial crisis that threatens both American credibility and the viability of the UN itself. Although the sums of money involved appear modest relative to other areas of U.S. government expenditure, the deep cleavages and layers of mistrust on all sides over financial arrangements are indicative of the underlying political differences that continue to erode the U.S.-UN relationship.

Building on these analyses of the eight key thematic issues, chapter 10 assesses the domestic political forces and trends that have done so much to define and shape U.S. policies toward the United Nations. The chapter opens with a critical appraisal of how the effort to discourage in-depth Senate debate of the UN charter in 1945—out of fear of repeating the League experience—in the end left several pivotal issues unresolved and open to heated debate decades later. It then contrasts the broad surface expressions of support reflected in public polling since the UN's founding with the much more mixed picture that emerges from an examination of trends among various demographic groups, especially the divergent worldviews that have splintered the Republican party. These differences, as expressed on the political level, account for much of the apparent ambivalence in American attitudes and policies toward the world body. Particular attention is given to questions of presidential leadership and UN finance.

In conclusion, chapter 11 draws a number of overall lessons from these thematic chapters, beginning with the caution not to expect miracle cures for such deep and stubborn problems. It calls for adjustments in the policies and attitudes of other member states and the UN secretariat, as well as in those of the United States. A principal recommendation proposes the development of two interactive political compacts—one domestic and one international—to place the U.S.-UN relationship on a new footing. In essence, parallel and mutually reinforcing political reforms within the United States and within the UN community will have to be undertaken if the deeply embedded factors pushing the United States and the world body apart are ever to be overcome.

At this point, a word about methodology would be in order. The scope of the study is largely limited to the League of Nations and the United Nations. As global political organizations, they have sparked more controversy in U.S. political circles than have regional arrangements, such as the North Atlantic Treaty Organization (NATO) or the Organization of American States (OAS), or functional bodies, such as the UN specialized agencies. The Bretton Woods institutions—the International Monetary Fund (IMF) and the World Bank family—with their weighted voting and widely accepted mandates, have traditionally enjoyed broad political support in Washington. With growing criticism of the IMF's role in the recent international financial crisis and with congressional uneasiness about the power of the World Trade Organization (WTO), however, world economic and financial institutions are increasingly subject to the kinds of funding cuts and political pressures from Capitol Hill that in earlier years were reserved for the UN. Therefore, although this study makes relatively few references to the WTO and the Bretton Woods institutions, its conclusions may be increasingly relevant to their future. Nor is international law a focus of this study, yet the implications for the future of the international legal order are also worrisome, because in many cases political support for its universal application and for its institutional base is eroding or under political assault.

The volume's analytical approach is largely thematic rather than chronological both because much of the history has been well documented elsewhere many times and because of the extraordinary, and rather disturbing, degree of continuity in the nature of the arguments on both sides of this core debate. Much of what is being said today on both sides was stated, often with greater eloquence and clarity, in the public discourse leading to the rejection of the League. The persistence of these opposing viewpoints and the lack of concerted efforts to reconcile them (other than during the unusually forward-looking days at the close of the Second World War) have far-ranging, if not reassuring, implications for current and future policies and strategies not only for the United States, but for the rest of the international community as well.

Other than in the discussion of public opinion data, which are of secondary importance to this account, the political and historical assessment presented in this book relies little on quantitative analysis. Also, the author has made little effort to contribute to political science theory, although he hopes that others may find the material presented here to be useful for theory building. The intent, instead, has been to tell the story of America's awkward and hesitant relationships with global political organizations over the course of the twentieth century. To tell this story, the narrative relies heavily on the words of the chief protagonists, particularly members of Congress, who have played a significant role in shaping and leading the national debate. The selection of whom to include has been based on three criteria: official position; representation of a major school of thought on the issue; and how well and concisely the quote captures the core of the argument. By presenting the protagonists in their own words, the book seeks to amplify their voices and clarify their arguments, in an attempt to capture the flavor and emotion, as well as the essence, of the discourse as it has evolved through the course of the century. Few questions of public policy have sparked such passionate, persistent, and polarized debate. To understand the depths of disagreement, one must listen to the words and voices, feel the anger and obstinacy with which they are expressed. Dry assessments of public opinion polls and congressional votes simply cannot begin to tell the whole story. As a result, the narrative includes a large number of quotes, rather than presenting the author's summaries of various points of view. The American political stage, at least until the homogenization encouraged by mass media coverage and concerns about political correctness, was filled with quotable, lively, and sometimes outrageous characters. Their views about international organization, though typically shy on facts, rarely lacked candor. Even today, few subjects produce such pungent rhetoric, particularly in Congress, as the United Nations and the U.S. role in it.

It is not the purpose of this book to weigh the various criticisms of UN procedures and performance, to add further fuel to the domestic debate, or to pronounce judgment about who is right or wrong on each question. There is no lack of partisan voices from both camps. Over the past quarter century this author has been one of these voices; in his view, the degree of antipathy in U.S. political circles toward international law and organization in general and toward the UN in particular has become dysfunctional, skewing policy choices and handicapping the nation's potential for international leadership and for achieving its core interests. It has been the author's experience, however, that much of this debate has revolved around the invocation of symbols and the caricaturing of opposing viewpoints. Frequently emotional, these exchanges have resembled the proverbial dialogue of the deaf, with little effort either to understand the other side or to define some common ground that might provide a more politically sustainable basis for national policymaking.

This book also represents a personal quest for clarity, for a better comprehension of why some prominent and thoughtful Americans—including those with whom the author has dueled verbally through the years—feel so strongly and stridently that the United Nations and other international organizations are bad for the United States. It is a phenomenon that seems doubly puzzling to the representatives of other countries, many of whom cannot imagine either a world without the UN or a UN without a vigorous American presence. One of the purposes of this book is to respond to the hundreds of queries the author has received over the years from foreign colleagues puzzled by U.S. policies and attitudes toward the global body.

The emphasis, therefore, is on the hard-core skeptics, who have been well represented—some would say overrepresented—in Congress, although undoubtedly the more internationalist and legalistic strain in American thinking has been persistent and politically influential as well. Its views, however, have been more widely represented in the writings of mainstream foreign policy analysts and in executive branch pronouncements, and hence are more widely understood, particularly in other countries. On the whole, the volume gives relatively little attention to the virulently anti-UN views of the more paranoid far-right fringe groups, with their xenophobic, antigovernment, and often racist and anti-Semitic messages. Although occasionally these groups may have a modest amount of influence in some states on some local issues, overall their impact on U.S. foreign policy has been marginal at best. Moreover, it would unfairly malign more mainstream and influential conservative views to pair them with extremist rhetoric, as have some UN supporters. This is not a book about straw men or, save one brief passage, about black helicopters. It seeks to gain a fuller understanding of the perspectives of those Americans who have expressed serious and thoughtful reservations about the United Nations, its affiliates and predecessor. At points, the book takes issue with the logic or factual base of some of the more extreme criticisms of the UN, but its primary purpose is not to defend the institution or to refute its critics.

By examining the evolution of American policies and attitudes toward international organization in some detail, the author hopes to throw some light on the larger question of America's place in a rapidly changing world. Several of the domestic factors discussed here, such as congressional-executive relations, partisanship, attitudes toward government, single interest groups, and the growing role of nonstate actors, are relevant to other areas of foreign policy as well. The actions and statements of U.S. representatives in world forums are bound to affect the way other countries view Washington's likely contributions, style, and attitudes on other levels of interaction and on other issues. Whether or not one considers the substance of what transpires at the UN and its affiliated bodies to be important, there is no denying that the world body serves as one of the most visible places in which to make a statement or set a tone about national priorities and preferences. America's ambivalence within and toward the organization has left its mark on relations with both friends and potential adversaries, reinforcing the image that the United States is as uncertain about its interests as it is assertive about its values. Other countries follow the ups and downs of U.S.-UN relations with considerable interest and, more often than not, some consternation and wonderment. The world body, after all, is a collection of nation states, not an abstraction, and it is the one place where each country deals both individually and collectively with almost all of the other nations of the world on an enormous variety of issues. It is, despite a number of structural distortions, a relatively good vantage point from which to take stock of how America views its place in the world on the eve of a new, and hopefully less ambivalent, century.

CHAPTER TWO

A Special Nation, Peerless and Indispensable

If peace is to endure it must rest upon justice no less than power. . . . That does not mean that each [nation] must enjoy an equal voice, but it does mean that each must be heard.

—PRESIDENT HARRY S TRUMAN, 1946

The democracies in the United Nations no longer can tolerate the adverse consequences of the imbalance between power and responsibility, between voting majorities and financial contributions, between obligations and benefits.

—ALAN L. KEYES, 1986

American exceptionalism cannot mean being the exception to the laws everyone else has to obey.

—JOHN WESTON, 1997

THIS CHAPTER ADDRESSES claims of American exceptionalism: whether the United States is—or is perceived by its people and leaders to be—so different in some important respects from other countries that it cannot (or will not) fit comfortably into the decisionmaking and norm-setting structures of global political bodies. This theme, the first of eight considered in this book, has proved to be one of the most common, yet least understood, obstacles to successful international cooperation in this century. The United States, of course, is not the only major power in the world, nor the only one to throw its weight around the halls of the UN from time to time. But the scope and reach of American power, as well as of its interests, are without precedent. Combined with deep strains of idealism and ideology, shaped by a singular history, and conditioned by a political system defined by the separation of powers and by partisan differences over foreign policy, American relations with the League of Nations and the United Nations have proven more persistently problematic than those of any other nation, large or small. For most Americans, moreover, the sense of exceptionalism has been so much a part of their outlook, values, and national character that it has received only occasional question or critical comment.

From this perspective, international law and organization have been expected to express, embody, and extend the American dream, not to challenge or modify it. For example, speaking in 1945 of the UN as if it were a solely U.S. creation, Senator Alexander Wiley, R-Wis., suggested that "for the American people it [the UN] is merely another experiment in a long line of great American experiments." Brimming with national pride, he declared that "America is embarking on a great new adventure. She is cutting her moorings with the past. She is setting forth on the rough and challenging seas of international cooperation, financial, political, and social."[1] Even internationalists have tended to see the United States as the center of the political and economic universe. In their view, America may need the world, but the world needs America even more. As President Woodrow Wilson put it, "the world will be absolutely in despair if America deserts it."[2]

Americans have always seen themselves as special.[3] The nation, carved out of wilderness, founded on democratic principles, protected by geography, and possessing great wealth and power, is blessed as no other. It is a nation of immigrants, a country populated by people drawn to or steeped in the imagery of a place without limits, without peers among the nations of the world. Despite the realities of global economic interdependence, a declining share of world output, continuing vulnerability to terrorism and weapons of mass destruction, and persistent domestic social problems, Americans tend to dismiss the prophets of decline and doom. A series of public opinion surveys conducted during the past decade, according to Seymour Martin Lipset, documents that Americans remain far more patriotic and far more optimistic than their counterparts in other developed countries.[4] As winner of the cold war and the last remaining superpower, the United States retains—at least in the eyes of most of its citizens—its position as a country of unsurpassed power and influence on a global scale. Some triumphalists, trumpeting America's unparalleled good fortune, have recently posited that U.S. hegemony is good for the world and that a true multipolar system would be less benevolent and less stable.[5] In this regard, it is worth recalling that one of the things that has made America exceptional has been its remarkable success in exporting its values and culture. In arguing for the United States to take the "lead in the 21st century as the dominant power of the Information Age," a former Commerce Department official in the Clinton administration asserts that "Americans should not deny the fact that of all the nations in the history of the world, theirs is the most just, the most tolerant, the most willing to constantly reassess and improve itself, and the best model for the future."[6]

America's singular worldview has been shaped, of course, not only by the heights at which it now finds itself, but also by the unique historical path that led it to this exalted vantage point. If the first half of America's history was a period of consolidation followed by geographical expansion, during which the nation engaged with others on a selective basis, then the last half has been a time of growing confidence and of increasing economic, political, and cultural influence around the world.[7] From the days of Manifest Destiny in the mid-nineteenth century, the United States has defined its foreign policy on a grand scale, launching one major diplomatic, economic, or security initiative after another. The United States, after all, has had a mission. In typically grand and inspiring tones, Woodrow Wilson phrased it best:

> The only immortal thing about America is her conscience. America is not going to be immortal because she has immense wealth. Other great nations had immense wealth and went down in decay and disgrace, because they had nothing else. America is great because of the ideas she has conceived. America is great because of the purposes she has set herself to achieve. America is great because she has seen visions that other nations have not seen, and the one enterprise that does engage the steadfast loyalty and support of the United States is an enterprise for the liberty of mankind.[8]

Even isolationists during the interwar years spoke of an America, free of entangling alliances and true to its superior values, that would be prepared to defend its core interests and principles whenever and wherever it deemed necessary.[9]

Two generations later, the spirit and essence of Wilson's vision was captured eloquently by Ambassador Adlai E. Stevenson II when he defended before Congress the U.S. role in the UN as an extension of America's historic mission:

> We have remained not only a great military and economic power but also, more fundamentally, a nation committed to certain universal moral ideals.

> What is still more important is our enduring determination to work toward an
> ever greater realization of those ideals, both at home and abroad. This is surely
> the deepest source of our national strength. If the United States had ceased to
> exert its share of moral and ethical leadership during the past decade, the
> world today would be a very tragic place.[10]

American foreign policy, as a consequence, for most of the last century has
been drawn with sweeping, at times messianic, strokes befitting what
President Clinton has termed "the indispensable nation."

America has been exceptional, however, not only in its immodest perception of its place and values in the community of nations, but also in how
it has viewed its options for dealing with the rest of the world.[11] No other
major power was so positioned geographically that it could have conceived
of isolationism as a realistic alternative, even in the first decades of this century.[12] Yet few peoples embraced the dream of the United Nations with the
faith and fervor of the American people. Tugged and hauled by these contradictory impulses, as well as by the demands of innumerable single-issue
constituencies, U.S. foreign policy has frequently looked ambivalent, if not
simply rudderless. For Washington's foreign affairs practitioners, a perpetual challenge has been to try to reconcile the idealism embodied in both the
isolationist and the internationalist extremes with the requirements of a
successful and sensible foreign policy in a world that does not fully correspond to either vision.[13] Reflecting on his years helping to fashion a realistic postwar foreign policy in the midst of such competing worldviews, former secretary of state Dean Acheson concluded that:

> Two contrary and equally unrealistic ideas about it [the world] competed for
> the national mind, both springing from our earlier history. From the
> American phases of the European wars of the eighteenth century—the domi-
> nant memory of the founders of this country—came the doctrine . . . called
> isolationism. From the experience of the long period of world peace and eco-
> nomic development in the nineteenth century . . . came the dream of univer-
> sal law and internationally enforced peace, embodied and embalmed in the
> League of Nations and resurrected in the United Nations.[14]

His history may have been both selective and simplistic, but Acheson's
recognition that each of the competing strains in American attitudes had
long historic roots seems right on target. Like other executive branch officials charged with the conduct of U.S. foreign policy, much of his career

was devoted to finding a third way, a more pragmatic blend of idealism, national interests, and realistic tactics, whether through unilateral action, ad hoc coalitions, standing alliances, or international institutions.

Although unilateralism has tended to supplant isolationism in an era of globalization, the fundamental domestic political struggles and schisms over the conduct of U.S. foreign policy remain. The core belief in American exceptionalism, moreover, has persisted with only episodic questioning, such as during the Vietnam War protests. In the ongoing debate between those favoring an interventionist or a minimalist foreign policy, using multilateral instruments or going it alone, all sides begin with the premise that the goal is to preserve and protect America's unique assets, historical values, and special place in the world. By and large, the major schools of thought do not doubt that the United States remains the land of opportunity, whose economic, social, and political system still serves as a model to be emulated the world over. They differ instead about the domestic social and economic consequences of a more integrated international economic and political system. In this sense the debate is about means more than ends, about priorities more than purposes. With largely undiminished expectations, America faces the world as a nation confident in its place and power but unsure precisely how to use them in a world in transition. Nowhere are these contradictions and uncertainties as evident as in multilateral institutions. America expects to lead but at the moment is not quite sure where or how, or what to do if others fail to follow. At the same time, other nations are unsure how, some even uncertain whether, to harness the qualities that have made the United States exceptional to common endeavors within and through international organizations. Ultimately ambivalence afflicts both sides of the equation.

The Burden of Exceptionalism

Throughout this century American policymakers and opinion shapers have tended to agree on the superiority of their country's physical, social, and moral attributes, yet they have disagreed sharply on its implications for America's role in the world and in international institutions. To some, the best way to preserve national strength is to use it cautiously and sparingly by avoiding unnecessary, open-ended, and possibly never-ending foreign entanglements and multilateral commitments. The United States, in other words, is strong and independent enough to stand above and apart from international organization, exercising its unparalleled power at times and places of its choosing instead of frittering it away on other nations' agendas.

Avoiding irreversible engagements is said to be the best way to ensure that America's ideals and aspirations are not compromised by the cynical give and take of old world politics. Others have argued quite the opposite for both moral and practical reasons. America's wealth and power, in their view, obligate it to be a leader among nations, to use its strength to assist not only those less fortunate, but particularly those with shared values and interests. To maintain its privileged position in a dynamic world, they would argue, the United States should actively work to build those international institutions and norms that can reinforce peace, stability, and democratic values.

During the 1945 Senate debate over the UN charter, Senator Homer Ferguson, R-Mich., asserted that "we can keep our heads in the clouds of idealism and also plant our feet squarely on the ground of realism. As a Nation, we are great enough for that."[15] In a 1947 message to Congress urging support for the United Nations "with all the resources that we possess," President Truman underlined that "the responsibility of the United States is a particularly heavy one because of the power and influence that our history and our material resources have placed in our hands. No nation has a higher stake in the outcome than our own."[16] A year later, Ambassador Warren R. Austin, U.S. representative to the United Nations, stressed in testimony to the House that "we cannot live alone." From a practical perspective, he continued, "we may be the leading country of the world, but we must live with the rest of the world in harmony and with their help. We need their help as much as they need our help."[17]

Testifying before the Senate in 1963, Ambassador Stevenson addressed the question of how to reconcile U.S. power with multilateral decisionmaking at the world body:

> The United States does not own or control the United Nations. It is not a wing of the State Department. We are no more and no less than the most influential of the 110 members. If we were less, we would be failing to exert the influence of freedom's leader; if we were more, we would destroy the effectiveness of the United Nations, which depends precisely on the fact that it is not an arm of the United States or of any other government, but a truly international organization, no better or worse than the agreements which can be reached by the controlling majorities of its members.[18]

Although Stevenson's analysis deserves high marks for its sensitivity to the requirements for credible international decisionmaking, it implies that the full-scale pursuit of immediate U.S. national interests should take a back seat upon occasion to the larger and longer-term purpose of preserving the legitimacy and effectiveness of the UN as a multilateral institution. This line of reasoning raises the ire of those who argue that American international-ists have tended to put the cart before the horse by forgetting that the United States participates in international institutions to advance its interests, not to support the organizations for their own sake.

Today, these unresolved questions continue to cast a shadow over U.S. relations with the United Nations. Paradoxically, at the founding of the League of Nations in 1919, its supporters and opponents based their argu-ments on the premise that it was America's unsurpassed material strength, its geographical distance, and its democratic principles that made it uniquely well or poorly suited for leadership in international institutions. None questioned whether the United States was a special nation, "the keeper of the conscience of democracy," in the words of Nicholas Murray Butler, the president of Columbia University.[19] At one point, President Wilson asserted that "the Government of the United States is the only government in the world that the rest of the world trusts."[20] At another point, he claimed that "the United States is the only Nation which has sufficient moral force with the rest of the world to guarantee the substitution of discussion for war."[21] Former president William Howard Taft, a Republican and president of the influential League to Enforce Peace, asserted in 1917 that:

> The position of our country is unique. We are the most powerful nation in the world with one hundred millions of people, of the highest average of intelli-gence, of great homogeneity and solidarity, and with greater wealth and greater variety of resources than any other nation. . . . The primacy of the United States among the nations of the world . . . , taken with its real neutral-ity, must give it a great influence in a council of nations which can and ought to be exerted for the world's benefit.[22]

The United States, in other words, could enter into international arrange-ments from a position of strength. It need not fear being manipulated by lesser powers, and its very attributes gave it an obligation to take a leader-ship position in efforts to build a more peaceful and orderly world.[23]

Using similar assumptions to reach very different conclusions, the Reverend Bishop Thomas Benjamin Neely of Philadelphia, a zealous far-right opponent of the League, contended that "if the United States remains independent, it can be arbiter of the world." Indeed, he concluded, "the United States of America since its birth has steadily grown in strength, prosperity, and influence, until the world generally regards this nation as the greatest and best of the nations, and in it has the greatest confidence."[24] William Jennings Bryan, the famed populist orator, antimilitarist, and former secretary of state to Wilson, cautioned that "we cannot afford to exchange the moral prestige of this republic for the martial glory of all the empires that have risen and fallen since time began."[25]

President Wilson, however, insisted that America, with truth and principle on its side, would lead the world to the League and to a new era of peace. In his last public speech as president, just hours before the onset of his disabling illness, Wilson told an audience in Pueblo, Colorado, that:

> There is one thing that the American people always rise to and extend their hand to, and that is the truth of justice and of liberty and of peace. We have accepted that truth and we are going to be led by it, and it is going to lead us, and through us the world, out into pastures of quietness and peace such as the world never dreamed of before.[26]

Given the rising tide of opposition to the League in the Senate and Wilson's unwillingness to compromise on what he saw as points of high principle, his words proved less than prophetic. Perhaps unfairly, Wilson's critics saw his devotion to lofty ideals as self-serving (much as representatives of other countries sometimes accuse the United States of selectively asserting principle as a cover for the pursuit of its own national interests). For example, Elihu Root, the widely respected former Republican senator from New York and former secretary of state in President Theodore Roosevelt's administration, told others in 1919 that he resented Wilson's "arrogant denial of anybody's right to criticise" him. In the words of his aide, Philip C. Jessup, Root "believed that Wilson was a man without convictions or moral principles and was more influenced by considerations of self-advantage than by the underlying principles upon which the American government was founded."[27]

Henry Cabot Lodge, the Massachusetts Republican and formidable chairman of the Senate Foreign Relations Committee who led the Senate opposition to the League, was also prone to invoke America's principles and traditions, but to a different end. Not the isolationist and extremist that he was sometimes accused of being, Lodge came closer to sounding like a unilateralist, nationalist, and pragmatist. He had been a strong supporter of the war against Spain and the occupation of the Philippines. The United States, through the League, had no interest in "meddling in Europe," he stressed, for "we are ready to go there at any time to save the world from barbarism and tyranny, but we are not thirsting to interfere in every obscure quarrel that may spring up in the Balkans." He fretted that the League's Article 19 on "mandatories" would entail the "very grave responsibility" of having to "take charge of some distant people." Although America's Monroe Doctrine responsibilities had required it to intervene in Haiti, Santo Domingo, and Nicaragua, this League mandate "is a demand to go out through Asia, Africa, and Europe, and take up the tutelage of other people."[28] In contrast, A. Lawrence Lowell, the president of Harvard University, found such mandatories "for a backward people" to be "highly meritorious" both "to prevent maltreatment of the native population" and "to prevent a selfish monopoly of products that may be essential to the industry and prosperity of the world."[29] From each of these perspectives, it is accepted both that America is exceptional and that this status poses certain burdens. Where they differ is on how these responsibilities should be determined and how selective or expansive they should be.

The Indispensable United States

When opinion in the United States is divided about the scope of its global responsibilities or about the degree to which it should be engaged in multilateral institutions, the political repercussions are bound to be felt throughout the world. That is as true today as it was in 1919. It is widely believed—rightly or wrongly—that American abstention fatally weakened the League of Nations so that it could not forestall the events that led to the Second World War. As Secretary of State James F. Byrnes lamented in a November 1945 speech, "after the first World War we rejected the plea of Woodrow Wilson and refused to join the League of Nations. Our action contributed to the ineffectiveness of the League."[30] Now, he said, "the situation is different. We have sponsored the United Nations Organization. We are giving it our wholehearted and enthusiastic support. We recognize our responsibility in the affairs of the world." Although it reflected a somewhat simplistic interpretation of the interwar years and of the League's capacities, this lesson of America's indispensability spurred the architects and supporters of the United Nations on both sides of the Atlantic during the 1940s.

    With the onset of the cold war, several prominent Americans called for an organization of like-minded democracies, free of Soviet vetoes. American allies worried that such calls could undermine the U.S. commitment to the new world organization. Testifying before Congress in 1948, Secretary of State George C. Marshall cautioned that by splintering the United Nations "we may be left in the unenviable position of being responsible for the loss of a highly useful world Organization with nothing to put in its place." He noted, moreover, that he was "under constant pressure from other nations to try in every conceivable way to avoid a rupture. They are very fearful, and they do not have the Atlantic Ocean, or our great power, or our great feeling of security to reassure them."[31] Marshall recognized, unlike many of his contemporaries, that for America's friends and allies, participation in strong multilateral organizations and arrangements was a matter of necessity, not choice. Only the United States could believe that it had the luxury of a never-ending domestic debate about the value of its participation in the United Nations.

Yet for the architects of international organization, both the image and the reality of America's uniqueness create uncomfortable and intractable dilemmas. Today, these dilemmas are compounded by the uncertainties of the current transition period in international politics. Lacking reassuring guideposts, many countries, not just the United States, are engaged in domestic and foreign policy soul-searching. As Europe moves ever closer to political and economic integration, America at times appears to be moving away from cooperation in global political organizations, and its once solid commitment to international economic and financial institutions has also been questioned more vigorously by congressional critics in recent years. According to Professor Lipset, in some ways "the United States is less exceptional as other nations develop and 'Americanize.' But, given the structural convergences in economy and ecology, the extent to which it is still unique is astonishing."[32] America's political culture apparently retains much of its distinctiveness.

All of this complicates the task of international organization, for ideally multilateral organizations would thrive in a multipolar world in which power, prosperity, and political values were distributed more evenly among member states. As Marshall commented in 1948, if there is "a complete lack of a power equilibrium in the world, the United Nations cannot function successfully."[33] A balance of power would ease the search for broadly acceptable formulas for voting, financing, and burden sharing. When one—or even two—member states are significantly more powerful than the rest, then it is difficult to ensure that the power relationships outside a multilateral organization are equitably reflected inside its decisionmaking processes. This dilemma has plagued international institutions throughout the twentieth century.

The League of Nations could not succeed, nor ultimately survive, without U.S. participation. Its successor, the United Nations, learned over its first forty years to cope with a world of two superpowers by scaling back its ambitions and shifting its priorities. Postwar U.S. leaders placed a premium on establishing both strategic rationales and political links between the UN and its most influential member. As John Gerard Ruggie of Columbia University and the United Nations has aptly observed:

> The conceptual bridge that FDR, Truman and Eisenhower built between America's sense of exceptionalism, on the one hand, and the international order, on the other, is a remarkable achievement—not only for keeping the United States engaged, but also for helping to transform Europe and to institute multilateral organizing principles globally to a far greater extent than would have been the case otherwise: in economic policy, decolonization, human rights, democracy promotion, and even in the sphere of security relations.[34]

Bridges, of course, are expensive not just in terms of their initial cost, but also because of the continual maintenance that is required year in and year out. More than a little rust and wear can be found on both sides of this U.S.-UN bridge these days. And now, with the collapse of the Soviet Union, the world organization is finding life with just one dominant power to be, in some ways, even more perplexing.

As New Zealand's prime minister said at the UN's fortieth anniversary commemoration, "this is first of all the Organization of the small countries." Reflecting a recurrent theme in the UN political culture, he claimed that "the small and the vulnerable have more in common with each other than with the big powers."[35] This prevalent perspective helps explain why it is sometimes said at the UN—at least in private—that it is impossible to live with or without the United States. In contrast, everyone likes Denmark. No less a source than Secretary-General Kofi Annan, speaking in Copenhagen on September 1, 1997, commented that "ever since the founding of the United Nations, Denmark has been a model Member State—devoted to the aims of the Charter and committed to their fulfillment."[36] But does a model member state have to be small and unthreatening, not to mention wealthy, democratic, and generous? No doubt it is easier to deal with principled small countries than principled big ones. The United States will never be a Denmark, of course, and each brings a distinctive set of qualities and capacities to the multilateral table. An organization of 185 Denmarks would also be unmanageable, leaderless and rudderless, especially when it comes to the maintenance of international peace and security. Its decisionmaking structure would probably look something like the General Assembly, not an entirely comfortable thought for those seeking a strong and decisive international organization. The United States ought to follow Denmark's example of fealty to its financial commitments, but leadership also sometimes requires taking unpopular stances and bucking the group-think mentality that tends to pervade the General Assembly.

Among America's harshest critics regarding its arrears, not surprisingly, are those nations most dependent on Washington's leadership to forward their common agendas at the UN. According to the *Economist*, "it is difficult to overestimate the disgust with the United States, even among its allies, at the U.N."[37] In a 1997 speech to the British-American Chamber of Commerce, John Weston, then British permanent representative to the world body, underlined the great "anger and exasperation, even among friends and allies" caused by the failure of the United States (and others) to pay its UN dues in full. "You complain the UN doesn't do the job, but you don't pay the UN the sum you voted to do that job . . . ," he lamented. "What a reputation to risk, for a nation of such traditional vision and generosity!"[38] Speaking to the Council on Foreign Relations in 1997, Ambassador Razali Ismail of Malaysia, the president of the fifty-first General Assembly and the official charged with trying to forge agreement among the member states on a UN reform package, emphasized that "United States–United Nations relations are a two-way street, and there is a danger that unilateral demands and conditions from Washington could trigger an equal and opposite reaction from other Member States. . . . Repeated financial withholdings, threats, the moving of goalposts and conditionalities have raised serious questions about the reliability of the United Nations' most important Member."[39]

Few at the world body would dispute that the United States is indispensable to the success of many international undertakings, given its economic, political, and military power. They recognize that their fates are tied to America's, and they fret when developments in Washington political circles threaten its potential for leadership. That may help to explain why President Clinton paradoxically received his first standing ovation at the UN when he appeared before the General Assembly in September 1998 during the midst of the impeachment crisis triggered by the Monica Lewinsky affair and accusations that he had committed perjury. Tellingly, the substance of his speech, which failed to address U.S. arrears to the world organization, received only tepid applause. Most world leaders, it would appear, want a strong U.S. president and a united America, even though they are quick to criticize the ways in which the United States employs its power and they at times bemoan the dangers of hegemony.[40] They, too, can sound ambivalent about the United States, just as the United States does about international organization.

If anything, many in the UN community seem to have an exaggerated sense of American wealth and power, contending that the United States could do much more to right the wrongs and inequities of the world. Those who feel marginalized by the system tend to resent the influential and affluent, of course, and the United States naturally qualifies as the prime target. A November 1996 editorial in a United Nations Staff Union publication charged:

> The current super power shows a dangerous split personality: what we witness at the UN is the result of multilateralist sentiments in Washington, battling the hegemonistic forces there. This is the only way to understand the US attitude of love it when it suits us, bash it when it suits us. It maximizes their influence in the UN, indeed in the world.[41]

Although the authors of this argument cannot seem to decide whether the U.S. policies stem from a sing-song struggle between two competing tendencies in Washington or result from a rational calculation of how to advance U.S. interests in the world, it reflects sentiments often expressed in private at UN headquarters.

Critics also claim that the U.S. government is anything but generous and that its policies are as self-serving as those of other member states. They point out that the United States ranks at the bottom of the industrialized countries in terms of the portion of gross domestic product (GDP) devoted to foreign assistance (0.12 percent, with much of that going to two countries, Israel and Egypt).[42] From 1976 to 1985, U.S. official development assistance (ODA) rose at an average annual rate of 1.7 percent, but it fell 3.4 percent a year from 1986 to 1995.[43] From 1990 to 1995, annual U.S. ODA shrank from $11.4 billion to $7.3 billion, as the United States slipped from being the largest to the fourth largest provider of aid, exceeded by Japan, France, and Germany.[44] These figures, it should be noted, exclude private contributions and the development and humanitarian efforts of non-governmental groups, which Americans favor as channels for assistance. It would be expected that high-tax nations would emphasize government-to-government aid, while relatively low-tax countries, like the United States, would have higher levels of private giving. According to figures collected by the Organization for Economic Cooperation and Development, it is true that a larger portion of U.S. ODA is directed through nongovernmental channels than is true for most other developed countries. As a percentage of GNP, however, the amount of aid provided by American nongovernmental organizations—0.03 percent in 1995–96—is only about average for industrialized countries.[45] (These themes are developed further in chapter 3.)

It is an old saw, moreover, not only at the UN, but also in the American foreign policy community, that the United States simply is not good at multilateral diplomacy, that it is uncomfortable in global political gatherings, and that it does much better one-on-one, where its power can be brought to bear more directly and fully. The breadth and diversity of the UN's membership, plus the skewed nature of the voting formulas in its plenary bodies, no doubt make it more difficult for the United States to exercise its power effectively. During the waning years of the Reagan administration, when U.S.-UN relations were on the upswing, a senior state department official lamented that "maybe we have come to believe our own rhetoric about being powerless in the UN, but there's a reason for that: too often we find that we really are powerless."[46] Though no doubt exaggerated, this perception of America as the helpless giant in UN forums is sufficiently prevalent to make many Americans fret about the apparent disparity between their power outside and inside of the world body.

Nonetheless, when push comes to shove, the United States remains the most powerful nation on earth, even in the UN. Given its raw power, as well as the strength of its political convictions, the United States has had less need to develop or rely on its diplomatic skills than have smaller or medium powers. For example, the American diplomatic campaign to deny Boutros Boutros-Ghali a second term as secretary-general was widely criticized by others at the UN as being clumsy and ham-fisted. But it also succeeded, even though the United States was the only member of the Security Council to vote against a second term in the first round of balloting. Richard Holbrooke, the Balkans troubleshooter, has contended that "although the American campaign against Boutros-Ghali, in which all our key allies opposed us, was long and difficult—especially for [then U.S. Ambassador, Madeleine K.] Albright, who bore heavy and unjust criticism for her role— the decision was correct, and may well have saved America's role in the United Nations."[47] Many other delegations were no doubt also pleased to see a change of UN leadership, even though they remained resentful of

American tactics. Boutros-Ghali himself, through painful experience, came to understand the contrast between diplomatic skill and political influence. In an analogy that was not entirely complimentary, Boutros-Ghali compared the United States to the Roman Empire. "Like in Roman times, they have no diplomacy," he commented, but "you don't need diplomacy if you are so powerful."[48]

The Universal United Nations

Given this imbalance of power, the principles of universality and democratic methods do not coexist comfortably in the United Nations. It has long been recognized that the democratic principles that are the bedrock of the American political system apply at best awkwardly to international machinery in which governments, not individuals, are represented and in which the responsibilities for policy implementation are spread so unevenly.[49] The founders of the United Nations, well aware of the dilemma of trying to reconcile in its decisionmaking processes the realities of power and the principle of universality, tried to have it both ways. On the one hand, the charter declares the sovereign equality of all its members, interprets this principle procedurally into the one-nation, one-vote rules of the General Assembly, and then limits the scope of the Assembly's power by declaring that its decisions are binding only on internal budgetary and administrative matters. In the smaller Security Council, with its unprecedented legal and enforcement powers, on the other hand, the charter gave the United States and its four principal wartime allies veto power over nonprocedural matters. Understandably, the United States, which was the prime champion of the Assembly from the late 1940s through the 1950s, came to prefer to do business in the Council once the pro-western majority disappeared in the Assembly in the 1960s.[50]

But where does the nation that likes to see itself as peerless and indispensable, as having other options, fit into this equation? Americans apparently have felt a recurrent obligation, given their perceived special status, to be in the vanguard of efforts to create new organizations and to reform the ones that exist. At the same time, once the institutions are created, U.S. officials find themselves in the awkward position of being only first among equals, in terms of sovereignty if not power. The very democratic principles practiced, however imperfectly, at home and preached so fervently by Americans abroad take on a very different meaning in one-nation, one-vote bodies, such as the General Assembly. There, national interests and grand principles often clash. In a grotesque role reversal, repressive regimes call for "transparency" and "democratization," while the United States defends the special prerogatives of the relatively rich and powerful.

Even at the UN's founding, U.S. leaders were divided on these core questions. For example, Dean Acheson, a prime architect of postwar U.S. foreign policy but a skeptic about the curative effects of international organization, contended that the tenets of American idealism helped to produce "a grand fallacy" in the structure of the world organization. It was mistaken, in his view, to believe "that one could—and should—apply to external affairs the institutions and practices of legalistic procedure in liberal democracies." Moreover, among the more dangerous fallacies was that "what was reasonable and right would be determined by majority vote; and just as the equality of man led to one man one vote, so the doctrine of the 'sovereign equality of states' led to one state one vote."[51] As discussed later, sovereign equality concerns the status of nations large and small before the law. It does not imply any particular voting system in international bodies. As Acheson correctly suggested, it has been the merging of these two distinct notions that has caused so much consternation by American critics through the years.

"The developing countries and ministates have the votes in the General Assembly," commented Representative John H. Buchanan Jr., R-Ala., in 1975, "but who, Mr. Speaker, speaks for the peoples of the Earth? Who speaks for human rights?"[52] Former U.S. permanent representative to the UN Jeane J. Kirkpatrick emphasized in 1996 Senate testimony that "the United Nations does not represent people . . . and it cannot be said to represent people until all the governments present there are representative democracies. That, of course, is not the case." In her view:

> It is extremely important that Americans and/or the U.S. government *not* come to think or speak as if it regarded the U.N. as the ultimate source of legitimacy. Our Declaration of Independence and Constitution identify very different sources of legitimacy. The Declaration of Independence says clearly: "To protect these rights governments are instituted among men deriving their *just powers* (that is, their legitimacy) from the consent of the governed.[53]

Her point is well taken concerning the "ultimate" source of legitimacy, and this is no doubt one of the reasons that Americans, despite all of the early talk of the UN being a "town meeting for the peoples of the world," have rarely looked to the General Assembly either as a font of wisdom or as the highest authority on international matters. At the same time, the Security

Council and General Assembly, as legally constituted, multinational decisionmaking bodies, can give greater international legitimacy in political and legal terms to actions undertaken by the United States or other member states on behalf of the international community. In this regard, the United States may seek, as it did before the Desert Storm operation against Iraq in 1991, the authorization of the Security Council as an international legitimizer even when the ultimate legitimacy of the U.S. government derives from its people. These two uses of the term legitimacy—one more political and the other more legal—are not inconsistent. If Ambassador Kirkpatrick's point is taken to the extreme, moreover, then international law would lose much of its meaning.

Former General Assembly president Razali correctly points out that "most Member States cherish the principle of sovereign equality,"[54] but over time views on the subject have become decidedly mixed in the United States. In an October 1945 speech, Secretary of State Byrnes resolutely defended the principle:

> The world system we seek to create must be based on the principle of the sovereign equality of nations. That does not mean that all nations are equal in power and in influence any more than all men are equal in power and influence. But it does mean equal respect for the individuality and sovereignty of nations, large and small. Nations, like individuals, should be equal before the law.[55]

Critics, while not so much challenging this classic formulation of the principle, have questioned sharply the way it has been translated into the voting practices and procedures of the General Assembly, based on the charter's one-nation, one-vote rule. Some skeptics also doubt the wisdom of having all the nations of the world debate the whole spectrum of global, and sometimes local, issues.

Senate Foreign Relations Committee Chairman Jesse Helms, Republican of North Carolina, is no fan of international organization, nor of the State Department for that matter. In a 1996 article he wrote that "the United Nations also complicates matters by giving states with no interest in a particular problem an excuse to meddle without putting anything concrete on the table." He questioned, for example, why "countries like Togo, Zaire, Panama, or Ireland, or China" should be involved in discussions about the Middle East peace process, in which "they have no legitimate role." In his view, "what the United Nations ends up doing is giving lots of countries a seat at the table who bring nothing to the table."[56] Senator Helms did not suggest how, or by whom, it should be determined which countries do or do not have a legitimate interest in the outcome of particular regional crises, some of which have wider explosive potential. Nor did he explain why the United States is entitled to a global role, when, according to his calculus, other large nations, like China, are not. His comments, however, reflect how little support there is in the United States for the notion that the Assembly should be regarded as anything approaching a global parliament.

Americans are not alone in their skepticism about the claim by many at the United Nations that the General Assembly's one-nation, one-vote formula is "democratic." Speaking to a 1957 dinner of the American Bar Association, Winston Churchill, one of the organization's principal founders, lamented that "justice was not being achieved in the Assembly." In his words:

> If the Assembly continues to take its decisions on grounds of enmity, opportunism, or merely jealousy or petulance, the whole structure may be brought to nothing. The shape of the United Nations has changed greatly from its original form and from the intentions of its architects. The differences between the Great Powers have thrown responsibility increasingly on the Assembly. This has been vastly swollen by the addition of new nations. . . . It is anomalous that the vote or prejudice of any small country should affect events involving populations many times exceeding their numbers, and should affect them as self-advantage or momentary self-advantage may direct.[57]

The U.S. permanent representative to the UN at that time, Henry Cabot Lodge—a moderate Republican and much more of an internationalist than his grandfather—came to similar conclusions. In a 1976 book, he urged his readers to "remember that the General Assembly is not an accurate mirror of world opinion and that equality in voting as between large and small nations has created such a sense of injustice that, although well aware of the difficulties, I support the proposition that the UN be changed so that voting more nearly corresponds with the ability to carry out the things which are voted." He went on to suggest that any state paying "less than one tenth of one percent of the budget . . . should become an associate member" without vote, and that "half of the ten elected seats in the Security Council should be rotated among the larger states."[58]

Since the early 1970s commentary along these lines has become pointed and even shrill, especially among Republican representatives, officials, and pundits. In 1971 Representative Louis C. Wyman, N.H., declared on the House floor that "U.N. voting is no place for the principle of one man, one vote, or one nation, one vote lest we be stark out of our mind. . . . If we do continue with such a voting structure in the U.N., we are bound to be stolen blind."[59] Equally bluntly, Representative Samuel L. Devine, Ohio, suggested in 1975 that American diplomats at the UN should "not yield so much to all of these pipsqueak nations that have the same vote as we do."[60] Burton Yale Pines of the Heritage Foundation likewise asserted that in a one nation, one vote system, "policymaking is divorced from policy responsibility."[61] Not to be outdone, Patrick J. Buchanan, the columnist and perennial presidential candidate, declared in a July 1998 column that "the New World Order is being built on a fallacy and a scam. The fallacy is that 'all nations are created equal' and each has an equal right to determine the world's destiny."[62] These comments, which constitute only the tip of the iceberg, tend to confirm polling data that Republicans are generally less comfortable with working in multilateral, one-nation, one-vote forums than are Democrats.[63]

To the representatives of other countries, the United States, with its many facets and its predilection for combining moral preaching with power politics and selective respect for international law, can be hard to fathom.[64] They may well see a messianic America, whose modern-day missionaries carry a confusing mix of political, economic, and cultural, as well as moral, messages.[65] After all, if one country is superior or perceives itself to be—whether in rights, values, or power—then others must be inferior in some respects, making the legal principle of sovereign equality difficult to translate into politically operational terms. The result is a persistent tension between the principles and realities of broad-based international arrangements.

Apparently these problems are not of recent vintage. Assessing the results of a Gallup Poll of July 1945, in the UN's first days, Martin Kreisberg of the University of Michigan warned that three public "prejudices" were influencing U.S. policymaking:

—Many Americans have a strong spirit of chauvinism; they are convinced that we are the most righteous and mightiest of all peoples.

—Many are prone to deep-rooted isolationism, arising from a mistaken belief in the self-sufficiency of America.

—Many are convinced that America is the most generous of nations and that what help we give abroad comes under the heading of charity—Christian charity is the term.[66]

Kreisberg went on to posit that chauvinism is hardly a peculiarly American trait. That is true. The American branch of chauvinism is different, however, both in its content and in its consequences. For much of this century, most Americans have actually accepted at face value the nationalistic boasts of their politicians and statesmen. We tend to believe the rhetoric. In our view, historical developments have, in fact, tended to confirm its validity. The United States, at least in overall material and quantitative terms, has indeed been the most successful nation of the twentieth century. That does not imply that American values and structures have universal applicability or that they are flawless, but the historical record does make it harder to dismiss American claims as pure chauvinism or to convince Americans to compromise their goals or principles for the sake of international cooperation. When you are sure that you are right, compromise does not come easily.

For all of these reasons, Americans have not found a comfortable way to reconcile their domestic democratic principles and their sense of exceptionalism with the realities of decisionmaking in intergovernmental bodies, particularly universal ones. At the same time, the architects of international organization have been unable or unwilling to find a way fully to reflect or take into account within intergovernmental decisionmaking structures America's preeminent position in the real world outside. These twin dilemmas have persisted throughout the century, contributing to the uneasiness that has continued to grip American attitudes and policies toward international institutions. It is hard to square being exceptional outside of the organization with being just one of many within its larger halls. Until other member states begin to take these concerns more seriously—at the very least to cease challenging the legitimacy of the U.S. veto power in the Security Council—American ambivalence is likely to persist or even grow.

Are Americans Out of Step with the Rest of the World?

Rather than coming to grips with these central constitutional dilemmas, it has become commonplace in UN circles to assert the somewhat more comforting proposition that the problem is simply attitudinal: given their prejudices and predilections, Americans just do not value the UN as much, nor understand it as well, as others do. What else could explain Congress' penchant for withholding assessed dues and the recurrent and seemingly insatiable chorus of criticism concerning UN performance voiced by U.S. opinion leaders? The image of American exceptionalism as the product solely of special features of its political culture and history, moreover, reinforces the view held both by representatives of less friendly member states and by U.S. critics of the UN that the United States is out of place in the world body and that its beliefs, values, and perspectives are fundamentally and irreversibly out of synch with those of the other members. The contention that a clash of incompatible political cultures is at the heart of the matter no doubt makes it easier for the more contentious partisans on both sides of the ongoing debate to identify who is to blame for the ailments that have afflicted U.S. relations with international organizations throughout this century.

Finger-pointing about political values, however, fails to account for why U.S.-UN relations have declined since the end of the cold war, nor does it give any hint about how the deepening rift might be healed. On the one hand, America's democratic political values have largely triumphed in UN debates during the 1990s, as they have in much of the world outside. On the other hand, the parallel rise in America's relative power standing among the nations of the world with the collapse of communism has not been reflected within the decisionmaking structures of the world organization. In fact, its influence appears to have declined over these years within the UN, widening the gap between U.S. power inside and outside the world body. Clearly, to ascribe American exceptionalism simply to its unique political culture would give insufficient weight to the extent to which strategic and substantive considerations also tend to set American policies and interests apart from those of others on a host of policy and constitutional issues. As discussed earlier, the United States is unique not only in its history, geography, and political culture, but also in terms of its power position in the contemporary hierarchy of nations. This suggests, in turn, that a search for the roots of the distinctive aspects of U.S. policies should not be limited to the realms of public attitudes, historic experience, and political culture, but should encompass a candid assessment of the ongoing struggle for influence within the UN as well. If Russia, Japan, Germany, or China happened to be the sole superpower, would their attitudes toward and policies at the UN be so different from those of the United States at this juncture? Such a hypothetical cannot be answered with any confidence, but a half century of poll data suggests that American attitudes toward the UN as a whole—although more polarized and partisan—are not so markedly different from those in other developed countries.

As documented in chapter 10, Americans were quick to become disillusioned with the new world organization in the late 1940s. But, according to survey data of that era, they were not alone in their disappointment. In

Canada, long thought of as a core UN supporter, a July 1946 survey by the Canadian Institute of Public Opinion found respondents dissatisfied with UN progress by a 44 to 31 percent margin. Australians, also known for their commitment to the world body, were evenly divided (34 to 34 percent) between satisfaction and dissatisfaction in their assessment of the UN's progress, according to a June 1946 survey conducted by Australian Public Opinion Polls. Belgians were also split down the middle—36 to 36 percent—when asked in June 1946 by the Academic Institute for Social and Economic Information if they had "confidence in the work of the United Nations for the maintenance of peace." Apparently French and Swedes were even more pessimistic. In France half of the respondents to a January 1946 French Institute of Public Opinion survey said that they did not have confidence "in the United Nations organization to avoid war," while one-third did. Queried by the Swedish Gallup Institute in June 1945 whether a new League of Nations "would secure the peace for at least 50 years," 26 percent of Swedes said "yes" and 45 percent "no." In contrast, almost one-half (49 percent) of those responding to a February 1946 British Institute of Public Opinion survey in Great Britain declared themselves to be satisfied "with the work the organization of the United Nations has done so far," while 20 percent were dissatisfied and 31 percent did not have an opinion.[67]

A generation later Americans were more favorably disposed to strengthening the UN than most. When asked in a December 1970 Gallup Poll whether they "would like to see the United Nations become a stronger organization," Americans responded favorably by an 84 to 8 percent margin, topped only by Australia (85 to 8 percent), and followed by Sweden (79 to 6 percent), Greece (75 to 2 percent), Great Britain (74 to 9 percent), Holland (66 to 10 percent), West Germany (65 to 5 percent), Spain (46 to 5 percent), and Uruguay (45 to 31 percent).[68] Similarly, Americans, by a 3 to 1 margin, favored a proposal for the United Nations to "establish a peace keeping army of about 100,000 men." Only Greece and Australia were more in favor.

At the end of the 1970s, a particularly tense decade for relations between the United States and the UN, U.S. attitudes toward the UN had once again plummeted. When Gallup International posed its classic good job–bad job question in 1979, the U.S. ratings of UN performance were near the bottom of the list, trailed only by France, the Federal Republic of Germany, and Japan (and no developing countries). Although the American results were no worse than three of its major allies, they were far more negative than those found in Italy, Canada, the United Kingdom, the Benelux countries, Scandinavia, or Western Europe as a whole. By the mid-1980s, the negative UN performance ratings given by most Americans were echoed in a number of developed and developing countries. When Gallup International asked the same question in seventeen countries between December 1984 and March 1985, nine nations gave the UN bad marks on balance. Ranging from the most to least negative, these nine were South Africa (white population only), Uruguay, Turkey, Great Britain, Japan, Germany, the United States, Greece, and Canada.[69] Argentines were evenly divided. On the positive side, from least to most favorable, were Portugal, Brazil, Australia, Belgium, Switzerland, the Netherlands, and the Philippines. The United States, in other words, was the seventh most negative out of seventeen.

What is most striking about the relative rise of American attitudes into the western mainstream between 1979 and 1985 is not that U.S. opinion about UN performance rose in this period—indeed it fell off slightly—but that attitudes toward the UN dropped more dramatically in most other western countries over that period. According to the Gallup figures, the most stunning reversal came in the United Kingdom, from a wide 53 to 22 percent positive margin to a negative margin of 26 to 47 percent.[70] Even in Canada, where the UN has always fared somewhat better in public eyes than it has in the eyes of its neighbor, opinion shifted from a 46 to 21 percent favorable margin to a 36 to 39 percent unfavorable edge. (Negative commentary from the Reagan administration and from U.S. media coverage of the UN may have helped spur this Canadian shift, although that cannot be documented.)

More recent international surveys also show that American attitudes toward the UN are similar to, if not more positive than, those in other developed countries. The latest effort, a thirteen-country survey by Zogby International and GfK Great Britain, conducted during the first three months of 1999, found the percentage of Americans having a favorable opinion of the United Nations (70 percent) as the second highest among the eight NATO countries polled and the fourth highest of the thirteen.[71] At the same time, more Americans (27 percent) had an unfavorable opinion of the world body than did those polled in any of the other twelve countries.[72] These results reinforce the impression that Americans are unusually polarized in their views of the UN.

In March 1994, major newspapers in four allied countries (*Der Spiegel* in Germany, the *Guardian* in Great Britain, *Asahi Shimbun* in Japan, and the *New York Times* in the United States) conducted polls using the same set of questions.[73] Of the four, Americans were the most positive about the UN's contributions "to keeping world peace in the last 50 years," more forthcoming than Japanese or Germans regarding their nation's "responsibility to contribute military troops to enforce peace plans in trouble spots around the world when it is asked by the United Nations," more favorable toward having the UN send troops on such missions than the Japanese, and more likely than the Germans and almost as likely as the Japanese to consider cooperation through the UN to be important after the end of the cold war.

A series of international opinion surveys in the mid-1990s, sponsored and overseen by *Yomiuri Shimbun* (Japan's largest newspaper chain), confirmed the impression that the American people are generally in tune with their allies in their views of the UN. In March 1993 people in France, Germany, Japan, the United Kingdom, and the United States were asked whether the UN should "have the leading role" in resolving conflicts around the world.[74] Of the five, only British respondents were more favorable than American ones toward a UN role. When asked in the same poll whether the UN's post–cold war peacekeeping operations had helped maintain peace, only Japanese respondents were more affirmative than those in the United States. In an April–May 1995 survey among the same five countries, Americans by a 2 to 1 ratio said that the role of UN peacekeeping operations was likely to increase in the future, a more positive figure than that in Germany or Great Britain, comparable to that in France, and less optimistic than that in Japan.[75]

The replication of these results, as unscientific as they might be, year after year makes a strong case for the proposition that in the aggregate Americans are not unusually negative in their view of the place and future of the UN. These polls, however, say little either about the intensity of feeling behind the responses or about the relationship between public opinion and government policymaking. As discussed at greater length in chapter 10, not only does the United States have more than its share of skeptics, but they seem much more passionate and ideological in their rejection of the UN than do the larger numbers of their countrymen who vaguely value the organization and its work. The UN does not seem to have inspired such zealous opposition in other countries. The rivalry in the United States between the executive branch and Congress for control of foreign policy, moreover, has done more to frustrate executive initiative and to spawn dual messages to the rest of the world than would be the case in a parliamentary system. From a strategic perspective as well, the interests, choices, and priorities of the United States are not identical to those of even its closest allies. These differences, which cannot be deduced from polling data, help explain why the governments of the United States and its allies have decided at times to adopt rather different approaches to the world body. For sound strategic and foreign policy reasons, the governments in Western Europe and Japan have chosen to champion the UN, even as their publics have cooled somewhat to the world body. In America the situation has usually been the reverse, as the public has been more amenable to international organization than their elected representatives throughout most of this century.

Nor do Americans necessarily see the future role and priorities of the world body the same way as their allies do. When respondents from the same five nations were asked in a March 1994 *Yomiuri Shimbun* poll to select those areas in which "the United Nations should devote its efforts more strongly," the differences were quite striking. Americans had relatively high response rates for famine, human rights, environment, medicine, education and culture, disarmament, and population. They were the least likely, however, to choose three of the organization's largest program areas: economic aid to developing countries, refugees, and conflict prevention. (Japanese, by the way, had the highest response rates for each of these three subjects.)

To the extent that poll results can be relied on—and in this case they seem consistent with experience as well—the problem is not so much that Americans as a whole are less bullish about the world organization, but that they see its areas of comparative advantage and its future priorities differently. At a point when the secretary-general is asking the member states for a cohesive sense of what kind of a UN they want for the twenty-first century, the prospect, instead, is for continued wrangling, even among allies, about what the organization should be doing and where its resources should be going. On most issues, of course, the gap between the United States and the rest of the membership is even wider than with its principal allies. These are differences of substance, not perception, that cannot be addressed through educational or public relations campaigns. It is not a question of who is "for" or "against" the UN, but of what kinds of mandates and agendas are seen to be most sensible at this stage of history. The existence of competing, even if not fully articulated, visions of what the UN of the future should be doing, furthermore, is a sharply limiting factor in efforts to design a far-reaching reform plan. As discussed in chapter 8, there is nothing close to a consensus among the membership on these essential matters.

From the foregoing analysis, it seems that Americans are less ambivalent about active participation in the UN than about what it is and is not doing. Most Americans *do* see a future for the world body, just not the same one favored by most member states. While no cause for celebration, this more nuanced understanding of American exceptionalism may suggest where one could begin to look for the elements of a new relationship between the United States and its fellow member states. If the debate ever gets beyond mutual recrimination, then it should be possible to see a ray or two of light at the end of what has been a very long and rather dark tunnel. At the same time, however, growing doubts about the equity and responsiveness of the multilateral decisionmaking process discussed earlier in this chapter will also have to be addressed, for they have tended to fuel parallel concerns—highlighted in the next chapter—about whether U.S. national sovereignty can be fully protected and its interests adequately reflected in global political bodies. The intensity with which these concerns are held, in turn, has long helped define the dividing line between those Americans who are skeptical and those who are downright hostile toward international organization.

CHAPTER THREE

National Interests, Sovereignty, and Global Governance

I am an American—born here, lived here, shall die here. I have never had but one flag, never loved but one flag. I am too old to try to love another, an international flag. I have never had but one allegiance, the allegiance of the United States. Personally, I am too old, I cannot divide it now.
—SENATOR HENRY CABOT LODGE, 1919

The science of weapons and war has made us all, far more than eighteen years ago in San Francisco, one world and one human race with one common destiny. In such a world, absolute sovereignty no longer assures us of absolute security.
—PRESIDENT JOHN F. KENNEDY, 1963

International organizations—whether the United Nations, the World Trade Organization, or any others—will not protect American interests. Only America can do that.
—SENATOR BOB DOLE, 1995

AS THE LAST CHAPTER emphasized, Americans do see themselves and their country as special. They are not shy about claiming that the United States is *the* indispensable nation, whose power and principles are essential to successful international cooperation. Yet, as this chapter details, a second and parallel theme has been that despite its unsurpassed national power, U.S. national sovereignty is a precious and fragile commodity that must be jealously guarded at all times within and from international organizations. As the logic and momentum for international integration seem to grow irresistibly, so do the forces of nationalism and resistance. Their concerns are understandable when seen in the context of the arguments by some UN supporters that nationalism and sovereignty are the twin evils that must be overcome by ceding wider and wider responsibilities to international bodies. Traditional ambivalence about government at the national level, moreover, has been projected by some onto a global screen, where the notion of a world government has been welcomed by a few Americans but rejected emphatically by far more.

Government: Big or Small, Near or Far

The United Nations was founded when public respect for and expectations of government were at a peak. President Franklin Roosevelt and his administration had used federal government spending and organization to pull the nation out of a severe depression and to produce unprecedented quantities of military supplies to support the allied war effort. Not surprisingly, the administration's vision of the postwar international system reflected New Deal values, with an emphasis on developing means for harmonizing and directing the efforts of sovereign states to tackle common problems.[1] After all, in questions of war and peace, more than in any other area of public policy, responsibility lay with the state, and the first task of the new world organization was to prepare for intergovernmental cooperation to resist aggression. In 1945 relatively few voices questioned the validity of the statist assumptions that underlay the new organization.

Yet historically Americans have sought to keep the power of central government in check, and today they appear to have decidedly mixed attitudes toward government.[2] They identify closely with their nation and its values, much less with the governmental structure established to implement national purposes and principles. Few see the government either as a savior or as an adversary. It provides essential services with one hand and levies burdensome taxes with the other. It ensures an orderly and predictable environment within which to pursue commerce, culture, and family life, yet places restrictions that some find intrusive on private enterprise and personal freedoms. It both organizes the national defense and undertakes military commitments in faraway places for reasons that are only vaguely understood by the citizens who are called upon to risk their lives to carry them out. Throughout American history, there has been a tug-of-war between the rights and prerogatives of individual states and those of the federal government. Although largely muted today, these questions sparked a bloody civil war only three generations before the Senate considered entry into the League of Nations.

Americans are often caricatured as being fundamentally and irreversibly antigovernment. As one bumper sticker recently spotted in a discount store parking lot put it: "I love my country, but I fear my government." According to John R. Bolton of the American Enterprise Institute:

> The entire history of the United States, from the first colonists through the Revolution, and forward until today, has been infused with a distrust of government and a belief in individual liberty. The United States is a land of low taxes, more private property, less government regulation and subsidy, greater freedom of speech and press, more toleration of diverse religious expression, and on and on. Although other individual countries may best the United States in one or another of these categories, in the aggregate, there is no real contest.[3]

At the same time, however, in times of national crisis—caused by threats to national security, economic well-being, or social stability—citizens have historically turned to the federal government as the organizer of a collective response. And its role in facilitating and providing the legal, financial, and material infrastructure for America's economic growth and private enterprise is too often overlooked. Perhaps in a time of relative security and prosperity, it is easier to denigrate the role of government—and of intergovernmental organization—whereas the drive for institution-building is likely to be greatest in or following periods of crisis.

The impression of widespread antipathy for government has been heightened in recent years by the extreme rhetoric and actions of the militia movement; the broad disillusionment with and decreasing participation in the political-electoral process; the emphasis in the platforms of both major parties on the need to limit spending, programs, and personnel in the federal government; efforts to devolve power from the federal to the state level on a number of domestic social issues; and White House scandal. It is said that the independent, pioneering, and self-reliant spirit of the American people, derived from their history, culture, and free enterprise economy, conditions them to distrust government and to seek to limit its roles to the bare necessities. This is a period in American history, moreover, when sustained economic growth is accompanied by the perception of a broad-based shift of spending and responsibilities from the federal to state or even local levels, and when privatization of formerly government-supplied services is invoked frequently as a political slogan and somewhat less frequently as a policy choice. Some are quick to see a link between current economic success and limitations on the government's place in the economy.

Like all caricatures, there is some truth to this one. Several surveys demonstrated a marked decline in public confidence in government institutions from the early 1960s to the early 1990s, apparently bottoming out in 1994.[4] Public opinion polls since then suggest that citizens have come to trust government more over the past few years of prosperity, but that a majority still express mistrust in the institutions of government.[5] Apparently even most politically mainstream Americans are ambivalent about government in general and about the federal government in particular. Clearly the welfare state model that is so prevalent—and popular—in much of western Europe and other industrialized countries would not fit well with the American character and economic system.[6] Indeed, this factor is often cited as one reason the U.S. economy seems to be doing a bit better than its chief competitors these days.

At the same time, efforts to eliminate the federal deficit have entailed service cutbacks or threats of future reductions that have stirred strong political resistance from affected groups, ranging from the elderly, to the arts, to educators, to labor, to welfare mothers, to governors and mayors, to industries and communities concerned about defense procurement cutbacks and base closings. "Bureaucracy" may be widely used as a pejorative term and government as a whole may be seen as too large, too intrusive, and insufficiently responsive, yet every citizen seems to be a constituent for one program area or another. Likewise, public opinion surveys in recent election years have tended to show a marked ambivalence toward Congress. At the same time that they support the good work of their own representative, respondents say that Congress as an organization is out of touch with average Americans, overly responsive to special interests, and doing a poor job of maintaining ethical standards.[7]

Although two recent polls suggest that Americans on the whole believe that the United Nations is less likely to waste money and more likely "to do what is right" than is their own federal government, American ambivalence toward government at home is paralleled, at least in broad strokes, in American attitudes toward global governance and intergovernmental institutions.[8] As would be expected, according to the results of numerous polls, the more local and accessible the level of government, the more comfortable citizens feel with it, and the better they understand what it does and why it does it.[9]

The United Nations system is actually much smaller than the government of a large city in terms of budgets and personnel, but it looks far away, inaccessible, expansive, and intrusive. It is a favorite target of those legislators concerned about threats both to American sovereignty and to congressional prerogatives. In 1971, for example, Representative John R. Rarick, D-La., proposed legislation "to remove the United States from the U.N. and the U.N. from the United States, thus freeing our people from the ever-tightening yoke of international controls and the erosion of national sovereignty and constitutional government."[10] More recently, Representative Ron Paul, R-Texas, has sponsored a series of similar bills to get the United States out of the UN and all of its affiliated organizations.[11] In March 1998 he told the House that such a step was needed because the UN "frequently acts in a manner contrary to the sovereign interests of the United States." During the same floor debate, Ken Calvert, R-Calif., objected to efforts to pay a portion of U.S. arrears to the world body, saying that "I am no fan of the United Nations, and do not trust that institution to respect American sovereignty. It is our job as constitutionally elected representatives of the American people to protect our sovereignty."[12]

In recent years, commentators from across the nation's political spectrum have voiced concerns about the lack of accountability in international institutions. Ralph Nader, a consumer advocate who had rarely ventured into foreign affairs, told the Senate Foreign Relations Committee in 1994 that the new World Trade Organization would be "antidemocratic" because it "would shift power from citizens and domestic legislators and regulators to international trade bureaucrats to an extent unprecedented in our history." He claimed that its governance "would be chronically secretive, nonparticipatory and not subject to any independent appeals process."[13] Similarly, in a 1996 article, University of Michigan law professor José Alvarez asked, "So who should be 'afraid' of the 'New World Order?' If fear motivates healthy scrutiny, the answer should be anybody who believes in accountable government." He cautioned that "there is no global freedom of information act that permits public access to 'restricted' documents issued by these organizations" and that "international secretariats, formally independent and guaranteed certain privileges and immunities to assure that independence, are not necessarily accountable to governments."[14]

From the right flank, columnist Patrick J. Buchanan warned in a July 1998 article about "the vast and elaborate superstructure that is rising. For what, ultimately, are all these transnational institutions—the U.N., WTO,

IMF, World Bank, etc., all about—but part of a veiled scheme for the transfer of money, prestige, power and sovereignty from America to a new class of parasite-mandarins, slaving to control the destiny of mankind."[15] Senate Foreign Relations Committee Chairman Jesse Helms has declared that "U.N. reform is about much more than saving money. It is about preventing unelected bureaucrats from acquiring ever-greater powers at the expense of elected national leaders."[16] Ironically, this concern is shared not only by Americans of quite different political persuasions, but also by the UN representatives of developing countries, which have a hard time trying to keep up with the numerous and varied UN programs and activities.

In reality, of course, it is the United States and other governments that have charged international secretariats with such a wide range of responsibilities, most essential—others less essential—to the smooth functioning of a highly complex and interdependent international system. International bureaucrats, rather than aspiring to be "parasite-mandarins" with sweeping powers, tend to think of themselves as international functionaries whose work is overregulated and underappreciated by the member states. Because much of this work is highly specialized and rarely publicized, however, only a handful of national officials and even fewer public opinion leaders follow what is going on in each area of international responsibility. Each constituency, moreover, sees only a small piece or two of a much larger and more complicated puzzle.

The kind of conspiracy theory favored by Buchanan seems far-fetched, for if there is a culprit it is technology, the Internet, and the explosion of knowledge in the latter decades of the twentieth century, not some cabal of ambitious bureaucrats. The problem is not so much that foreign-born international civil servants are plotting to steal American sovereignty, but that the management of a growing array of transnational problems demands so much timely and specialized knowledge, such expertise and concentration, that most national legislators—whether in the United States or in other countries—cannot understand or keep track of all of the interactions and developments. Whether they are from international secretariats, national or local governments, nongovernmental organizations, academia, the private sector, the media, or individual citizens, those who choose to follow particular issues become the self-selected transnational constituencies (or epistemic communities) for each realm of policy. Given America's advantage in information technologies and analytical capacity, the keys to penetrating these mazes, Americans, individually or collectively, should be unusually well placed to maintain their voice in shaping international developments for years to come.

Although these trends carry an air of inevitability, some, like Senator Helms, have declared that "this process must be stopped." In Helms's view, the domestic process of devolution of power from the federal to the state level "must be replicated at the international level. Reining in the U.N. bureaucracy goes hand in hand with Congress' domestic agenda of devolution."[17] In the UN's early years, some southern members of Congress worried that the codification of global human rights standards would encourage federal civil rights legislation and compromise states' rights (see chapter 4). More recently, the twin processes of devolution of power and the globalization of the economy have led individual states within the United States to be more assertive on matters of trade and even economic sanctions.[18] These debates continue to rage on the floor of Congress today.

It has not only been in the United States, of course, that calls for devolution or subsidiarity in governance have been heard in recent years.[19] In the ongoing intergovernmental deliberations about reforming the UN system, long-standing arguments about the lack of coordination in a highly decentralized collection of UN agencies and programs have had to contend with growing interest in placing management authority closer to the level of program implementation, under the principle of subsidiarity (see chapter 8). Many western countries have emphasized the latter approach. In seeking to square this circle, Secretary-General Annan in July 1997 called for "decentralization and delegation of authority, coupled with full accountability" in UN management and "decentralization of decision-making at the country level and consolidation of the United Nations presence under 'one flag.'"[20]

The far right and the far left have at least one thing in common: a resentment of well-established western governments, none more so than the U.S. government. By extension, the international legal and institutional order that is perceived to be western-dominated has become a target of the rhetoric of both political flanks. Some see the UN, like the League before it, as fundamentally anti-interventionist, as the tool of those satisfied with the status quo and determined to thwart change.[21] According to Professor Alvarez, the American "militia member who despises the UN shares with Libyan President Quadaffi a fear that international organizations create a layer of regulation by an unaccountable elite that diminishes national sovereignty."[22] This has become a favorite theme of Iraq's president Saddam Hussein as well. All of these concerns—whether American, western, or third world—stem from a common concern about international decisionmaking processes that no single national government, not to mention domestic political group, can fully control. That, of course, is the nature of multilateral institutions, even relatively transparent and accountable ones. All member states are likely to feel some level of discomfort at the prospect of participating in processes involving the input of hundreds of countries, yet none of the others seems nearly as ambivalent as the one that can and does exert the greatest leverage: the United States, where the skepticism about government at any level seems most pronounced.

The grandiose rhetoric and sweeping agendas that are so popular at the UN, moreover, permit critics to caricature the world organization as the epitome of overly ambitious governance, even if it lacks the resources, personnel, and programs to implement these grand schemes. Senator Helms, for example, has claimed that "a United Nations that can recognize its limitations . . . is worth saving," but "a United Nations that insists on imposing its utopian vision on states begs for dismantlement."[23] (He might think differently, however, about the UN that imposed on Iraqi sovereignty to seek out and destroy Saddam Hussein's stash of weapons of mass destruction or that set standards that inspired the launching of independent trade unions in Poland and now China.) Because most Americans know relatively little about the world body's structure, operations, or finances, they tend to be susceptible to exaggerated claims—positive or negative—about it.

Global Governance: Promise or Threat?

Apparently the subject of international organization received more attention in secondary school education in earlier years than is the case today. In 1921–22, high school debate teams from across the country focused on a straightforward query: "resolved, that the United States should enter the League of Nations." The handbook prepared for the North Carolina High School Debating Union, in enumerating the principal points for the affirmative and negative sides of the debate, gives the flavor of the priority issues of the day. The affirmative arguments were that (1) "the League of Nations will prevent future wars," (2) it "will lead to economic benefits of disarmament and industrial peace," (3) it "will prove to be in harmony with American ideals," (4) it "will prove a useful organ of international justice and comity," and (5) "America as the world's greatest democracy owes it to herself and to the world to become a member and a leader in the League of Nations." The negative response asserted that (1) "the League of Nations will involve us in European Wars," (2) it "will infringe upon our sovereignty," (3) it "will disturb our Pan-American relations," (4) it "is not in harmony with American ideals and stands in the way of results it [the United States] seeks to accomplish," and (5) "America as the world's greatest republic can best make her contribution to the world by living her own life and by keeping clear of entanglements."[24]

Both sets of arguments are overstated and overly dramatic given the limited powers that had been assigned to the League. They both revolve, moreover, around issues of sovereignty and whether America's freedom of action would be multiplied or restricted by its participation in the League. Supporters and detractors of the new body in the Senate debate engaged in no less hyperbole than their counterparts in secondary schools. Senator Seldon P. Spencer, R-Mo., cautioning that the covenant was "brimful of glittering generalities," noted that although he favored a League of Nations in theory, "I don't want it if it means for us the abandonment of our nationalism." The staunch isolationist, William Borah, warned that the covenant constituted "a renunciation of the Monroe Doctrine." Adding a note of bipartisanship to the negative chorus, Senator William H. King, D-Utah, pronounced that the American people would never "abdicate any of their sovereign rights. In my opinion, the Sermon on the Mount, the Ten Commandments and the Monroe Doctrine are good enough for them."[25] Such sweeping denunciation of the League left an exasperated A. Lawrence Lowell to remark that "criticism seems to have been left almost wholly to those who object to a League of Nations altogether." He complained that "we have heard little or nothing of the way this plan could be improved to meet their views."[26]

Yet many of the League's advocates, including President Wilson, were also not above grandiose and deeply emotional appeals. In a speech delivered just hours before his physical collapse in September 1919, President Wilson claimed that "in the Covenant of the League of Nations the moral forces of the world are mobilized."[27] Charles Nagel, who had served as Taft's secretary of commerce and labor, asserted that "the President has thrown upon the international screen a dream of democracy so alluring that the demand for its realization can at best be guided and directed, but can never again be silenced. . . . [T]he dream of universal political peace will never be dismissed from public consciousness."[28] An editorial in the *Nation* of July 12, 1919, accused opponents of the League of having abandoned the moral high ground.[29] Supporters of the League, like its opponents, were not shy about suggesting a religious, as well as a historic, aura for the covenant.

Wilson's secretary of the Navy, Josephus Daniels, went so far as to declare that the Covenant was:

> . . . a document which makes the Magna Carta and Declaration of Independence mere forerunners of an immortal instrument that blesses all the world for generations. . . . The draft of the League of Peace is almost as simple as one of the parables of Jesus and almost as illuminating and uplifting. It is a time for churchbells to peal, for preachers to fall upon their knees, for statesmen to rejoice, and for the angels to sing, 'Glory to God in the Highest!'[30]

Such hyperbole and self-righteousness, of course, served only to polarize the debate over the League, making a reasonable political compromise between the president and his critics that much more difficult to obtain. The League of Nations was in reality a rather modest vehicle, yet few of its supporters or detractors wanted to admit, as Lowell did, that the organs of the League would have relatively little authority and that it represented a compromise. It was, he noted, "both the most effective and least adventurous method of preventing war."[31]

Four generations later, the American political discourse about international organization retains much of this rhetorical, moralistic character. More moderate claims tend to get lost in the clatter. The media, seeking to sell the high drama of ideological conflict, tend to be more interested in highlighting points of difference than in noting areas of common ground. The UN, for its part, finds grand goals and sweeping mandates hard to resist, no matter how modest its resources for implementation. It, too, thrives on symbolism. For example, despite the decidedly modest results of the summit-level conclave convened for its fiftieth anniversary, the UN General Assembly has called for a "Millennium Summit and Assembly," because "the year 2000 constitutes a unique and symbolically compelling moment to articulate and affirm an animating vision for the United Nations in the new era."[32]

The U.S. debate, in turn, usually revolves around political symbols and philosophies. Abstract and ideological questions, such as whether some hypothetical image of global governance represents a promise or a threat to American values and freedom of action, are more at issue than current realities, such as what organizations actually do or whether U.S. national interests are being served. In fact, there is ample reason to believe that the proliferation of intergovernmental organizations and arrangements has not significantly compromised state sovereignty. For example, based on a series of case studies in different issue areas, Gene M. Lyons and Michael Mastanduno of Dartmouth College concluded that "a significant transfer of political authority from states to the international community has *not* taken place."[33] Nonetheless, in the overheated and largely symbolic debates in the nation's capital, the day-to-day realities of the existing international organizations receive less attention than do the images and implications of what they might become some day.

A Global Tax Man?

Nowhere has this phenomenon been better illustrated than by the furor in recent years over proposals to give the United Nations taxing authority. Americans, naturally, find nothing more obnoxious about government than its power to tax. As many others had before him, William Jennings Bryan pungently noted in 1917 that "the power to tax has been characterized as the power to destroy."[34] The notion that a world government could add a fourth layer of levies on top of those charged by the local, state, and federal governments is, to most Americans, a prospect that is worrisome at best. In a 1996 survey conducted by the Wirthlin Group for the United Nations Association of the USA, respondents rejected by a 2-to-1 margin "the idea of dedicating specific taxes or charges to fund U.N. activities."[35] (When "charges" on unpopular activities, such as tobacco, oil, arms sales, and currency transactions, were tied to supporting popular purposes, such as health care, environment, peace, and development, without mentioning the UN, more favorable responses were recorded.)

The basic concern is as old as the Republic. As Bryan queried, "is it safe for any nation to transfer to a Council controlled by others the all-embracing power to tax, and bind its people to meet any assessment that may be levied by the Council?"[36] Representative John T. Wood, R-Idaho, an outspoken foe of the UN, suggested in a House debate in 1952 that it was treasonous for Congress to accept the assessments voted by the General Assembly, because these constituted an "annual tax." "Who is going to hold the tax strings in this Nation?" he asked rhetorically. "Is this Congress going to hold these strings, or is the United Nations?"[37] He did not comment on whether the presumed alternative—to let each member state decide its own dues level—would be either workable or desirable.

Daniel Gouré, a policy analyst at the Center for Strategic and International Studies, contends that it would be harmful to both the United

Nations and its member states to give the UN taxing authority beyond the assessment of dues:

> To grant the U.N. the power to levy taxes of any kind is to begin a process that will ultimately lead to the destruction of that institution. No matter how worthy its causes, no matter how successful its efforts, and no matter how efficient and cost-effective its operations, people will resist taxation without representation. They will closely measure each expenditure with an eye toward any hint of inequity. They will constantly criticize U.N. activities while seeking to turn decisions and programs to their benefit.[38]

Cautioning that none of the current proposals for reforming the world body "would address the central issue of adequate and proper representation as a precursor to taxation," he warns that expanding "the reach and responsibility of the U.N. . . . would only add to the problem." According to Gouré, because "the power to tax implies the power to coerce" and would require some sort of UN enforcement mechanism, advocates of a UN tax have sought "to make the tax as inconspicuous, if not covert, as possible" through indirect levies such as a value-added tax on airline tickets.[39]

Washington's acute sensitivity to any suggestion of a UN taxing power was vividly demonstrated in 1996 when a personal comment made by Secretary-General Boutros-Ghali in the academic confines of Oxford University triggered a firestorm. Discussing the UN's debilitating financial problems, the secretary-general noted that scholars had proposed a number of possible revenue-raising schemes, such as user fees or a tariff on airline tickets, that could be considered by the member states.[40] The comments, although politically inept, could hardly have been mistaken for the pronouncement of a new policy initiative. The notion of giving the world organization an independent source of funds has been raised from time to time by individual diplomats at the UN but has never gained broad political favor outside of some academic circles.[41] Large and small member states alike have shown a consistent determination to keep the UN secretariat on a short financial leash and fully accountable.

Nevertheless, Senate Majority Leader Bob Dole of Kansas, no fan of the secretary-general and himself a Republican presidential candidate, called Boutros-Ghali's statement "an outrageous attempt [to create] an international Internal Revenue Service," designed "not just to alleviate a current funding shortfall, *but explicitly to evade the control of member states.*"[42] Dole and Helms cosponsored legislation to ban funds for any UN body that advocated or developed schemes for international taxation. Similar legislation was introduced in the House, and commentators from the Heritage Foundation, the American Enterprise Institute, and the Cato Institute joined the chorus.[43] The White House, with President Clinton also preparing his reelection campaign, was no more enthusiastic. Referring to the "abysmal idea" of a global tax, Clinton's spokesperson, Michael McCurry, declared that the notion "is not going to get very far here in the United States."[44]

The specter of taxation, like so many other worries of those fearful of the potential powers of world organization, is another camel's-nose-under-the-tent concern. Speaking on the floor of the House in 1998, the influential Gerald Solomon, R-N.Y., expressed his pleasure that proposed legislation linking payment of arrears to UN reforms "would prevent any arrearages from going to the U.N. if that body attempts to create taxes on American citizens, and they are talking about that, as my colleagues know. We know that U.N. bureaucrats would like to do exactly that." He went on to warn that "this legislation is a shot across the bow. Do not try it."[45] Apparently several members of Congress view their vigilance—and threats of further unilaterally imposed penalties—as the first line of defense (or deterrence) against encroachments on American sovereignty on the part of aggrandizing international civil servants.

Pat Robertson, the religious right leader and sometime presidential candidate, paints an even more sinister scenario. Asserting that "the new world order is going to cost plenty," he cautions that "if you like the Internal Revenue Service you will love the tax police of the new world order." In good populist fashion, Robertson warns of an alleged conspiracy against the American people, hatched by "one-worlders" and "Establishment bankers":

> A worldwide IRS under a banking oligarchy would become the American citizens' worst nightmare. But remember, before the financial bloodsucking begins in earnest on the newly minted American citizens of the world, the monopoly bankers will have placed themselves and their central banks above the law and out of the reach of the taxing power.
>
> They did it in 1913 in America, and, rest assured, they plan to do it again in the new world order.[46]

The logic of his conspiracy theory gets a bit strained, of course, with the United States losing all of its military and political muscle yet with its potent central bank—the Federal Reserve System—apparently retaining great power, even as it sheds every ounce of patriotism. The battle, according to

Robertson's treatise, is not only with mischievous foreigners, but also with those privileged Americans who seek to profit from globalization and the strengthening of international institutions.

It is tempting to dismiss the hand-wringing of those warning so vociferously about the dangers of global tax schemes. Their scenarios are largely fanciful, their arguments politically self-serving, and their rhetoric overheated. The United Nations has never had taxing authority and has no plans to seek it; the prospects of sovereign member states ceding such power are nil in any case. Yet it is true that developing countries have sought repeatedly to come up with some politically salable formula or mechanisms for requiring the transfer of resources from the North to the South. This goal has long been—and continues to be—a tendentious issue in debates between developing and developed countries at the United Nations. For example, in early 1970 President Nixon's Task Force on International Development bluntly rejected the notion of a target level for international aid.[47] Yet that fall the General Assembly set precisely such a target for official development assistance at 0.7 percent of GNP for "each economically advanced country" by 1975.[48] Because such Assembly resolutions do not constitute binding legal commitments, the United States generally has accepted them with a caveat about the limited utility of such targets.[49] They have, however, been treated as a moral obligation, as well as a standard, by those who preach about the need for the United States and other wealthy countries to do more to help the least developed countries. Targets may be closer to tithes than taxes, but either way they sound to some Americans more like coercion than appeals for voluntary giving. Echoing a conservative critique of domestic social programs, Professor Samuel Huntington of Harvard, a member of the Nixon task force, commented that "there is something clearly wrong with a program when its goal has to be expressed in terms of how much should be spent on it rather than what should be achieved by it. . . . A percentage can be a target, but it is not a purpose."[50]

Ironically, the congressionally mandated withholdings of U.S. dues payments to the UN since the mid-1980s—something that has been supported by many of those warning about the danger of UN taxes—has encouraged some national delegations to the UN to take a fresh look at the question of alternative funding sources. For example, at the 1995 special commemorative meeting of the General Assembly to mark the UN's fiftieth anniversary, Sweden noted that "mandatory contributions should continue to be the backbone of the financing of the core activities," but that "the dependency on one large contributor must be reduced. . . . [T]he time has come to seriously discuss alternative methods of getting the necessary resources to the United Nations system."[51] During the Assembly's general debate that year, Gareth Evans, then foreign minister of Australia, discussed the pros and cons of new revenue sources in some detail and called on the secretary-general to appoint a high-level advisory group "to think explicitly through what has hitherto been more or less unthinkable: how to fund the United Nations system in a way that reaches out beyond the resources that Member States are prepared to put directly into it."[52] The representatives of several smaller and middle-size countries agreed that further study was needed, and Malaysia urged consideration of "a tax on the trade in weapons of war."[53]

None of these proposals has received detailed study by the member states or gained broad support. UN staff experts, aware of how controversial such notions are among the member states, have by and large steered away from them, even though many individuals within the secretariat may well be personally sympathetic to finding new sources of revenue. The degree of interest in these ideas, however, has been related to the worsening of the UN's financial crisis caused by the mounting arrears, especially those of the United States. If member states were more reliable payers of their obligations, then the specter of a global tax man—as remote as it is today —would disappear completely from the intergovernmental agenda. It is, after all, only in extremis, when the financial viability, even survival, of the UN system appears to be threatened, that such proposals receive even modest attention from governments.

Nationalism and Global Institutions

Americans have long debated whether one can be both an ardent patriot and a farsighted internationalist. Does one have to choose? Is one perspective necessarily incompatible with the other? At what point does nationalism conflict with the goals of international engagement and cooperation? Do nations with a strong sense of identity tend to make, or break, effective international institutions? Is the effort to develop cooperative arrangements among the world's disparate nations likely to require significant compromise of America's interests, influence, or values? Do international institutions, on the whole, serve to advance America's agenda or to make it hostage to priorities that are foreign in their content as well as in their geographical origins? Have the League of Nations and the United Nations, in other words, been essentially un-American activities? Conversely, must the allegedly narrow national interests of the United States (or of other countries) be jettisoned before a more durable peace and a deeper cooperation among nations can be achieved? Is nationalism inherently the enemy of internationalism, and vice versa?

In the debate over the ratification of the League covenant, Senator Lodge left no doubt where he stood. He lamented that the Senate was being asked "in a large and important degree to substitute internationalism for nationalism and an international state for pure Americanism."[54] Posing the matter as a Manichaean choice between the League and his country was, of course, politically convenient for the leader of the League opposition in the Senate. Whether tactic or belief, this argument has surfaced repeatedly, and often simplistically, throughout this century in public and congressional debates about international organization. Writing in 1927 about his experiences as one of President Calvin Coolidge's unofficial representatives at the Geneva World Economic Conference, A. Cressy Morrison asserted that "to destroy nationalism and to substitute a universal brotherhood of nations may be ideal, but the millennium is not yet here. The New Testament teaches 'brotherhood,' but we still have policemen."[55] In a 1952 floor debate Representative Wood of Idaho warned that UNESCO would teach American children to revere not "our country and its beautiful Star-Spangled Banner," but rather "a world government and the spiderweb banner of the United Nations."[56]

Not all of America's opinion leaders, of course, have perceived an inevitable tension between national and international sentiments. In a 1915 address Columbia University President Nicholas Murray Butler noted that patriotism emerged only with the modern nation state and asserted that "there is no necessary conflict in the mind of the wise, well-instructed patriot, between the cause and purpose and aim of this nation and the cause and purpose and aim of the whole great group and family of nations."[57] In an August 1950 editorial in the Saturday Review of Literature, Norman Cousins, long a leading spokesman for world federalism, claimed that "it is inconceivable that there should ever be any real conflict between the welfare of humanity and the welfare of the American people. If such a conflict does arise, then American democracy will have lost its meaning as we know it." In fact, he suggested that U.S. delegates to the UN "can best represent the American people by regarding themselves as representatives of the human community."[58] A dozen years later, A. J. G. Priest, a leader of the United World Federalists, similarly told a Senate hearing that because "the United States is primarily interested in an orderly world" and is "the most idealistic nation," he "would hope there would be no clash between our ideals and what is in the best interests of the planet."[59]

From this idealistic perspective, it appeared that the world wanted what America wanted and that America's values were universally held by the world's people. Reared with faith in the basic goodness of the American people, Butler, Cousins, and Priest were confident that the national interests of the United States would be best served by an orderly, law-abiding, predictable international system, buttressed by networks of international law and cooperation. They yearned for a world order, in other words, that would reflect in practical ways the more positive aspects of their own law-based society. This assumption of a symmetry between U.S. goals and those of other countries also made it far simpler to conclude that patriotism and internationalism were completely compatible, since their objectives converged. Yet how would their assumptions apply to current policy dilemmas, such as when should the United States participate in international interventions in virulent subregional crises? To what extent, and where, do U.S. national interests and transnational humanitarian impulses overlap? As discussed in chapters 7 and 9, in cases where there does appear to be a coincidence of U.S. and global interests, how should the burdens and risks of intervention be shared among countries? Should American notions of national interest be reconfigured to encompass moral and humanitarian imperatives that transcend boundaries and national identities? Unfortunately, the simple assertion that America's core interests and values are shared by others does not begin to answer the complex challenges confronting contemporary policymakers.

Some advocates of a more peaceful and cooperative world seized on nationalism and unfettered sovereignty as the sources of the most destructive conflicts and hence as the enemies that must be overcome. In calling for the establishment of a "League of Peace" to forestall a return to "the anarchy of sovereign nationalities," the *New Republic* in 1915 noted that it would serve as "the first rallying point of a world citizenship."[60] At the conclusion of the Second World War, this view understandably was on the ascendancy. Philip C. Jessup, the noted Columbia University law professor and later a World Court judge, commented in 1947 that "sovereignty has been the chief obstacle in the way of the elimination of war" and that "the danger of war is so terrible and so acute in this atom-splitting age that we are forced to take the risk of too much rather than too little international control of sovereignty." For the United States, he asserted that "our new position of world primacy has also led us to accept the United Nations as the key to our foreign policy. A foreign policy based on the United Nations is a policy of multilateral decision and action, not a policy of unilateral decision and action."[61]

In his August 1950 editorial, Cousins contended that the world needed "law-making, law-enforcing, and law-interpreting agencies," as well as strict limits on sovereignty:

> Unlimited national sovereignty cannot be retained—if we sincerely want peace.
> No nation can be a law unto itself in the common affairs of the world community—if we sincerely want peace.
> No nation can expect to retain sole jurisdiction over the size and nature of its arsenals—if we sincerely want peace.[62]

From the vantage point of this strain in American thinking, the choice between nationalism and internationalism is clear, as it was for Senator Lodge, although Jessup and Cousins would pick the latter.

From the UN's earliest days, however, key U.S. officials stressed that the UN was needed not to preside over a world without national interests, but precisely because of national differences in interest and perspective. Following the Assembly's first meeting in London in 1946, for example, Secretary of State Byrnes reported that "all was not calm and peaceful at the meetings in London." Comparing these clashes of interests to those in "our national and state legislatures," he contended that "if these conflicts of interest did not appear in the forums of the United Nations, these forums would be detached from reality and in the long run turn out to be purposeless and futile."[63] Sixteen years later, in 1962, Adlai Stevenson, then permanent representative to the United Nations, assured the Senate that "on virtually all vital questions we and the majority of members find common ground." Stevenson went on to assert that "in all the history of the United Nations I know of not one case in which the United Nations has injured the vital interests of the United States." Although the United States had never sought "to control the United Nations," he noted, its "position in the United Nations is preeminent" because it was the "host country" and "largest single contributor to its regular budget."[64]

Could the UN ever aspire to control the United States? Although farfetched, this idea nevertheless constituted the premise for what reportedly had been the most expensive miniseries ever produced for American television, the week-long 1987 ABC series "Amerika." The storyline assumed that by 1996 the Soviet Union would have usurped control of the UN and then would employ UN peacekeeping troops to conquer and occupy America, destroying the Capitol and brutalizing American citizens along the way. In the months before the series was aired, the United Nations, the United Nations Association of the USA (UNA-USA), and a host of other nongovernmental organizations protested the depiction of the world organization and the use of the UN symbol and blue helmets. Concerned that Congress had already slashed funding both to the UN and to its peacekeeping operations in Southern Lebanon, a series of former top U.S. officials, including Alexander Haig, Jeane Kirkpatrick, and Robert McFarlane from the first Reagan administration, signed a UNA-USA statement complaining of "the portrayal of U.N. peacekeeping forces as brutal aggressors" and calling for additional programming that "presents a balanced picture of the U.N.'s real-life efforts to keep peace in troubled regions of the world." The controversy generated a great deal of media attention both for the UN and for the series. In the end the series suffered from poor reviews and from low and then declining ratings. It was striking, nevertheless, that a scenario normally identified with the more extreme and paranoid fringes of the American political spectrum could have provided the basis for a week of programming on one of the major networks.

More troubling was the fact that at least one top Reagan administration official was ready to give credence to the notion that the UN could pose a mortal threat to the American way of life. In February 1987 Alan L. Keyes, the ranking State Department official in charge of UN affairs, reminded a House subcommittee that he was "not known as a fan of the United Nations system per se," in part because "it poses some very difficult challenges and dangers to the interests of the United States." In his words,

> It is *probably* going too far to do what was done in the recent series "Amerika," and portray the United Nations as the rubric under which the liberties of this country are finally subverted and destroyed. You do not have to sit in too many General Assemblies to know that those tendencies exist and those intentions exist on the part of some countries. I do not think that it is farfetched at all to believe that on the day that we desert the field that we will certainly leave that stamp to be placed on whatever actions our enemies may see fit to take against our interests.[65]

Although Keyes concluded that the United States should remain engaged in the UN, his emphasis on how threatening the UN could be to American values certainly could have served to reinforce the anxieties and antipathies toward the UN of more radical and paranoid observers. Coming from a top State Department official, these concerns had to be taken seriously. One would not have had to stretch his rhetoric too far to visualize the UN black helicopters featured in the "Amerika" series and later in the lurid visions of far-right militia groups.

So it is not surprising years later that conservative commentators still fret that a strengthened UN could threaten U.S. sovereignty. As Jeffrey R. Gerlach of the Cato Institute wrote in 1993:

> A United Nations endowed with more military power than any single country would have very few restraints placed on its actions. No country, acting alone, would be able to defend itself against a U.N. mission, even an unfair or unwise one. That could even place the sovereignty of the United States at risk. Since the purpose of U.S. foreign policy should be to protect the sovereignty and territorial integrity of the United States, thus ensuring that the liberties of the American people are not imperiled by external threats, the "logic" of proposals to make U.N. military power superior to that of the United States should be firmly rejected.[66]

His dual premise—that the member states would someday permit the UN to control forces more powerful than those of the United States and that they could be employed independently of the wishes of any of the five veto-bearing permanent members of the Security Council—is surreal to say the least. Based on a strawman, on an imaginary, all-powerful, and willful world government, his argument is really a response to the theoretical treatises of those more radical advocates of a world without nations who offer equally unrealistic notions of a world military force capable of defeating the forces of any single national government.[67] This "debate" is a classic case of the two ends of the political spectrum arguing over a hypothesis that is utterly far-fetched and beyond the realm of political possibility in the existing interstate system.

Two dimensions of Gerlach's argument are worth noting, however, because they illustrate why some Americans have grave misgivings about international organization. One is the camel's-nose-under-the-tent syndrome—seen earlier in worries about taxes—which focuses less on current realities than on the potential threats to national sovereignty that could be posed by international arrangements that accrue unanticipated powers over the years. How that will come about is rarely addressed, but the fear of the unknown future seems to have been palpable enough through the years to have fed a persistent sense of unease, even paranoia, on the far right. A second implication of his argument is that the United

Nations has an identity, corpus, and cognition that are somehow independent of its most powerful member states and that somehow this entity can be turned—how and by whom is unclear—against its creators. The underlying fear is that the UN's founders have given life to some kind of an institutional Frankenstein with powers and an independent volition far beyond anything they had contemplated.

Inhibiting U.S. Freedom of Action or Multiplying Its Reach?

Testifying before the Senate Foreign Relations Committee in 1965, Secretary of State Dean Rusk spoke of his wariness about the term sovereignty, "because immediately people wrap the American Flag around themselves and resort to that form of patriotism which Samuel Johnson once had referred to as 'the last refuge of the scoundrel.'" In the practice of U.S. foreign policy, Rusk noted:

> We are every day, in one sense, accepting limitations upon our complete freedom of action. . . . We have more than 4,300 treaties and international agreements, two-thirds of which have been entered into in the past 25 years. . . . Each one of which at least limits our freedom of action. We exercise our sovereignty in going into these agreements.[68]

Rusk went on to argue that "law is a process by which we increase our range of freedom" and that "we are constantly enlarging our own freedom by being able to predict what others are going to do." Pointing to particular policy concerns, he emphasized that "there are no such things as sovereignty with respect to epidemic diseases, for example, because disease does not recognize political borders."[69]

Proponents of multilateral initiatives, especially in the peace and security realm, have frequently emphasized their multiplier effect, through which the United States can enlist other member states to join it in a common effort to address common interests. In addition to the benefits of sharing the burden and spreading the risks, such joint initiatives, especially when conducted under an international legal umbrella provided by the Security Council or an established regional organization, offer the prospect of greater political support at home and abroad.[70] Advocates assert that multilateral undertakings almost always gain broader domestic political support, as well as legal legitimacy, than do similar actions carried out unilaterally. The coalition effort, authorized by the Security Council, to expel

Iraqi forces from Kuwait is often cited as a successful case. According to former president George Bush, Security Council Resolution 678, which authorized the use of force, helped to gel both international and domestic political support:

> It eased some of the problems of coalition maintenance and resolved the debate about the need for provocation before we could act. Although we didn't realize it at the time, it also changed the debate with Congress, creating a context for the use of force which helped bring it aboard. The Security Council had voted to go to war.[71]

On Capitol Hill, legislator after legislator, including some normally quite critical of the UN, cited the Security Council's authorization as reason to support President Bush's decision to use force in the Gulf.

Less than a decade later, however, prominent members of Congress, such as Senator John Ashcroft, R-Mo., were warning "of a growing arrogance of a United Nations that has grown accustomed to dictating American foreign policy toward Iraq." In his view, Clinton administration policy was drifting to the point at which "the President of the United States will find himself asking permission of U.N. bureaucrats before he takes action to secure the interests of the United States. That cannot be allowed."[72] From this perspective, the danger of the tail wagging the dog is ever present—that in trying to pursue its national interests through the complex political dynamics of multilateral organizations, the United States will lose its freedom to maneuver and will end up lending support to the separate agendas of other countries and blocs. These critics see, in the give-and-take among large numbers of countries that characterizes the multilateral decisionmaking process, the temptation, if not the inevitability, of compromising U.S. interests and values. According to this school of thought, large multilateral institutions, even if they are not pernicious and corrupt, tend at the very least to seek courses of action that represent the lowest common denominator of the disparate interests of their member states. In the process, individual national purposes often get homogenized and generalized beyond recognition.

In opposing the plan for the League of Nations, Senator Lodge eloquently voiced deep reservations both about the ill-defined nature of U.S. commitments and about potential restrictions on its freedom of action:

> I cannot forget America. . . . I cannot but keep her interests in mind. I do not want the republic to take any detriment. I do not want dangers heaped upon

us that would only cripple us in the good work we need to do. I want to keep America as she has been—not isolated, not prevent her from joining other nations for these great purposes—but I wish her to be master of her fate. . . . I want her left in a position to do that work and not submit her to a vote of other nations with no recourse except to break a treaty she wishes to maintain.[73]

Complaining that the draft covenant was "very loosely and obscurely drawn" including on such key questions as how the executive council would reach a decision, Lodge stressed that "whatever a country agrees to, that the country must maintain. The sanctity of treaties lies at the basis of all peace, and therefore we must be as careful as possible to remove all chances of disagreement arising out of conflicting interpretations of language." The problem was compounded, he said, by the lack of any "provision for withdrawal or termination," making the treaty, and the U.S. commitment, "indissoluble."[74]

Aware of the criticism that the League covenant was too loosely drawn, which was voiced by some of the proponents of the League as well as by its opponents,[75] the architects of the United Nations charter sought to draft a tighter document that defined more precisely both the multilateral decisionmaking process and the obligations of member states. These efforts, in turn, led to complaints by some UN observers, such as James T. Shotwell and Marina Salvin, about the rigidity of the charter text.[76] As supporters of broader international cooperation, their perspective, based in part on frustration that Soviet vetoes were narrowing the range of UN action, ran in quite the opposite direction from Senator Lodge's concern that the United States would not have been in a position to block unwanted commitments in the League because of its loose structure. Recognizing this dilemma to some extent, Shotwell and Salvin, writing in 1949, argued that "the idea that the United Nations would be strengthened by binding its members to legal obligations that are stricter and more far-reaching than those in the Charter of the United Nations is proceeding along the very line which strengthens the hand of the objector by offering him more points on which to object."[77] The effect of these contradictory strains in American thinking has been to place international institutions in an uneasy position of imposing obligations that are seen as either too strict or too loose on their member states.

Some irreconcilable objectors have asserted that a cabal of internationalists has pushed America into international arrangements that can only sap its resources on the agendas of other countries. In a 1950 statement critical of the Korean conflict, Representative Clare E. Hoffman, R-Mich., cautioned

his House colleagues that "for years financially and politically powerful individuals and groups have been attempting to force us into some form of a
world-wide organization. They have succeeded to such an extent that they
now claim that we must continue to furnish the munitions of war and the
men to fight in every way to which the United Nations may commit us."[78]
According to this theory, even the U.S. veto could not preserve the nation's
volition once it joined the UN, because internationalist Americans would
control the U.S. vote in the Security Council. Under these assumptions,
there can be no satisfactory guarantees of American sovereignty once it
agrees to participate in an international organization, because the problem
stems more from domestic politics than from international structures.

Another of Senator Lodge's concerns—that multilateral diplomacy
consisted of walking a tightrope between asserting national interests and
getting along with the other delegations—was reiterated in 1927 by
A. Cressy Morrison in his reflections on the World Economic Conference. It
is difficult "for any nation, and more especially the United States," he commented, "to meet the majority opinion and be courteous and friendly without yielding something to his international idea when in our hearts we feel
we should not yield."[79] Morrison's cautions may sound rather quaint now
that U.S. negotiators have accumulated more than a half century of active
engagement in a wide variety of multilateral forums. His words do express,
however, a sense of uneasiness that U.S. representatives often seem to feel in
multilateral negotiating frameworks.

In the early years of the Reagan administration, for example, U.S. representatives frequently appeared to be uncomfortable in UN bodies, toward
which they had been highly critical and in which their views were out of step
with the majority. During those years the United States often seemed more
like an in-house gadfly, seeking to protect its values by keeping a certain
distance from the other member states and from the daily give-and-take of
multilateral diplomacy, than like the preeminent and confident power
described by Ambassador Stevenson. A case in point was the somewhat
petulant remark by Ambassador Charles Lichtenstein in a meeting of the
UN host committee in 1983 that if other members did not like the way they
were being treated in the United States, then they should "seriously consider removing themselves and this organization from the soil of the United
States." Should his point be missed, he added that "we will put no impedi-
ment in your way and we will be at dockside bidding you a fond farewell as
you set off into the sunset."[80] Keyes, who was handpicked by Ambassador
Kirkpatrick to be the U.S. ambassador to the UN Economic and Social

Council and then became assistant secretary of state for international organization affairs, had no doubt about the task at hand and no qualms about
undertaking it with gusto. As he later boasted during his unsuccessful run
for the Republic presidential nomination in 1996:

> What we did at the United Nations was to fight the battle against those who
> were seeking to destroy America's interests and values. . . . I went there as a
> warrior on behalf of this people, to make sure that our values would not be
> destroyed, that our partnerships around the world would not be vilified, and
> that our enemies would not be able to pretend that they had the moral high
> ground over us on any policy question.[81]

Even given the excesses of campaign rhetoric, it is clear that the Reagan team
at the UN was not there to blend in and get along, but—in their view—to
do battle against multiple adversaries in diplomatic garb.

A related problem for a global power like the United States is whether
the political dynamics of near-universal multilateral organizations might
not complicate relations with allies, as well as restricting American freedom
of maneuver in other ways. It may become more difficult, for instance, to
manipulate either carrots or sticks unilaterally.[82] This has no doubt been a
problem from time to time in American ties to Israel and Taiwan, but much
less so with other allies, who have been better positioned to protect their
interests and less likely to face political assaults in the General Assembly and
other UN forums. Ironically, as noted in chapter 2, America's allies have
been among those most critical of its withholding of dues payments as a
means of forcing reform on the world organization. They have seen it very
much in their interests to encourage U.S. delegates to be more fully
enmeshed in the multilateral decisionmaking process so as to decrease the
possibilities for unanticipated unilateral actions as well as to buttress their
own interests and policies in global bodies.

Some Americans have questioned whether the U.S. role as leader of the
free world, particularly during the cold war years, was compatible with
dependence on the United Nations and its multilateral decisionmaking
processes. As Senator John G. Tower, the influential Texas Republican,
asserted in 1962, "We must not allow it [the United Nations] to dictate our
foreign policy. The responsibility for free world leadership is ours. We should
not abdicate that leadership."[83] Yet would not its allies and friends look to
U.S. leadership, and power, within the United Nations, as well as outside it?
Could the West have afforded to cede the political battlefield offered by the

UN to the East? If the United States had taken that course, would it not have eliminated one of its options for competing effectively during the cold war: employing multilateral diplomacy when needed? This, in effect, would have lessened American freedom of action, not expanded it. Senator Tower's prescription might well have become a self-fulfilling prophecy.

More recently, Bob Dole, writing in 1995, emphasized that "U.S. sovereignty must be defended, not delegated." Neither an isolationist nor a fan of the United Nations, he underlined that:

> International organizations will, at best, practice policymaking at the lowest common denominator—find a course that is the least objectionable to the most members. Too often, they reflect a consensus that opposes American interests or does not reflect American principles and ideals. Even gaining support for an American position can involve deals or tradeoffs that are not in America's long-term interests. . . . Subcontracting American foreign policy and subordinating American sovereignty encourage and strengthen isolationist forces at home—and embolden our adversaries abroad.[84]

The target of Dole's criticism, of course, was less international organization than the nature and conduct of U.S. policies within these bodies. While that was to be expected from a likely presidential candidate on the eve of an election year, his arguments also expressed deep doubts about the value of the multilateral decisionmaking process, especially because he questioned the extent to which other member states share American interests and values. In his view, moreover, for the United States to depend on multilateral organizations is ultimately tantamount to feeding isolationist impulses because the mandates set by international bodies usually do not coincide with American interests and because the organizations lack the power to implement them in any case.

A prime purpose of international organizations, of course, is to provide a forum for identifying points of common interest among member states and then for facilitating joint action to advance them. As the base of common interests narrows, so too does this rationale. At the same time, however, the corollary purpose—to find a means of resolving differences—comes to the fore. In this way, the UN has found a raison d'être in good times and bad, taking on a different guise according to the ebb and flow of world politics and surviving postwar euphoria, cold war tension, post–cold war optimism, and more recent reassessment and retrenchment. The divergent perceptions of the extent of shared values with other countries, as illustrated by Senator Dole's concerns, nevertheless have fueled the sense of ambivalence that characterizes American attitudes and policies toward the world body.[85] These views persist even though three-fourths of all General Assembly resolutions in the past five years (1994–98) have been approved by consensus and the degree of voting coincidence on other Assembly resolutions between the United States and other member states tripled between 1988 and 1995.[86] Nevertheless, it is certainly true that multilateral decision-making necessarily entails some trade-offs to gain the support of others for one's national positions. That is the nature of the business.

A central fallacy in this line of reasoning, however, is the assumption that acting unilaterally would always permit complete freedom of action. Domestic politics may—and frequently do—limit a government's ability to pursue international initiatives, particularly those that lack the support and participation of other countries. If individual nations or groups of countries oppose in the United Nations a course of action being considered by the United States, is it not reasonable to assume that they would express their opposition, one way or another, depending on how much it matters to them, outside of the world body as well, thus raising U.S. costs or constraining its options? It is far too simplistic to assume full flexibility in one case and none in the other. Both entail shades of gray, depending on the circumstances of each situation. As suggested earlier, there may be times, as in Kuwait and Haiti, when international and domestic political support can be rallied by first gaining Security Council blessing for an essentially American initiative. According to former president George Bush and his national security adviser Brent Scowcroft, the choice of a multilateral course of action for forcing Iraqi troops from Kuwait was a matter of realism not ideology:

> We also believed that the United States should not go it alone, that a multilateral approach was better. This was, in part, a practical matter. Mounting an effective military counter to Iraq's invasion required the backing and bases of Saudi Arabia and other Arab states. Building an international response led us immediately to the United Nations, which could provide a cloak of acceptability to our efforts and mobilize world opinion behind the principles we wished to project.[87]

In such cases, the scope of action that is politically, geographically, and materially feasible may in fact be expanded, not narrowed, by taking the multilateral route.

Evolving Notions of Sovereignty

To many of the harsher critics of American participation in multilateral bodies, there is an inevitable, zero-sum, trade-off between the strengthening of international institutions and the loss of U.S. sovereignty. During the debate over the League of Nations, Senator Borah eloquently invoked an image of:

> a free, untrammeled Nation, imbued anew and inspired again with the national spirit; not isolation but freedom to do as our people think wise and just; not isolation but simply the unembarrassed and unentangled freedom of a great Nation to determine for itself and in its own way where duty lies and where wisdom calls.[88]

Bishop Neely stated flatly that "the United States of America cannot put itself under this super-world-government without losing its sovereignty, which it would do the moment it took the league obligations."[89] From his stark perspective, the very act of accepting international commitments constituted an unacceptable diminution of national sovereignty. Others, of course, saw these questions very differently. The League covenant "does not create a super-sovereignty—it is only a loose obligation among the nations of the world," said former president Taft, who then asserted:

> It does not impair our just sovereignty in the slightest—it is only an arrangement for the maintenance of our sovereignty within its proper limits: to wit, a sovereignty regulated by international law and international morality and international justice, with a somewhat rude machinery created by the agreement of nations to prevent one sovereignty from being used to impose its unjust will on other sovereignties. Certainly we, with our national ideals, can have no desire to secure any greater sovereignty than this.[90]

In equating sovereignty with just principles, Taft seemed to be suggesting that national sovereignty was not an absolute and that the task of international organization was to protect that sovereignty which is just from that which is not. To him, there was no contradiction: America's exercise of sovereignty would be an extension of its fundamental values, which would naturally coincide with the system of international norms and laws that would guide international organization. America and international organization need not fear each other, for they would stand for the same things.

President Wilson tended to speak of sovereignty in the kind of sweeping and relative terms that worried his more nationalistic critics. In a March

1919 speech, for example, he looked forward to a time "when men would be just as eager partisans of the sovereignty of mankind as they were now of their own national sovereignty."[91] More modestly, A. Lawrence Lowell, in his debate with Senator Lodge, asserted that the covenant of Paris provided only for the "minimum essentials of such a League."[92] (President Truman seemed to echo him twenty-seven years later in telling Congress that the UN only "represents a minimum essential beginning."[93]) In Lowell's view, "the fear of a super-sovereign body, to which we are asked to sacrifice our independence, is the creature of an over-heated imagination. . . . No organ of the League has any authority to give commands to this country that need give us a moment's anxiety." In a less dismissive tone, however, Lowell did note the lack of "an express statement in the Covenant that internal affairs are not subject to interference by the Council," although he said that could easily be added and would conform to "recognized principles of international law."[94] (The drafters of the United Nations charter, apparently having learned this lesson, did add such a clause in Article 2, paragraph 7.)

In such polarized debates, more down-to-earth, common-sense voices sometimes can be heard from middle America. Also writing in 1919, F. R. Clow, a professor of history and economics at the State Normal School in Oshkosh, Wisconsin, recognized that the League's power and reach could grow over time, but that this would occur only with American public support. In his scenario, neither the United States nor its people would lose their volition by joining the League:

> The great importance of the League of Nations is not in what it can be or do at the outset but in what it may become. . . . But the League can thus grow into a super-national state only by serving us better in some respects than our national governments do. There is no reason for being afraid of it on that account.[95]

It is notable, however, that Clow's basis for assessing international organization is how well it serves the needs of people in general, not simply the interests of individual nation states. In his comments appear to be the seeds for a kind of transnational, or global, populism. Unlike those, such as Bishop Neely, Pat Buchanan, or Pat Robertson, who mix populism and nationalism with right-wing ideology in a potent brew, Clow based his assessment on the straightforward criterion of whether or not international organizations were acting in a way to benefit people everywhere and anywhere. If so, they should grow; if not, they should fade away. Whichever level of government performs best, whether national or international, would be deserving of his support. Clow's view suggests, as many have contended through the years, that true sovereignty rests with the people, not with national governments. Professor Clow seems almost to be asking: whose sovereignty is it to lose in any case?

Eight decades after the great debate over the League, Americans still have not resolved their differences over the effect on national sovereignty of participation in international arrangements. Although more than fifty years of active participation in the UN system seem to have reassured most Americans that the sovereignty of their nation is sturdy enough to survive such extended and extensive international involvements, not everyone is yet convinced. In his book *The Great Betrayal*, Pat Buchanan targets his wrath on those free-traders and globalists who, in his view, are more than ready to exchange American sovereignty for the material benefits of the global economy. In order "not to awaken the sleeping giant of American patriotism," Buchanan writes, they have chosen "to proceed by subtlety and indirection" and "by stealth":

> Like a shipwrecked, exhausted Gulliver on the beach of Lilliput, America is to be tied down with threads, strand by strand, until it cannot move when it awakens. "Piece by piece," our sovereignty is being surrendered. By accession to NAFTA, GATT, the UN, the WTO, the World Bank, the IMF, America has ensnared itself in a web that restricts its freedom of action, diminishes its liberty, and siphons off its wealth.[96]

To raise such notions, he acknowledges, "is to provoke ridicule as a reactionary caught up in conspiracy theories." Like a true populist, however, what he describes is not the calculated conspiracy of the few, but the clash of interests between the affluent internationalists and the working class that has been left behind by global economic competition.[97]

Senator Jesse Helms, as well, continues to see substantial tension between nationalism and internationalism and between his views and those of international secretariats:

> The United Nations has moved from facilitating diplomacy among nation-states to supplanting them altogether. The international elites running the United Nations look at the idea of the nation-state with disdain; they consider it a discredited notion of the past that has been superseded by the idea of the United Nations. In their view, the interests of nation-states are parochial and should give way to global interests. Nation-states, they believe, should recog-

nize the primacy of these global interests and accede to the United Nations' sovereignty to pursue them.[98]

In some respects, Helms's conclusions are understandable, even if greatly exaggerated. It *is* the responsibility of international secretariats to look for answers that transcend the interests of specific member states and that could form the basis of agreement and common ground among them. It *is* their job to be "international" rather than to represent the interests of any country. In reality, however, this duty requires that they be ever cognizant of the perspectives and positions of member states, especially of powerful ones such as the United States. Nation states define both the context within which and the mandates for which international secretariats work. Nation states also shape and approve budgets and exercise administrative oversight, sometimes amounting to micromanagement, of the secretariat. More fundamentally, it is the nation states, not the UN secretariat, that have the capacities for carrying out the decisions reached in the intergovernmental bodies. For these reasons, the past half century of experience has demonstrated the degree to which the "United Nations" is dependent on its member states, even if some members of the secretariat and some private commentators would have it otherwise.

Although questions of sovereignty have not disappeared from American debates about participation in international organizations, what has changed dramatically over the years is the context within which the arguments are pursued.[99] Isolationism was abandoned as a viable option with World War II, and questions of sovereignty received much less attention at the time of the founding of the UN than they had in the debate over the League. As Senator Joseph L. Hill, D-Ala., declared during the 1945 debate on charter ratification:

> When we ratify the San Francisco Charter and become a member of the international organization, we lose no American rights, we surrender no American sovereignty, we invite no interference or meddling with American domestic affairs, we continue [to be] the masters of our own household. And force cannot be used without our consent, since force is used only if we are in agreement with the other nations to do for our peace and for the peace of the world the things which we cannot do alone.[100]

In 1945, these sentiments were accepted without question by almost all of the Senate.

Today, not only does the United States readily participate in many hundreds of multilateral arrangements of an intergovernmental character, but the dynamics of commerce, investment, communications, culture, science, education, technology, and public policy issues has required the private sector, nonprofit and nongovernmental organizations, and individual citizens to think, plan, and act in transnational and global terms. As conditions have changed, so have notions of sovereignty. Long ago it ceased to be an absolute. Relatively few aside from the far right argue anymore that there is a zero-sum tug-of-war between internationalism and sovereignty, especially on nonmilitary issues. Even security is most often seen as a shared commodity to be pursued through alliances, arms control accords, economic sanctions, peacekeeping, and international diplomacy, as well as ultimately by means of national military power and will. Despite all of these developments, it would be a mistake to conclude that sovereignty is no longer an issue in domestic debates about U.S.-UN relations. The issue has simply undergone a metamorphosis, assuming new forms under changing conditions and attracting new advocates to different sides of the continuing debate, not always along party lines.[101]

Zero-sum arguments about gaining or losing national sovereignty miss two of the most fundamental ways in which conceptions of sovereignty are evolving with the times. One stems from the growing role of nonstate actors in shaping and implementing public policy, and the other from the ways in which international institutions assist, rather than erode, the ability of nation states to maintain their sovereignty. In domestic as well as foreign policy, there has been an unrelenting tendency for nonstate actors of all kinds—corporations, nonprofits, nongovernmental organizations, religious, cultural, and educational institutions, professional and technical associations (what scholars call "epistemic communities"), unions, and individuals—to become more and more involved in matters once considered affairs of the state. It has been reported, for example, that George Soros's personal philanthropy to strategically important Russia exceeds official U.S. assistance, not to mention his much larger for-profit investments there.[102] Ted Turner in 1997 pledged $1 billion to the UN system over ten years, to be implemented through a private UN foundation with an international board that he has established; Turner's pledge will exceed all but a handful of UN member states in terms of annual giving to the world body. And in late 1998 Microsoft chairman Bill Gates announced a $100 million gift to expedite the delivery of children's vaccines to developing countries, with a Seattle-based nonprofit organization to work with international agencies, such as the

World Health Organization (WHO), United Nations Children's Fund (UNICEF), and the World Bank, in carrying out this initiative.[103] Private capital flow to developing countries ($244 billion in 1996) is six times as large as the official development assistance of all donor countries and international institutions, including the World Bank, combined ($41 billion in 1996).[104] In recent years nongovernmental groups have played catalytic, even decisive, roles in issues as varied as environmental protection and sustainable development, human rights, humanitarian affairs and refugee relief, and arms control (land mines, nuclear testing, and chemical weapons in particular). Not only have these independent groups worked alongside whichever governments happened to share their views, regardless of geography, but the scope of their efforts in terms of substance, structure, and participation has been transnational, focused on issues, not national boundaries.

None of this, of course, implies that governments no longer matter or are going out of business. They remain the essential building blocks and ultimate decisionmakers of any plausible scenario for world order. For all their claims of autonomy, moreover, much of the political energy of nonstate actors is directed toward influencing the decisions and actions of governments and intergovernmental institutions. What is increasingly evident, however, is that sovereignty is not some sort of exclusive or finite property of either nation states or intergovernmental organizations that can be traded off between these two levels of governance without being shared by others, particularly the peoples from whom sovereignty is delegated to states to begin with. In practical, if not legal, terms, sovereignty has become an increasingly inclusive and elastic concept.[105] As a result, squabbles about whether sovereignty is the property of member states or the UN tend to miss the point: a place in the global priority-setting process, as well as at the national level, will also have to be found for nonstate actors in the future.

Despite the emphasis on the importance of civil society in Secretary-General Annan's reform report of July 1997, the UN member states, many of which still have decidedly statist orientations, are still struggling to define an appropriate role for nonstate actors in what is a quintessentially intergovernmental organization. Perhaps over time the UN system can gain stronger public constituencies through the greater involvement of civil society in its operations, as has happened to some extent with environmental, arms control, humanitarian, and human rights constituencies. The place of civil society in decisionmaking and governance structures, however, is much more problematic. How to move forward on both fronts without alienating those member states that are already perturbed by the advances made by nongovernmental organizations is anything but clear.

Simplistic arguments about a perceived U.S.-UN tug-of-war over sovereignty overlook the many ways in which international institutions have been the friends, not the enemies, of national sovereignty. The interdependence of sovereign nation states was widely recognized as a fact of life during the debates preceding the formation of the League of Nations.[106] And the United Nations was created by nation states to serve their needs, not to be their competitor. Their chief need, and the fundamental purpose of the organization, was to discourage aggression by one state against the territorial sovereignty of another. Although it has often fallen short in the effort to achieve this through collective security, the UN system has proven very useful as a durable instrument with agreed rules and procedures that permit member states to combine their efforts to deal jointly with a wide array of issues for which no unilateral or bilateral solution has been found. In today's world even the strongest nation state is incapable of handling on its own any number of economic, environmental, social, humanitarian, and security challenges that defy borders and easy answers. International organizations have helped to fill this "sovereignty gap." Since the development of weapons of mass destruction and intercontinental delivery systems, security itself— once closely identified with sovereignty—has required negotiating with potential adversaries; building alliances; developing international norms and institutions, including multilateral monitoring and inspection regimes; and taking joint action when possible to encourage compliance with these rules and arrangements.

Rather than eroding national sovereignty, the United Nations and other international arrangements have generally served to foster the kinds of rules, conditions, and negotiating opportunities that have permitted the safe and productive exercise of national sovereignty, thus extending the life of the nation state era of history. As Fareed Zakaria has pointed out, it is important to distinguish the ambitions of state structures from those of nations. He is reassured that "states today are simply not as autonomous or as powerful as they were 150 years ago" and that "the long absence of great-power war and the growth of the global economy have weakened the state and intertwined it in structures that will make the once-straightforward rise and fall of great powers a complex, friction-filled process." In his view, moreover, these complications "could help blunt the otherwise aggressive temperament of great powers and tame the fierce nature of international life."[107]

At the same time the United Nations system itself has been affected by these developments, caught in the web of international arrangements that it had helped to spur in the first place, turning into a remarkably different institution than that envisioned in 1945 as a security-oriented vehicle for the victorious allies of World War II. Not only have its membership, substantive scope, and range of activities expanded enormously, but, as an intergovernmental organization, it has confronted many of the same questions that national governments have about how to involve nonstate actors in its structure and work, as well as how to address the host of issues that are intrastate or transnational rather than strictly intergovernmental in character.

The world body, moreover, with its mandate to find ways to harmonize the actions of nations toward common ends, inevitably tends to advocate a broader understanding of the boundaries of national interest. As Secretary-General Annan phrased it in his first annual report on the work of the organization, "the twentieth-century project of international organization is all about how to stretch national interests and preferences, temporally as well as spatially, so as to produce in greater quantities the public goods that the political market place of inter-State behaviour would otherwise underproduce."[108] Perhaps one of the great tasks of the twenty-first century will be to try to convince those resistant to being "stretched," including many members of Congress, of the merits of a more expansive view of the scope of national interest. Until this is accomplished, the twentieth-century project identified by the secretary-general will remain incomplete and precarious.

CHAPTER FOUR

Enemies Within,
Enemies Without

As it seems to be a universal opinion in Europe and other countries that
the United States is unduly prosperous, so is there a united sentiment that
anything which can be done to distribute our prosperity throughout the
world, and advance other nations by tapping our sources of income is a
perfectly normal and proper thing to do.

— A. CRESSY MORRISON, 1927

We are just like neophytes in a professional poker game, and have just
about as much chance of coming out even.

—SENATOR GEORGE MALONE, 1950

This is the last nation on the face of the earth to shun diversity, or to reject
the open forum, or to fear the growth of democratic practices.

—SECRETARY OF STATE DEAN RUSK, 1965

Of course Kofi [Annan] would see it that way. After all, he hails from an
inconsequential little country on a mendicant continent that has distinguished itself lately for coups, massacres and AIDS.

—PATRICK J. BUCHANAN, 1998

GIVEN THE SPIRIT of American exceptionalism and the worries about governance and sovereignty traced in the last two chapters, it is not surprising
that a sizable number of Americans have also harbored doubts about the
intentions of others. This chapter, then, considers my third theme: the
tendency to see within global bodies unfriendly and irresponsible factions
that could use these organizations to milk America's wealth and power or to
challenge its values. These suspicions have proven remarkably resilient
through the years, even as the principal targets of these concerns have
shifted with major geopolitical realignments. From decade to decade, congressional debates about U.S. participation in and support for global orga-

nizations have voiced persistent doubts about the motivations and intentions of the other member states.

Strangely enough, for years it has also been a common refrain in United Nations circles that nothing is wrong with the world organization except for its members. This may seem an odd claim for a body created by, of, and for sovereign nation states—after all, what would be the alternative? When seen in a different context, however, this old saw does reflect one of the principal sources of American ambivalence: the mistrust, at times even disdain, that a sizable minority of Americans have felt toward the political and social systems of other member states. This tendency has been compounded by the practice of large numbers of countries to cluster together in geographical or political blocs, in part to counteract the power of the United States and its allies. The very existence of blocs from which the United States has been excluded has raised the ire and doubts of influential Americans from time to time. If one is suspicious of the motivations of other countries, sees their objectives as incompatible with those of the United States, or lacks respect for the legitimacy of other governments or blocs, then one's enthusiasm for institutions designed to promote greater degrees of intergovernmental cooperation is bound to be tempered at best.

Usually these doubts about the leaders of other countries are coupled with expressions of sympathy for their citizens. Americans are not, on the whole, mean-spirited about other peoples, but they do tend to be wary of the machinations of other governments, which are often caricatured as corrupt, undemocratic, and even less trustworthy than their own. So it is not completely incongruous to see the simultaneous growth of people-to-people, Peace Corps, and student exchanges and of anti-foreign-government rhetoric, as is the case today.[1] As some Americans gravitate to the internationalist pole, others are attracted to chauvinistic explanations for their problems.

During the course of the twentieth century, the primary targets of xenophobia have shifted from the intrigues of Old World Europe, to the malevolence of Soviet communism, to the demands of third world autocrats. The constant for those Americans most skeptical of international organization, however, has been persistent doubt about the compatibility of the goals and priorities of other member states with American values and purposes. Without some minimum threshold of mutual trust and respect, of course, the prospects for any intergovernmental organization will be sharply limited. As John Foster Dulles, then a U.S. representative to the General Assembly, phrased it in 1948, speaking of the difficulties of developing "a wholly adequate world organization" when some powerful member states do not respect political liberties, "it is impossible to combine, in one order, the idea that the state is the *servant* of the people and the idea that the state is the *master* of the people."[2]

Those Wily Europeans

A recurrent, but fading, theme among American critics of international organization has been that other countries—particularly the Machiavellian Europeans—have had base and ulterior motives for creating these institutions, in contrast to the lofty, if allegedly naive, principles that moved presidents Wilson, Franklin D. Roosevelt, and Truman. In isolationist circles, this theme had gained nourishment from more than a century of reverence to a narrow and selective interpretation of George Washington's Farewell Address of 1796, in which he asserted that:

> Europe has a set of primary interests which to us have none or a very remote relation. Hence she must be engaged in frequent controversies, the causes of which are essentially foreign to our concerns. . . . Why, by interweaving our destiny with that of any part of Europe, entangle peace and prosperity in the toils of European ambition, rivalship, interest, humor, or caprice?[3]

Washington called for the extension of commercial relations to Europe but warned the United States "to have with them as little political connection as possible." He urged that existing "engagements be observed in their genuine sense. But in my opinion it is unnecessary and would be unwise to extend them." Arguing against "permanent alliances," Washington acknowledged that from "a respectable defensive posture, we may safely trust to temporary alliances for extraordinary emergencies."[4] After all, the alliance with France had just proved to be a considerable asset in the struggle for freedom from British colonialism. Displaying more than a little realism tinged with understandable cynicism, he cautioned against naiveté, not against dealing with others to further the national interest:

> It is folly in one nation to look for disinterested favors from another; that it must pay with a portion of its independence for whatever it may accept under that character. . . . There can be no greater error than to expect or calculate upon real favors from nation to nation. It is an illusion which experience must cure.

A balanced understanding of the founding father's words—with their subsequent Monroe Doctrine corollary—had served America well during its first century as it focused on domestic expansion and development.[5] In that process, the young nation engaged in extensive international diplomacy and commercial relations, dealing with interstate political and security questions on a case-by-case basis as national priorities dictated. For most of that period, the growing nation was in little position to interfere in European politics in any case. It was more concerned, and properly so, with limiting the reach of European ambitions in the Western Hemisphere.

By the late nineteenth century, fueled by a sense of Manifest Destiny, America's growing role and ambitions began to extend far beyond the continent, or even the hemisphere.[6] The widely popular war with Spain established the United States as a global, some said imperial, power. In parallel with these expanding conceptions of national and strategic interests, public interest in international law, arbitration, and limitations on armaments also swelled, resulting in active American participation in the first Hague peace conference in 1899 and in the second in 1907.[7] President Theodore Roosevelt's successful mediation of the Russian-Japanese war in 1905 added to the prevailing sense that the United States had emerged as an important and engaged global power. Given these dynamics, by the early years of the twentieth century many Americans had come to see isolationism as anachronistic and unilateralism as inadequate—and potentially risky—for an America coming to take its natural place as one of the leading nations of the world.

Along these lines, William Howard Taft, speaking in Salt Lake City in February 1919, declared that:

> The men who advocate our staying out of the League by reason of a policy against entangling alliances laid down by [George] Washington, for a small nation struggling for existence, whereas to-day we are one of the most powerful nations in the world—I say that these men belittle the United States and its people.[8]

Taft's forward-looking vision of a dynamic America casting off the shackles imposed by its former weakness no doubt fit the optimistic outlook of much of the body politic. Washington's cautions, however, better corresponded to the prevalent cynicism about the motives and conduct of the Great War and, more immediately, about the way in which European leaders had reacted to

President Wilson's high principles and bold plans for a new era of international cooperation. America, in other words, needed a strategy for getting
beyond its isolationist tendencies without submitting to the control of
Europe, with its intrigues and petty quarrels.

Wilson claimed that the League structure would ensure that nations
would no longer be dependent on alliances for security because "this project
of the League of Nations is a great process of disentanglement."[9] But, as historian Elmer Bendiner has noted, "events in Europe seemed to conspire to
further America's suspicions that it was the honest country bumpkin being
taken by the wily city con man of internationalism."[10] Wilson, through his
frequent and self-serving complaints about the cynical, short-sighted, and
nationalistic machinations of his European negotiating partners, tended to
confirm rather than deny this view.[11] In his oft-quoted September 1919
speech in Pueblo, Colorado, he went so far as to assert that "it is only certain
bodies of foreign sympathies, certain bodies of sympathy with foreign
nations that are organized against this great document which the American
representatives have brought back from Paris."[12] In his controversial public
letter of March 1920 to Senator Gilbert M. Hitchcock, D-Neb., Wilson
underlined that "for my own part, I am as intolerant of imperialistic designs
on the part of other nations as I was of such designs on the part of
Germany."[13] In a private note, he complained of "the constant militaristic
intrigues" that he felt had been under way within the French delegation at
the Paris peace conference.[14] Earlier, upon Wilson's return from Paris,
Senator Key Pittman, D-Nev., had exclaimed that "the President has won the
greatest diplomatic victory recorded in history. He has overcome the cynical diplomat, the skeptical statesman and the hopeless materialist."[15]
Speaking of the causes of war, William Jennings Bryan concluded that "the
League's diagnosis of the disease is faulty; . . . the real difficulty with Europe
is that the governments reject the moral standards that regulate individual
life. . . . There is neither a system of international law nor an accepted international code of ethics enforcible by common agreement and united
action."[16]

Cautioning his readers that "the atmosphere surrounding this pact is
one of secrecy, compromise and exchange," Charles Nagel, Taft's secretary of
commerce and labor, said that "in effect it is an alliance, to which we are to
become responsible parties, to enforce for others what we refuse to claim or
to accept for ourselves. . . . The only altruistic contribution is to come from
us." He concluded that "instead of committing ourselves to this Unholy
Alliance, it will be well to keep our hands free, prepared at all times and

under all circumstances to give aid to true champions of Freedom and Independence."[17] Bishop Thomas Benjamin Neely, the pungent right-wing commentator, put it succinctly: "true Americanism cannot support the so-called League of Nations, for anything that is against the democratic idea is against this democratic nation."[18] The Republican party, in its 1928 platform, extolled the virtues of a dual policy under which the United States had refused to accept any obligations under the League covenant but had "most usefully assisted by cooperation in the humanitarian and technical work undertaken by the League, without involving ourselves in European politics by accepting membership."[19]

It could be argued, as Senator Kenneth B. Keating, R-N.Y., an internationalist, did in 1947, that better global organization was needed precisely because "lasting peace . . . cannot be left to the mercy of Old World powers still harboring the hatreds of generations." In his view, "some organization with a very great deal of power is necessary to persuade the countries of Europe, and of the Orient too, to drop their hatreds and suspicions and pull together."[20] Yet for many Americans, the nation's ideology, with its stress on independence, free enterprise, and personal liberty, provided a counterbalancing rationale for going it alone. From their perspective, a strategy of unilateralism (or, for some, isolationism) offered a way to project these core values onto the foreign policy screen without becoming encumbered with unnecessary entanglements. America's geographical and geopolitical position, separated by vast oceans from those who could threaten its territorial integrity, provided the ideal setting. And its growing economic and military power permitted its citizens to believe—at least until the era of intercontinental delivery systems for weapons of mass destruction and of economic and ecological interdependence—that they had a choice about whether, as well as to what degree, the United States should become engaged in world politics. Calling isolationism "an understandable by-product of American history," Professor Martin Kreisberg noted in 1949 that "the great majority of early settlers came here to get away from Europe and Europe's problems. They wanted to forget Europe and to get along by themselves. America's size and vast resources made such a prospect plausible."[21]

These suspicions of European craftiness and ulterior motives have subsided in mainstream thinking over the years, but they remain favored themes of far-right rhetoric about the dangers of international cooperation. They are often combined with a populous, antiestablishment, anti-Eastern elite message—much like this one from evangelist, TV commentator, and sometime presidential candidate Pat Robertson:

My wife, Dede, was born in the Midwest and raised as a Taft Republican. Her comment on foreign affairs a few years ago was very perceptive: "I don't trust anyone running the foreign affairs of America who speaks with a foreign accent." In fact, how can anyone understand the family life, the shared values, the history of free enterprise and free speech, and the intense patriotism of people born in Columbus, Ohio? For that matter, how can a native-born American, educated at Groton, Harvard, and Oxford, who then goes to work on Wall Street, understand what goes on in the hearts of people in Iowa, Nebraska, Texas, or Florida? The Atlanticists on Wall Street may be willing to sell out America, but Main Street wants no part of their plan.[22]

Of course, wariness about the sinister designs that the Old World may have on the New dates back to the American Revolution, the vulnerable early years of the Republic, and the articulation of the Monroe Doctrine. But whereas these concerns originally had a solid strategic rationale and were at least understandable at the time of the League debate, they seem curiously out of place today when voiced by opinion leaders in the last superpower as it helps to reshape the geopolitical map, as well as the cultural landscape, of Europe.[23]

In his 1998 book, *The Great Betrayal,* Patrick J. Buchanan casts Europe as a threat only to the extent to which it is setting a bad example, one Americans should avoid emulating at all costs. "Look at Europe," he cautions. "Nations there are meekly transferring control of their defense and foreign policy, of trade and immigration policy, to a superstate called the European Union." Further, he concludes, "what is happening to France, Britain, Germany, Italy, will happen here if we do not wake up. Once a nation has put its foot onto the slippery slope of global free trade, the process is inexorable, the end inevitable: death of the nation-state."[24] In his view, the once-dominant Europeans have foolishly permitted their national sovereignties to implode in favor of the false promise of regional integration. By resisting the trap of global integration, it seems, the United States can stand back and watch the snare meant to bind it to the Old World engulf the European perpetrators in their own illusion.

Writing in 1954, historian Richard Hofstadter provided one sociological explanation for the prevalent phobias of Europe that still rings true. He identified "the incredibly bitter feeling against the United Nations" as one of the "unintelligible figments of the pseudo-conservative ideology," and commented:

Is it not understandable that such a feeling might be, paradoxically, shared at one and the same time by an old Yankee-Protestant American, who feels that his social position is not what it ought to be and that these foreigners are crowding in on his country and diluting its sovereignty just as "foreigners" have crowded into his neighborhood, and by a second- or third-generation immigrant who has been trying so hard to de-Europeanize himself, to get Europe out of his personal heritage, and who finds his own government mocking him by its complicity in these Old World schemes?[25]

The final section of this chapter considers the political consequences of the potent, if not entirely accurate, perception that there is a growing tide of immigration, bringing with it increasing competition for jobs, education, turf, and social services at lower socioeconomic levels. At the fringes of the body politic, the xenophobic appeals of the radical right have found a ready constituency among some of those disenfranchised and marginalized by the globalization of economic competition. When the current economic boom subsides and unemployment rises, these political pressures are bound to grow. As discussed in greater depth in chapter 10, a consistent socioeconomic pattern has been evident through the years in American public opinion surveys about the UN. The better educated (presumably including many of Hofstadter's Yankee Protestants) are both more critical of specific aspects of UN performance and more supportive of staying engaged with the organization and its activities. Those who reject U.S. participation in the world body altogether—the "get the U.S. out of the UN and the UN out of the U.S." crowd—largely come from the less-educated and lower socioeconomic strata of American society.

Communists at Turtle Bay

If the image of European monarchs maneuvering to entangle the United States in Old World squabbles through the League of Nations haunted many Americans in the early decades of the twentieth century, then its more sinister counterpart in mid-century was the fear that the Soviet Union would use the United Nations as a bridge for speeding communist infiltration of American society. Although a few voices from the right, such as Bishop Neely, could be heard in 1919 casting the League as part of a Bolshevik plot, this was at best a minor theme in the debate. With the cold war, however, the issue took a more urgent, concrete, and threatening tone. In the words of

Dean Acheson, himself the target of suspicion in some quarters, "waves of fear of communism spread over the country, reaching hysterical proportions. They were assiduously stirred by persons in authority."[26] The sort of high-minded sentiments voiced so eloquently at the UN's founding were little in evidence when a Senate Judiciary investigations subcommittee held hearings in 1952 on the "Activities of United States Citizens Employed by the United Nations." Only seven years old, the world organization was, according to one strain of opinion in its host country, already beginning to look, if not like an institutional Frankenstein, at least like the breeding ground for potentially harmful un-American activities.

The question of divided loyalties, to the United States and to the UN, arose early and often in the inquiry, which was chaired by Senator Patrick McCarran, D-Nev. Much of the hearing was devoted to an attempt to identify communists among a long list of Americans employed by the UN. Alfred J. Van Tassel was one of those so accused. Asked whether he considered his "obligation to the United Nations superior to that of your obligation to the United States," Van Tassel, not surprisingly, responded that he did not "consider them in any sense whatsoever incompatible. I consider that I can be a perfectly loyal United States citizen and a loyal member of the Secretariat of the United Nations, and I think I am both."[27] To the question of whether he was a party member, however, he was more circumspect, pleading the Fifth Amendment like the others who testified before the subcommittee. According to Communist party doctrine, full-fledged members were obligated to put party loyalty above that either to country or to an international organization.

The campaign to root out American communists from UN headquarter in New York City's Turtle Bay had a dual negative effect on relations between the United Nations and the United States that commentators have largely overlooked. In Acheson's words, "the result was a highly unfavorable opinion of the United Nations in the United States and of the United States in the United Nations."[28] Each became more suspicious of the other. Hardcore anticommunists, of course, came to see the UN as a modern-day Trojan horse, offering a means for spies and subversives to infiltrate American soil and even its foreign policy elites. The McCarran hearings and investigations may have produced little public evidence of subversives in the UN secretariat, but those addicted to conspiracy theories would have expected such a result. In their view, deeply entrenched Communist party cells would have known how to escape detection and might well still exist long after the subcommittee completed its work. For some anticommunists, this is a case that has never been closed.

The growing disillusionment of many Americans with the world body only a few years after its triumphant inauguration is understandable in the context of their concomitant worries about the threat posed by global communism. In the UN's first five years, China—one of the five permanent members of the Security Council—had fallen to the communists (some said, rather improbably, as a result of a conspiracy among China hands in the State Department); Eastern Europe had slipped behind the iron curtain; the Soviet Union had exploded an atomic device, possibly with the aid of spies in the United States; and South Korea was invaded from a communist North. Meanwhile, the much-touted UN Security Council, rather than maintaining international peace and security, was immobilized by repeated Soviet vetoes. To add to suspicions about the reasons for this unfavorable and unanticipated course of events, Alger Hiss, who had, as a State Department official, headed the secretariat at the UN's founding conference at San Francisco and organized the Dumbarton Oaks preparatory conferences, had been charged by Whittaker Chambers of heading a Communist party cell in the department and then was convicted in 1950 for perjury in the infamous "pumpkin papers" case.[29]

For many commentators and legislators, Hiss came to personify what was wrong both with the United Nations and with the State Department's handling of U.S. foreign policy. Representative Clarence J. Brown, R-Ohio, pulled these themes together when he told his House colleagues in 1952 that:

> There is no agency or department of Government that has shown a more rapid increase in expenditures than the State Department; and there is no agency of the Government in which the American people have less faith and confidence. . . . And I am not unmindful of the fact that the man who presided over the opening of that conference in San Francisco at which the United Nations was born, was a man named Alger Hiss. I am not unmindful of the fact that it was he who counseled the American delegates to that conference that whatever they did they should give to Soviet Russia the veto power which has resulted in the United Nations organization being impotent to do any really constructive work in behalf of world peace.[30]

Adding fuel to the developing conspiracy theories, Hiss at the time of his trial was president of the Carnegie Endowment for International Peace, a leading private research organization with strong UN ties. The chairman of its board, moreover, was none other than John Foster Dulles. No less a figure than Dean Acheson declared that he would not turn his back on Hiss—whose brother Donald had been Acheson's assistant—even after his perjury conviction.[31] To say that Hiss was well connected would be an understatement.

Many years later, individuals and groups with a penchant for believing in conspiracies within the foreign policy elite still cite Hiss's role in the founding of the UN as evidence of the world body's anti-American orientation. Such references are not restricted to the John Birch Society and fringe elements by any means. Two recent candidates for the Republican presidential nomination have also reminded their readers of Hiss's sinister presence behind America's postwar internationalist leanings. According to Pat Robertson, after the UN's founding conference in San Francisco, "the official documents were then transported to the White House by none other than Alger Hiss, the presidential adviser who was later charged with giving state secrets to the Soviets and was convicted of perjury in 1949."[32] In a 1998 anti-free-trade book, Patrick Buchanan points out that the executive committee chairman of the Citizens Committee for Reciprocal World Trade in 1946 was "the rising young diplomatic star who had been at Roosevelt's side at Yalta—Alger Hiss."[33]

Although Hiss was hardly as influential in shaping the postwar world architecture as the Yalta reference suggests, apparently Buchanan wanted to imply that the creation of the UN, the emphasis on free trade, and accommodation to the Soviet Union all went hand-in-hand as parts of America's immediate postwar strategy. As Louis Wyman, R-N.H., declared on the House floor following the 1971 seating of the People's Republic of China in the UN, "frankly, ever since the days of Alger Hiss, the charter and structure of the U.N. has been suspect in the minds of many in relation to the best interests of the United States of America."[34] The events of these troubled early years—long forgotten by most Americans and ignored by centrist decisionmakers—continue to shape the context within which a segment of American society places the United Nations and other efforts at international organization. This remains a part of Hiss's legacy.

To those most devoted to the ideals of international organization, however, the heart of the matter was not Alger Hiss, but the relationship between the host country and the international civil service. Here, as well, lasting damage was done by the attempt to identify and expel Americans in the UN secretariat suspected of being communists. According to the report of Senator Alexander Wiley, R-Wis., on his experience as a delegate to the 1952 session of the General Assembly, the goal was simply "to maintain the highest possible confidence of the American people in the United Nations, by . . . making sure that the U.N. so conducts its own affairs as always to be fully worthy of such confidence." Noting that the FBI had screened all Americans in the UN secretariat plus all those on the staff of the U.S. mission to the UN, Wiley pointed out that only a relatively small number were under suspicion. He emphasized, however, that:

> There is no room for a single American Communist or individual with Communist sympathies or affiliations inside the United Nations. . . . The American people would not tolerate for one moment a requirement on them to continue to pay one-third of the salary of a single individual who refuses to state on the witness stand (a) whether he is now or has ever been a member of the Communist Party; (b) whether he is now or has ever been engaged in espionage against the United States; (c) whether he would or would not support the United States in a possible war against an aggressor state.[35]

Loyalty oaths were required of all Americans working for the UN, and the FBI was permitted to open an office in UN headquarters to facilitate the interviewing and fingerprinting of American nationals in the secretariat. The employment of scores of Americans was terminated, and many more resigned under pressure.

Although perhaps understandable in the political context of the times and arguably appropriate to a military alliance, such as NATO, these unilateral rules and activities were grossly out of place in a virtually universal political organization like the UN. According to article 100 of the charter,

1. In the performance of their duties the Secretary-General and the staff shall not seek or receive instructions from any government or from any other authority external to the Organization. They shall refrain from any action which might reflect on their position as international officials responsible only to the Organization.
2. Each Member of the United Nations undertakes to respect the exclusively international character of the responsibilities of the Secretary-General and the staff and not to seek to influence them in the discharge of their responsibilities.

The secretariat, in other words, was to remain wholly independent of individual member states, which, in turn, were to respect its independence. According to Dean Acheson, the charges mounted by senators McCarran and Joseph McCarthy, R-Wis., "kicked up quite a row and soon had both the State Department and the Secretary General taking embarrassing positions inconsistent with those they had previously maintained."[36] Author Shirley Hazzard argues passionately in *Defeat of an Ideal: A Study of Self-Destruction of the United Nations* that because neither side of this independence principle was respected during this ordeal, a long-term decline of the UN's capacities and operations was set in motion. She contends that "in allowing themselves to become the implements of precisely those oppressive forces the United Nations had been created to contend with, and in contravening the very liberties held to be basic in the UN Universal Declaration of Human Rights, the Secretary-General [Trygve Lie] and his associates made a mockery of the Organization itself and of everything that took place there."[37] Apparently the pressures from East and West to distort these principles persisted throughout the four decades of the cold war. Former secretary-general Javier Pérez de Cuéllar has acknowledged that even when he assumed office in 1982, "the malevolent influence of the cold war extended to the secretariat." Yet he contended that, "with few exceptions, secretariat personnel retained the impartiality that is the duty of an international civil servant."[38]

In retrospect, it is evident that the American campaign to root out communists at the UN served both to heighten the concerns of those who saw the UN as a potential threat to U.S. security and to dampen the enthusiasm of those who believed in the internationalist ideal. It displayed for all to see the limits of international cooperation in a sea of nationalism, mistrust, and insecurity. More subtly, it brought to the surface the difference in attitudes toward international cooperation of different segments of American society (a topic discussed more extensively later in this chapter and in chapter 10). Acheson, the epitome of the Eastern establishment, labeled the whole affair as "the attack of the primitives" and called McCarthy "a lazy small-town bully."[39] UN enthusiasts had looked to the international civil service through idealistic eyes, seeing in it a partial antidote for the Machiavellian machinations of the member states. But for just these reasons, others saw in the secretariat the embodiment of an international conspiracy to thwart American interests and erode its sovereignty. As article 100 underlines, it was the secretariat that was to remain above the organization's inevitably turbulent political waters, maintaining faith in and commitment to the highest purposes and principles of internationalism.

Under the best of circumstances that would have been a trying task, but the violations of that principle by both East and West in the cold war made it nearly impossible to attain.

Over the years, as British author and journalist Rosemary Righter has wryly noted, "the quality of UN staff is the question on which governments . . . are most critical, most hypocritical, and most fatalistic."[40] The effort to maintain the integrity and competence of the UN secretariat has been an uphill battle ever since these early blows to the notion of an independent international civil service. While the principles of article 100 are still cherished by much of the staff and Secretary-General Kofi Annan has endorsed the development of a staff code of conduct,[41] the cross-pressures on the secretariat and the competition among member states, including the United States, to see their nationals appointed to key posts can be fierce at times. Recently, perhaps reflecting its declining influence in the world body, the United States has not fared well in getting American officials placed in either top or mid-level positions in the secretariat.[42] Yet no matter who wins this competition, in the long run it has been the quality and independence of the secretariat and the reputation of the organization that have suffered as the result of the claims many nations have laid on what were to have been international posts.

Race, Class, and Their Legacies

The xenophobic elements that have contributed to Americans' ambivalence about international organization have not been limited to suspicions about wily Europeans and insidious communists. More subtle and complex has been the effect of racial attitudes and of stereotypes about the legitimacy of developing countries. Undoubtedly, the least researched, understood, or discussed factor in the evolution of American attitudes toward international institutions is race. After a century of change—largely for the better—in racial relationships within the United States, it is hard (and painful) to recall the extent to which racial attitudes once openly shaped the perspectives of many Americans. Even Woodrow Wilson's worldview was tainted with the endemic paternalism that underlay the doctrine of Manifest Destiny, the impulse for missionary work, and the League's proposed mandates over some colonial territories. In defending the latter, the president commented that "we have put the same safeguards, and as adequate safeguards, around the poor, naked fellows in the jungles of Africa that we have around those peoples almost ready to assume the rights of self-government in some parts of the Turkish Empire, as, for example, in Armenia."[43] In those times, nativism, racism, and fear of the influx of hordes of immigrants, particularly from Asia, came together in American politics in a politically potent combination. Racism and ethnic prejudice were as much a part of American culture as apple pie and motherhood.

Nevertheless, George Wharton Pepper, a prominent and apparently optimistic Philadelphia lawyer, argued in 1920 that America's ethnic and racial diversity made it a natural leader in the League: "The United States of America is itself a league of many nations. Every European dispute presents issues which tend to array one racial group against another." In his view, "circumstances are compelling the people of the United States to work out within their borders the racial problems which underlie the world's unrest. Great racial groups that find it possible to live together in unity under one flag may have something of value to contribute to the settlement of overseas disputes between their brothers in blood."[44] True enough, but there was little evidence either in the events of the times or in the content of the Senate debate over the League to justify Pepper's assumption that America had worked out its racial problems.

Undertaken at a time of race riots and lynchings, the debate in the U.S. Senate over entry into the League of Nations was as ugly in terms of racism and xenophobia as it was instructive about the depths of antipathy some Americans felt about the prospects for close international cooperation.[45] Prominent senators openly cautioned against participating in international bodies on an equal basis with nations and peoples thought to be inferior in some way. Even as austere and venerable a New England gentleman as Henry Cabot Lodge was not above racial appeals for staying out of the League. One of his favorite themes in a series of speeches and debates from 1917 through 1919 was that the United States could lose control over its immigration policies—at that point a hotly contested issue—under the League since it was a question with both domestic and international dimensions. "Are we ready to leave it to other nations," he asked, "to determine whether we shall admit to the United States a flood of Japanese, Chinese, and Hindu labor?" He, for one, could not "consent to putting the protection of my country and her workingmen against undesirable immigration, out of our own hands. We and we alone must say who shall come into the United States and become citizens of this Republic, and no one else should have any power to utter one word in regard to it." Speaking of "the vital question of the exclusion of Mongolian and Asiatic labor," Lodge warned that these "are actual, living questions of the utmost vitality and peril to-day.

In them is involved that deepest of human instincts which seeks not only to prevent an impossible competition in labor but *to maintain the purity of the race.*[46] These themes, centered on the prevalent fear, especially on the West Coast, of a vast flow of Asian laborers, was echoed in a number of anti-League journals.[47]

If Lodge had not been explicit enough in his racial appeals, the low point came when James A. Reed, D-Mo., a senator known for his virulently racist views, took to the floor of the Senate on May 26, 1919. He warned his colleagues that this would be "a colored League of Nations. That is to say, the majority of the nations composing the league do not belong to the white race of men. On the contrary, they are a conglomerate of the black, yellow, brown and red races, frequently so intermixed and commingled as to constitute an unclassifiable mongrel breed." Brandishing a table of illiteracy ratios, Reed intoned that there was a danger not only of bringing "to the council board races which are dark skinned, but also those so low in civilization that they constitute the very dregs of ignorance. . . . They are the victims of superstition and are steeped in barbarism." Turning to Haiti and the practice of voodoo, Reed cautioned that "these baby murderers, these creatures of the forest who sacrifice children to their idols, are to have a place in the councils of nations, and their vote is to be the equal of the vote of the United States."[48]

Just warming to his subject, Senator Reed showed little more respect for the nations of Asia. The senator reminded his colleagues from West Coast states that they had called Japanese and Chinese "totally unfit for citizenship," that Asian immigration to the United States was restricted, and yet that in the League China and Japan would "each cast a vote equal to the vote of the United States." He did commend Australia to senators from the South and West, though only for its opposition to the Japanese proposal for an amendment calling for racial equality (something President Wilson, for all his high-mindedness, had squelched in any case).[49] When James D. Phelan, D-Calif., meekly noted that the monarch in Siam was Oxford educated, Senator Reed asked whether he would want the Siamese to populate California. Phelan was quick to assure his Senate colleagues that he was "bent on preserving her [California] for a white man's country" and that Siamese are not "assimilable."[50]

Did others rush to condemn such blatant racism? Hardly. According to the *Congressional Record*, Reed's performance elicited frequent laughter from an amused and apparently supportive gallery. In his book, Bishop Neely, warning against a "league of foreign nations," quoted Reed's racist comments approvingly and at length.[51] Rather than objecting, the defenders of the League in the Senate adopted a strikingly defensive posture. Senate Minority Leader Hitchcock, President Wilson's point man for League ratification, responded timidly that the United States "largely controlled" and "dominated" "little half-baked countries," such as Liberia and Haiti. "The league has very little to do," he continued, because "practically all of its powers . . . are in the hands of the executive council" and its five permanent members: the United States, Great Britain, France, Italy, and Japan. Senator Philander C. Knox, R-Pa., assured his colleagues that "these little nations could not put over an injustice in their own favor, yet they could, by their vote, prevent justice from being done to the greatest nations of the world."[52]

Racism did not kill the League, and Senator Reed's extreme rhetoric probably won few converts to the anti-League forces. Xenophobia, especially fear of manipulation by crafty Europeans, was far more prominent and politically potent in the League debate than racism in any case. Other "irreconcilable" senators sought, with some success, to build on these prevalent fears and prejudices: Borah of Idaho rallied Irish-Americans against the League by claiming that it would be dominated by Britain; Lawrence Y. Sherman, R-Ill., charged that the pope would control the votes of the majority of League members, which were largely Catholic; and Hiram W. Johnson, R-Calif., invoked anti-Japanese sentiment.[53]

More than a generation later, the Senate debate about participation in the United Nations showed that Americans had matured markedly in terms of both racial and international attitudes. The senators avoided direct racial, religious, or xenophobic appeals. At one point, in fact, Tom Connally, D-Texas, chairman of the Senate Foreign Relations Committee, interrupted the testimony of a speaker—who had warned of a Soviet-inspired world government turning the United States into "a feeding trough for the 'have nots' of the world"—to caution that "we want to have your views, but we do not want in these discussions any gratuitous references to any other government or people."[54] At later points, however, this discipline lapsed. For example, in discussing the proposed International Trade Organization, Senator George Malone, R-Nev., complained on the Senate floor in 1950 that under its one-nation, one-vote system:

> The United States would have one vote, just as would Siam, that little nation, many of whose people live on canals, using the canals for sewage disposal, for cooking, for bathing, for fishing. One battalion of United States Marines could

take over the whole nation in 3 or 4 days, and half of its people would not know it.[55]

Although his prose was a shade less graphic, the thrust of his remarks fully echoed those of Senator Reed three decades before: the United States should not be equated with peoples and nations deemed inferior. Again, none of his fellow senators were moved to object to such language or arguments. Given the persistence of such views, it is not surprising that the legacy of racism still lingers—consciously or unconsciously—beneath the surface of American attitudes toward international institutions.

Race was rarely mentioned during the 1945 floor debate, except to underline that it was an irrelevant consideration given the unity and pluralism of America. Nonetheless both the establishment of the UN and the subsequent creation of NATO, plus the Marshall Plan and Truman Doctrine, gave a distinctly Eurocentric cast to postwar U.S. foreign policy. During the 1945 debate Senator Walter F. George, D-Ga., commented that "the Anglo-Saxon race and all other races which have been transplanted to our shores have a distinct and special mission to perform on this earth, namely that of giving political government to mankind."[56] Similarly, Senator Wiley extended American racial pluralism as far as Europe, but no further, when he suggested that the ideas in the Constitution "stabilized our American race, which had stemmed from every racial group in Europe, into a people fit for a people's government."[57] Some well-placed Americans, however, apparently had their doubts about how well that would work. Dean Acheson, for example, would have preferred to see the headquarters of the world body situated in Geneva, Copenhagen, or San Francisco, rather than placing it "in a crowded center of conflicting races and nationalities."[58] Fortunately his fears were misplaced. Because multilateralism in postwar America came to be seen as a trans-European enterprise, it tended to unify, rather than divide, the nation's multiple ethnic minorities.[59] Although this limited conception of an integrated and principled America was highly Eurocentric, it did not encourage the kinds of base and mean-spirited racial assaults that were so prevalent in 1919.

Nevertheless, even in contemporary America attitudes toward international organization appear to be correlated with attitudes toward race. For example, John Gerard Ruggie has recently cited both historical evidence and the demographic breakdowns of public opinion surveys to support the hypothesis of "a relationship between interethnic accommodation at home and multilateral organizing principles abroad." According to his reading of public opinion studies, "nativism, when it is not isolationist, is closely associated with a preference for unilateralism in foreign policy, and a more expansive identity with multilateralism."[60] It is no coincidence, then, that the public and congressional debate over the UN has intensified during a time of sharpened differences over immigration, multiculturalism, and affirmative action. Americans divided over how to handle diversity at home are also uncertain of how their nation should fit into universal international organizations.

Through the years, moreover, the results of public opinion surveys in the United States have usually found minorities to be more supportive of the United Nations than whites.[61] For example, in a series of national surveys during 1995–96, minorities rated the UN more favorably (6.3 on a scale from 0 to 10) than did whites (5.6); a larger portion of minorities (83 percent for African Americans and 85 percent for other minorities) than of whites (77 percent) agreed that UN peacekeeping affected U.S. national interests; and minorities also articulated greater support than whites for foreign aid (as well as for assistance to poor people within the United States) and for UN peacekeeping operations in Burundi and, by a smaller margin, in Bosnia.[62] Hispanics and Asian Americans, according to many recent polls, have been the most supportive of the UN. Enthusiasm for the UN appears to have ebbed somewhat among African Americans during the 1990s, although they remain markedly more committed than whites to paying UN dues in full.

North-South debates in the world body fall, to a certain extent, along racial as well as economic and political lines, a division that may reinforce the perception that national interest is correlated with racial identity. Many of the more extreme critics of international organization, moreover, tend to combine virulently racist and anti-Semitic attitudes with their xenophobia, chauvinism, and antigovernment rhetoric. Such views, of course, are no longer considered acceptable in the political mainstream and are relegated to alienated fringe groups. With race no longer discussed openly in foreign policy circles, however, it is hard to judge from public evidence the extent to which America's racial legacy contributes, even subconsciously, to its ambivalence toward international institutions and toward support of aid programs and military interventions in the developing world. The evidence is mixed on congressional and presidential support for U.S. participation in UN military operations, but there is little reason to believe that race has been a consistent or decisive factor. President George Bush, in fact, was the leading advocate for the U.S.-led interventions in Somalia and Kuwait but was reluctant to put U.S. forces on the ground in Bosnia. Yet race may have contributed to the rapidity of the U.S. withdrawal from Somalia following the release of graphic pictures of Somali abuse of American troops. And the Congressional Black Caucus was much more enthusiastic about the prospect of U.S. intervention in Haiti than were most other members of Congress.

There is some evidence that through the years Americans opposed to civil rights legislation and racial integration at home have also tended to be critical of the United Nations, which may be seen to represent similar values on a global scale. For example, a 1958 national study of public opinion commissioned by the Carnegie Endowment for International Peace found some suggestive, if sketchy, correlations when it focused a special survey on Los Angeles, where "vociferous anti-UN sentiments had been repeatedly manifested." Among those polled, "those who opposed the United Nations were only a small minority but within this group four-fifths favored racial segregation and a third voiced anti-Semitic sentiments." Two-thirds of those interviewed were favorable to the United Nations, and of those, only 15 percent and 3 percent, respectively, held such views. In an area of the city "into which Negroes were moving in large numbers, there was much more opposition to the United Nations among white adults than was found in other areas of the city."[63]

From time to time, members of Congress have objected to multilateral arrangements that might have even an indirect linkage to domestic social and civil rights questions. To Senator Forrest C. Donnell, R-Mo., the connection between the principles and aspirations voiced in the UN charter and the push for civil rights at home was all too direct. In 1949 he objected to the following language in Senate bill 984, introduced on March 27, 1947, which prohibited discrimination in employment because of race, religion, color, national origin, or ancestry:

> This act has also been enacted as a step toward fulfillment of the international treaty obligations imposed by the Charter of the United Nations upon the United States as a signatory thereof to promote universal respect for, and observance of, human rights and fundamental freedoms for all without distinction as to race, sex, language, or religion.[64]

Noting that the sponsors of the bill were largely from the North, he reminded southern senators and those concerned with protecting states' rights that the prerogatives of states in matters such as "suffrage, schools, segregation, poll tax, freedom from seizure, and many other fields" might be affected by such international undertakings.[65] The following year Senator Donnell drew the Senate's attention to a California appeals court ruling that the state's alien land act could not be enforced because it then applied only to Japanese and a few other "Asiatics" and was contrary to the universal human rights and antidiscrimination clauses of the UN charter. Well ahead of his time, Senator Homer Ferguson, R-Mich., worried that the effect of the charter's provisions, at least under the interpretation given by the California court decision, "may be to nullify or make void all statutes in any State in relation to distinctions made between the sexes."[66]

In 1947 Democratic senators George of Georgia and Harry F. Byrd of Virginia objected to the appointment of Mark F. Ethridge, a "New Dealer" and UN delegate, to a foreign aid post, reportedly because they were "not enthusiastic about Mr. Ethridge's views on social and economic problems in the South."[67] After that, according to the New York Times, "no more has been heard of the Ethridge appointment." In 1971 Representative Rarick of Louisiana objected to the UN's "aggressive program . . . to mobilize the people of the world to combat racism," something that "can be eliminated only if freedom is destroyed." Railing against "the forced integration of public schools and the busing experiment," he complained that the UN, by asserting that racism had to be eliminated to achieve peace, was suggesting "that anyone opposing the combating of racism is against peace."[68]

During the UN's first decade, anti-Semitic, anticommunist, and anti-United Nations sentiments were sometimes combined, even on the floor of Congress, in a combustible mixture. In 1948, for example, Representative John E. Rankin, D-Miss., who often spoke against civil rights efforts, commented on "this international Sanhedrin up here in New York, shown as the United Nations, attempting to subordinate the United States to its domination." Claiming to be "speaking now for the real Americans" and referring to "this Zionist group, the hand of the Communist movement," Rankin stated that:

> They have no right to drag us into a race war in Palestine. They have no more right to go in there and set up a racial state in Palestine than they have to set up an Indian state in Ohio or Pennsylvania or to set up a Negro state in Virginia, Texas, or Mississippi.[69]

Although Pat Robertson claims that only "the Christian United States" stands in the way of Satan and his world government plot,[70] the kind of direct anti-Semitic and anti-UN rhetoric Rankin indulged in is rare these days (at least on the House and Senate floors) and confined to extremist circles. It is worth noting, however, that hate groups seem to find it natural to combine their racial, ethnic, and religious prejudices with an extreme distaste for anything appearing "foreign," and the UN usually tops the list.

In the contemporary debate about international institutions, it would be unthinkable for any mainstream faction to raise the question of race as frontally and as energetically as had been the case during the League debate. In some cases, however, the style of expression seems to have changed more than the underlying message. For example, while Robertson eschews direct racial comments in his 1991 book on *The New World Order,* the case he cites as evidence against a standing UN army is certainly suggestive:

> As I mentioned earlier, I cannot forget the bloody picture in *Life* magazine of the young Belgian settler in Katanga whose wife and children lay dead behind him in a little Volkswagen, brutally killed by black African soldiers serving in a United Nations contingent.

In case his readers should miss the point, he added that "if it happened there, it can happen here."[71]

Patrick Buchanan referred to "Kofi and his global parasites" in a July 1998 column criticizing Kofi Annan, the first black African to serve as secretary-general of the UN, for his advocacy of an International Criminal Court. It is curious, perhaps suggestive, that the secretary-general is the only person in the column to be referred to by his first name. Referring to "Kofi, et al.," Buchanan asked: "How should we deal with these snake-oil salesmen? The same way that the town dealt with the phony Duke and Dauphin in *Huck Finn*—tar and feather 'em, and ride 'em out on a rail.'"[72] Coming just three months after Gerald Solomon, R-N.Y., declared that the secretary-general "ought to be horse whipped" for comments that he made during his mission to Baghdad,[73] Buchanan's tar and feathering proposal and Huck Finn references hark back to a period in American history when racial and political differences were too often handled by mobs and extra-legal methods.

Others sometimes invoke a reverse form of racism as a justification for very different perspectives on the world body. In 1996 Ali A. Mazrui, a professor at the State University of New York, Binghamton, complained that Africa was still underrepresented in UN bodies that, like the Bretton Woods institutions, "continue to be disseminators of Western ideas and values. . . . The Security Council is still primarily a 'white man's club' with nonwhite visitors."[74] At the UN, of course, racism cuts both ways, particularly in terms of interregional struggles over numbers of secretariat posts and of slots on intergovernmental bodies. The conversation may be about geographical distribution, but the subtext concerns varying perceptions about what constitutes an appropriate racial, as well as political, balance within the UN's principal organs. The whole question of race, geography, and representation at the UN is driven by the pursuit of power and prerogatives in a world body that became far more diverse and representative with the surge in membership following the decolonization movement.

Among American critics of the UN, its shifting and growing membership brought sharp questioning of the legitimacy of many of the new governments. They, not the people they claimed to represent, were said to be inferior. Indeed, too many of these regimes proved to be neither representative nor viable. Yet the crude stereotype applied to the developing world sounded at least chauvinistic if not racist. True, as noted above, at different points UN critics had been just as outspoken in their fears of European or Soviet domination in the UN. In those cases, history, politics, and ideology, not race, were the motivating factors. Differences on policy questions have no doubt played a role as well. To some extent, lack of public support at the UN for the economic agendas of developing countries has paralleled similar misgivings about welfare programs at home. Given Americans' preference for self-reliance over government handouts, opponents of the UN have sought to convey the image of the world body as a global welfare agency seeking to promote a North-to-South transfer of wealth. Certainly there has been a persistent concern in congressional debates, as well, about foreigners of any race telling Americans what to do. Yet the cries of resentment about having "uncivilized" peoples and governments judge America and run the UN have seemed just a bit more shrill and indignant.

During a 1962 House debate, for example, Representative Thomas H. Pelly, R-Wash., claimed to be a past supporter of the UN but warned that "if any sinister attempt is made through the United Nations, as one hears it may be, to destroy our nationhood or to put our country at the mercy of others, including the peoples of backward nations, then I and many others will move to kill it."[75] Earlier that year, Senator John Tower gave a lengthy speech on the Senate floor about the dangers of taking too strong and sweeping a stance against colonialism, as he believed the UN and the Kennedy administration had, because "no importance is given to the primitive state of millions of tribesmen, or their age-old feuds which will erupt as the Afro-Europeans are driven out." In his words, "it will be a long while indeed before many of these new African nations become a real factor in the world power struggle. A vote in the General Assembly of the U.N. does not make Chad, Dahomey, Gabon, Somalia, Mauritania, and so forth strong countries."[76] Following the 1971 General Assembly vote to seat the People's Republic of China, Representative Robert H. Michel, a prominent Illinois Republican, claimed that "there are 41 African 'states' which in reality are little more than aggrandized principalities, all carrying full voting rights in the U.N."[77] Concerns about the political implications of the growing number of African nations in the General Assembly were certainly not limited to Capitol Hill. Acheson fretted in *Present at the Creation* that the "proliferation of states" had contributed to the UN assuming overly ambitious roles, commenting that "it has become a possible instrument of interference in the affairs of weak white nations, as Rhodesia is experiencing as I write."[78]

In his 1984 book, *A World Without a U.N.*, Burton Yale Pines contended that:

A majority of today's U.N. members are ill-prepared to address the issues that come before the U.N., for these nations stand only on the threshold of political and economic development. They have no experience in international matters and can boast little knowledge of any history but that of their own transition from colonialism to independence.[79]

Seven years later, foreign policy critic Alan Tonelson went even further. Commenting on "the social, economic, and political disorganization and the official corruption from which Third World countries suffer," he suggested that:

Indeed, many of these places are not real countries—at least not in the sense that states in the industrialized free world and parts of the Far East are. Third World countries may belong to the UN, they may have their own flags and airlines and armies and postage stamps, but many of them lack the critical attributes of statehood—the institutional structures and the bedrock cohesion needed both to generate resources and to use them productively.[80]

More recently, following the 1998 U.S. cruise missile strikes in retaliation for the bombing of the U.S. embassies in Kenya and Tanzania, Robert Kagan, a senior associate of the Carnegie Endowment for International Peace and an editor of the *Weekly Standard*, remarked to the *New York Times* that a serious antiterrorism campaign would require more "than bombing two primitive nonstates like Afghanistan and Sudan."[81]

Even when not questioning the sovereignty and legitimacy of smaller and less developed countries, conservative critics have frequently questioned their role in the United Nations. Writing in 1991 Pat Robertson complained that "tiny, unsophisticated nations which hold 80 percent of the voting power pay less than 1 percent of the budget."[82] In a 1996 article Jesse Helms asserted that the United Nations would resist reform because "many of the smaller and lesser developed members . . . benefit from the current system and gain influence by selling their sovereignty to the organization."[83] In his view, not only are many less developed nations corrupt, but the world body itself has had a corrupting influence on them. If most of the UN's member states lack legitimacy, as these critics contend, then surely the organization cannot serve as a legitimate place for the United States to do its global business.

Starkly divergent attitudes toward developing countries define one of the fault lines underlying American ambivalence toward international institutions. The dismissive tone in the quotations cited above contrasts starkly to America's historic sense of obligation to assist—at least rhetorically— peoples seeking to escape oppression, as reflected in President Wilson's emphasis on the principle of national self-determination and U.S. support for the decolonization movement in the early years of the United Nations. As Ambassador Adlai Stevenson expansively phrased it:

> The American people have rejoiced to see the people of the old colonial empires attain their independence. This movement is in our tradition. It fulfills on a grand scale that prophetic phrase in our Declaration of Independence that all men—not just Americans, but all men—are created equal and have unalienable rights. . . . Our posture in the United Nations is based on the belief, so amply justified year after year, that the interests which we hold in common with the great majority of nations—regardless of size, power, population, race or region—are so much stronger than the interests which divide us that we generally find common ground with them on the vital issues.[84]

Seeing global institutions as reflections of American values, proponents of international organization tended, rather paternalistically, to assert that the newly independent countries were going through a struggle not unlike that which the United States had experienced in exerting its independence less than two centuries earlier.

During the cold war years, UN supporters would often defend the dissenting views of developing countries as a natural part of the give-and-take discourse of democratic forums. In 1962 congressional testimony, Secretary of State Dean Rusk contrasted the two opposing "views about the future of human society": the Marxist belief in "a drab one-world of gray uniformity," and the western "view of a pluralistic world—a world of color, variety, and movement." Admittedly, he continued, the latter "view is much more difficult, for its essence is diversity. It is not so tidy as a uniform world and its behavior is unpredictable precisely because it will be influenced by flesh-and-blood men." Expressing his strong preference for diversity, Secretary Rusk noted that:

> The operations of the United Nations are based on consent, illumined by debate, and conformed by majority decision expressed by men, most of whom demonstrate daily their independence of mind and spirit. If it does not always perform exactly the way we want it to, that is the price of a world in which independence is valued as highly by others as it is by us.[85]

To Rusk, this was not so much a case of principle versus interest as one of short-term versus long-term interests. Losing a few votes in the General Assembly, he seemed to be saying, was a small price to pay for winning the larger war against communist ideology. The kinds of arguments put forward by Rusk and Stevenson, of course, lost much of their persuasive power with the demise of the Soviet Union and the easing of the East-West competition. Now that that war has been won, the redeeming value of being on the short side of votes in the General Assembly is less apparent, as is the utility of courting the support of those recalcitrant developing country governments that are themselves profoundly undemocratic.

Over the years, the question of race in America has also shifted to new ground, with less emphasis on civil rights and integration and more on immigration, affirmative action, welfare, and economic opportunity. Who is considered "different" or "foreign" in American society is changing, with potentially profound implications for attitudes toward greater international integration. It may be more than coincidental, in that context, that Hispanics and Asian-Americans are emerging as the UN's biggest supporters and that blacks are beginning to express some uncertainty about its value. Adopting a sense of economic determinism worthy of Marx, Patrick Buchanan contends that "America is no longer one nation indivisible. We are now the 'two nations' predicted by the Kerner Commission thirty years ago. Only the dividing line is no longer just race; it is class." And the class distinction, in his analysis, is between those who profit ("Third Wave America") and those who don't ("Second Wave America") from the globalization of the economy. According to his critique, the precedence given to commerce, in turn, has led to "ethnic solidarity," "the deconstruction of the United States," and "resegregated student dorms, ethnic gangs, a revival of ethnic and racial politics, secessionist movements in the Southwest, all the way over to the white militias and the Southern League."[86]

According to Buchanan's economic and class model, race is no longer the problem: immigration is. "No sooner had the Civil Rights Act of 1964 been passed than America threw open its doors again—with the Immigration Act of 1965," he notes, "in thirty years, 30 million immigrants, legal and illegal, poured in." Lamenting that the immigrants who arrived in the early years of this century had "moved ahead of the black men and women who had been here for centuries," Buchanan approvingly quotes Booker T. Washington's concerns about the pending arrival of "those of foreign birth and strange tongue and habits." Asserting that there is nothing "racist, immoral, or xenophobic" about repatriating illegal aliens, Buchanan declares that "America must halt illegal immigration and impose limits on legal immigration." Who opposes such a moratorium? Buchanan's answer: "cultural, social, and economic elites who do not compete with immigrant workers and benefit from an endless supply of low-wage labor."[87]

Buchanan's nativist platform is not based on direct and open appeals to race in a traditional sense, but it is certainly race-conscious and profoundly antiforeign. It is no coincidence that his rhetoric, echoing that of many of the League's adversaries, combines anti-free-trade, anti-immigration, and anti-UN slogans, nor that his followers tend to have highly unfavorable attitudes toward the UN, even relative to the supporters of other conservative presidential candidates (see chapter 10). Ross Perot, for example, has made similar economic arguments but has not made the UN a bête noire in his populist campaign rhetoric, so his followers appear less strident about the world body. Although still a modest portion of the electorate—probably fewer than 20 percent—those who feel economically and socially marginalized by the globalization of the economy tend to be active politically and vocal in their opposition to further steps toward international integration. In legislative terms, their numbers may be too few to propel new initiatives but large enough to block the funding of international institutions and to stall ratification of a growing backlog of international agreements and treaties. And they have had a disproportionate voice within the Republican party and its majority in Congress. As such, they have helped to shift the terms of the American debate about international organization and, in the process, have contributed significantly to the growing sense of ambivalence about the United Nations.

The stark differences in outlook toward other countries and the UN between a Stevenson and a Buchanan, moreover, are founded on divergent views of American society. As such, they cannot be easily reconciled. It is a fundamental premise of Buchanan's politics that U.S. society is divided, and increasingly so, along sharply defined class lines. This analysis contrasts with the more traditional mainstream image of America as the great melting pot, the place—unlike the old world—where class, race, religion, and ethnicity no longer need define one's place in society. As John Ruggie has noted, rather than having an "'organic' basis in either land or people":

> American nationalism . . . is a civic nationalism embodying a set of inclusive core values: intrinsic individual as opposed to group rights, equality of opportunity for all, antistatism, the rule of law, and a revolutionary legacy which holds that human betterment can be achieved by means of deliberate human actions, especially when they are pursued in accordance with these foundational values.[88]

Although these values have been achieved only imperfectly at home, Ruggie postulates that a "direct link between the character of American nationalism and the political efficacy of multilateral world order principles exists through the mechanism of accommodating differences of ethnos, race, and religion among Americans in keeping with the concept of civic, as opposed to organic, nationhood."[89] From this vantage point, a foreign policy that seeks to encourage free trade, the transnational flow of people, information, and ideas, respect for human rights and fundamental freedoms, the peaceful settlement of disputes, and the primacy of international law and organization would seem best to reflect these core values.

For much of the postwar era, these values in fact did serve to buttress the bipartisan consensus on the overall shape and purposes of U.S. global strategies. Doubts about the international law and organization plank of this strategy, however, began to grow with the realization that many UN member states—first eastern communists and then southern socialists—shared neither these values nor this worldview. What was good for America might not be seen by everyone, after all, as good for them or for the world, and vice versa. Now, the uneven effects of economic interdependence and globalization are leading a significant minority of Americans to question the domestic model as well. U.S. policies toward international organizations, then, are shaped, in part, by the answers to a series of interlinked questions about the nature of contemporary American society, the effects of an increasingly global economy, and the degree to which U.S. interests are perceived to be compatible with those of other countries and peoples. Since the standing assumptions in each of these cases are being challenged in the domestic political arena, and since these are a priori questions, the derivative matter of developing a coherent and sensible stance in international organizations may take some years to be resolved. In the process, some old prejudices will need to be aired and exposed to the light of day. The result may well be a greater sense of national purpose in the world, but it will not come easily. In the meantime, as so often in the past, the world will have to wait for the resolution of America's domestic divisions. At the same time, as discussed in the next chapter, the tendency of other UN member states to gang up on the United States—or at least the perception among American diplomats and commentators that this is the case—can only aggravate lurking suspicions that the United Nations, as presently constituted, is not a friendly place.

CHAPTER FIVE

America in Loyal Opposition

Today, I am no longer able to rise in defense of the United Nations. I am no longer optimistic about the future of that one-time community of nations that has now fallen so far.

— SENATOR ABRAHAM RIBICOFF, 1975

I do not believe in retreat . . . . I believe in standing and fighting and pursuing the course we believe is right. While votes may be disappointing, they can be reversed.

— SENATOR HUBERT H. HUMPHREY, 1975

People give a lot of lip-service to the importance of the United Nations, but in fact they're not prepared to defend it from attacks on its basic principles. If they were prepared to stand up for these principles as we are, the UN would prove to be a much more valuable organization, and one that was more true to its own ideals.

— DENNIS GOODMAN, 1987

What a strange and distant planet the United Nations inhabits.

— MARC THIESSEN, 1998

BUILDING ON THE THEMES of exceptionalism, wariness, and suspicion introduced in the last three chapters, this chapter looks at some of the specific historic and contemporary controversies that have fueled the American sense of being isolated in UN forums. This fourth theme puts considerable emphasis on the often dysfunctional interplay between domestic and international issues. It asks, in essence, whether the UN can be as united as its name implies and whether a unity of purpose also can be forged domestically in an era of single-issue, localized politics. To do this, the chapter first traces the evolution of the UN into what is sometimes regarded as an unfriendly place for U.S. interests and values, then considers the domestic consequences of General Assembly actions against two of America's allies during the turbulent 1970s, and finally looks at two more recent developments in U.S. politics—judging foreign governments by their democratic virtues and the rise of single-issue constituencies—that are contributing to ambivalence about the UN. In each case, the question arises whether America's unique qualities—its exceptionalism—has not contributed to the perpetuation, almost institutionalization, of America's minority status in UN organs other than the Security Council. This larger question is addressed in the brief concluding section of this chapter.

An Unfriendly Place?

Founded as the outgrowth of a wartime alliance, the world organization was sundered first along East-West and then North-South lines. In the late 1940s and early 1950s, as the cold war worsened, repeated Soviet vetoes in the Security Council led many to question whether an organization based on the premise of great power unanimity could play a useful security role, or even remain intact, as East-West tensions grew. Soviet ideology, moreover, seemed to preclude significant cooperation on central questions of peace and security. Nevertheless, as discussed in chapter 6, the effort to integrate the Soviet Union into the expanding system of international institutions remained a core element of U.S. postwar strategy. According to historian John Lewis Gaddis, "the American attitude was less that of expecting to impose a system than one of puzzlement as to why its merits were not universally self-evident."[1] Yet, as U.S. officials continued to make the argument for a broad-based United Nations despite the frustrations of dealing daily with Soviet tactics and rhetoric, many Americans began to have serious doubts about the wisdom of relying solely on the new "united" organization, when it was in fact badly divided. The charter, after all, made no claims for universality. The organization was to include the fifty-one founding members from San Francisco—allies during the war—plus "all other peace-loving states which accept the obligations" in the charter and are deemed worthy by the other members (article 4).

During the early postwar years, several opinion leaders and members of Congress called for the creation of a league of like-minded democracies, reviving the old notion of an Atlantic Union, although most saw it as a supplement to, not a replacement for, the United Nations. The establishment of the North Atlantic Treaty Organization in April 1949 served these purposes, at least in terms of organizing a credible collective defense effort among the chief western democracies. Between the UN and NATO, bipartisan support for the postwar international architecture could be sustained, because there was something for internationalists of every stripe. Those mainstream voices calling for a new, more homogeneous, body did indeed subside (temporarily) after the founding of NATO. Nonetheless, the underlying concern—that the UN, by its very nature, is too diverse to advance western values or to meet American security needs with any consistency—has persisted in critiques of the world body ever since.

During the UN's first decade, U.S. officials naturally touted the importance of the General Assembly, where, beyond the reach of Soviet vetoes and assured of a favorable response to most western initiatives, they could pursue U.S. interests in a propitious and largely supportive atmosphere. As John Foster Dulles phrased it from a realist's perspective in 1948 testimony before the House:

> The present United Nations, with all of its weaknesses, is an asset rather than a liability. . . . On the basis of my experience—and I have participated in all of the regular sessions of the Assembly—these "town meetings of the world" have served to enlighten world opinion about the nature of Soviet leadership. Soviet tactics, obstructionism, boycott, and smear have alienated many who were originally disposed to be friendly or neutral. General Assembly debate promotes world-wide moral judgments that are influential even though their implementation is not well-organized.[2]

With the success of the U.S.-encouraged and UN-shepherded decolonization movement and the subsequent rapid expansion of UN membership during the 1950s and 1960s, however, things began to change for the worse from a short-term American political perspective. As General Assembly debates took on North-South as well as East-West dimensions, American values and interests were more readily challenged and pro-western voting majorities became more difficult to assemble on a range of issues. As early as 1952, Secretary of State Dean Acheson reported to President Truman that "the outstanding fact of the Assembly so far is its dominance by the Arab-Asian bloc."[3] In 1961 Ambassador Adlai Stevenson warned against "that pleasant illusion of omnipotence to which we Americans have clung for so long," which could "now swing the other way . . . from disillusion to despair, from an illusion of omnipotence to a myth of impotence."[4] The following year, he asserted that "there is a great power which is regularly outvoted in the Assembly, but it is not the United States. It is the Soviet Union, whose aims and actions so often inspire widespread distrust."[5] During the next decade or two, however, it became more and more apparent that the Assembly no longer resembled the friendly, pro-western forum that the United States touted in the early years as an alternative to the Council.

Ironically, by getting its way in supporting the decolonization struggle, the United States helped to transform the General Assembly into a far more diverse and contentious place. To many, it appeared to be a classic trade-off between grand principles (decolonization) and short-term national interests (control of the Assembly).[6] American diplomacy assumed a more defensive character in UN forums during the 1960s and early 1970s. More and more, as the United States began to lose the initiative, its strategies within multilateral institutions came to center on "damage limitation," rather than seeking to accomplish major positive gains. As America's capacity to control the course of General Assembly debates and the content of its resolutions declined, a growing number of American observers came to the reluctant realization that not only did the organization suffer from ineffectiveness in carrying out its founding purposes but, more ominously, that its pronouncements could do real harm both to America's values and to its friends. In their eyes, an American creation—"our" organization—was being turned against its founders and diverted from its original rationale and principles. (The degree to which this should be attributed to anti-Americanism rather than to divergent interests and political philosophies, however, is open to question.)[7]

As addressed in chapter 2, the Assembly's one-nation, one-vote rule and sovereign equality principle gave smaller countries a voice in world affairs unmatched anywhere outside of its walls. As a result, with the influx of scores of newly independent developing countries, the weight of opinion in the Assembly on issue after issue tipped away from U.S. national interests, at least as they were currently defined in Washington, D.C. The new member states, moreover, quickly came to realize that their best chance of maximizing their influence in the body, especially in the face of America's historic dominance of the Assembly, was to band together in regional and political blocs. For small delegations caught in the middle of cold war politics, the group identification permitted them to pool their staff resources and to lessen their individual political risks when their collective positions riled one major power or another. To the United States, however, the tendency toward bloc voting compromised its ability to exert the kind of power it possessed outside of UN halls, offered the Soviets a backdoor route to greater influence within the world body, and made a mockery of the one-nation, one-vote rule.

Viewing the world through the prism of East-West relations, which in the UN from the early 1970s involved Beijing as well as Moscow, Washington officials were slow to comprehend the implications of the political sea change under way at the United Nations. They were preoccupied, in any case, with the conduct of the war in Vietnam and with the growing domestic dissent it was spawning. The war had a dual effect on U.S.-UN relations, neither for the good. First, most member states saw the conflict from a North-South perspective, reinforcing their conviction that American power needed to be checked. In that regard, Washington's determination to keep serious discussion of the war out of UN forums only served to re-inforce that conclusion. Second, the domestic consequences affected U.S.-UN relations even more profoundly. The failure of the war effort served to undermine more than two decades of bipartisanship on major questions of foreign policy, to destroy both the credibility and the unity of the foreign policy establishment, to sharpen congressional-executive differences over war powers and the conduct of foreign policy, and to cast doubts on the basic internationalist assumptions that had undergirded American leader-ship in the construction and operation of the post-1945 system of interna-tional institutions. The stunning triumphs of the secretive bilateral diplo-macy conducted by the Nixon-Kissinger team, moreover, contrasted favorably to the plodding and indeterminate debates at the UN, where the U.S. voice seemed increasingly lonely, muted, and defensive, as well as to the tenets of open diplomacy championed by Woodrow Wilson. Henry Kis-singer "never gave a thought to the U.N. save on the odd occasion it caused him trouble," Daniel Patrick Moynihan once said.[8]

When the UN began to veer off track—at least from an American perspective—during the 1960s and more sharply during the 1970s, the U.S. response was uneven and uncertain. Much depended on the personalities and predilections of the U.S. permanent representative of the moment and the style of the administration (it hardly seemed, for example, that ambas-sadors Moynihan in 1975 and Andrew Young in 1977 were accredited to the same UN). Citing a 1975 Chicago Council on Foreign Relations poll that showed the general public far more likely than opinion leaders to believe that the UN should play a "very important" role in U.S. foreign policy, Ambassador Moynihan contended that on UN matters "elites were exhausted, but the country was not."[9] Most elites and foreign policy "real-ists" simply looked the other way as newly independent and developing countries used the General Assembly as a rostrum from which to voice their complaints about the existing world order. Its resolutions, after all, were nonbinding, and the media had grown tired of its endless debates. Little of consequence was heard from establishment figures on the subject.

Ironically, while the American people eventually largely overcame the well-publicized post-Vietnam syndrome about nonintervention abroad, the

sundering of bipartisanship and the fissures that developed within the foreign policy elite over Vietnam have had more lasting effects on support for
international institutions. According to Godfrey Hodgson, writing in 1973,
the American foreign policy establishment had come together "to combat
the rising tide of isolationism after the Senate defeated American membership in the League of Nations in 1920." In his view, the less-hawkish wing of
the establishment—interested in developing countries and international
institutions, and including prominent figures such as Adlai Stevenson and
Chester Bowles (he might have added George Ball, John Kenneth Galbraith,
and Cyrus Vance, among others)—was always a distinct minority. It is
telling that McGeorge Bundy, the former national security advisor and
putative dean of the establishment, did not include the UN or any other
global institution in his list of seven "major undertakings of post-war
American foreign policy" cited for the Hodgson piece.[10] To most foreign
policy opinion leaders, the UN was to be maintained as an essentially symbolic expression of America's global engagement, but it was rarely seen as a
place to do serious business.

Into this intellectual and political hodgepodge strode Daniel Patrick
Moynihan, fresh from a stint as ambassador in New Delhi and armed with
a prescient analysis of why things had gone sour at the UN and of why that
mattered, and with some hard-headed ideas about how to reassert American influence, if not leadership. In a provocative and influential article, entitled "The United States in Opposition," in the March 1975 *Commentary*,
Moynihan examined the historical roots and ideological tenets behind "the
tyranny of the UN's 'new majority'" (a phrase that President Gerald Ford
had employed in his 1974 speech to the General Assembly). According to
Moynihan's analysis, the new member states had remarkably uniform views
drawn from British socialist traditions that favored equity and redistribu-
tion of wealth over economic development and that entailed a pervasive
anti-American bias. The triumph of the nonaligned bloc in the UN, however, stemmed, in his view, not only from the coherence of its position, but
also from "a massive failure of American diplomacy." Chronicling what he
deemed to be a persistent assault on American values and interests in a
series of UN forums and on a wide range of subjects, Moynihan argued that
it was high time for U.S. policy to recognize that "world society and world
organization have evolved to the point where palpable interests are disposed
in international forums to a degree without precedent." Given the "enormous" stakes involved, the only choice was for the United States to go pur-
posefully "into opposition," aggressively asserting its social, economic, and

political values. "Speaking for political and civil liberty," he emphasized, ". . . is something that can surely be undertaken by Americans with enthusiasm and zeal."[11]

Moynihan's proactive approach appealed to many Americans, especially to neoconservatives, as more realistic than paying deference to outmoded dreams of a united UN that never was and as a more forward-looking and positive approach than that offered by defensive, damage-limitation strategies. Moynihan, at least, seemed to be taking the UN, and its member states, seriously. He never wavered, moreover, on the importance of the United States staying in the UN, putting up a good fight for what it believes, and meeting its financial and legal obligations. His stormy and brief tenure as permanent representative to the UN from mid-1975 through February 1976 was marked by the achievement of consensus at the Seventh Special Session of the General Assembly on an ambitious range of North-South economic and development targets; the Zionism-racism debacle, discussed below; and persistent controversy about the effectiveness of his assertive, many said undiplomatic, rhetoric. As a consequence, his successors, William W. Scranton in the remainder of the Ford administration and Andrew Young and Donald McHenry in the Carter administration, adopted less confrontational styles. Yet the North-South battle lines had been drawn irreversibly by the attempts of the nonaligned, with Soviet encouragement, to fashion new world economic, information, social, and political orders out of the nonbinding resolutions produced by their Assembly majorities. In terms of combative tactics, it was then left to Jeane Kirkpatrick and the Reagan administration in the 1980s to pick up where Moynihan had left off. But it had been during the turbulent 1970s that the notion took hold in much of Washington that the UN was no longer a hospitable place either for America or for some of its less popular friends.

Beijing In, Taipei Out

America's first of several shocks from Turtle Bay in the 1970s came when the General Assembly decided on October 25, 1971, that Beijing rather than Taipei should occupy the Chinese seat in the UN. It was a stunning defeat for the United States, which had fended off this Soviet and nonaligned effort for many years, made worse when several delegates took to the Assembly's aisles to dance in celebration of this hard-fought victory. The Assembly in effect added a second communist power to the Security Council's permanent members and expelled a long-time U.S. ally in the Pacific. Predictably, congressional reaction was swift and heated. Many legislators called for financial retaliation against the UN, questioned continued U.S. participation, and urged cutbacks in aid to member nations that voted "against" the United States. "Now that the Communist influence has become dominant in the U.N.," railed Representative Ovie C. Fisher, D-Tex., "let the Communist nations pay in accordance with the number of people they claim to represent." Senator Robert C. Byrd, D-W.Va., declared that Congress should reexamine "U.S. commitments to this organization which has failed so miserably in this hour of testing, and should definitely reduce U.S. contributions to the United Nations." "The time has come," said Senator Barry Goldwater, the former Republican presidential candidate from Arizona, "for us to cut off all financial help, withdraw as a member, and ask the United Nations to find a headquarters location outside the United States that is more in keeping with the philosophy of the majority of voting members, someplace like Moscow or Peking." According to Senator Paul J. Fannin, R-Ariz., "America's contribution should not be any larger than that of any other major nation such as the Soviet Union or the new member, Red China."[12]

Such sentiments, of course, had often been heard from the more anti-internationalist members of Congress. Some favored cutting funds for the UN, while others preferred either targeting those aid recipients that showed inefficient "gratitude" in the way they cast their votes on the question of Chinese representation or somehow expelling nonpayers and late payers from the world body. What was different and new about the 1971 chapter of the ongoing and gradually escalating crisis in U.S.-UN relations, however, was that the anti-UN minority on Capitol Hill had a chance to flex its political muscles as never before. Within a week of the vote in the General Assembly, the Senate for the first time voted, 41 to 27, to defeat a foreign aid bill—legislation that President Nixon had labeled the "absolutely vital" bulwark of bipartisan foreign policy.[13] Spite about the UN vote was not the only factor in the defeat of the foreign assistance measure, but it was, by all accounts, an important and perhaps decisive one.

For all of the outpouring of anti-UN emotions, support for the global organization was still reasonably broad and deep in Washington in 1971. Since 1953, according to the Gallup Poll, more Americans had responded that the UN was doing a "good job" than a "poor" one, although the gap in the September 1970 survey had narrowed to 44 to 40 percent, respectively.[14] Bipartisan support for including the People's Republic in the UN had been growing for some years both in Congress and in the general public.

According to a May 1971 Gallup Poll, a plurality of Americans favored Beijing's participation by a 45 to 38 percent margin.[15] Many mainstream legislators, while expressing dismay at the ousting of Taipei, saw the inclusion of Beijing not as a threat, but as an opportunity for better bilateral relations and as a step toward the dream of a more universal UN. They questioned what would be gained by withholding financial support for the UN, especially in light of the fact that several U.S. allies had voted to give Beijing the seat. Given the narrowing margin on this issue in the Assembly with each passing year, there was already a sense of inevitability about the eventual seating of the People's Republic. Had it been known, even to the U.S. team at the UN, that President Nixon was already deeply engaged in secret diplomacy with Beijing, then the U.S. resistance in the General Assembly would have appeared even more futile.

George Bush, the U.S. permanent representative, had already reassured the Assembly's finance committee that "the Administration of President Nixon is not threatening the United Nations, or planning financial reprisals for any political contingencies here. On the contrary, . . . we want the U.N.'s finances to be rescued from their present precarious state."[16] Moreover, the Senate defeated by a 2 to 1 margin, a proposal to cut voluntary funding— payments to UN programs and agencies that are not assessed or legally obligated and hence have long been Congress' preferred form of UN funding.[17] The 1971 crisis, therefore, was marked not only by the degree of congressional anti-UN rhetoric it occasioned, but also by the expression of continuing commitment to the organization by its long-standing advocates in both the executive and the legislative branches. Washington, in short, was divided about the implications of the Assembly's move and about what, if anything, should be done about it.

Rock Bottom? The Zionism-Racism Fiasco

Although the base of UN support on Capitol Hill still appeared reasonably solid in 1971, warning lights of far greater trouble ahead should have been flashing when Arab and African delegations, with Soviet encouragement, turned next to lumping Israel, South Africa, and anticolonialism into a combustible package. In resolution 3151G (xxviii) of December 14, 1973, the General Assembly condemned "the unholy alliance between Portuguese colonialism, South African racism, zionism and Israeli imperialism." Criticizing the passive and retiring U.S. government stance in the face of this worrisome step, Professor Leon Gordenker of Princeton wrote in the

Washington Post in July 1974 that "surely a government that can negotiate with China and the Soviet Union can organize enough persuasiveness to reduce the production of pernicious symbolism" in the UN.[18]

The next year, the floor underneath congressional and public support for the UN largely gave way when the General Assembly determined, in resolution 3379 (xxx) of November 10, 1975, that "Zionism is a form of racism and racial discrimination." By equating Zionism with racism, the Assembly in effect declared that one of its members was illegitimate. In response, Ambassador Moynihan issued his famous rebuttal that the United States "does not acknowledge, it will not abide by, it will never acquiesce in this infamous act."[19] Contending that, through the resolution, "the abomination of anti-Semitism has been given the appearance of international sanction," he spoke of the ominous "realization that if there were no General Assembly, this would never have happened." Noting that people were beginning to say "that the United Nations is a place where lies are told," he warned that in the "real world . . . there are real consequences to folly and to venality." In other words, as Ambassador Moynihan had stated on other occasions, in his view the world organization had become "a dangerous place," not just an inefficient or ineffectual one.

Congress, which had earlier voted overwhelmingly to express its opposition to the proposed Assembly resolution, wasted no time in condemning the action. The next day, November 11, the Senate approved, without opposition, Senate Concurrent Resolution 73, which sharply condemned the Assembly resolution, strongly opposed any U.S. government involvement in the UN's Decade for Action to Combat Racism and Racial Discrimination as long as the Zionism-racism resolution was associated with it, called on the Assembly to reconsider its action, and resolved that the House and Senate foreign affairs committees "begin hearings immediately to reassess the United States' further participation in the United Nations General Assembly."[20] The House passed a similar resolution, House Resolution 855, that same day by a vote of 384 to 0 (although it deleted the call for hearings).[21] The implications and procedures that would have been involved in suspending U.S. participation in the Assembly were not at all clear: was this to be a boycott or a withdrawal, and could it be limited to the Assembly given the scope of UN activities addressed there?

The very notion of selective U.S. participation in the UN's primary organs, however, was a telling departure from past policies. Ironically, a decade after many members of Congress had sought to punish the Soviet Union and other debtors to the UN by denying them voting rights in the

Assembly, Congress was now threatening to punish the UN members by doing the opposite, by refusing U.S. involvement in that same body. From a congressional perspective at least, participation in the Assembly seemed to be a privilege for other countries but a burden for the United States. As Moynihan had pointed out, if the Assembly did not exist, then the Zionism-racism resolution could not have been produced or given so much global attention and apparent sanction. In the end, of course, nonparticipation in the Assembly, given its broad-ranging responsibilities, including setting the UN's budget and dues scale, was not an attractive or viable option. Non-participation in the Assembly made sense only in the context of a with-drawal from the organization as a whole, something that, for all their anger, mainstream Americans could not yet contemplate. Any talk of nonpartici-pation, however, was an ominous sign for the future of U.S.-UN relations and an indication of the depth of dissatisfaction with, even alienation from, the world body.

Many representatives and a few senators spoke of financial reprisals against the UN or, more to the point, against recipients of U.S. aid that had voted for the Assembly action. Uncharacteristically, however, the final House and Senate resolutions did not threaten or mandate financial with-holdings or aid cutbacks. Nor, however, did anyone rise to assert U.S. finan-cial obligations either. This debate was a turning point, not just one more chapter in the continuing saga of U.S.-UN relations, and it was handled in Congress in a more concerted and focused manner than earlier crises had been. The leadership of each chamber offered its resolution at the beginning of debate, having already won the backing of large and growing bipartisan groups of their colleagues. Rather than quibbling about funding or offering to buy influence among UN members through augmentations of aid—something many legislators accused some Arab states of having done in New York—the congressional leadership chose to pose the ultimate ques-tion: whether the United States still considered the UN, or at least its Gen-eral Assembly, to be a body with which it wanted to be associated. Although it was an awkward time in the annual budgeting cycle to begin revising UN and foreign aid numbers in any case, Congress wanted to deliver a deeper message. Most legislators, for this round at least, wanted to make it clear that they were not seeking a financial discount on their UN membership, but instead were reconsidering whether they wanted to pay the escalating polit-ical price of remaining a member of the club.

Some of the congressional rhetoric, particularly in the House, was nowhere close to being diplomatic. Robert E. Bauman, R-Md., stressed that "we should make these thugs and scoundrels in the United Nations account for their actions." Calling the Zionism-racism resolution "brazen," "reprehensible," "divisive," "inflammatory," "crude," and "banal," Mario Biaggi, D-N.Y., concluded that the UN had "become a house of conspiracy and infamy," many of whose members were "hypocrites." Suggesting that "the U.N. is now controlled by essentially nondemocratic states which regularly endorse terrorism as a desirable life style," William E. Frenzel, R-Minn., urged a review of foreign aid and UN funding programs should the world body continue "to be the international public playpen for nonelected heads of regimes created or sustained by terrorism." Tom Downey, a young Democrat from Long Island, warned supporters of the Assembly resolution that "with respect to additional foreign aid for those countries who supported that resolution, they should be aware of the feeling in the Congress during this Christmas season. We will be making a list and checking it twice to determine who has been naughty and nice."[22]

A tone of finality infused much of the debate in both chambers. In the House Sidney R. Yates, D-Ill., intoned that it was "difficult to conceive that the General Assembly will ever again serve any useful purpose, so thoroughly did it discredit itself." "Unless there is a reversal of this vote," warned Donald W. Riegle, D-Mich., "the United Nations runs the very great risk of becoming another League of Nations." Suggesting that the Assembly vote "symbolizes the end of an era" and that Congress had "taken a stand to put the U.N. on notice," Matthew J. Rinaldo, R-N.J., concluded "that lack of moral character led to eventual demise of the League; the lack of courage in the United Nations in 1975 demonstrates the lack of moral force in that body. Without such force, the United Nations cannot remain a viable organization." Robert Nix, D-Pa., said that the Assembly's actions "mark what may well be the beginning of the end of the United Nations. An organization founded on the principles of peace, brotherhood, and reason has now officially adopted violence, prejudice, and wild irrationality as its new credo."[23]

Perhaps the most telling commentary was voiced on the Senate floor. Robert Packwood, R-Ore., for example, remarked that "by their action last night the United Nations has shown that it does not take itself seriously as a body designed to try to keep the peace in the world, let alone world morality, and I think the time has come when we can well ask the question: Does this nation any longer belong in that body?" As a long-time supporter of the UN, John Glenn, D-Ohio, regretted that the beliefs of those in Congress who still felt that the UN remained "a viable worldwide forum" had been "rendered less defensible after votes such as occurred at the U.N. this week." Internationalist Charles Mathias, R-Md., said for "those of us who have consistently supported efforts to make the United Nations a more viable organization, the vote must be taken as a signal to rethink the basic assumptions on which such support was based." Terming the Assembly resolution "heinous," "abhorrent," and "stupid," Joseph R. Biden, D-Del., contended that "the 72 nations that supported this resolution need the U.N. more than we big powers do. In the long run it will hurt them more than the United States, the Soviet Union or China." Robert Taft Jr., R-Ohio, cautioned that "if the U.N. is to be a showplace for the immaturity and irresponsibility of certain Third World states, and a propaganda forum for the Communist powers, then it will be utterly useless for the purpose of promoting peace. If that is so, what possible justification can there be for having a United Nations, or for continuing U.S. membership in the organization?"[24]

There were, of course, a few moderating voices in the congressional debate. Democratic Senator Edward M. Kennedy, D-Mass., strongly condemned the substance of the Assembly action, but pointed out that "it is not the U.N. which instigated yesterday's vote—it is those member states which favored the passage of this resolution that rightfully deserve to be the target of our protests." For the shrinking portion of Congress that still placed a high value on the overall work of the UN, Kennedy's points may well have been persuasive. The problem, however, is that Senator Ribicoff, D-Conn., in stressing his unwillingness anymore "to rise in defense of the United Nations," better captured the tone of the times.[25] While the 1971 crisis over the seating of Beijing and the expulsion of Taipei stirred the UN's adversaries on the Hill, the 1975 Zionism-racism uproar cut deeper and far more broadly, for it sapped the enthusiasm of many of America's strongest proponents of international organization. It made them question the basic assumptions on which the organization had been founded and to hesitate to come to its defense.[26] Even Claiborne Pell, D-R.I., who had been a proud member of the U.S. delegation at the founding conference in San Francisco, declared that "the prestige of the United Nations and the perceived value of that organization to this country is probably at its lowest ebb today."[27]

For long-time skeptics, the temptation to say "I told you so" was great. As Representative Walter Flowers, D-Ala., commented: "to our new disapproving colleagues, 'Welcome to the club' from those of us who have for some time been suspect of the United Nations and our continued participation in it." Senator James B. Allen, D-Ala., was pleased to note that "the Congress and the people of the United States are coming to realize just how

harmful the United Nations can be to peace."[28] Among its various and
largely odious outcomes, the Zionism-racism debacle gave an unprecedented degree of moral and political legitimacy to the UN's doubters, while
leaving its advocates to defend its virtues as well as its effectiveness. The
political "balance of forces" had begun to tip. More than twenty years later,
in a March 1998 speech in Jerusalem, Secretary-General Kofi Annan noted
that the resolution marked the low point in Israel's relationship with the UN
and that "its negative resonance even today is difficult to overestimate"—
this even though the Assembly finally took the unusual step of rescinding
the resolution in 1991.[29]

A League of Democracies?

When unhappy with the UN's actions, or inaction, Americans have frequently attributed its failings to its allegedly undemocratic ways. From the
outset, anomalies in its voting procedures and membership criteria have
been called into question. For example, during the 1945 debate about the
charter in the Senate, Burton K. Wheeler, D-Mont., a reluctant supporter of
ratification, suggested that its devotion to true democracy set America apart
from many of the other founding members:

> The trouble with so many idealistic Americans is that they judge all the other
> countries on the face of the earth by the same high ideals and principles which
> we have here in the United States. They do not realize that the people of many
> of the countries in Europe and Asia do not even know what democracy means,
> because they have never understood it. They have been ruled by an iron hand.
> Democracy means one thing to a Chinaman or a Russian, and it means quite
> a different thing to the people of the United States.[30]

He went on to ask: "What other power on earth is going to sacrifice itself to
guarantee the strengthening and perpetuation of our way of life if not
America?" Wheeler, like Henry Cabot Lodge a generation earlier, questioned
whether the incompatibility in political belief systems of the various member states would not preclude a workable and productive international organization of near-universal proportions. American exceptionalism, in Lodge
and Wheeler's view, revolved around its democratic principles and practices, things that were far too precious to be compromised, much less sacrificed, at the alter of international cooperation.

During the UN's early years members of Congress repeatedly questioned its utility because of the "obstructionist" role played by the Soviet Union and its frequent vetoes in the Security Council. In 1955 Senator George Malone,R-Nev., for example, asserted that the UN "will never maintain the peace so long as Red Russia, with 3 votes, and some of her satellites, with 1 vote each, are members."[31] In his view the world body had become "a debating society or club, in which the outlaws and bandits have equal privileges with the decent members. That policy has never worked with any club or society in the world." The founders of the organization, including the Soviet Union, were well aware of the differences of values and interests within the victorious alliance, but they hoped that the UN would provide a means of working them out peacefully, in part by identifying areas of common interest. As the charter underlines, a central purpose of the new body was to provide a forum for encouraging harmony and tolerance among nations with different political and social systems.

Nevertheless, Americans who had come to see the world body as an extension of American values and interests felt betrayed and alienated by the shifting political climate in the General Assembly. As Senator Ribicoff bemoaned in 1975, "the United Nations, set up on democratic foundations and with democratic procedures, is constantly being overwhelmed by countries that are neither democratic in scope or in philosophy."[32] In 1986 Assistant Secretary of State Alan L. Keyes wrote that:

> The welfare state socialism of some European states cooperates unwittingly with the tyrannically oriented statism of many developing countries. . . . It is a world of easy trade-offs and accommodations where most lack the political courage and clarity of purpose needed to remember, much less defend, the meaning of free democratic principles. The world-weary moral relativism that has become second nature in many free democracies sits all too well with the resentful moral hypocrisy of the unfree UN majority.[33]

Americans, in his view, had to confront political adversaries from both the Old World and the New, since neither shared their values or objectives. By bringing these worlds together, the UN was serving principally to unite ideological opponents rather than to facilitate cooperation among those with common goals and priorities. Similar themes were voiced by a chorus of conservative critics, including John R. Bolton, Charles M. Lichenstein, Burton Yale Pines, and Pat Robertson.[34]

The UN, however, was never intended to be a body of like-minded democracies, as these critics imply. Some of its most prominent founding members, most pointedly the Soviet Union, would not have been eligible under these revised and narrowed criteria. The product of the victorious coalition in World War II—allies temporarily united because of strategic necessity rather than deeply shared values—the UN charter established neither a democratic club nor a universal forum. According to its so-called "enemies" clauses, in articles 53 and 107, military action against World War II adversaries in order to maintain peace or prevent aggression would not require prior Security Council authorization. And new members were to be "peace-loving," not necessarily "democratic," a term never used in the Charter. Some confusion in the minds of critics and supporters alike, however, is understandable both because the resulting organization was something of an amalgam of competing visions and because America's leaders have tended to oversell its virtues and to cast them in a variety of shades, depending on the audience. This, too, has added to a sense of ambivalence about an organization that seems to represent different things to different groups.

Global Programs, Domestic Agendas: Acting Globally and Thinking Locally

Most Americans regard the UN and other international institutions as policy instruments for advancing specific causes—for good or ill—rather than as ends in themselves. In that context, although internationally minded groups have long urged Americans to "think globally and act locally," U.S.-based interest groups of all stripes have tended to reverse the slogan: to be concerned about how UN debates and programs will affect pet domestic issues. These concerns have only been reinforced by the growing recognition of how the globalization of communications, economics, and politics has further tightened the links between local and global events and developments. Interest groups tend to focus on those global issues that appear to mirror or impinge upon aspects of particularly contentious domestic debates. What matters, in their view, has less to do with what the organization does around the world than with how its words and deeds might affect the outcome of U.S. domestic policy struggles. The world body, from this perspective, serves as a two-way instrument for disseminating some views and limiting others. For example, some see parallels between international arms control and disarmament and local gun control, between development assistance and welfare, between human rights abroad and civil rights at home, between population planning and abortion politics, and between global and local environmental questions. If you don't like one, you probably won't like the other.

Others worry that the lowest common denominator will prevail. Consumer advocate Ralph Nader, for example, fretted in 1994 Senate testimony that the expansion of GATT rules and the creation of the World Trade Organization would work against U.S. environmental, consumer, and worker health and safety regulations under the pretense that they serve as nontariff barriers. Although subsequent experience makes his worries now seem overdrawn, he warned at that time that:

> The GATT rules envision placing a ceiling on health, safety and environmental protection, but provide no minimal floor beyond which all nations must rise (except against prison labor). One does not have to guess which country's standards are most likely to be pulled downward.

As a self-styled grass-roots activist, he cautioned that the "percolating-up process for advancing crucial non-commercial values that shape living standards will be stifled by the WTO, with bottom-up democratic impulses replaced by pull-down mercantile dictates." Nader espoused a domestic agenda markedly different from that offered by traditionally conservative critics of international organization, but he seemed to share their concerns for sovereignty when he dramatically declared that the WTO would "undermine citizen control and chill the ability of domestic democratic bodies to make decisions on a vast array of domestic policies from food safety to federal and state procurement to communications and foreign investment policies."[35]

Ralph Nader aside, on most of these issues, it should be stressed, the UN—reflecting the views of most member states—usually comes down on the "liberal" and statist side of the debate, at least from the perspective of American conservatives. Those worried about governments playing too intrusive a role in society are unlikely to be pleased with the programmatic and normative decisions of hundreds of governments gathering to weigh sensitive social and economic matters, particularly when these appear to impinge upon domestic policy choices and national sovereignty.[36] It would be remarkable if the results of UN deliberations did *not* have statist leanings. Moreover, the United States, even during Democratic administrations, tends to be one of the most "conservative" countries in the General Assembly on most of these questions (human rights often being a big exception). Yet from the perspective of hard-core conservatives who feel underrepresented in international bodies, the positions taken by American representatives may look quite "liberal." Conservatives' views do not get voiced often in UN debates, because they tend not to fit within the range of perspectives embraced by member state governments or traditional internationalist nongovernmental organizations (NGOs). Given this political context, it should come as no surprise that American conservatives tend to greet the outcomes of most UN deliberations with restrained enthusiasm at best. They look, instead, to Congress, where their influence is far greater and where they can be much more confident of getting a sympathetic hearing from a body that often shares their distrust of executive power.

The range of subjects being addressed by the UN at any point in time, moreover, produces such a quantity of dialogue, papers, decisions, and programs that some of it is bound to be construed as offensive by one domestic constituency or another within the United States (and often within other member states as well). Even if the final outcomes are not deemed obnoxious, the positions and comments voiced by individual countries or groups during debates may well be, especially if taken out of context. The growth of single-interest politics within the United States has made a difficult situation that much worse. It has fostered the development of advocacy groups—pro or con—for each subject. They, in turn, tend to see the UN system through a narrow lens, focused on the debates and programs in that single-issue area. In this way, UN forums have become the setting not only for intergovernmental dialogue, but also, on another level, for the magnification and amplification of domestic disputes over highly contentious issues, with each side seeking international blessing for its positions. This is a formula for intense reactions—some favorable, many unfavorable—and for substantive distortions through judging a large enterprise by a small sample. It is not a promising means for developing broad understanding or support.

Since the Reagan administration, the most visible and consequential overlapping of domestic and international agendas has been between those promoting family planning, particularly in developing countries, for economic, social, and environmental reasons and those engaged in the highly charged tug-of-war between pro-life and pro-choice groups at home. The latter battle has been especially divisive because it has been cast by both sides in stark moral and constitutional terms. The international dimensions of the population issue have combined much of this righteous fervor with a far-reaching philosophical and policy debate about the nature of economic and social development, the historical record concerning the relationship between overpopulation and poverty, and the role of the state in family planning.[37] The most recent round in this struggle over population policy between the Clinton administration and the Republican-led Congress resulted in October 1998 in the president's veto of the UN reform-for-arrears package, leaving U.S.-UN relations in limbo and inching the United States closer to the brink of losing its vote in the General Assembly (for greater detail, see chapter 10).

Two ironies have fueled the ambivalence that many Americans feel about these matters as the focus of public policy attention. For one thing, the question of choice versus government regulation tends to cut in opposite directions on the domestic and international levels, with pro-choice proponents at home often supporting population control abroad and with those concerned about statism and the rights of women abroad tending to favor restrictions on a woman's right to choose in the States. Paradoxically, moreover, it was the United States that took the lead in the 1960s to warn the world about the population bomb and to urge the creation of the UN Fund for Population Activities. Two decades later, it was American policy shifts and legislation that sought to limit the agency's funding and activities.

One of the quirkier, but not inconsequential, developments of recent years has been the National Rifle Association's (NRA's) discovery of the United Nations. This coincides with two related substantive trends in the world organization. First, many member states, including the United States, have shown renewed interest in addressing the potentially destabilizing flows of small arms into areas of tension or intrastate conflict, by seeking means to curb illegal transnational arms shipments to terrorists, local warlords, and parties to civil war. Not since the late 1970s has either the U.S. government or the UN paid serious attention to controlling the international arms trade, although growing awareness of the enormous human, social, and economic costs of even localized conflict has refocused public, media, and governmental concern on what has now been coined "microdisarmament" and even on the possibility of "preventive disarmament." Second, the United States and several other member states have urged the world body to develop both norms and programs for dealing with what the secretary-general has called "uncivil society": transnational drug smugglers, money launderers, gun runners, and crime networks. At the June 1997 Denver Summit of the Eight, the heads of the seven leading industrial countries and the Russian Federation called for standard systems for firearms identification and for a stronger international regime for licensing the import and export of firearms.

This transnational momentum toward finding ways to monitor the international trade in small arms understandably has made the NRA nervous, given its repeated clashes with the Clinton administration over gun control legislation, its declining public support, and its recognition that U.S. regulations are among the laxest in the industrial world. Particularly worried that the UN Commission on Crime Prevention and Criminal Justice in Vienna may develop a declaration of principles on the regulation of firearms, the NRA gained NGO consultative status with the UN's Economic and Social Council in November 1996 so that it could attend regional workshops and comment on the issues before the commission.[38] NRA representatives have been outspoken at UN meetings, but they lack the kind of clout in intergovernmental forums that they had exercised in Congress in the past. "Make no mistake about it," NRA lobbyist Tanya K. Metaksa warned its members, "the United Nations' growing interest in firearms regulation is a direct and serious threat to you as an American gun owner."[39] In her view, a "U.N. declaration on gun control would be used by every anti-gun group on the planet to influence governmental bodies from parliaments and congresses to city councils." While the secretary-general's March 1998 report on measures to regulate firearms has several caveats about the need to respect the sovereignty, customs, and legislation of each country,[40] it is clear enough why the NRA finds the UN to be a dangerous place: the NRA's agenda of minimizing restrictions on gun ownership and use is facing growing public opposition within the United States, which will only be reinforced if the codification of international standards is accomplished.

UN actions in two additional areas—human rights and environmental matters—have proven to be lightning rods for conservative criticisms. Ironically, these are two areas in which most Americans would like to see greater international cooperation. The United States has stood virtually alone (Somalia is the other holdout) in its failure to ratify the Rights of the Child Convention, negotiated during the Bush administration and signed by President Clinton in February 1995. Although UNICEF, the chief advocate for the convention, remains the American people's favorite UN agency, the conservative opposition to ratification in the Senate has been adamant. In his run for the presidency in 1996, Alan Keyes labeled the convention "the most explicit assault on the authority of parents and the integrity of the family we have ever seen. We absolutely never should ratify it."[41]

An early proponent of the Republican-led "family values" campaign, Pat Robertson cited a long list of objectionable "'protections' the lawyers and sages of the United Nations have prescribed for children." Of these, his chief concern was the following:

> A key provision is the right of each child to "mass media" intended for his or her social, moral, or intellectual good. This "right" would prevent parents from prohibiting their children from being indoctrinated by government-sponsored mass media—an alarming precedent. This tactic has always been uppermost in totalitarian regimes. Strip children from their parents, then propagandize them by the state, so that children become agents and inform-ers against their parents.

Oddly, Robertson then expresses abhorrence over the "filth and violence" of the popular media and questions whether they should be "the custodians of morality and mental hygiene."[42] It is not clear which he finds to be the greater evil, free enterprise or government control of the media. In any case, the convention requires parties to "respect the responsibilities, rights and duties of parents" (article 5) and states that "a child shall not be separated from his or her parents against their will" except in cases of neglect or when the parents are separated and appropriate legal action is required (article 9). Rather than seeking to impose a state monopoly on information, article 13 has quite the opposite intention in seeking to ensure that children have the "freedom to seek, receive and impart information and ideas of all kinds, regardless of frontiers."

Although generally proponents of UN human rights monitoring around the world, some Americans get distinctly uncomfortable when those investigations come too close to home, as has happened in recent years con-cerning questions of capital punishment, religious intolerance, and violence against women in prison. [43] For example, in the fall of 1997, the UN's spe-cial rapporteur on extrajudicial, summary, or arbitrary executions, Bacre Waly Ndiaye of Senegal, decided to conduct an on-site investigation of the use of capital punishment in the United States.[44] International norms do not explicitly prohibit the death penalty, but the UN Human Rights Com-mission has called for limits on its use and scope. A former official of Amnesty International who had carried out similar fact-finding missions to a number of countries, Ndiaye saw no reason why the United States should be an exception or why he should not criticize America's extensive use of capital punishment in his 1998 report to the commission in Geneva. The Clinton administration initially approved of the trip but then largely snubbed him when he sought to meet with high-level U.S. officials. Ndiaye was able to meet with political and judicial leaders in several states, however. To Senator Helms, the mission was "an absurd U.N. charade" and "a perfect example of why the United Nations is looked upon with such disdain by the American people."[45] Bill Richardson, then the U.S. permanent representative to the UN, predicted that Ndiaye's report would "collect a lot of dust."

It is a testament to how far the environmental movement has come in the United States to witness how much opposition it stirs up at times. So it was not surprising in June 1997 when Senator Mike Enzi, R-Wyo., sought, unsuccessfully, to amend the UN arrears-for-reform bill to "ensure that the United Nations does not spend U.S. taxpayer money to sponsor conventions that result in stricter—and more expensive—environmental standards for Americans than other members have to bear." On the proposition that developing countries should get a break on standards, he quipped that "they don't buy it in Wyoming." In any event, Senator Helms said, the amendment was unnecessary because under his bill the administration would have to certify "that the sovereignty of the United States has not been violated." He, too, was concerned "with the increasing number of United Nations treaties that impose regulatory burdens and . . . infringe on the rights of the American people."[46]

More remarkable was the October 1997 approval of the American Land Sovereignty Protection Act by the House of Representatives in a vote largely along party lines. The bill sought to require congressional approval for the designation of any place in the United States as a Biosphere Reserve or a World Heritage site. The bill would have rescinded the sixty-seven designations that had been nominated by successive presidents over the past quarter century and approved by UNESCO. The chief sponsor of the legislation, Representative Don Young, R-Alaska, emphasized "our congressional duty to keep international commitments from abridging traditional constitutional constraints" and reminded his colleagues that "we are not a one-world group. We are the sovereign Nation of the United States of America." To Helen Chenoweth, R-Idaho, this was "a simple bill on American sovereignty" and so "let us let the sun shine on this, let us let the people have their say, and let us let the Congress act." "We are the best arbiters of these kinds of issues," added Frank Riggs, R-Calif., "not some faceless international council."[47]

In opposition, Bruce Vento, D-Minn., asserted that a World Heritage designation served primarily as a boost to tourism and the Man and Biosphere Program as a facilitator for international scientific cooperation on environmental matters. Noting that the UN "has absolutely no authority whatsoever to dictate Federal land management decisions within or for the United States," he lamented that "what is most ironic about this debate is the fact that the United States has been the leader in establishing these programs." In the view of Sam Farr, D-Calif., "this bill would be setting a very dangerous precedent by Congress overreaching, by fearing fear itself." Pointing out that "environmental protection has to be global in order to be effective," Maurice D. Hinchey, D-N.Y., contended that "this legislation is the product of an overactive imagination, one which has the ability to see a problem where none exists." Mincing no words, George Miller, a twelve-term Democrat from California, declared that "this may be the craziest damned bill I have ever seen. . . . This is not about sovereignty, this is about extremism run amok."[48]

Perhaps Representative Miller was right. Why a quiet program that had the blessing of Republican and Democratic administrations for a quarter of a century should suddenly be considered a threat to national sovereignty is not evident. Less than a decade earlier, the Reagan administration, in the person of Richard S. Williamson, the assistant secretary of state for international organization affairs, testified before Congress that, with the inscription of three new American sites by the UN, "I am pleased to announce that . . . the United States now has the most sites inscribed on the World Heritage List."[49] That an action considered to be a cause for national pride by the Reagan administration is now seen as something sinister illustrates the enormity of the shift in congressional attitudes during the past decade. It is a sign of the times, moreover, that the bill passed the House by a comfortable forty-five-vote margin (236 to 191), although it did not become law.[50] Just the day before, October 7, 1997, the House also voted—again along party lines—to limit President Clinton's authority to declare federal lands to be national monuments. [51] In part, these actions can be read as a reaction to the president's adept use of these powers to curry environmentally minded votes prior to the 1996 election. In part, they repeat the pattern of the interminable struggle for turf between a Republican Congress and a Democratic White House, with the UN caught helplessly in the middle.

Helms spokesperson Marc Thiessen, however, also had a point. The gulf in understanding and perspective between Congress and the UN often seems so wide and so difficult to bridge that, indeed, they appear to occupy "strange and distant planets." From Turtle Bay's vantage point, the ever-shifting and rarely consonant voices from different parts of America—with its contentious brand of pluralism—at times make it hard to tell who, if anyone, speaks for the whole. Listening to the pleadings of civil society may not help much, given the political imbalance that is endemic in NGO representation at the world body. By a largely self-selecting process, it is the internationalist wing of civil society that is likely to be both present at and attentive to the United Nations. Whatever their nationality, NGO representatives at the UN may be no better placed to understand what makes Jesse Helms or Pat Buchanan tick than would a career international civil servant or the representative of a developing country. There are not many NRAs among the UN corps of several thousand NGOs,[52] but the number of more conservative groups represented appears to be growing as they come to see UN meetings and conferences as forums whose decisions make a difference in their subject areas. The prospect, then, is for growing controversy and dissent within NGO deliberations at the UN. Yet without more of these verbal and ideological clashes on a wider range of issues between the representatives of these very different planets, not to mention political philosophies, prospects for narrowing the conceptual gaps will remain decidedly dim. So, too, will be the UN's chances of "harmonizing the actions of nations" or America's prognosis for overcoming the ambivalence that is crippling its conduct of foreign policy.

Permanent Opposition?

The common thread that runs through all of these sample episodes, spanning three decades of U.S.-UN interaction, is that American representatives, official and unofficial, very often find themselves in a minority position in global institutions. These few examples could be multiplied many times. Even when other highly developed countries are on the same side of the question, the United States often serves as point man, receiving the most hits and leading the counterattack. In commenting on this phenomenon in 1987, Dennis Goodman, the senior deputy assistant secretary of state for international organization affairs, stated that he "would lay the blame especially on our OECD colleagues. They know better, but they are too often unwilling to take the necessary stand." In response, America's friends at the UN question the tendency of U.S. officials to see grand principles in what

others see as modest matters of national interest and perspective and to prefer confrontation to compromise. Believing that the UN was created in the
image of the United States—for example, Goodman asserts that both the
United States and the UN are "based on the principles of a liberal
democracy"—some U.S. representatives are still confounded at times to
find themselves repeatedly in a minority status in "their" world body.[53]

As suggested in chapter 2, America is different. Its interests, as well as its
history, culture, values, size, location, wealth, and power, have tended to set
it apart from most UN member states on a host of issues, again and again
through the years. Its tactics tend to be a bit rougher and its tolerance for
UN customs and rituals a bit thinner than those of its partners. U.S. diplomats have gotten used to their minority status and have learned ways to
protect and further American interests and values in the whirlwind that is
multilateral diplomacy. The spirit of appeasement and passiveness that
Ambassador Moynihan railed against in the 1970s is long gone. In its place,
foreign commentators would suggest, Americans have become the perpetual gadflies, the habitual in-house critics, of international organization.
Some observers even infer that U.S. representatives to the UN have come to
savor the role of the lonely defender of western values in the face of overwhelming opposition. It is a stance of seemingly heroic dimensions, and
one that has served to bring two U.S. permanent representatives considerable public and political acclaim at home, if not in UN circles.[54]

One's perspective depends, of course, on where one sits. From the vantage point of long-term American interests, it looks as if Moynihan's assessments and prescriptions were basically on target. The United States and its
partners faced a very serious political challenge that threatened not only
their interests, but also the viability of the UN as an institution. As many
nonaligned representatives came to appreciate, they had become so intoxi-
cated with the power of their numbers within the organization as to attempt
to compel changes in the real world order outside of the UN's halls that
were neither feasible nor, in retrospect, desirable in terms of their own long-
term national interests. Outspokenness by U.S. representatives was called
for when real questions of principle were at stake. Even the Assembly came
to recognize how pernicious and debilitating was the Zionism-racism resolution, rescinding it, in an almost unprecedented move, in 1991.

Yet Americans must learn to listen, as well as to preach, to the other
member states. For example, only very slowly and reluctantly did the U.S.
government come around to the majority viewpoint—both in the UN and

among the U.S. public—that it was high time to exert real pressure on the apartheid regime to step aside in South Africa. Through much of the 1980s, conservative critics of the UN would cite resolutions on South Africa as one more example of the inequities of bloc voting in the Assembly. It should be recognized, moreover, that at this point the developing countries have no where else to go, given the dearth of North-South forums and the growing role of the Group of Eight and other North-only arrangements, to voice their concerns and to pursue their interests before the world's peoples and governments. Where else, for example, can they try to draw the world's attention to the political and social costs of globalization and falling commodity prices for many fragile developing societies?

American candor on human rights, democratic values, and free enterprise has undoubtedly helped to spur extraordinary changes in the world, not to mention in the UN system. Words linked to enduring principles and backed by concerted action and coherent strategies can have enormous power. The last decade of the twentieth century has seen the collapse of communism, the disaggregation of the nonaligned movement, the globalization of the economy, and a surge in democratic values throughout much of the developing and formerly socialist worlds. As a result, moderation has come to the UN (though whether it will stay depends on developments both inside and outside the organization). Name-calling has all but disappeared from UN debates, and the Assembly regularly passes the bulk of its resolutions by consensus, the rule that has held for a decade on UN budgets and has governed ongoing reform efforts. Democracy, a term not even mentioned in the charter, has become the proclaimed goal of much of the UN's operational activities and the subject of one of the three "agendas" articulated by former secretary-general Boutros-Ghali. A United Nations that once sought to tame and restrict multinational corporations now preaches the value of private enterprise and foreign investment.

Although important skirmishes continue in many areas, the United States and it partners have largely won the battle for hearts and minds at the UN, as in the world outside. Ironically, as the political atmosphere at the UN on major substantive questions has improved, the relationship between the United States and the world body on institutional matters, on internal "turf" questions, has deteriorated. During those years when the United States was singled out by name in critical Assembly resolutions, when its values were trashed and its friends threatened in UN debates, the United States largely paid its dues without question. Yet the wider the base of agreement between the United States and the majority in Assembly votes and the tamer the rhetoric, the more Congress has insisted on withholding assessed contributions from the world body for all sorts of reasons. As a result, U.S. arrears to the UN are peaking during the period when the voting coincidence between the United States and other member states in the General Assembly is at one of the highest levels in decades. From a low point of 15.4 percent in 1988, voting coincidence rose steadily to a high of 50.6 percent in 1995.[55] It is worrying, however, that the numbers have slipped each year since, to 44.2 percent in 1998.

Perception and reality, unfortunately, have been out of synch for some years now, with the former usually lagging behind the latter. Driven by domestic political and social developments, congressional initiatives toward the United Nations often seem to bear little relationship to what is actually happening in the world organization. The cases cited in the preceding section suggest that some of the UN's more implacable critics are placing symbolic issues and domestic agendas—such as World Heritage sites, gun control, and abortion—ahead of the more fundamental questions of national interest and strategy that understandably propelled neoconservative critiques in the 1970s and 1980s. This is a puzzling turn of events that makes America's friends nervous, both because of what it says about the quality of U.S. leadership and because some developing countries could well conclude that they, and the institution, are being penalized for good behavior. Surely principled dissent by American representatives on issues of core national values and interests is to be expected and welcomed. But it appears as if some members of Congress are simply taken with the act of defying and denigrating the UN. They seem to relish thumbing their noses at the rest of the membership, just as some member states appear to go out of their way to oppose and frustrate U.S. initiatives.

Perhaps there is an element in the American ethic that takes comfort in standing alone, in asserting individuality for its own sake. If so, then Americans may well earn the reputation of being sore winners, as well as poor team players. The anti-Americanism that many perceived in the 1960s and 1970s was largely issue-driven as part of major ongoing debates about the Middle East, South Africa, arms control, and economic questions.[56] Over the past few years, however, there have been disturbing signs that a vicious cycle is under way. Because of its financial withholdings and what others perceive to be bullying tactics, the United States and its behavior within the organization are themselves becoming the issue in the eyes of too many delegations. It would be most ironic if anti-Americanism over U.S. tactics and attitudes were to blossom in the world body now that the larger strategic and normative battles have been fought and largely won. Perhaps a self-fulfilling prophecy is at work, to everyone's detriment. In particular, these squabbles have tended to distract attention from the more consequential questions of peace and security addressed in the next two chapters. In the final days of the twentieth century, as in its early years, Americans are badly divided over the contributions that international organization can be expected to make to the maintenance of international peace and security.

CHAPTER SIX

Dilemmas of Force

The one error, which we must not, above all others, make, is to assume that this organization is the final word. On the contrary, it is certain to be merely the first modest and hesitant step, sufficient to point the direction, but utterly inadequate to achieve the goal of lasting peace.

—SENATOR WILLIAM FULBRIGHT, 1945

As far as actually doing anything, the UN is about as valuable to putting down invasions as a fifth wheel on a wagon.

—REPRESENTATIVE USHER L. BURDICK, 1950

Perhaps the most fundamental failure of the UN is this: there can be no confidence that even if a clear and unambiguous case of aggression were to come before the Security Council or the General Assembly, a majority of the members would treat it as such and would come to the aid of the victim.

—HENRY CABOT LODGE, 1976

EVEN IF NONE of the doubts and suspicions described in the last four chapters existed, questions about the appropriate role of global bodies in achieving international peace and security would still persist in the minds of many Americans. These fundamental queries, of course, are not uniquely American concerns. Nor are they of recent vintage, since they both impelled and troubled the architects of the League of Nations and those of the United Nations. Chapters 6 and 7 lay out some of the principal themes that have defined the divergent schools of thought in America on these fundamental challenges to international organization. This chapter addresses the core dilemma—how to achieve reliable collective security without abandoning national freedom of action—that has sparked such ferocious, searching, and ultimately inconclusive debate throughout this century.

Too Weak or Too Strong?

From the concerns cited in chapter 3—that interventionist and intrusive international organizations could compromise U.S. freedom of action, values, and even sovereignty—it would seem that Americans would generally prefer international bodies to be small, weak, and passive. Yet the record has been mixed, with internationalists vexed by the relative weakness of existing bodies and some skeptics claiming that they would support stronger organizations more capable of enforcing international law and order.[1] Praising the UN charter as a reasonable compromise between these divergent tendencies, Senator Edwin C. Johnson, D-Colo., told his colleagues during the 1945 ratification debate that "America has followed the middle course in the past between isolationism on the one hand, and rabid internationalism on the other. The San Francisco Charter follows that middle course."[2] Yet this has proved to be an uncomfortable compromise. Ultimately, the League of Nations and the United Nations were each chided by some Americans for being too weak to accomplish much and by others for embodying the potential for being too strong and controlling. This catch-22 political dynamic has been a persistent source of American ambivalence toward international organization throughout the twentieth century.

It was striking, in this respect, to see conservative, male, and Republican support for the United Nations surge in a public opinion survey after the Security Council–authorized Desert Storm operation expelled Iraqi forces from Kuwait in 1991.[3] All three groups, traditionally skeptical about the world body, seemed to be saying that they liked this refurbished image of a get-tough, militarily supportive United Nations rallying behind U.S. leadership to teach a local bully like Saddam Hussein a lesson about the need to respect international norms. The organization, for the first time in four decades, was beginning to resemble the one that Franklin Roosevelt and Harry Truman had championed in 1945. In retrospect, however, this case appears to have been something of an anomaly. It occurred at a special moment: when the United States dominated the Security Council whose members strongly preferred to work by consensus whenever possible. The United States, moreover, was willing to provide the bulk of the forces and to take the largest political and human risks. A few years later, with President Bill Clinton in the White House, the Republican Congress turned its collective back even on low-risk peacekeeping operations. A closer look at the short-lived poll results, moreover, tells a more sobering story: while some traditional critics gave the UN a fresh look after Desert Storm, traditional supporters—including women, minorities, Democrats, and liberals—were markedly less enthusiastic after such a massive use of UN-authorized force. This persistent division contributes significantly to the overall sense of ambivalence, for one lesson of the

Desert Storm experience was that a major strengthening, or at least reorientation, of the UN toward its founding mandate as an enforcer of international law would be likely to lose some support from those reluctant to trade a "soft" UN for a "hard" one, even as it gained favor from more hawkish Americans.

The outlines of this fundamental dilemma, posed by the disjunctures in American attitudes, were clearly articulated in 1949 by Clyde Eagleton of New York University in testimony on behalf of the American Association for the United Nations before the House Committee on Foreign Affairs:

> It was the United States which at San Francisco made the United Nations weak to begin with. The Government did that because they were afraid that the people, or more especially, the Senate, would not take anything stronger than was proposed there. Now, since that time, I am afraid that the American people have shown little if any willingness to pay the costs, that is to say, the costs in limitations upon the freedom of national action, to pay the costs to make the United Nations any stronger.[4]

In Eagleton's view, it would therefore be "illogical to hope that the American public, who are willing to accept no more restrictions upon their national sovereignty than the UN Charter, would be willing to accept in place of it some far more restrictive undertaking."[5] His words were particularly troubling when considered in their historical context; he spoke in the late 1940s, when public enthusiasm for the world body had begun to wane amid rising concern about whether repeated vetoes by the Soviet Union were effectively disabling the Security Council. One could not have both a stronger United Nations and absolute national sovereignty, Eagleton seemed to be saying. As long as the American public is torn by this classic dilemma—of wanting to have one's cake and to eat it too—international organization will not be able to enlist broad and durable public support.

At times the debate over U.S. participation in the League of Nations had much of this same sing-song flavor. In 1915 the editors of the *New Republic,* including Walter Lippmann, called for a strong organization, because "there is no stopping short at a league to prevent war. Such a league would either grow to world federalism, or it would break up in civil war."[6] Yet for others, the circularity of arguments reflected deep-seated uneasiness with the whole conception of the proposed experiment in international cooperation. Writing in 1917, William Jennings Bryan expressed his discomfort either way:

There is no international law-making power [proposed for the League]; and,
if such a law-making power existed, there are certain questions upon which it
would not assume to act—certain questions which each nation, whether large
or small, is conceded the right to decide for itself without regard to the views
or interests of other nations. . . . and yet these are the very questions out of
which wars grow.[7]

Bryan's dilemma is clear: he did not favor interference in essentially domestic affairs, yet he recognized that peace cannot be guaranteed without some
international power to address domestic developments that might hold the
seeds to international conflict. So he saw little point in a League that lacked
such powers, yet would have opposed one that was granted them. His arguments are remarkable not only for their candor, but also for their prescience
in anticipating one of the hottest political debates of the closing years of the
twentieth century.

Some of the League's opponents, however, claimed that they would
support a substantially strengthened international body. For example,
Senator Borah, the determined isolationist, claimed that:

If a body of international law is established, I would give the court compulsory
jurisdiction. . . . I would give it the same power that the Supreme Court has in
controversies between states. That is the only system which will give the
smaller nations any hearing, when they are in controversy with large nations.[8]

Henry Cabot Lodge declared in 1919 that he would not oppose a world
body that could actually bring about disarmament and enforce the peace,
but that "in trying to do too much we might lose all." Questioning the
strength of the ties among the potential member states, Lodge scoffed that
there had been some thirty such leagues throughout history, "none of them
very successful."[9] In responding to Senator Lodge, Harvard president A.
Lawrence Lowell complained of the lack of specific suggestions "from those,
and there are many, who profess to believe in a League of Nations, but not
in this particular plan."[10] Although Senator Lodge led the charge against the
League of Nations, he and other prominent Republicans had endorsed the
principles and proposals of the League to Enforce Peace, based on the
enforcement of international arbitration decisions, at its first national
assembly, held in Washington on May 26–27, 1916.[11]

In his 1930 book, *The United States of the World*, Oscar Newfang, a pro-
lific author and proponent of stronger international organization, thought

that he had the explanation for this seeming dilemma. Based on their historical experience, he conjectured, Americans saw in the League all of the
shortcomings of the Articles of Confederation and would be supportive of
a stronger system patterned on the U.S. federal form of government:

> Underneath and behind all the specific objections that were made in America
> against various sections of the League Covenant, when the question of joining
> the League was before the country, there lay the overwhelming and historical
> conviction that a mere confederation, a mere alliance of governments, acting
> only by unanimous decision and upon states as political units, is totally inad-
> equate as a machinery for establishing justice and suppressing warfare
> between states. We have tried that method in this country and found it a fail-
> ure. Before we could achieve peace and prosperity among our states we were
> obliged to form a more perfect union.[12]

The United States, according to Newfang, was "far more sympathetic toward
the Permanent Court of International Justice than toward the Assembly or
toward the Council of the League." Asserting that the American people sought
"the establishment of a body to lay down international law, a body to apply
the law, and a body to enforce the law," he concluded that they would favor a
"world judicial authority" similar to the U.S. Supreme Court.[13] Indeed, in
1917 former president William Howard Taft, a leading proponent of a strong
League, argued for the establishment of an international judicial tribunal that
would function like the U.S. Supreme Court in the way it handles disputes
between states. Over time, he asserted, nations would contract "the habit of
arbitration" to settle their differences, as had the United States and Canada.[14]

John Foster Dulles, hardly known as weak-kneed or soft-headed, especially concerning the communist threat to American values, was one of a
long line of U.S. policymakers who, like Newfang and Taft, expressed greater
faith in international law than in international institutions. He had been a
student of Woodrow Wilson at Princeton and later served the president on
the U.S. staff at the Paris Peace Conference. Testifying before the House in
1948, Dulles contended that "the American people do not want world government, which can be had only by accepting despotism. . . . They seek the
rule of law, not of men." He then went on to a sweeping and surprising conclusion, placing the value of law above that of national sovereignty:

> They [the American people] would define aggression, establish control of
> atomic energy, regulate armament, and then enforce such laws through an

international council in which no nation would have a right of veto. That approach to the problem of world order is basically sound and the moral stature of the United States would be increased if the Congress were to make it clear that, at this critical time, when the fate of humanity hangs in the balance, our great Nation is ready to take the lead in surrendering its sovereignty to the extent necessary to establish peace through the ordering of just law.[15]

Dulles's distinction between the legitimacy of law and the illegitimacy of institutions is puzzling, especially given the sweeping powers that he would entrust to a vetoless international council. He tended to defend the United Nations, moreover, not so much as an instrument for building international law but as a political forum that has "served to enlighten world opinion about the nature of Soviet leadership."[16]

Although Newfang's hypothesis about Americans' disillusionment with confederation may offer some encouragement to those in favor of world federalism, there is reason to doubt its validity as an explanation for the virulent opposition of conservatives and isolationists to American participation in the League.[17] The colonists' experience with the Articles of Confederation was rarely mentioned in the debate and surely was not on the minds of average Americans. The controversies over sovereignty and nationalism, moreover, were far more emotional and polarized than such a good-government explanation would allow. To some of those who feared that America might be moving toward imperialist aspirations, the League did not look sufficiently strong to keep nationalism in check. Scott Nearing, for example, dismissed the new organization in his 1919 tract, *Labor and the League of Nations:* "The organization of the League is undemocratic. Its machinery is impotent. The Council is vested with authority but it has no real power. The League is little more than a voluntary association of governments."[18] Viewed from the perspectives of a dedicated anti-Bolshevik, however, the League was pictured as an entirely different animal. Bishop Neely claimed that "the so-called League of Nations is not to prevent war but to rule the world in many things, and, we may say, in everything, and that it is intended to be the supreme government and a permanent over-government."[19]

A quarter century later, the Senate debate over the UN charter showed that neither the dynamics nor the content of the left-right debate had changed much. Several charter supporters, for example, found different ways of saying that the UN was a largely hollow instrument, but better than nothing. In essence, the new organization was damned with faint praise.

While stressing the historic opportunity offered by the charter and affirming that he would vote for it "wholeheartedly and proudly," Senator Wiley of Wisconsin also pointed out that "the Charter is merely a collection of 10,000 words. They can become empty words." Choosing to join the UN, he noted, "does not mean that the United States is going to rely exclusively on the charter for her protection from war. It does not mean that America will be putting all her security eggs in the basket of the charter. On the contrary, we ourselves must keep our powder dry."[20] Senator Johnson of Colorado also considered himself to be a strong supporter of the new organization, although he suggested that "it is a pretty weak reed" in some respects because of the veto power. Considering that fifty "cooks" had created the charter, he commented that it was "a pretty good dish. Not enough meat in it and perhaps a little too much froth, but as a compromise it is excellent."[21]

The problem with compromise, of course, is that it provides a convenient target for both ends of the political spectrum. As the product of a series of concessions by all sides during the course of the intergovernmental negotiating process, neither the League of Nations nor the United Nations could fully satisfy everyone.[22] Perceived as too weak by some and too strong by others, both world bodies have been caught in the unceasing rhetorical crossfire between the left and right in American politics. Given the highly political mandates of these institutions, this may well have been inevitable.[23] So in the years ahead, the UN will continue to have little choice but to attempt to steer clear of the political shoals on either side, while aiming its messages whenever possible to the political center, whose support remains critical.

Peace through War?

Americans of all persuasions agree that the core purpose of the United Nations, like the League before it, should be to bolster international peace and security. How that should be achieved, however, has divided supporters, as well as detractors, of international organization. Skeptics, of course, have had little faith in the capacity of international organization to deliver on its core promise of international security and none in its ability or willingness to serve unilateral U.S. national security needs. But even advocates of the UN and the League have been unable to find satisfactory answers to the questions of whether, how, and by whom force should be used to preserve or restore peace. Those attracted to international cooperation as an alternative to violence between nations find the notion of securing peace by applying force to be an oxymoron. This seeming perversity is compounded by the fundamental dilemmas involved in the proposition that global organizations will be in a position to mobilize power to enforce their decisions and norms in a world of sovereign nation states.

The architects of international organization found it exceedingly difficult to square the circle: legal authority to mandate the use of force theoretically resides primarily with the global body, yet the possession and control of military force reside almost solely with independent and sovereign member states, or, to a lesser extent, with subnational rebel groups that answer neither to national nor international authorities.[24] One of the core attributes of sovereignty, embodied in article 51 of the UN charter, revolves around the right and the capacity to use military force to protect one's citizens and territorial integrity. Yet if international organizations and the system of international law on which they are founded are to fulfill their essential responsibility of enhancing international peace and security, then their existence must affect the way in which nation states and subnational actors employ military force. Although the relationship between the use of force and the nature of international institutions is a defining issue, it is not one on which there has been any substantial convergence of thought among Americans, even among the proponents of the League and of the UN.

American advocates of international organization have tended to coalesce around three broad schools of thought about the use of force and about what is, and is not, appropriate. Each of these positions has distinct implications for attitudes toward international law and organization, for what is sought in and expected of security arrangements among sovereign nation states, for relationships between security alliances such as NATO and global institutions, and ultimately for how the performance of international bodies is to be judged. These three schools are based on fundamentally different sets of assumptions:

The problem is war. If war itself is the enemy, a dysfunctional and destructive aberration that must be eliminated, then the chief goal of international organization must be its prevention.[25] According to this perspective, prevention should be accomplished through nonmilitary means, including not only economic sanctions, but also inducements and noncoercive measures such as education, persuasion, norm-setting and consensus-building, or through removing the root causes of tension and conflict. All of these, along with the methods of peaceful conflict resolution noted in chapter VI of the UN charter, such as mediation, arbitration, and judicial settlement, correspond to areas of comparative advantage for international organizations. The fewer the wars and the fewer the casualties, the more successful international organization will have proved to be. If force has to be utilized in defense of peoples or principles, then international institutions have failed. Since the two great experiments in international institution-building in this century have followed devastating world wars, it was to be expected that the elimination of war would be among their central purposes. In the stirring opening words of the preamble to its charter, the United Nations was founded "to save succeeding generations from the scourge of war, which twice in our lifetime has brought untold sorrow to mankind."

The problem is the unilateral use of force. If the problem is not war per se, but rather the unauthorized unilateral use of force by a nation state or a sub-national group in a manner that could precipitate war, then the purpose of international organization is to deter, discourage, or make unnecessary the unilateral employment of force. From this perspective, the only way to eliminate war is to prevent, or, if deterrence fails, to defeat through collective political, economic, and military action, the unilateral use of force. Borrowing a page from domestic political and legal structures, this school holds that unilateralism breeds chaos and undermines the framework of international law and order that is necessary to ensure long-term peace and security. The goal of international organization, then, is to foster multilateral security cooperation and to develop international arrangements in a way that provides incentives for working together and disincentives for going it alone. This school sees nationalism and unilateralism, not war itself, as the adversaries to be overcome. The covenant of the League of Nations, for example, opens with an acceptance by the signatories "of obligations not to resort to war" as a way of handling relations among countries. A critic of this school, Alan Tonelson, recently jibed that for liberal internationalism "purely U.S. national interests were never its top priority. In fact, they were not even supposed to exist."[26]

The problem is justice. A third group, rather than rejecting the use of force altogether or condoning its use only by multilateral bodies, believes that the litmus test should be the purposes for which and the proportionality with which force is employed. Some wars are just, others are not. The purpose of international organization, as well as of national military forces, in this school's view, should be to deter or defeat the illegitimate use of force. International institutions, rather than banning the use of force, should facilitate the organization of an effective collective military response to threats to international peace, security, and core principles (as chapter VII of the UN charter was to help accomplish). Should a multilateral response be insufficient or unachievable, then there should be legal provisions—such as article 51 of the UN charter—to permit unilateral or ad hoc international military action to uphold recognized international norms and principles. From this perspective, the decision-making procedures and rules of international bodies matter a great deal, as does the degree of automaticity in the reactions of member states to calls to collective action. These institutions, moreover, are seen to have very important roles in creating and disseminating, as well as in defending, universal norms that should govern the behavior of nation states both internationally and domestically. Organizations should be judged by what they stand for and by how far they are willing to go to preserve their principles. Their purpose, according to this school, is neither to preserve an unjust status quo nor to pursue peace at any price.

Although not mutually exclusive, these three perspectives do offer remarkably different visions of the roles and purposes of international organization. The failure of American proponents of international institutions to achieve anything approaching a consensus on these core matters has added to the prevailing sense of ambivalence about the utility of international arrangements in the key realm of national and international security.

These divisions were highly visible in the debates leading to the founding of the League of Nations. One of the most telling criticisms of the first school was that it would tend to preserve a status quo that might be unjust and more reflective of the interests of imperialist European powers than of independent-minded America. In 1915, for example, an editorial in the *New Republic* cautioned against a "League of the Satisfied," to which dissatisfied powers, such as Germany, might protest that "you bar the future, and you call it peace."[27]

The second school was well represented by the most influential private group favoring a strong international organization, the League to Enforce Peace, founded (as was its British counterpart, the British League of Nations Society) in 1915.[28] Its first president, former president William Howard Taft, was a strong advocate of an international institution with real teeth in the security realm. In its platform, the league emphasized the need for the development of international law, called for the submission of "justiciable questions" to a judicial tribunal and other issues to a council of conciliation, and mandated the joint use of both "economic and military forces against any of their number that goes to war, or commits acts of hostility, against another of the signatories" before utilizing these other remedies. According to Taft, this "third or Force plank gives vitality to the platform. It provides for economic pressure and a Police Force to hold off members of the League from war until the cooling and curative influence of the League's judicial procedure may have time to operate." His reference to a "police force" to buy time for diplomacy to work sounds like the kernel of a peacekeeping concept, while his emphasis on "economic pressures" seems to presage the Security Council's recent dependence on economic sanctions as a way station between words and war. Apparently an early believer in deterrence as well, Taft added that "fear of police action is usually effective without actual use of force. 'They also serve who only stand and wait.'" In his view, "the League is to be a world alliance."[29]

Yet some proponents of this second school, while advocating the collective use of force, drew the specter of the destructiveness of modern warfare so vividly as to raise the question whether the risks inherent even in multilateral military action were not intolerably high, thus feeding into the pacifist tendencies of the first school. Taft himself, for example, warned in a 1919 speech in San Francisco:

> If, in ten or twenty years, we are called into another war, that war will be world suicide. The instrumentalities now capable of being used in war are far more destructive than they were when this war began; we have discovered explosives and poisonous gases which can destroy a whole community.[30]

His argument, while technically overdrawn, and overwrought, anticipated the much more credible threats posed in 1945 by the discovery and use of atomic bombs soon after the creation of the next great experiment in international organization. Speaking in 1925, former Supreme Court justice John H. Clarke similarly intoned that "resort to science has rendered modern war so destructive of life and property that it presents a new problem to mankind, such, that unless our civilization shall find some means of making an end to war, war will make an end of our civilization."[31] Under such conditions, if one accepts Clarke's rendition of a scientific and military judgment, the best choices for enhancing security would seem to be based on deterrence, arms control, reliable alliance structures, and preventive diplomacy, not on the vague obligations incurred through membership in the League (see chapter 7). Despite its best efforts and some modest diplomatic successes, the organization, in the end, excelled in none of these core security tasks.[32] Why would Americans want to be drawn into international conflicts, which were potentially so deadly, before the development of a truly reliable set of collective security arrangements? The prospect would stir ambivalence at best.

Philadelphia lawyer George Wharton Pepper cautioned that "all the machinery of the League is carefully planned to give effect" to Wilson's ideal of applying force "to attain a righteous end." In Pepper's view, "a coercive alliance based upon unassailable force has in it nothing but the promise of disaster." Foreseeing a far brighter future "for a league of nations organized for conciliation," Pepper suggested that "it is in such an organization that the moral influence of a peace-loving nation can be exerted with maximum effect." In such an organization, Pepper concluded, "the United States may be of maximum use to other nations" and in it would be "America's greatest opportunity."[33] Reflecting the first school of thought, Pepper stressed the need for prevention but rejected the most feasible way of achieving it—deterrence through military means—in effect, criticizing the League for even endeavoring to do that which critics from the other side correctly deemed it poorly equipped to accomplish in any case.

A. Lawrence Lowell asserted, in its defense, that the League would indeed seek to prevent war, not leave the United States with the sole option of joining one under way, as in the First World War, with the likelihood of huge casualties.[34] Rejecting this line of reasoning, the populist William Jennings Bryan responded that the prospect of American military participation, rather than deterring conflict, "might encourage other members of the League to acts which would precipitate war." He questioned whether "force" can be considered a "preserver of peace. Do not reason and experience combine to prove that it provokes rather than prevents war?" In its ultimate reliance on force, Bryan continued:

> The League's plan is not new in principle; it merely extends and enlarges a plan which the world has outgrown—a plan which has written history in characters of blood and filled the earth with unutterable woe. . . . The fundamental error lies in the fact that a plan which relies upon "Force" for its "vitality," *cultivates the spirit that breeds wars.*[35]

In essence, Bryan would have dismissed the second and third schools of thought, since he found no historical basis to believe that the use of force would produce either deterrence or a justifiable outcome.

Those skeptical of giving the League coercive powers did not come only from the ranks of populists and pacifists. Originally a member of the League to Enforce Peace, Herbert Hoover came to have doubts about key provisions of the League covenant, joining the growing ranks of those who favored extensive reservations. Specifically, the future president expressed reservations about the collective security aspects of the covenant because in his view the League's role should be "the pacific settlement of controversies among free nations."[36] In October 1915, a committee of the Chamber of Commerce of the United States warned that:

> Power to coerce by economic or military force once created is apt to be employed. The proposed league is almost sure to have within itself the elements of separate combinations based upon distinct interests and aims. . . . It is not clear that a powerful league would rest content with the moral influences of the proposed council's advice. In other words, the question is whether the proposed employment of force for peace is not more apt to increase than to decrease disorder.[37]

Foreshadowing conservative concerns about the League a few years later, and about the United Nations generations later, the chamber was already questioning not only the logic of depending on coercion to achieve peace, but also the prospects for exercising effective control over international forces once they are established.

In his rejoinder to William Jennings Bryan, Taft contended that the threat to use force in retaliation served both pragmatic and moral purposes:

> Fear of forcible restraint and punishment is often an indispensable motive to strengthen moral impulse to obey the law and follow the right. . . . Force used for selfish, vicious or improper ends is, of course, to be deplored. But is there any method of defeating force used for such ends, except superior force threatened or applied for the common good?[38]

While Taft's analogies appear to have been drawn from a domestic law-and-order context, they might also have applied to a balance-of-power as well as to a collective security system. Like many other commentators of his time, Taft and other supporters of the League to Enforce Peace linked the justifiable use of force to a bolstering of international law and to the development of an international judicial and conciliation system to handle disputes among nations, to be backed up by the threat of force applied through unspecified international procedures.

As discussed in chapter 7, the League of Nations that finally emerged from the give-and-take of trans-Atlantic diplomacy fell far short of the expectations either of those, like Taft, who favored a collective security system with teeth or of those, like Bryan and Pepper, who were seeking an alternative to the use of force.[39] Taft's secretary of commerce and labor, Charles Nagel, regretted that the plan of the League to Enforce Peace "to employ military and economic power for the preservation of world peace" was not realized.[40] "There is no safeguarding of peace," lamented the *New York Tribune*. "There is no limitation of armaments, no international police force under the control of the League."[41] In contrast, President Wilson's own secretary of state, Robert Lansing, "wanted a League that would be virtually without powers of enforcement at all" and "the press was symptomatic of country and Congress—passionately divided or else a bit bored."[42] The spirit of ambivalence was in the air.

From the first school of thought, American (and British) pacifists tended to gravitate toward the League as an alternative to the horrendous violence of the First World War. This tendency, which grew when Congress rejected League membership, may have dampened the prospects for mainstream public support. As the British historian F. S. Northedge commented in his history of the League,

> Much of the anti-war sentiment which clung to the League had more than a tinge of pacifism of the unconditional variety about it: many of those enrolled in the League cause (and the League *was* a cause, in a sense in which its successor, the United Nations, never became) so hated war that they never wanted to fight another, not even a League war, a war to defend the Covenant. Such a war they considered to be a contradiction in terms, a commission of the sin the League was supposed to eliminate.[43]

Neither pacifism nor isolationism fared well during the interwar period. The hard-core opponents of the League were widely seen as short-sighted and reactionary at a time when the United States should have been accepting its inevitable international responsibilities, including participation in the League. Yet to the extent that the League—hampered by weak machinery and huge holes in its membership—was seen as ill-prepared to cope with the global threat posed by fascism, it, too, appeared to be an utterly inadequate answer to international and national security needs.

Neither of the alternatives posed in 1919 retained much credibility a generation later, when few doubted that the new United Nations would need to be endowed with what the League most tragically lacked: a realistic system to organize the collective use of national forces for ends widely accepted to be legitimate. To Walter Lippmann, writing in a 1943 volume, any collective security regime would need to be backed by strong alliances and national defense preparedness, two things that he felt Taft and Wilson had ignored out of misplaced idealism. According to Lippmann, "in them the idealism which prompts Americans to make large and resounding commitments was combined with the pacificism which causes Americans to shrink from the measures of force that are needed to support the commitments."[44] Despite their reluctance to arm or develop strategic alliances, he noted that "both favored a League of Nations in which the United States assumed the obligation to enforce peace." As Lippmann understood, the first step toward collective security is to do what is necessary to ensure national security. Yet to this day, many of the UN's more ardent supporters cling to the notion that the world organization should serve as an alternative to national defense preparedness, while defense hawks tend to be dismissive of its security relevance. Those who recognize the symbiotic relationship between the two—the politically moderate pro-UN, pro-defense segment of the population—are often caught in the political crossfire.

The Veto, National Security, and the Use of Force

Throughout the century Americans disagreed about how the international community should make decisions about the use of force. On the one hand, a true collective security system should work with some sense of automaticity, that is, an attack on one should, without too many caveats, exceptions, and delays, be considered an attack on all. It would be the relative certainty of a collective military response that would constitute the most credible and effective deterrent to aggression. On the other hand, the United States, like other nations, wants to retain the sovereign right to decide when, where, and how its national military forces are to be employed. Former senator Bob Dole, for example, has asserted that once the president has proclaimed America's interests, they "should not be second-guessed, modified, or subject to the approval of international organizations."[45] In the words of Senator Jesse Helms, "the security policies of the United States are not run by the United Nations, nor by the U.N. Security Council, nor by Kofi Annan."[46] As noted at the outset of this chapter, this inherent tension between automaticity and flexibility, between international and national levels of decision, has defined one of the fundamental dilemmas that have thwarted the most carefully negotiated plans for maintaining international peace and security. It has also, in turn, been one of the sources of American ambivalence toward international institutions.

No doubt many Americans would like somehow to blend national freedom of action and a reliable international security system. For example, Tom Connally, chairman of the Senate Committee on Foreign Relations, and a member of the U.S. delegation at San Francisco, commented in 1945 hearings on the charter that "we wanted to have it like it is; an organization that could not increase our obligations, that would not add obligations that we know not of without the consent of the United States." When drafting the charter, he noted, "we thought we could hear the eloquent voices of Senators lifted in protest, at tying ourselves to this Organization endowed with authority to adopt amendments to send our boys to war when we do not want them to go and to do this and that and the other—we did not agree to do that."[47] Michigan Senator Arthur H. Vandenberg, a leading Republican voice at San Francisco, had opposed extending the veto to questions of pacific settlement, considering it incompatible with the principle of sovereign equality and "immoral and indefensible" beyond issues involving the use of force. Yet he wrote in his diary that "every cloud has a silver lining" because:

> the irony of the situation is that the greater the extent of the "veto," the more impossible it becomes for the new League to involve America in *anything* against our own will. Therefore, the greater the "veto" the easier it becomes to fight off our critics in Congress, in the country, and in the press when the new Treaty faces its ratification battle.[48]

It was certainly understandable that the architects of 1945, especially the congressional ones, would be haunted by the voices of 1919. But the resulting effort to mix two irreconcilable tenets—like oil and water—was bound to produce an unsatisfactory and unstable compound. As a result, the public was left confused, caught between high expectations and spotty results.

The question of international decisionmaking has arisen repeatedly in American public and official debates about the nature of international organization and the U.S. role in it but has never been treated, at least in mainstream discourse, as the central and decisive issue. From the nationalist flank, international organization is often pictured as a threat to American freedom of action, including on core security matters. From the internationalist flank, the concern has been the opposite: that narrow national interests will steer international decisionmaking, rather than vice versa. But for most Americans, the bottom line question has been more about performance than about control of decisionmaking. International organizations are more likely to be judged on the extent to which they are perceived to have played a positive role in helping to maintain international peace and security.

Assessing UN performance on security matters has turned out to be a murky business. For several reasons, American citizens have tended to receive a muddled message. For one thing, the UN's degree of involvement has varied enormously from place to place and time to time. Its failures—and they are myriad—are usually much more visible than its successes, which often consist of helping to prevent outbreaks of violence. The UN, moreover, does very little on its own, and it is hard to parse where credit and blame lie when many hands are involved in shaping the outcome. At times, there may be a dissonance between national and international purposes. For example, some Americans have chided the United Nations for not doing more to save lives in the Rwandan genocide, when in fact this inaction was the result of national decisions in Washington, D.C., and other key capitals that were reluctant to become too deeply involved in a situation that posed considerable risks and no easy or quick solution. In the former Yugoslavia the Security Council committed peacekeepers on the ground to implement an ever-changing mandate, subject to the disparate and wavering interests of the United States, Russia, the major Western European powers, and the Islamic states, among others.

Relatively few Americans, of course, have looked to international organizations to serve as the mainstay of U.S. national defense. The mainstream, "realist," position has been to look to collective action as, at best, a supplement to U.S. military strength. Former president Theodore Roosevelt, for example, although expressing disdain for "professional internationalists," said that he would support the plan put forward by the League to Enforce Peace "as an *addition to,* but not as a *substitute for* our preparing our own strength for our own defense."[49] More recently, the Clinton administration asserted in its 1994 review of U.S. policy toward multinational peace operations that "when our interests dictate, the U.S. must be willing and able to fight and win wars, unilaterally whenever necessary. . . . UN peace operations cannot substitute for this requirement."[50] In a July 1996 report, the Commission on America's National Interests, a self-appointed but influential group of mainstream opinion leaders, rated the maintenance of "a strong UN and other regional and functional cooperation mechanisms" as a third-tier priority.[51] International organization, in their view, does not threaten U.S. interests, but in strategic terms it also does not matter very much one way or the other.

Some prominent Americans have argued either that, contrary to the emphasis on collective military action in its charter, the United Nations is not good at security tasks or that it is not good for the organization itself to focus too heavily on them. From the latter perspective, Senator George D. Aiken, R-Vt., worried out loud at a 1962 hearing about "United Nations military operations overshadowing the real and permanent good which is being done in other ways" and queried whether "it is becoming regarded as a military institution. . . . How long can you let that go on without destroying the United Nations itself?"[52] Typical of the former perspective, that same year Senator John Tower asserted that "the theory that the United Nations has preserved and is preserving world peace is . . . preposterous. . . . On the occasions when it claimed victories for peace, the United States manipulated the strings."[53]

Although sometimes asserting that participation in the United Nations can have reformative qualities, defenders of the organization often lament that it can be no better than its member states allow it to be, particularly in the peace and security realm. Yet this answer is hardly reassuring to American skeptics, who judge the organization on its performance in the real world, not under idealized conditions. After all, if the UN is to remain a virtually universal body, these member states cannot be traded in for better models. One of the assumptions behind international law and organization, moreover, is that they will bring out the best and prevent the worst from an otherwise unruly pack of sovereign nations. If the world body is going to succeed, it will have to make do with its existing imperfect members. It will also need to broaden its institutional perspectives and culture, as embodied in its staff and expressed in its doctrine, so that the charter's enforcement provisions are regarded as every bit as legitimate as those on peaceful settlement. This does not mean that the organization will be as effective in, or as well suited to, employing one set of peace and security tools as the other. The collective security side of the organization obviously became very rusty through disuse during four decades of cold war, and now many smaller member states (and some big ones like China and Russia) appear anxious about the ways in which an American-led and interventionist Security Council has or might employ its powers to authorize military action and economic sanctions in places like Iraq and Kosovo.

The UN's own ambivalence about the use of force has been displayed for all to see in the former Yugoslavia. Richard Holbrooke, the architect of the Dayton accords, has chronicled the organization's chronic reluctance to take military action to compel the parties to live up to various agreements or to support the diplomatic process. He notes, however, that "the tortured half-measures of the United Nations and the European Union had been inadequate, to be sure, but they had kept the Bosnian Muslims from complete destruction for several years." Explaining why he and Madeleine Albright, then the U.S. permanent representative at the UN, felt that it was necessary to exclude the UN from the Dayton negotiations, Holbrooke states that "telling the U.N. that its involvement would weaken the search for peace was painful, especially for those of us who had grown up believing in the importance of the world body." At the same time, Holbrooke stresses the critical role of the economic sanctions that the Security Council had imposed on Serbia and Montenegro, asserting that without them "we would have begun the negotiations with almost no bargaining chips." According to Holbrooke, "Milosevic hated the sanctions. They really hurt his country, and he wanted them lifted. This gave us a potential lever over him."[54] In Kosovo it has been NATO, not the divided Security Council, that has sought to exercise leverage over Milosevic's choices.

Perhaps drawing from the lessons of Yugoslavia, where he handled the transition from UN to NATO control, Secretary-General Annan has declared that "the United Nations does not have, at this point in its history, the institutional capacity to conduct military enforcement measures under Chapter VII." At the same time, he notes, "in recent years, the Security Council has called, with increasing frequency, for economic sanctions as an enforcement tool under Chapter VII. The universal character of the United Nations makes it a particularly appropriate body to consider and oversee such measures."[55] Yet, here too, many member states and NGOs are questioning whether the UN should carry out sanctions measures with large humanitarian costs for the civilian populations in target countries, such as Iraq. If the critics from the left get their way, despite talk of carefully targeted sanctions that only hurt elites, soon the Security Council will find it politically impossible to undertake any kind of effective coercive measures, returning the world body to its cold war posture of having little other than peaceful settlement options to rely on.

The irony is that, despite this shift in emphasis at the UN from military to economic enforcement measures, in the United States the public and most critics still judge the organization on its capacity to carry out effective military operations. In that regard, its track record during the post–cold war period has hardly lived up to the expectations engendered by the U.S.-led effort to expel Iraqi forces from Kuwait in early 1991. At a 1995 forum Jeane Kirkpatrick expressed an across-the-board disappointment with the UN's security performance:

> The United States has tried very hard to build and use structures for collective security and collective defense over the last few decades. Most recently we have tried to use to the maximum the United Nations as an instrument for security—not for consultation, not for discussion, but for security. But that doesn't work, not as in Somalia, not as attempted in Bosnia or Croatia as a solution to military problems. . . . So far we have seen that the United Nations doesn't function effectively militarily when confronted with security problems.[56]

Kirkpatrick's blanket dismissal of a UN security role is too sweeping given the organization's emphasis on economic sanctions and on the "softer" side of security: preventive diplomacy, peaceful settlement, postconflict peace building, arms monitoring, arms control, and disarmament. Nevertheless, her pronounced tone of disillusionment with UN peace operations is characteristic of a great deal of American commentary since peacekeeping peaked in 1994.

If the United Nations is as enfeebled in security affairs as Kirkpatrick and other skeptics suggest, however, then it would also follow that the world body is not much of a threat to American security interests. In their view, the United States would simply be wise not to depend on this weak reed for its national security needs. Although this is widely understood today, at the birth of the League of Nations in 1919, its adversaries contended that the new organization could compromise America's core strategic interests, including the Monroe Doctrine.

Senator Henry Cabot Lodge repeatedly warned his colleagues that the global obligations inherent in the League would be the death knell of the Monroe Doctrine, which "rests upon this proposition of separating the Americas from Europe in all matters political . . . It was the fence that we put around to exclude other nations from meddling in American affairs, and I have never been able to get it through my head how you can preserve a fence by taking it down."[57] If the Monroe Doctrine is founded on permanent factors, it is not immediately obvious how the League could undo it, yet Lodge's passionate pleas were persuasive, no doubt in part because of their appeal to longstanding assumptions about the nature of world affairs. With dire predictions that, once the League was launched, Japan would establish bases in Mexico or the Panama Canal, Bishop Neely asserted that

League membership would hinder a U.S. response because "it would no longer be the independent United States, free to think her own thoughts and to carry out her own noble purposes."[58] To the contrary, A. Lawrence Lowell asserted that, unless the Monroe Doctrine were to be used to justify American imperialism in this hemisphere, the League would serve to extend the Doctrine globally rather than to contradict it in the New World.[59] His arguments, although frequently invoked by the League's advocates, seemed to carry relatively little weight with key senators.

The simplest way to deal with the Monroe Doctrine and with similar concerns that other prospective members no doubt had regarding their neighborhoods, it seemed to many, was to have the League's council decide on the basis of unanimity, thus giving each council member a veto over its actions. In the process, however, the concept of collective security was largely sacrificed. The League would no longer be threatening to America's interests and doctrines—or to any other major power's—but it also would be impotent in most cases, except where a consensus for action could be achieved. It would not be the last time that the high principles of collective security would have to be sacrificed at the alter of geopolitical realities.

In planning for the United Nations, the Roosevelt administration was determined not to repeat the mistakes of President Wilson in terms of either the architecture of the new body or the way it was to be sold to the Senate and the American people.[60] One of the principal lessons derived from Wilson's failures concerned how to handle the collective security, or article 10, controversy. It was recognized that superior force would have to be employed to deter or resist aggression and that the four big powers—FDR's "four policemen"—would have to work together to ensure peace. Each of the four would need some sort of veto power over the collective use of force, however. In this way, the question was finessed in an ambiguous manner that in the short run quelled potential opposition from those worried about American sovereignty, but that in the long run fostered substantial public confusion and uncertainty. Writing in 1946 journalist James B. Reston asserted that "it was not clearly understood, at least in the United States . . . that there was never any intention that the United Nations should have power to coerce one of the great states."[61] Although the administration had downplayed the importance of the veto in its public pronouncements, in private it had stressed that the veto was needed to protect American interests, as well as to secure Russian and British participation. At a May 1944 private meeting with the congressional Committee of Eight, a bipartisan group formed to facilitate executive-congressional dialogue about the shape of the proposed world organization, Secretary of State Cordell Hull went so far as to declare that "our Government would not remain there a day without retaining its veto power."[62]

The public was understandably confused and divided about the charter's veto provision—the unanimity principle—because U.S. leaders were as well. In selling the UN, supporters tended to claim that the veto would eliminate the League's fatal flaw. For example, Senator Connally noted during the 1945 ratification debate that "one of the most compelling arguments against the League was, in effect, 'If we adopt this Charter it will mean that we will send our troops to distant lands to fight in foreign wars without our consent.'" The UN's veto provision, in his view, "is a source of strength for the Charter in that it gives absolute assurance to each of the Big Five that they will not be asked to use their armed forces in some military enterprise in which they do not concur."[63] In actuality, however, the League's council was granted no binding authority; it was to act by unanimity, effectively giving each member of the Council a veto over the commitment of forces. The League's adversaries in the Senate, however, did their best to obscure this point. Two generations later the younger Henry Cabot Lodge still claimed that "there's one great difference" between the United Nations and the League of Nations:

> The Covenant of the League, under Article X, gave the League the power to put the troops of a country into combat. This was the rock on which the League foundered. My grandfather, in the Senate, insisted that the U.S. reserve this right, with the result that this country didn't join the League. The founders of the UN remembered this, and the UN can't put a country's troops into combat without its consent. . . . The UN, in short, is more realistically based than the League.[64]

In reality, decisionmaking structures of the League and the UN differed in two key respects: first, only the five permanent members of the Security Council were given veto power in the UN; and, second, under article 25 of the UN charter "the Members of the United Nations agree to accept and carry out the decisions of the Security Council in accordance with the present Charter." Therefore, for 180 of the UN's 185 members, the obligations under the charter are much more explicit than under the League covenant. Chapter 7 of the UN charter, moreover, contains detailed provisions for enforcement machinery to facilitate the collective use of political, economic, and military sanctions, while the covenant was virtually silent on the subject of how the members of the League would go about organizing a collective response to aggression. All of this suggests that, despite the younger Lodge's claim to the contrary, the United Nations came a good deal closer to institutionalizing the vision of collective security than had the League.

In testimony before the House Committee on Foreign Affairs in 1948, Secretary of State George C. Marshall provided a practical rationale for the veto provision in the charter—something which by then had become controversial because of its frequent employment by the Soviet Union:

> I feel that the veto, in certain respects, is as essential to us as others seem to feel that it is to them. I am referring again to the fact that I once was a soldier. I am very much concerned that the people of the United States do not find themselves committed to the use of this great power in a military way on a basis of a two-thirds vote. They must have an opportunity for a decision in relation to that.[65]

He went on to suggest, however, that he favored modifying the veto provision "in connection with pacific settlements." This explanation did not entirely mollify some legislators, who continued to press for a charter amendment to restrict use of the veto. Representative Lawrence H. Smith, R-Wis., told of "receiving a lot of mail from constituents wanting to know what can be done while this veto situation exists in the United Nations Organization." He attested to "a great deal of confusion . . . in the minds of Members of Congress to say nothing about the general public." Could the State Department, he asked, "set forth in simple terms just what is involved in this matter of the veto. You have stated that the veto should be retained in one part of the Charter and eliminated in another. That is what puzzles us and the public."[66]

Representative Smith was not the only one confused. Noting that he "did not know that the United Nations was based upon power relationships," Representative James G. Fulton, R-Pa., quizzed Marshall on why he had spoken "of power relationships as being the basis of the United Nations."[67] His query was not as naive as it sounds half a century later. The new world organization had been presented to the American people as the embodiment and extension of the wartime alliance, which would largely work by consensus, given its members' fundamentally congruent interests and shared high principles. The veto would act as a safeguard, reserved for the relatively infrequent instances of divergence. Now the message was becoming more nuanced and more mixed, adding to public consternation about a deteriorating relationship with America's most powerful wartime ally. As James Reston phrased it in a 1946 *Foreign Affairs* article: "The most important of all the basic assumptions about the United Nations has not been fulfilled. This assumption was that the great states would manage to have a little faith in each other; not much, maybe, but at least enough to operate an association that depended on unity."[68] While Reston was not ready to give up on the infant organization, clearly his preliminary prognosis, after only one General Assembly session, was not encouraging. Apparently a sizable body of American opinion perceived the veto power as a kind of political insurance policy: something one needed to have but hoped not to have to use. Like life insurance, the veto was to be employed only in extremis.

Opposing a bill in 1949 that sought to develop the United Nations into a world federation, Representative Smith cautioned that the unanimity principle would sow "more confusion in the public mind." Having initiated the veto power in the UN, "our own body," the United States, in his view, was "stymied, and the great hope that we had is not being realized, we are frustrated. Our foreign policy since the war has been a dismal failure." Distancing Congress from the establishment of the unanimity rule, Representative Fulton in the same hearing underlined that it "was a decision of President Franklin D. Roosevelt . . . made by the man in constitutional power over the foreign policy of the United States. It was not a decision of the representatives of the people."[69] Though leaders of Congress from both sides of the aisle had played active roles in the U.S. delegation in San Francisco and in selling the charter to their colleagues in the Senate, none had foreseen how quickly the veto provision would become controversial both in Congress and in public commentary.

It soon became apparent that the functioning of the Security Council, the linchpin of hopes for the postwar security regime, rested on a paradox: the Security Council could not work with the Soviet Union but could not succeed without Soviet participation. These realities were understood by the public, which, in turn, was divided by them. In a May 1945 poll by the American Institute of Public Opinion, 78 percent said that the new body could not succeed without U.S. participation and 64 percent said the same about Russian participation.[70] Both, they reasoned, were essential. By the spring of 1948, following the Czech coup and the twenty-third Soviet veto in the Security Council, 46 percent of poll respondents agreed that it was "hopeless to try to work along with Russia in the United Nations," while 45 percent believed that "there is still a chance we can make the UN work with Russia in it."[71] The public was split down the middle on this core question.

From the outset, many foreign policy practitioners had also questioned the validity of this very premise of common interests between Moscow and Washington. Acting Secretary of State Joseph Grew wrote in a private memorandum in May 1945 that the veto would leave the UN "powerless to act against the one certain future enemy, Soviet Russia," making the UN's "power to prevent a future world war . . . but a pipe dream."[72] The public, however, had been led to believe that one of the purposes of the new organization was to help cement the wartime alliance between Moscow and Washington. It was hardly reassuring to hear that the UN would only work under ideal conditions that did not exist. As relations with Moscow soured and the Soviet representatives in the Security Council increasingly relied on the veto to protect their interests, skepticism about the value of the world body soared in Congress. "With this Russian veto always in prospect, the United Nations can accomplish just exactly nothing," complained Representative Burdick. "After one veto the members argue for another week only to be squelched with another veto."[73] Representative Chester E. Merrow, R-N.H., called in 1948 for the elimination of the veto provision, but "if this cannot be accomplished and if the Kremlin continues in its refusal to cooperate, we must abandon the UN and form at once a new international organization of liberty-loving democratic states without the presence of the impeding Soviet Union."[74]

The deterioration in congressional enthusiasm for the young organization was illustrated by the changing attitudes of Senator Johnson of Colorado, who, as noted earlier, had been a vocal booster for the charter during the 1945 ratification debate. Although he had expressed some hesitation about the veto provision at that time, he had concluded that "our only hope . . . to maintain world peace is that none of the big five nations will choose to make war." And the greatest virtue of the charter, in his view, had been that "it continues the life of the United Nations Organization. The organization that did such a magnificent job of winning the world's greatest war. Under this Charter, these successful war-winning nations will try their hand at winning the peace."[75] Just three years later, he urged the elimination of the veto and blamed the UN for the growing tensions in the world:

> The United Nations under its Charter has demonstrated its inability to cope with the problem of maintaining world peace. Frustration and panic are its

achievements to date. Hate has displaced hope in the world, and fear has sup-
planted confidence. Due to its impotence, world unity has disintegrated into
two bristling armed camps ready to strike. War is on everyone's lips.[76]

It would have been more accurate to say that international tensions created
the UN's stalemate, rather than the other way round, but neither Congress
nor the public doubted that the UN had failed to deliver on its great
promise.

More moderate voices asserted that the UN was the best that the world
could produce under the circumstances and that everyone should strive to
make the best of a difficult situation. Contending in 1947 that "the United
Nations as it is now set up is probably the most effective organization we
could hope to have at the present time and still retain the Soviets and their
satellites as members," Senator Francis J. Myers, D-Pa., lamely suggested that
"it is important to try to hold them as members in the hopes that this present intransigence may be merely a passing period, a sort of adolescence in
international cooperation."[77] James Reston, writing in the *New York Times*,
commented that "the United Nations is a poor scapegoat. It cannot be
blamed for failing to deal with problems it never was designed to solve. And
its principles are not invalid just because the Soviet Union will not abide by
them."[78] Sumner Welles, one of the original State Department architects of
the UN, acknowledged in the *Washington Post* "that the exaggerated use of
the veto by the Soviet Union has frequently hamstrung the United Nations,"
but he underlined that "we ourselves have known from the outset that the
United Nations, as a universal organization, cannot succeed unless Soviet-
American cooperation can be achieved."[79]

Reston and Welles were technically correct, but the public and congressional uneasiness about the veto reflected the persistent ambivalence that
shaded the attitudes of one administration after another toward decisionmaking in the Security Council. During the early years of the cold war, the
United States found it easier to conduct its business in the General Assembly
than in the Security Council. The Council did authorize the coalition
defense of Korea—the most important demonstration of collective security
in the postwar era—but only managed to do so because Moscow's representative was boycotting its sessions at the time. When the Soviet delegate
returned to his seat and sought to frustrate the continuation of the war
effort, the United States and its allies resorted to the constitutionally creative
device of the "uniting for peace" resolution, which reasserted the Assembly's
potential role in the peace and security realm when the Council was unable

to discharge its responsibilities. Given the key role that the use or the threat of use of the veto has played in defending U.S. positions at the UN in recent years, the words of Ambassador Arthur Goldberg in 1965 sound both dated and ironic: "my Government has never been prepared, and is not prepared, to accept a situation in which the capacity of the United Nations to act for peace could be stopped by the negative vote of a single member."[80]

But would the United States have accepted a veto-less Security Council in 1945? No one knows, since it had been the Soviet Union, acutely aware that it would be outnumbered in the new Council, that had insisted on the provision for an unqualified veto.[81] Ambassador Andrei Gromyko, who represented the USSR at the Dumbarton Oaks planning meeting, had referred to the veto as the bedrock of Big Four unity. In September 1944, President Roosevelt personally pleaded with Gromyko to soften his position, to no avail, and then cabled Premier Joseph Stalin that "we and the British both feel strongly that in decisions of the Council, parties to a dispute should not vote if one of the parties is a permanent member of the Council. I know public opinion in the United States would never understand or support a plan . . . which violated that principle."[82] Stalin, sensing tension within the alliance and the emergence of markedly different visions of postwar Europe, was unmoved. Three years later, with the new organization still in its infancy, Secretary of State Marshall told the General Assembly that "the United States would be willing to accept, by whatever means may be appropriate, the elimination of the unanimity requirement with respect to matters arising under Chapter VI [pacific settlement] of the Charter and such matters as applications for membership."[83] In January 1948, U.S. Ambassador Warren R. Austin convened the five permanent members to consider such a step but found that only the United States "was ready to modify the veto provisions of the Charter."[84]

The following exchange at a 1949 hearing captured the mixed emotions triggered among the public and their representatives by the notions both of a UN-authorized force and of the provision for veto power (the speakers were Clyde Eagleton of New York University, speaking for the American Association for the United Nations, and Representative Walter H. Judd, R-Minn., known for his expertise on East Asia, his staunch anticommunism, his advocacy of overseas postwar relief, and his oratory):

Eagleton: I worked in the State Department on the making of the Charter. While I was there, I was always working to make it stronger. . . . Then after I left the State Department I went out and lectured considerably over the country and I would ask questions of the audience and I was shocked at the response I got.

For example, if I asked about an international police force, they would say, "we are all for it." Then I would say, "Do you realize that that police force can be used against us?" Their mouths would drop open and they would not be so sure. I would say, "Do you realize that your boy might be called upon to fight in that police force?" The ladies would sit down and say no more. . . .

Judd: When I asked that question of audiences I always said, "Yes, it could be used against us if we were violating the law, but we do not intend to violate the law and therefore I am not fearful." Then I got a different answer. If they thought that at somebody's caprice it could be used against us, they naturally recoiled from that. We could organize a United Nations police force if people had confidence in the organization. Is not the reason for that the realization that it would not be under the control of the Assembly by two-thirds vote, but its actions would be under the control of the Security Council with the Big Power veto?

Eagleton: I doubt if the people, if you are asking what the people thought, I doubt if they thought that far.[85]

As discussed in chapter 10, the barnstorming sales approach of the Roosevelt and Truman administrations was hardly designed to encourage careful public reflection about the implications of the charter's principles and procedures. Perhaps Eagleton's account of his public encounters was exaggerated, but such relatively uninformed initial reactions should not have been surprising. This was a case, after all, of a major shift in national policy—one that entailed radical new approaches to security, yet that was preceded by relatively little public debate and scrutiny. For all of the visionary speculation during the war about the postwar world, the actual structure and procedures of the UN that emerged from San Francisco did not receive sufficiently rigorous or critical analysis in public. Moreover, Eagleton's line of questioning must have seemed puzzling to some in his audience, given that he represented the UN's principal support group in the country, one of whose foremost leaders was none other than Eleanor Roosevelt. With these basic matters still unsettled in the public's mind, it is not surprising that these fundamental issues continued to haunt American attitudes and policies toward the world body for years to come.

Concern about the Soviet Union's overuse of the veto and disappointment with the UN's failure to hold the wartime alliance together during the early days of the cold war soon contributed to a sharp decline in public support for the UN. According to public opinion surveys, support reached some of its lowest levels ever in the late 1940s. This pattern of growing disillusionment could also be seen in the declining expectations of key American policymakers. John Foster Dulles, for example, had headed the Commission to Study the Bases of a Just and Durable Peace, which in March 1942 called for a world government with a parliament, court, and operating agencies, and which would control all military forces beyond those required to maintain domestic values.[86] Six years later, Dulles explained the need for continuing reliance on national military power based on his experience at the founding conference:

> Those who made up the American delegation at San Francisco, as your chairman will recall, realized that, in view of the veto power, the Security Council could not itself be relied upon to provide effective protection and that being so the nations ought to be free to organize effective protection of their own. Consequently, at San Francisco, we proposed that the Charter authorize collective self-defense.[87]

In succeeding years, of course, Dulles gained a reputation as a hard-line anticommunist, with grave doubts about the possibilities for international cooperation given the nature of the Soviet Union. His intellectual metamorphosis was complete: from a one-worlder and former student of Wilson at Princeton to a unilateralist and cold warrior.

For those with a classically Wilsonian vision of collective security, accepting the necessity of a veto to protect sovereign freedom of choice in matters of national defense was the equivalent of crossing the Rubicon. Defying geography, Wilson himself had crossed the Rubicon at the Paris Peace Conference. As Dulles pointed out, and as Lippmann had argued earlier, this step would and should entail increasing dependence on national defense preparedness and on military alliances outside of the United Nations structure.[88] According to James Reston:

> It may be charged that Mr. Truman has repeated the mistake of Woodrow Wilson, and to a certain extent of Franklin Roosevelt, in that he has not emphasized to the American people the necessity of making clear that now, as before, the United States will fight any nation that consistently seeks to destroy the principles and purposes on which world order rests, even if there is no express commitment to fight for them under a legal charter.[89]

In light of the Soviet veto, Reston argued that it was incumbent on the United States to stand up—unilaterally if necessary—for the principles on which international law and order were to have been based. The veto provision, in his view, had opened a possible split between these purposes and the enforcement decisions (or lack of them) emanating from the Security Council. Under his formula, it was up to the United States to assess whether such a split existed and, if so, to act to close it, unilaterally if necessary. Multilateral options were to be preferred, but—harking back to the third school of thought outlined at the outset of this chapter—the first priority was to protect these unspecified principles and purposes. Among the first casualties of the cold war, therefore, were the very notions of collective security and broad-based international cooperation on which the world body was founded.

CHAPTER SEVEN

Keeping the Peace: National Interests and International Commitments

I ask the fathers and mothers, the sisters and the wives and the sweethearts whether they are ready yet to guarantee the political independence and territorial integrity of every nation on earth against external aggression, and to send the hope of their families, the hope of the nation, the best of our youth, forth into the world on that errand.

—SENATOR HENRY CABOT LODGE, 1919

It is one thing when we are attacked; it is one thing when American citizens are attacked or American property is being destroyed, and quite another thing when Bulgaria is being attacked, or some Hindu is being attacked, or a person of some other nationality is being attacked.

—SENATOR BURTON K. WHEELER, 1945

If we do not want to use our troops or anybody else's troops, all we have to do is say no. But if the Security Council, with our vote, decides to use force in a certain situation, I do not see how we can in good faith refuse to contribute our quota and go along with the enterprise.

—SENATOR THOMAS T. CONNALLY, 1945

THE DILEMMAS RAISED in the last chapter are doubly difficult to resolve when the national interest is not self-evident. At points when the American people are uncertain or divided about the nature and extent of U.S. interests and obligations in crises overseas, questions of command, costs, and war powers tend to rise to the surface; that is particularly true when the interventions are to be undertaken in partnership with others through international institutions. Such doubts have been especially evident during the post–cold war years, as the shape and nature of both conflict and interests are evolving in uncertain directions. Yet the evidence suggests that similar concerns and doubts haunted the public and their elected representatives during the establishment of the League and the UN.

Uncertain Interests, Open-Ended Commitments

For most Americans, the searing experience of the Second World War removed any remaining doubts about the importance of national military preparedness and about the legitimacy of international arrangements for organizing a collective defense. Yet difficult questions remained about when and where the joint use of force is in the U.S. national interest. The answer—somewhere between nowhere and everywhere, never and always—could be found neither through unrelenting isolationism nor unceasing interventionism. As Senator Henrik Shipstead, R-Minn., put it during the charter ratification debate of 1945: "we have got to find a middle way between ever-recurring interventionist wars and allowing, by indifference or appeasement, the strangle hold of tyranny to engulf a greater and greater part of the earth."[1] Defining the principles and drawing the lines, however, have proven largely illusive, magnifying the doubts and uncertainties that have clouded the attitudes of many Americans toward the United Nations. While these debates continue to rage today, their roots can be traced to the highly polarized exchanges about article 10 of the League covenant.

Article 10 consisted of two sentences:

> The Members of the League undertake to respect and preserve as against external aggression the territorial integrity and existing political independence of all Members of the League. In case of any such aggression or in case of any threat or danger of such aggression the Council shall advise upon the means by which this obligation shall be fulfilled.

These simple words took on starkly different meanings to different readers. Some focused on the sweeping, if general, undertaking of the first sentence, which expressed the essence of President Woodrow Wilson's conception of collective security as the moral basis for world peace and stability. With this solemn pledge on the part of the major powers, Wilson said, "you have absolutely stopped ambitious and aggressive war." He was quick to assure the American people that this core provision would not apply to the "right of revolution" within countries or to "the choice of self-determination." However, he continued, "as against external aggression, as against ambition, as against the desire to dominate from without, we all stand together in a common pledge, and that pledge is essential to the peace of the world."[2]

Given the nation's traditional respect for international law and the relatively large number of League members, it was understandable that some might interpret article 10 as an unprecedented American commitment to preserving the global status quo, a morally binding obligation to protect a new kind of world order. Others saw the article as little more than a vague statement of good intentions. They focused on the enormous, some thought unbridgeable, gap between the ringing words of the first sentence and the hollowness of the second. To them, the vagueness of a phrase like "shall advise upon the means" seriously undermined the credibility of the rhetorical commitment contained in the opening sentence.

One of those who had counseled President Wilson against such general obligations before the drafting of article 10 was Elihu Root, the respected former secretary of state, secretary of war, and Republican senator from New York. At the urging of Wilson's aide Colonel House, Root wrote a long letter to House and the president on August 16, 1918, containing his views on a possible league and advising that:

> No agreement in the way of a league of peace . . . should be contemplated which will probably not be kept when the time comes for acting under it. Nothing can be worse in international affairs than to make agreements and break them. It would be folly, therefore, for the United States . . . to enter into an agreement which the people of the United States would not regard as binding upon them. I think that observation applies to making a hard and fast agreement to go to war upon the happening of some future international event beyond the control of the United States. I think that the question whether the people of the Country would stand by such an agreement made by the President and Senate would depend upon the way they looked at the event calling for their action at that future time when the event occurs—that they would fight if at that time they were convinced that they ought to, and they would not fight if at that time they were convinced they ought not to.[3]

In other words, Root saw little sense, and considerable risk to American credibility, to signing onto a vague and open-ended collective security commitment. Such a blank check on issues of war and peace, in his view, would be inappropriate and unworkable in a democratic system because its automaticity would eclipse the public's role in deciding such life and death questions.

It could also be argued, however, that if article 10 was meant to embody collective security, it was a rather pale shadow of the real thing. No means to accomplish its high-minded goals were specified. No machinery was established, or even proposed, to implement the decisions of the League's council. No binding authority was granted to the council, whose role was to be advisory. Moreover, according to article 5, unless otherwise specified "decisions at any meeting of the Assembly or of the Council shall require the agreement of all the Members of the League represented at the meeting." Not only was each member of the council to have veto power, but this would also be extended to the parties to a dispute, since any member of the League was to be invited to participate, with vote, in council meetings when its interests would be affected (article 4). This was hardly the formula to ensure decisive action to preserve world peace, with or without American membership.

The debate over article 10 nevertheless engendered impassioned rhetoric from all sides. Because the article offered little more than a hint of what a new security system might look like, onto its vague provisions were projected all of the hopes, fears, ambitions, and nightmares of the protagonists, whose struggle was really for the soul of American foreign and security policy at a turning point in its history. As has often been the case in debates about the UN, much of the controversy was about symbols, with both sides exaggerating the impact that the League would have, rather than about its actual procedures and capabilities. The formlessness of article 10's provisions, moreover, left lots of room for interpretation and caution. Writing for the Council on Foreign Relations in 1935, Columbia University's Philip C. Jessup asserted that "it was chiefly the vagueness and uncertainty of this commitment that caused alarm."[4] President Wilson's passionate and expansive defense of the centrality of the article, which he termed "the test of the honor and courage and endurance of the world,"[5] served only to feed these doubts. After all, was the new structure of world order to be based on the assumption of agreement among all the members of the Council? And had the European powers, in particular, absorbed the same lessons from the ravages of world war that Wilson had?

Some roundly criticized article 10 for buttressing an unjust and eventually indefensible status quo that was tied to a badly flawed peace treaty. Others complained that it constituted an open-ended commitment to participate in rash interventions throughout the world in matters of little relevance to U.S. national interests. Elihu Root proposed that article 10 be limited to a five-year term initially. In his view:

> If perpetual, it [the League] would be an attempt to preserve for all time unchanged the distribution of power and territory made in accordance with the views and exigencies of the Allies in this present juncture of affairs. . . . It would not only be futile; it would be mischievous. Change and growth are the law of life, and no generation can impose its will in regard to the growth of nations and the distribution of power, upon succeeding generations.[6]

Expressing similar concerns, a number of disillusioned liberals and intellectuals, such as Walter Lippmann and John Maynard Keynes, also came to oppose a League they once had seen as a great hope for a better world.[7] In 1915 the *New Republic*, with Lippmann as one of its editors, cautioned that in trying to prevent war, such schemes "take a static view of the world. They come quite naturally from citizens of satisfied powers, weary of the burden of defending what they have got. They ignore the fact that life is change."[8] Even as President Wilson claimed that article 10 "constitutes a renunciation of wrong ambition on the part of powerful nations with whom we were associated in the war,"[9] the narrow interests and bitter divisions so evident in the Paris negotiations seemed to belie this hopeful claim. For those concerned about the fate of democratic movements elsewhere, Wilson's assertion of the League's disinterest in domestic affairs cut two ways. Although the League would not seek to quell efforts to assert self-determination, it also would not intervene to discourage their oppression by authoritarian or imperialist regimes. As a result, and as so often since, the article 10 debate found international organization whipsawed between rhetorical attacks from the right and the left of American political discourse.

As always, partisanship accounted for much of the hyperbole. As a senator from Ohio, Warren Harding had voted for the League covenant with reservations, as had most of his colleagues. Once he became the Republican presidential nominee in 1920, however, his stance hardened and his rhetoric escalated. In late October, on the eve of the election, he declared that "we are never going to have anything to do with a League with Article X in it." The article in his view, not only was "the heart of the League," but was also "the steel heart, hidden beneath a coat of mail. Article X creates a world government, puts America in alliance with four great powers to rule the world by force of arms and commits America to give her sons for all the battlefields of the Old World."[10]

Harding may have been the standard bearer, but the point man for the opposition was the powerful chairman of the Senate Foreign Relations Committee, Henry Cabot Lodge. With passion and skill, the Massachusetts

Republican led the assault on article 10 from the right flank. Appealing to those who felt that article 10 would freeze the status quo, Lodge suggested that "if that League with that article had existed in the eighteenth century, France could not have assisted this country to win the Revolution." More of a unilateralist than an isolationist, Lodge went on to postulate that "if that League had existed in 1898, we could not have interfered and rescued Cuba from the clutches of Spain; we should have brought a war on with all the other nations of the world."[11]

The chief complaint of the anti-League forces, however, was that article 10 embodied an open-ended commitment of security guarantees to "every nation of the earth," as Senator Lodge phrased it.[12] According to Elihu Root, America could do more for peace by "keeping out of the petty quarrels that arise than by binding ourselves to take part in them."[13] At another point, Root claimed that "nothing has been done to limit the vast and incalculable obligation which Article X of the Covenant undertakes to impose upon each member of the League."[14] As for the United States, Lodge asserted in 1919 that "we ask no guarantees; but we are asked to guarantee the territorial integrity of every nation practically in the world. . . . Now, guarantees must be fulfilled. They are sacred promises."[15] Clearly Lodge was not about to give America's solemn vow to fulfill whatever fool's errand the League might come up with.

President Wilson countered that there was little likelihood that U.S. forces would be called upon to quell conflicts in other parts of the world and that it could always refuse to give its consent:

> If you want to put out a fire in Utah, you do not send to Oklahoma for the fire engine. If you want to put out a fire in the Balkans, if you want to stamp out the smoldering flame in some part of central Europe, you do not send to the United States for troops. The council of the League selects the powers which are most ready, most available, most suitable and selects them only at their own consent, so that the United States would in no such circumstances conceivably be drawn in unless the flame spread to the world.[16]

Wilson's interpretation of article 10 met the objection that it was an open-ended commitment but undermined his grand claims for its centrality and transforming power. For if Europe was to be left to the European powers, Asia to the Asian powers, and the Western Hemisphere to the United States under the Monroe Doctrine, then what would have changed? What is the meaning of globalism if it must rely on hegemonic regional power for its enforcement? Silent on these matters, the League covenant, unlike the UN charter, failed to clarify relationships between global and regional security arrangements.[17]

Following a well-worn path of late nineteenth century American thought, A. Lawrence Lowell emphasized the importance of compulsory arbitration of disputes to buy time before resorting to arms and of collective security through which the members of the League "should bind themselves jointly and severally to resist the aggressor at once." He asserted that "war, like fire, has a tendency to spread, and no one in a community has a right to start a conflagration which his neighbors have not a right to put out."[18] The question in the mind of critics—then and now—however, is how broadly the neighborhood should be defined and how small or localized a flame might be that would still need to be extinguished by global institutions rather than by regional or local means. Thoughtful critics, moreover, suggested that the automaticity implied in article 10 "would be to surrender the moral power of the United States in favor of justice," in Root's words, "which is the only sure basis of peace."[19]

Disappointed by the lack of enforcement machinery, William Howard Taft nevertheless was an ardent defender of article 10. Denying that it would compel the United States to undertake "burdensome expeditions to protect countries in which it has no legitimate interests," Taft wrote that:

> If a stronger nation were to attack a weaker nation, a member of the League, our immediate and selfish interest in the matter would be determined by the question whether it would develop into a world war and so drag us in. But we are interested as a member of the family of nations in maintaining international justice in the interest of international peace everywhere, and we should share the responsibility and burden. It was a mixture of all these motives which carried us into this war and we accepted as a slogan the cry: "The world must be made safe for democracy. We make this war to secure the liberty and independence of nations against the doctrine that 'might makes right.'" This is all that Article X proposes.[20]

This may be all, but it certainly was a lot. Taft, like Wilson, painted an expansive and ambitious vision for the League, with America's role defined by a mix of altruism, idealism, and national interests. Their canvas made a broad and unmissable target for critics ready to charge that the League was an invitation to endless commitments of America's blood and treasure.

Despite his grand vision, Taft also argued that there was "little, if any" chance that article 10 would "involve us in war":

In the first place, the universal boycott, first to be applied, will impose upon most nations such a withering isolation and starvation that in most cases it will be effective. In the second place, we will not be drawn into any war in which it will not be reasonable and convenient for us to render efficient aid, because the plan of the Council must be approved by our representative.[21]

Much of this line of argument seems to anticipate recent debates about U.S. commitments to United Nations peacekeeping and peace enforcement operations. What is most striking, however, is the contrast between Taft's all-inclusive notion of collective security and his narrow defense of the U.S. veto as a method of avoiding unpopular or untenable commitments. Neither Wilson nor Taft reconciled their conceptions of collective security, which assumed some degree of automaticity, with their acknowledgment that the United States would retain its prerogative to say no to collective action. Because the rules of the League required consensus, the new system was to have been built on a most unlikely marriage between collective responsibility and unit veto decisionmaking.

Through the years, tensions and contradictions between grand theories on the one hand and caveats about national interest on the other have persistently bedeviled U.S. policymaking and sown dissonance in public perceptions about the use of force. Burton K. Wheeler, a reluctant supporter of UN charter ratification, put it bluntly before the Senate in 1945: "I say that under the Constitution we have a right to protect American property and American interests wherever they may be; but we have no right under the Constitution of the United States, without a vote of the Congress, to send American troops anywhere in the world to protect foreign interests."[22] Eight years later, during the Korean conflict, Representative Cliff Clevenger, R-Ohio, sounding very much like Henry Cabot Lodge, declared that:

I want young Americans, if they have to go to Korea or some far-flung country in which they have no interest in order to die, to go there to die with an American declaration on their lips as to the reason why they give their lives; then there will not be the necessity for so many of them dying.[23]

For all of their high and universal principles, international organizations have always found it difficult to replicate the emotional appeal—as articulated so well by Wheeler and Clevenger—generated by plain, old-fashioned nationalism and patriotism.

Today, proponents of international intervention are still troubled by the task of defining guidelines and criteria for American involvement that, even if lacking emotional appeal, will at least reflect both national interests and broader international principles.[24] The Clinton administration sought to address these issues systematically midway through its first term. Stung by harsh criticism, especially from Capitol Hill, of its handling of the U.S.-led international intervention in Somalia, the administration conducted an intensive interagency review of U.S. policy toward UN peacekeeping, and to a lesser extent toward peace enforcement, operations. The resulting Presidential Decision Directive (PDD-25) concluded that the United States should make more "disciplined and coherent choices about which peace operations to support" and that "U.S. and UN involvement in peacekeeping must be selective and more effective."[25] The review stressed the changing nature of security threats in the post–cold war era, pointing out that "territorial disputes, armed ethnic conflicts, civil wars (many of which could spill across international borders) and the collapse of governmental authority in some states are among the threats to peace." It concluded that "while many of these conflicts may not directly threaten American interests, their cumulative effect is significant."[26] The administration's reluctance to draw definitive and permanent lines in the sand demarcating where U.S. interests start and stop was both realistic and practical given the unique factors involved in each case. Yet, despite the many cautions and caveats included in PDD-25, terms such as "cumulative effect" did not reassure those concerned about open-ended commitments.

Critics of U.S. military involvement in United Nations operations have persistently questioned whether such missions are in America's national interests. When preparing for his 1996 presidential campaign, Bob Dole wrote that:

> Placing American soldiers, sailors, airmen, and marines in harm's way is the gravest decision a president can make . . . American lives should not be risked—and lost—in places like Somalia, Haiti, and Rwanda with marginal or no American interests at stake. Such actions make it more difficult to convince American mothers and fathers to send their sons and daughters to battle when vital interests *are* at stake. The American people will not tolerate American casualties for irresponsible internationalism. And like overreliance on the United Nations, such adventures ironically end up reinforcing isolationism and retreat.[27]

In a similar vein, Ted Galen Carpenter of the Cato Institute has warned that "an activist United Nations . . . would constitute a dangerous entanglement for the United States" and has cautioned against making "parochial conflicts a matter of global concern and intervention." As he asserted, echoing Senator Dole, "the lives of American military personnel should be put at risk only to defend America's vital security interests. Their lives should never be sacrificed for the abstract and unattainable principle of global collective security."[28] According to Cato's Jeffrey Gerlach, "the pursuit of global collective security is likely to enmesh the United States in a myriad of complex and costly operations that have little to do with its national interest, and that will ultimately fail."[29]

The more fundamental questions, of course, are not whether U.S. policies should reflect its interests—which presumably is a given—but where do those interests lie, who should define them, and to what extent and where do they overlap with those of other countries? Both proponents and critics of international organization have had some difficulty providing clean, consistent, and operationally useful policy guidelines. This has been especially evident in addressing complex situations, such as the multiple crises in the former Yugoslavia, most recently in Kosovo, about which neither camp has spoken with a unified or consistent voice. On the whole, proponents tend to describe American interests in a broader geographical context, and skeptics tend to take a more circumscribed view, particularly regarding crises in the developing world. Alan Tonelson has suggested that "internationalism's genius for focusing U.S. attention on sideshows has nowhere been more evident than in America's relations with the generally weak, poor, politically fragile nations of the Third World."[30] Christopher Layne agreed that "American policymakers have been historically unable to distinguish between vital and peripheral interests, precisely because they equate security with world order. The post–Cold War infatuation with international peacekeeping/peacemaking reflects this habit of equating . . . security at the core with security at the periphery."[31]

According to Tonelson, critics "sardonically accuse" liberal internationalists "of favoring military actions only when no serious purely U.S. interests are at stake." Even worse, in his view, liberals tend to be "firmly committed to a timorous, often paralyzing, multilateralism when key American security interests are at stake."[32] He is no doubt correct that some Americans, particularly those with a post-Vietnam hangover, are attracted to the idea of multilateral interventions because they are uncomfortable with the use of U.S. military power for the pursuit of its unilateral national interests regardless of international law or opinion. Yet at a point in history when threats, risks, and opportunities slide so readily across national borders, when a number of security concerns are widely shared among many nations, it is hard to think of an issue or a place in which "purely U.S. interests are at stake." In fact, it is the lack of clear definitions or lines of demarcation between the interests of one nation and those of another that has made interest-based strategic calculations so perplexing in the ill-defined post–cold war era. There are not, and cannot be, wholly objective and quantifiable standards by which to assess the "national interest," especially of a highly pluralistic society such as the United States. In the murky act of defining the national interest, the old adage that "where you stand depends on where you sit" aptly applies. The scope of shared interests among various nation states, moreover, appears to be expanding in the absence of cold war rigidities, leaving even larger areas covered by shades of gray.

There is considerable reason to believe that it was the United States that pushed the UN into interventions in the cases cited above, as well as in Haiti, rather than vice versa; yet the argument that America's participation in international institutions has tended to draw it into conflicts of marginal importance to its core national interests is widely accepted among conservative foreign affairs legislators and commentators. In his presidential bid in 1996, Alan Keyes stressed that "we need to go to the UN to promote the interests of America, *not* the internationalist agenda of globalists who favor world government. . . . It is America's responsibility to take care of America's interests."[33] While the main target of such partisan attacks is surely the policies and priorities of the Clinton administration, which flow from a different interpretation of America's national interests, the United Nations itself ends up absorbing much of the blame because often it is the vehicle or instrument through which the administration's policies are played out in these cases. With the end of the cold war, the UN, as a global forum, is the place where most crisis situations, including those tangential to central American strategic interests, are addressed politically and sometimes diplomatically. The very scope of the world body's mandate, in the critics' view, offers too many temptations for those American policymakers with internationalist and interventionist tendencies. In this case, they would prefer to restrict or remove both the carpenter and his UN tools.

The skeptics about UN intervention cite several characteristics of the post–cold war era that make it, in their view, a particularly inauspicious time for an activist UN security role, particularly in the developing world. Conflicts there are now less likely to involve U.S. strategic interests or—with the demise of the Soviet Union as a global competitor—to escalate into global struggles.[34] The coming years, they argue, are likely to be characterized by instability and localized violence in many parts of the world, potentially providing never-ending opportunities for international intervention and UN peacekeeping.[35] In such a fluid geopolitical environment, they assert the importance of focusing U.S. military and strategic assets on potential challenges from major power rivals rather than on open-ended crusades for world order.[36]

Depending on one's assumptions about the nature of national interests, international military operations look either like a force multiplier or a force eroder, like a financial bargain or a diversion of precious resources. John F. Kennedy, like presidents before and since, argued that spending on UN peacekeeping represented a modest and sound investment, especially compared with overall U.S. defense outlays. In defending the purchase of United Nations bonds in 1962, President Kennedy pointed out that the United States would "spend this year nearly one-half of the Federal budget for national defense. This authorization represents an investment of one-tenth of 1 percent of that budget in the peacekeeping capacity of the United Nations."[37] Kennedy's UN ambassador, Adlai E. Stevenson, cautioned Congress:

> If the United Nations, even in its present imperfect form, were ever subtracted from the arsenal of our diplomacy, I think many times its costs in dollars would then have to be added to our defense arsenal. Nor do I care to contemplate the possible loss of life in avoidable conflict. . . . It costs a lot of money to fight a war. It costs some money at least to avert it, and I am sure that you have often heard that on a per capita basis each American spent only $1.06 on the United Nations in 1961 contrasted with about $300 on defense.[38]

Clinton's directive, PDD-25, concluded that "in the new strategic environment such operations can serve more often as a cost-effective tool to advance American as well as collective interests." The review urged a reduction in the U.S. share of peacekeeping costs and a monitoring of UN management improvements and efficiencies, although it noted that "peacekeeping can be a good investment for the U.S."[39] Issued against the backdrop of congressional qualms about the rapid growth of UN peacekeeping efforts from 1990 to unprecedented levels in 1994, PDD-25 sought to reassure skeptics that rather than launching an open-ended commitment to interventionism, the Clinton administration would assess each new proposed operation individually, carefully, and soberly.

Critics, extrapolating from the expansive trend lines of the early 1990s, asserted that costs and policymaking were out of control. Charles Lichenstein of the Heritage Foundation wrote of "the wild proliferation of U.N. peacekeeping," charging that "the U.N. has recently engaged in the promiscuous use of force under the authority of resolutions that may violate its own charter." He warned that the UN "peacekeeping budget and its expansive peacekeeping agenda are escalating out of control," a trend that he said "has contributed to a state of unreadiness in the U.S. military."[40] What the more vociferous opponents of peacekeeping failed to notice, however, is that PDD-25 marked a turning point. The United States, which had been in the vanguard of efforts to expand the scope of Security Council–authorized missions, had reversed course. The scale of UN peacekeeping operations contracted as rapidly from 1994 to 1997 as it had expanded over the previous four years. Yet Jesse Helms was still writing in late 1996 that "peacekeeping is the United Nations' fastest-growing industry."[41] In reality, by that point, it was the fastest-shrinking dimension of the world body's work. (After peaking at about $3.2 billion in 1994, peacekeeping costs were under $1 billion in 1998. The contraction of deployed peacekeeping personnel has been even more rapid, from about 70,000 in 1995 to 14,814 in 1998.) Whatever one thought of the wisdom of an ambitious peacekeeping agenda, evidently Washington, with the veto in its pocket, still maintained an impressive degree of control over Security Council decisionmaking.

The President, Congress, and War Powers

Few issues relating to the interpretation of the U.S. Constitution have as persistently divided Congress and the executive branch as that of war powers. While Article I, Section 8, reserves to Congress the right to declare war, throughout American history the president's executive authority has been interpreted as extending to the repeated employment of armed force for a range of purposes short of "war." The executive has undertaken most of these actions without significant congressional challenges. The question of what action might constitute an act of war has involved an ill-defined gray area open to endless scholarly and political debate and repeated reinterpretation. The tendency over the years has been toward an expansion of presidential authority and greater flexibility of executive action. By and large, Congress has accepted not only that the president should be free to deploy force rapidly in cases in which national security is endangered, but also that some circumstances may require American forces to engage in hostilities for short periods before the president can bring the matter to Congress.

Formal declarations of war have become increasingly rare, even in cases, such as the wars in Korea and Vietnam, in which large numbers of American forces were actively engaged in combat over extended periods and suffered heavy casualties. During the Korean conflict, some members of Congress questioned why American soldiers had to bear so much of the burden of "the UN's war" and called for reductions in the U.S. assessment.[42] Yet the United States still could not convince the UN Contributions Committee to lower its assessments for the regular budget to 33⅓ percent. Others criticized the White House's handling of the conflict, but relatively few legislators expressed constitutional concerns about congressional prerogatives.[43]

The controversial conflict in Vietnam, however, sparked a much wider questioning of the potential dangers of the abuse of executive authority, raised doubts about the wisdom of interventions in regional conflicts far from home, provoked a chorus of calls for closer congressional oversight of the use of force, and resulted in the 1973 war powers resolution.[44] Strikingly, however, the experience did not lead Congress to reassert in any binding or durable way its war powers authority under the Constitution, and even the constitutionally controversial war powers resolution permits the president to commit U.S. forces for sixty days without congressional authorization. In serious crises in the intervening years, such as in the Persian Gulf, Korean Peninsula, and the former Yugoslavia, Congress has tacitly acknowledged, by not posing serious challenges to presidential authority, that it wants a voice but not the ultimate responsibility for the commitment or welfare of U.S. forces deployed in areas of potential hostilities. This has held whether Congress was in Democratic or Republican hands. This issue remains a murky and unsettled matter, however, one in which practice, rather than law or principle, is shaping the relative roles of Congress and the executive in determining whether and how American forces will be engaged in international crisis situations.

The ongoing and inconclusive struggle between the legislative and executive branches over war powers has necessarily affected the related question of who has the authority to commit U.S. forces to multinational military operations. The ambivalence that some scholars, commentators, and legislators express about the executive's growing flexibility in military affairs often has taken on a pointed and hostile tone when the subject turns to the employment of American forces in operations undertaken or authorized by international organizations. Those members of Congress concerned about perceived usurpations of authority by the president in using military means to pursue unilaterally defined national interests are doubly sensitive to commitments that he might make to fulfill military obligations to international organizations and causes. Congress may have ceded ground to the executive on the unilateral employment of force, but in recent years under Republican leadership it has moved in the opposite direction—toward a reassertion of its authority—in matters involving multilateral commitments.

The sharp criticisms voiced by legislators who complained that they had not been properly consulted before U.S. votes for new UN peacekeeping and enforcement operations stung the Clinton administration, which used PDD-25 to try to assuage congressional concerns about notification and consultations. Acknowledging that "traditionally, the Executive branch has not solicited the involvement of Congress or the American people on matters related to UN peacekeeping," PDD-25 announced a series of steps to address the problem, including regular bipartisan consultations with leaders of Congress, monthly staff briefings on the UN's upcoming calendar, timely notification of Congress of upcoming Security Council votes on new or expanded peace operations, briefings of Congress on command-and-control arrangements, providing congressional committees with UN documents, submission to Congress of an annual report on UN peace operations, and support for legislation "to amend the War Powers Resolution to introduce a consultative mechanism and to eliminate the 60-day withdrawal provisions."[45] These measures, although opening the door to fuller congressional input into executive decisionmaking, did not satisfy Republican leaders, who included curbs on peacekeeping as part of the "Contract with America" platform on which Republican candidates ran in the 1994 congressional elections. Efforts in early 1995 to legislate drastic cuts in U.S. peacekeeping payments and severe restrictions on the president's ability to deploy U.S. forces as part of UN-authorized coalitions ultimately failed, but it was painfully evident that these issues had become highly politicized.[46]

There are many explanations for the degree of congressional hostility to UN military operations in the mid-1990s. Partisanship is a good place to start. In January 1995 the Republicans assumed control of both houses when a Democrat was in the White House for the first time since 1947–49. At that time, the Republican congressional leadership was a bit more cautious in its attacks on the new world organization, focusing instead on shelving President Truman's initiative to create an International Trade Organization. The mid-1990s, true to form, proved to be a period of intense bickering between the Republican Congress and the Democratic White House on a wide range of public policy issues. The real target, in many cases, appears to have been the president's handling of foreign policy more than the United Nations itself.

As mentioned earlier, legislators on Capitol Hill were worried about open-ended commitments and about the incompatibility of U.S. and UN interests. But this phenomenon should also be understood in the historic context of congressional concerns about loss of control over the deployment and employment of American forces overseas. In Charles Lichenstein's words, the legislators had "raised a genuine constitutional issue: the commitment of U.S. armed forces—arguably, the ultimate exercise of public authority—without the explicit consent, or even involvement, of Congress."[47] Members of Congress are understandably wary of being held responsible by their constituents—the voting public—for decisions over which they have no voice, but for which they can then be held accountable. In this regard, international decisionmaking, in which only the executive branch of government is represented, places members of Congress in just such an uncomfortable and potentially untenable position. Legislators, still vying with the executive for control over unilateral troop commitments, feel doubly removed from the possibility of exercising effective oversight over UN decisions and military operations potentially involving U.S. forces.

These concerns, it should be recalled, are not of recent vintage. Like the congressional-executive tug-of-war over war powers, complaints that international organizations would strip Congress of its war-making authority have been part of the fabric of American political discourse throughout this century. In 1917 William Jennings Bryan, emphasizing that "the Constitution vests in Congress, and in Congress only, the right to declare war," posed the rhetorical question: "Is it likely that Congress would consent to any plan that would entirely surrender its right to a voice in deciding when the country should be plunged into war?"[48] Bryan's query exaggerated the facts of the case, but it was nonetheless both powerful and prescient.

A year later, in 1918, Elihu Root expressed his conviction that the constitutional clause on war powers precluded the United States from entering into agreements that would entail an automatic obligation to commit American forces without explicit congressional authorization in each case.[49] The *New York Sun*, in an editorial of December 29, 1918, contended that "any plan . . . for an enlistment in a world police, subject to assignment to military or naval duty by another authority than the Congress of the United

States, requires an amendment of the Constitution if the Constitution continues to be valid and respected."[50]

Some figures in the League debate, of course, did speak in defense of executive authority. Charles Nagel, for example, characterized the complaint that "a league would deprive Congress of its control over questions of peace or war" as "too comprehensive." In his view, "it serves no purpose to deny that our Executive may at any time deprive Congress of its discretion to pass upon questions of war and peace."[51] A. Lawrence Lowell pointed out, moreover, that the executive had long entered into arms limitations and other guarantees through international agreement and hence that U.S. participation in the League would neither deny Congress any of its powers nor violate the Constitution.[52] These arguments, however, lacked emotional appeal, especially in a Senate that would naturally be concerned with protecting its constitutional and political prerogatives. By defining the issues for debate— the terms of political battle—the skeptics in 1919, as in 1994, won the day.

U.S. participation in the League was ultimately precluded by Senate concern over war powers. In explaining its proposed reservation to article 10, the Senate Foreign Relations Committee in 1919 reported that:

> This reservation is intended to meet the most vital objection to the League covenant as it stands. Under no circumstances must there be any legal or moral obligation upon the United States to enter into war or send its Army and Navy abroad or without the unfettered action of Congress to impose economic boycotts on other countries. Under the Constitution of the United States the Congress alone has the power to declare war.[53]

President Wilson had stressed that the League was nothing without article 10 and that any reservations concerning the article would be tantamount to nullification of the treaty, whereas influential senators argued that their role and that of their body would be next to nothing if it was adopted without qualification. Seen in these terms, the Senate debate was hardly conducted on a level playing field. President Wilson and the proponents of the League had permitted its opponents to shape the terms of the debate in such a way that it almost appeared to be a choice between the prerogatives of the Senate and those of the League. For many senators, this was a fairly simple choice.

The founders of the United Nations learned from President Wilson's tactical and political mistakes. As discussed at greater length in chapter 10, by enlisting the participation of top Republican and Democratic legislators in the U.S. delegation at the San Francisco founding conference, the Roosevelt and Truman administrations ensured a better-informed, less partisan, and much more sympathetic hearing in the Senate than the League was able to muster.[54] The spirit of bipartisan and interbranch cooperation extended not only to the Senate, but to the House as well (a chamber to which the Clinton administration, to its regret, has not always given sufficient attention in seeking to enlist congressional support for its policies toward the world body).[55] On the Senate side, this approach paid off handsomely in the debate over the Security Council and congressional war powers. During the 1945 Senate Foreign Relations Committee hearings on the UN Charter, Senator Eugene D. Millikin, R-Colo., asked whether it would violate the charter for Congress to reserve "the right to decide in each instance, in advance, whether or not it will contribute force to an expedition of force."[56] This was, and is, a core constitutional question.

The response from those Senate leaders who had been part of the San Francisco team, however, was strong, consistent, and bipartisan. They spoke to the Senate as statesmen as well as colleagues, as advocates for the new world organization as well as representatives of the legislative branch of government concerned about preserving congressional prerogatives and the system of checks and balances. Committee Chairman Tom Connally replied that such unilateralism:

> ... would, in my opinion, violate the spirit of the Charter, because if every country who is a party to the Charter did that, we would be almost right where we are now, dependent upon the individual action of each nation in case a dispute arose. This is what happened in the last war and in the present war. It seems to me that if we are going to join this organization, we ought to live up to our obligations and responsibilities.[57]

Senator Millikin then turned to Arthur Vandenberg, once an isolationist figure, who had also served on the San Francisco team and earlier on the delegations to the preparatory conferences at Dumbarton Oaks. Vandenberg gave a constitutional interpretation that would be pleasing to the ears of any president:

> I think that if we were to require the consent of Congress to every use of our armed forces, it would not only violate the spirit of the Charter, but it would violate the spirit of the Constitution of the United States, because under the Constitution the President has certain rights to use our armed forces in the

national defense without consulting Congress. It has been done 72 times within the last 150 years. It is as much a part of the Constitution as is the congressional right to declare war. . . . [T]he constitutional practice of 150 years . . . allows the President to use our armed forces externally for purposes of national defense, but ultimately requires, when the situation reaches the point of war, that the Congress is the only power and authority that can determine it. That may be a no man's land, but it has been a no man's land for 150 years.[58]

Senator Connally added a practical point. "The very usefulness of the Security Council," he noted, "is that it is supposed to have at its disposal forces that it can use immediately and quickly in emergencies. If we have to wait to get somebody's consent, the war will be on, and we will not be able to control it."[59]

Clearly a lot had changed between 1919 and 1945. As Senator Scott W. Lucas, D-Ill., told his colleagues in 1945, "we all realize that we are no longer an isolated republic protected by the grim hands of nature. . . . [I]f that third war should come, we shall see robot bombs and other weapons capable of reaching every point of the earth."[60] Jolted into World War II by a surprise attack from halfway across the globe's widest ocean, by 1945 Americans were far more attuned to the need both for preventive measures and for the capacity to take quick and decisive military action as needed. This, in turn, underlined the necessity of broad presidential authority over both diplomatic and military matters, at least in the early stages of an international confrontation. In this spirit the Senate in December 1945 decisively defeated an amendment introduced by Senator Wheeler that "would have required the President to obtain congressional approval before U.S. military forces could be used to implement a decision of the Security Council."[61] Earlier that year, Wheeler had unsuccessfully called for a national referendum on whether to amend the Constitution to prohibit the delegation of "war-making power" to a single U.S. representative on the Security Council.[62] Shipstead, one of two senators to vote against the charter, urged that the U.S. delegate to the Council "be subject to legislative as well as to Executive control."[63] This, too, got little response at the time.

With the onset of the cold war, the questions about congressional prerogatives, while never fully settled, tended to fade from view for two principal reasons.[64] One, the military competition with the Soviet Union and the advent of nuclear weapons and intercontinental delivery systems tended to reinforce the contention that decisionmaking authority should be vested in the president and the executive branch to permit a rapid and unified response to the growing threats to U.S. national security. And two, with the Soviet-American split and the repeated use of vetoes by the Soviet Union, the prospects for military action by the United Nations seemed less and less likely. Outside of academic circles, the effect of Security Council decision-making on congressional prerogatives pretty much remained a nonissue for the duration of the cold war.

The rapid growth in UN peacekeeping and military operations that followed the end of the cold war left very little time to adjust from one mode to its opposite, from low to high gear, from one set of expectations and principles to another. There was almost no transition period, and, as a consequence, little reflection or reassessment of where things stood or of what the political consequences would be of a growing reliance on UN-authorized or -led operations. Only after the rapid expansion in UN missions did PDD-25 promise "to develop a comprehensive policy framework suited to the realities of the post–Cold War period."[65] But by that point, the long-dormant question of war powers and intergovernmental institutions had again emerged with a vengeance, fueled, as in 1919, by the partisanship produced by the unusual circumstance of having a Democrat in the White House and a Republican majority on Capitol Hill. (During the latter stages of the Vietnam War, the situation had been the reverse, with a Republican in the White House and congressional Democrats, led by Senate Foreign Relations Committee chairman William Fulbright of Arkansas, equally partisan and passionate about the need for closer congressional oversight of the use of U.S. military power.)[66]

For the moment, the rift over war powers has quieted down. The second Clinton administration is more diligent about congressional consultations than was the first one, and the UN secretariat, under a new secretary-general, is more conscious of the need for transparency in its operations across the board. The biggest factor, however, has been the sharp decline in the level of UN peacekeeping activity noted above. Since the United States, in the wake of PDD-25, began to discourage the Security Council from mandating large new operations, the world organization has dramatically curtailed the scale of its recent missions. Congress, therefore, has little to dispute. Although the United States agreed in June 1999 to the UN's deployment of a few hundred civilian police officers and military liaison officers to help oversee the referendum in East Timor on its future relationship to Indonesia, Washington was adamant about putting the much larger and more volatile peacekeeping operation in Kosovo under NATO, not Security Council, command.[67]

Although this trend has temporarily eased congressional tempers, in the long run the effect could well be to deepen American ambivalence toward the United Nations. First, historic differences over war powers have not been resolved, only set aside to rise again with the next controversial crisis requiring major U.S. troop commitments. Second, rather than confronting congressional criticisms of multilateral operations and taking its case to the public for a serious debate, the Clinton administration largely acquiesced to congressional concerns without grappling with the core issues. As a result, no new consensus position has emerged and public sentiment has not been tested. Third, although a lower UN profile on security issues may please some in Congress, the public has always primarily judged the value of the UN on the basis of its performance on core peace and security issues. This was confirmed by a December 1998–January 1999 Zogby International survey in which almost one-half of the respondents could identify no UN activities other than peacekeeping.[68] If the UN comes to be perceived as irrelevant to security, as when the U.S. government itself worked to keep the organization on the sidelines during the Rwandan genocide, then the UN, like the League before it, will come to be seen as increasingly marginal to those questions that matter most.

Moreover, if the alternative is for the Security Council to delegate its charter role of overseeing, as well as authorizing, the collective use of force to ad hoc coalitions of willing member states, then the Council's authority and legitimacy in the eyes of the majority of member states are bound to diminish. Over the past few years, with the increasing tendency of the United States and others to assume the security roles assigned to the Council by the charter, there has been ample evidence that this deterioration of respect for the Council is already well under way. Perpetrators of genocide and aggression from the Great Lakes region of Africa to Baghdad to Kosovo have felt free to ignore the Council's solemn declarations, while even the Organization of African Unity in 1998 urged its member states to violate the Council's sanctions on Libya.[69] In the General Assembly debates about reforming the Security Council, developing countries have persistently questioned the wisdom and authority of Council decisions given its current composition and their perceptions of U.S. domination of its decisionmaking processes. Over time, if this downward spiral accelerates, then the credibility and utility of the Council will be increasingly questioned in American eyes as well.

Who's in Control?
The Question of Foreign Command of U.S. Forces

No issue concerning U.S. participation in international organization has triggered more emotion and less understanding than the question of foreign command of American forces. Should one have any doubts about this proposition, one need only look to the perplexing case of Army Specialist Michael New. Reportedly a quiet, religious, and unexceptional medic and Persian Gulf War veteran, New gained international notoriety in 1995 when he refused an order to add a UN patch and beret to his uniform when his unit was ordered to Macedonia to serve in the UN-authorized and -led peacekeeping operation there.[70] Court-martialed and given a bad-conduct discharge for failing to obey a direct order, New soon became the poster boy for anti-UN and anti-Washington groups and commentators across the United States. Not only was his case an irresistible subject for conservative radio talk show hosts, but it became a favorite theme for four candidates seeking the 1996 Republican presidential nomination. One of these, Pat Buchanan, usually received standing ovations when he called Specialist New "a hero of conscience," promised to pardon him on the first day of his presidency, and declared that "from that day forward no American will ever be sent anywhere to wear a blue beret for Boutros Boutros-Ghali."[71]

Moved by New's predicament, House Majority Whip Tom DeLay, R-Tex., introduced, with the support of one hundred members of Congress, a bill to "prevent the president from forcing American soldiers to wear the uniform of the United Nations."[72] Representatives Roscoe G. Bartlett, R-Md., and James A. Traficant Jr., D-Ohio, introduced similar amendments. Seeing the need to "put some sanity back into this whole operation of so-called peacekeeping," Traficant stressed that "when our troops are dispatched on official business, in harm's way, they will wear an American, United States of America, uniform, and they will wear only that uniform because the Congress today said so."[73]

New's father, Daniel, made it his mission to popularize the case, while running, ultimately unsuccessfully, in a Texas Republican primary for Congress. Though his son remained out of the limelight, Daniel New made the talk show and congressional rounds, declaring that "internationalists of every stripe are determined to eliminate loyalty to one's country as an evil of the worst kind." Sounding remarkably like Senator Lodge four generations before, Daniel New said that "it is time to end this bait-and-switch tactic of recruiting American Youth to one flag, and then changing the terms of the contract once they are in."[74] One of Specialist New's most ardent supporters, Representative Bartlett, claimed that, "I don't know any American who wants their son or daughter fighting and dying as a U.N. soldier."[75] He cautioned against placing U.S. soldiers "under the operational control of a U.N. commander who has not taken an oath to defend the Constitution, but has rather taken an exclusive oath of allegiance to the United Nations."[76] Apparently among New's objections was that a Finnish, rather than American, general was in charge of the forces in Macedonia,[77] although both UN and U.S. officials stress that he exercised only operational control and that the ultimate U.S. chain of command remains inviolate from the president on down.

In his 1991 book Pat Robertson had addressed this issue in his characteristically pointed and stark fashion. He reasoned that "the world government would also need a standing army," "personnel for such an army would have to come from somewhere," and "if America wanted a voice in the action, it would either have to provide volunteers or draftees." Then he asked,

> But what would happen if young Americans did not want to participate in a United Nations war against one of our allies, such as Israel? The answer is simple, they would be forced to serve under penalty of prison. What would happen if United Nations sanctions were levied against America? Would young Americans serving in a United Nations Army be forced to fire on their own countrymen? If not, who would do the job?[78]

This absurd and fanciful scenario ignores America's enormous influence in world affairs, as well as its veto power over any such decisions by the Security Council. Those with little knowledge of how the UN works, however, might find Robertson to be persuasive.

As this suggests, the story of Specialist New, for all of its unique features, may tell us something about the educational and socioeconomic fault lines that from time to time create fissures in the foundations of U.S. relations with the United Nations and other international organizations. Although a nonevent for most Americans, for whom the temporary service of U.S. military units in UN operations does not raise great problems of principle,[79] the New case became a cause célèbre for many on the anti-internationalist right. The Washington Post, in reporting the story in its "Style" section rather than on its news pages, pointed out that the lack of mainstream press attention to Specialist New's predicament illustrates "how separate the information pathways have become in this country. . . . A Michael New can be all the rage in one America, and virtually unknown in another."[80] This polarization, in which Americans do not even agree on which issues are worthy of debate, has contributed powerfully to the pervasive sense of ambivalence and uncertainty that has come to characterize U.S. policies and attitudes toward international organization.

Assuming a populist mantle, Alan Tonelson has posited that "our foreign policy debate increasingly pits social and economic classes against each other" and that "polls repeatedly show that the best educated and wealthiest Americans are the staunchest internationalists on both security and economic issues." He goes on to complain that:

> A remarkable share of our foreign policy debate still consists of affluent internationalists searching for new opportunities for risking their countrymen's lives and resources, and developing ever more arcane justification for doing so, and then lamenting the public's determination to put America's needs first.[81]

There is nothing unusual in historical terms, of course, about elites sending the masses off to foreign interventions and war. In this case, however, poll results do not bear out the picture of an elite minority dispatching the sons and daughters of a reluctant majority to do their dirty work. Support for UN peacekeeping, and U.S. participation in it, is far too broad to justify such a hypothesis. Tonelson's apparent resentment of the internationalist foreign policy establishment is suggestive of the views of an increasingly vocal and visible subculture in American politics, however (see chapter 4). The followers of Pat Buchanan and Pat Robertson may not know a lot about the United Nations, but they do know that they do not want to serve, nor do they want their children to serve, under its flag.

Specialist New was hardly the first American to have doubts about the foreign command of U.S. forces. Both supporters and opponents of the League of Nations rejected this possibility. Objecting to "the surrender of the right of each League nation to control its own military and naval policy," William Jennings Bryan declared that "no nation, however small, could for a moment consider such an abandonment of sovereignty." More to the point, in his view "for this nation to exchange its moral prestige for the expensive privilege of putting its army and navy at the command of European monarchs, to be used in settling European quarrels, would be retrogression, not progress—a stepping down, not ascent to a higher plane."[82] Writing in 1920, George Wharton Pepper questioned both the feasibility and the desirability of trying to organize an international army:

The question accordingly recurs whether it is actually feasible so to organize international force as to make nations afraid to go to war? If adequate international force is to be available, it must be either through the agency of a standing international army or police force at the disposal of the alliance or through the united response of member states to the appeal of a central council. An alliance with an adequate force at its disposal is necessarily a super-state. An alliance which depends for its force upon the response of member states is in effect a super-state if they respond and an impotent failure if they do not.[83]

This dilemma of how to assemble and command a force in a world of sovereign nations remains an Achilles heel for the United Nations today and a persistent source of American ambivalence about the organization.

The proposition that the League should organize and command forces, either of its own or contributed by its member states, had few backers. Even Wilson and Taft, the League's two most prominent proponents, opposed the notion. From his comments in a 1918 letter to Colonel House, it is not clear whether President Wilson's concerns were based on principle or tactical necessity: "The United States Senate would never ratify any treaty which put the force of the United States at the disposal of any such group or body. Why begin at the impossible end when there is a possible end and it is feasible to plant a system which will slowly but surely ripen into fruition?"[84] The following year Wilson sounded more resolute and principled in responding to French proposals in the Commission of the League of Nations. He contended that it would be unconstitutional to place American armed forces under international control, which he characterized as a step toward "substituting international militarism for national militarism."[85] Taft said that it was a "misconception" to assume that "the so-called international police is to be a permanent body under an international commander and subject to orders without involving consent of the nations contributing to the force." Instead, he continued, the "Great Nations" would agree "to furnish forces when necessary to accomplish a legitimate purpose of the League."[86] What he had in mind sounds much like the standby system that was eventually mandated for the United Nations under article 43 of its charter but that has never been fully implemented by the member states, most of which retain mixed feelings about creating either a standing or standby UN force under international command.

The sheer technical difficulty and political sensitivity of the task of designing workable arrangements for the command of international forces were attested by the fact that this question could not be resolved at the UN's founding conference. According to Ruth B. Russell's account, "the difficulties of choosing the chief commanders for wartime Anglo-American Combined Commands made it evident that this would be a matter for resolution at the highest level in the great-power governments."[87] The charter established a military staff committee composed of the chiefs of staff of the permanent members of the Security Council to advise the Council on military matters, but the committee was not to exercise command over UN forces. That critical question, according to article 47, paragraph 3, of the charter, "shall be worked out subsequently." In planning for the postwar organization, the Roosevelt administration concluded that "the question of command and control would pose an irresolvable political problem" for any major force and that the Joint Chiefs of Staff would go no further than to accept the kinds of negotiated standby arrangements eventually incorporated in article 43.[88]

Because of the vague and inconclusive nature of the relevant charter provisions and the experience of conducting joint operations among the allies in the Second World War, the question of command and control of international forces was not a highly controversial issue during 1945 congressional debates about the new world body. For the duration of the cold war, moreover, this remained a secondary question, because U.S. (and Soviet) units were largely excluded from UN peacekeeping operations. In the one large-scale military enforcement operation, in Korea, the Security Council specifically ceded command of the ad hoc coalition to the United States, which provided the bulk of the forces in any case. There was considerable grousing in Congress, however, about the modest contingents supplied by other member states, and a few of the UN's harsher critics expressed unease about the whole notion of an international command structure, even one dominated by the United States.[89] In 1991, in the first large-scale UN-authorized enforcement operation following the end of the cold war, American officers again led the command structure for the ad hoc coalition that expelled Iraqi forces from Kuwait. This time, however, modest casualties and quick success on the battlefield left American critics with little about which to complain.

It took an ugly and murky incident on the dusty streets of Mogadishu, Somalia, in October 1993 to bring the long-simmering debate on U.S. participation in UN peacekeeping missions to a boil. U.S. Army Rangers—acting under U.S. command but striving to fulfill a Security Council mandate to capture a local warlord—were caught in a bloody ambush.[90] The televised pictures of American soldiers being dragged through the streets by taunting Somali tribesmen galvanized the opposition to placing U.S. forces under UN command. Initially even the Clinton administration, which not only had approved the Somali operation as a follow-up to President Bush's original commitment of U.S. forces to Somalia to protect a humanitarian mission, but had urged an "uneasy" Boutros-Ghali to make it a UN operation in May 1993, blamed UN commanders for the debacle, opening the floodgates for a spate of UN-bashing on Capitol Hill and in the media.[91] Although the truth of the matter—that all of the U.S. forces involved in combat in Somalia had been under U.S. command and operational control at all times—eventually seeped out, the public impression remained that it was reckless "UN" commanders who put the U.S. forces in jeopardy.[92] The Clinton administration, for obvious political reasons, was slow to dispel this prevalent misimpression and assume the blame itself. Boutros-Ghali meanwhile seemed resigned to the political reality that one of the services the UN could offer to member states was to serve at times as a scapegoat for their own mistakes.[93]

At times in both Somalia and the former Yugoslavia, Boutros-Ghali had been reluctant to see the UN given responsibility for missions, such as the protection of "safe havens" in Bosnia-Herzegovina, for which it was ill-prepared. It is thus ironic that the secretary-general came to be caricatured by some American critics as a power-grabbing empire builder seeking a militarily ambitious United Nations. His general reluctance to use force assertively in the former Yugoslavia, coupled with his insistence on something close to a veto over the use of NATO airpower in the theater as long as UN peacekeepers were on the ground, made him increasingly unpopular in Washington. Richard Holbrooke, President Clinton's point man on the former Yugoslavia, wrote that "more than any other issue, it was his [Boutros-Ghali's] performance on Bosnia that made us feel he did not deserve a second term—just as Kofi Annan's strength on the bombing [of Serb positions] in August had already made him the private favorite of many American officials."[94] Despite Boutros-Ghali's palpable uneasiness with the use of force, some Americans still saw dark designs in his rather modest *Agenda for Peace* report mandated by the Security Council in early 1992 and in his rueful reassessment in January 1995. When he suggested the development of a small rapid reaction force in the latter report, Ambassador Madeleine Albright accused him of attempting to "arrogate more power" to himself.[95] Hampered by limited communication skills and a diffident manner that at times seemed arrogant, Boutros-Ghali became the Darth Vader of the new world order to commentators worried about an expansive UN.[96]

Several former officials picked up the refrain. For example, John R. Bolton—who ironically had been assistant secretary of state for international organization affairs when President Bush first ordered U.S. forces to Somalia in December 1992—warned that the UN secretary-general should not act like "the commander in chief of the World Federalist Army."[97] Similarly, Jeane Kirkpatrick and former assistant secretary of defense Richard Armitage suggested that Boutros-Ghali was striving to become "chief executive of the world" and "the world's commander-in-chief."[98] Kirkpatrick told the House Committee on International Relations in January 1995 that "the idea that U.N. forces . . . should be placed under the command of the United Nations Secretary General is unprecedented, it never existed, never really was recommended until the current Secretary General and the current U.S. President, after the recommendations of Secretary General Boutros Boutros-Ghali to President Clinton." Noting that "the Secretary General is not trained to command forces," she concluded that "placing forces under U.N. military command and control is a recipe for failure, as we have seen in Somalia."[99] Campaigning in 1996, Alan Keyes told a California audience: "don't let them fool you. Don't let them send our troops into war under the rubric of peacekeeping, especially not when it provides an ideal excuse to take a step toward putting our troops under the command and service of the United Nations, which is what I think this whole thing [sending U.S. troops to Bosnia] is about."[100]

Clinton's PDD-25 went to great lengths to reassure Congress and the public that the expansion of UN peacekeeping operations and the growing role of U.S. forces in them had not altered the long-standing U.S. policies and doctrines concerning the command of American forces engaged in a multinational operation. "No President has ever relinquished command over U.S. forces," it noted, and "if it is to our advantage to place U.S. forces under the operational control of a UN commander, the fundamental elements of U.S. command still apply." As the document asserted:

> The President retains and will never relinquish command authority over U.S. forces. On a case by case basis, the President will consider placing appropriate U.S. forces under the operational control of a competent UN commander for specific UN operations authorized by the Security Council. The greater the U.S. military role, the less likely it will be that the U.S. will agree to have a UN commander exercise overall operational control over U.S. forces. Any large

scale participation of U.S. forces in a major peace enforcement mission that is likely to involve combat should ordinarily be conducted under U.S. command and operational control or through competent regional organizations such as NATO or ad hoc coalitions.

There is nothing new about this Administration's policy regarding the command and control of U.S. forces. U.S. military personnel have participated in UN peace operations since 1948. American forces have served under the operational control of foreign commanders since the Revolutionary War, including in World War I, World War II, Operation Desert Storm and in NATO since its inception. We have done so and will continue to do so when the President determines it serves U.S. national interests.[101]

Yet, for all of its citations of historical precedent and standard operating procedures, PDD-25 failed to assuage the doubts of many critics, especially on Capitol Hill. For example, in 1996 Senate testimony Ambassador Kirkpatrick asserted that the president's "constitutional responsibilities as commander-in-chief for the well-being of U.S. forces . . . is not consistent with assigning U.S. forces to unfamiliar commanders to operate under U.N. rules of engagement."[102] Years later, the incident in Mogadishu is still cited as an example of the dangers of entrusting the lives of American servicemen and women to the whims of a foreign commander.[103]

Part of the explanation for the persistence of these concerns is simple partisan politics: this remains an easy way to try to embarrass a president who never served in the military about his handling of his responsibilities as commander-in-chief. But such partisan appeals would not trigger such an emotional response unless some deeper chord had also been struck. For some Americans—although certainly not for all—the notion of ceding the fate of young soldiers to the decisions of a foreign commander operating under a UN flag to achieve a mandate drafted by a fifteen-nation committee is simply unpalatable. Along with the chimera of the global tax man, the evocative images from Mogadishu raised deep-seated worries, particularly among those already feeling marginalized by the trend toward globalization, about loss of control and loss of sovereignty. It raised the specter of an expansive new world order that could threaten the lives of the nation's greatest asset, its youth, called to fight in other peoples' wars.

In its historical references and technical explanations, PDD-25 may have been on the mark, but its tepid defense of multinational military operations also laid bare the Clinton administration's profound ambivalence about one of the core tenets of the multilateralist vision. Even this century's most internationalist presidents—Taft, Wilson, Roosevelt, Truman, and Bush among them—have been unwilling to relinquish command authority over U.S. forces in harm's way. Bush and his national security adviser Brent Scowcroft have written candidly of the advantages and limits to the UN's role in driving Iraqi forces from Kuwait in 1991:

> Soviet support against Iraq provided us the opportunity to invigorate the powers of the Security Council and test how well it could contribute. We were, however, unsure of the council's usefulness in a new role of actively resisting aggression, and we opposed allowing the UN to organize and run a war. It was important to reach out to the rest of the world, but even more important to keep the strings of control tightly in our hands.[104]

Although highly practical in the short term, this stance contrasts starkly with Washington's frequently lofty rhetoric about the value of international cooperation. By insisting on maintaining firm control over any multilateral operation in which it participates with more than a token force, the United States ensures that it will usually be unable to recruit partners that are as fully committed as it is to the end goals. Further, by retaining the option of countermanding the orders of any international command structure that they do not fully control, U.S. officials demonstrate their lack of faith in the very notion of multinational leadership of international coalitions. Other national capitals, of course, have been all too eager to demand the same rules for their forces in UN peace operations, further eroding confidence in multinational security options. Through their circular reasoning, some critics of international operations have created a self-fulfilling prophecy by insisting on conditions that make international arrangements less likely to be workable when push comes to shove. For example, legislation approved by the Senate, 98-1, in June 1999 would condition the payment of arrears to the UN on a certification by the secretary of state that the UN had not entered into article 43 standby arrangements with *any* member state.[105]

Another irony stems from the general rule of thumb, referred to in PDD-25, that the commander of an international force will generally come from the nation that contributes the largest contingent to the joint operation. In other words, for an American to be placed in command, as in Korea and Kuwait, the United States needs to supply the bulk of the forces. In Kosovo, where the United Kingdom is supplying the most troops, a British general has been given command. The critics cannot have it both ways: to have America in command and to expect other countries to carry more of the burden of joint operations. Demands for greater burden sharing are incompatible with placing American officers in command unless one takes the argument to its extreme: that there simply should be no U.S. participation in international military operations. Yet it would hardly seem to be in U.S. strategic interests to encourage other nations to get in the habit of organizing multinational military ventures without some degree of American involvement and control. In any case, large-scale military missions will in most situations require substantial U.S. involvement given its preponderance in airlift, sealift, logistical support, intelligence, air support, and special operations.

The twentieth century has failed to find a workable and politically satisfactory resolution to the quandary of how international forces should be commanded. Who will ultimately be responsible for the lives of those serving under an international command? Who should be credited for their successes or blamed for their failures? Internationalists offer technical distinctions between operational control and command authority. Unilateralists issue hollow assurances that we will do it ourselves if it really matters. Isolationists pretend none of it really matters anyway because our interests rarely extend far from our borders and the crises are always someone else's to worry about. In the end, all three postures, by failing to address the core questions, tend to reinforce American ambivalence about international organization and its capacity to serve its fundamental security purposes. The self-fulfilling circle of doubt is thus complete: a deeply ingrained lack of faith in international military cooperation breeds a lack of will either to use the machinery that exists or to try to develop something better, thus ensuring that international mechanisms cannot perform effectively and confirming the initial doubts.

Who Owes Whom?
Paying for Peacekeeping Support Costs

One of the more curious, but potentially more serious, episodes in the ongoing debate between the United States and the other member states over burden sharing has been the brewing controversy over how the support costs for UN peace operations are defined, accounted, and shared. According to an appropriations bill amendment that passed the Senate on March 25, 1998, by an overwhelming 90 to 10 vote, it is the sense of the Senate that "the United Nations should acknowledge publicly the financial and military support of the United States in maintaining international peace and stability." Among the findings on which the amendment is based is the calculation that the Department of Defense had spent almost $8.5 billion during the last three fiscal years "for the incremental costs of implementing or supporting United Nations Security Council resolutions for which the United States received no credit at the United Nations." The amendment reiterates that U.S. law since 1994 has prohibited payment of more than 25 percent of UN peacekeeping costs and that "the United States is not obligated to pay those amounts" above that ceiling that have been counted by the UN as arrears. Noting that the United Nations would not even "exist today had it not been for the United States and for the generous support provided by the American taxpayers through good times and bad times," Senator Helms, the author of the amendment, said that it "stresses this obvious truth and suggests that the United Nations tone down its cry-baby rhetoric and acknowledge the plain truth." Helms argued that the arrears accumulated since 1994 for assessed amounts over 25 percent represent "hundreds of millions of dollars that we do not owe and that we should never pay, and I respectfully suggest that somebody should inform the international diplomatic corps that the United States controls the U.S. Government purse strings, not the United Nations."[106]

Taking a similar tack in the House, Representative Bartlett moved in September 1997 to strike the first arrearage payments to the UN from the appropriations bill.[107] While ultimately unsuccessful, Bartlett did manage to raise the visibility on the Hill of an issue that had long been discussed by conservative critics of peacekeeping. Despite the large Senate vote, which was no doubt inflated because it was a cost-free, nonbinding resolution, relatively few U.S. legislators appear likely to actually press for reimbursement of past support expenses. As Senator Rod Grams, R-Minn., commented, "it neither makes sense nor is practical to retroactively seek reimbursement for past 'in-kind' contributions. However, a better system for accounting for such contributions and seeking reimbursement from the U.N. is clearly necessary."[108] One problem with seeking reimbursement is illustrated by the senator's own figures, $1.5 billion in 1995 "in-kind" contributions and $4 billion "in recent years," which are substantially lower than those cited in the Senate bill. The latter includes costs for American troops deployed in the NATO-led peacekeeping operation in Bosnia-Herzegovina as well as for those stationed in the Persian Gulf to fulfill U.S. strategic objectives as much as for implementing Security Council mandates.

The United States, like any other member state, is reimbursed (at least to the extent that the precarious UN financial situation allows) for services rendered in direct support of Security Council–mandated missions.

Differences of opinion about the proper reimbursement levels have occurred from time to time, but the system of payments is well established. The UN, of course, has never agreed that individual member states can undertake their own actions in these theaters without Council authorization and then bill the UN for them, a point made by several members of Congress in the 1997 debate.[109] It is impossible to sort out, moreover, whose interests are being served by a particular UN mission, since the core assumption is that it serves the common interests of many member states. If the United States feels that a specific operation would not serve its interests, but rather the "UN's," then it has the option of vetoing the mission in the first place or of insisting that the funding of the operation should be voluntary.

The flurry of legislative initiatives calling for some sort of recognition of U.S. military efforts to support UN peace operations is significant less for financial than for symbolic reasons. The 1998 Helms amendment, in fact, was specifically aimed at gaining respect and appreciation, not financial offsets, from the UN and other member states. In introducing the amendment, the ever-quotable chairman bristled at what he termed "the familiar anti-American drumbeat out of the United Nations," the references to the United States as a "deadbeat," "the disingenuous, even dishonest arguments being floated to misrepresent the United States of America," and the "outrageous charges from those who do not represent American taxpayers." He took particular umbrage to a *New York Times* op-ed article by Kofi Annan that called for U.S. payment of its arrears and declared that "Fiji has done its part. What about the U.S.?," a comparison that the senator found "both absurd and untruthful."[110] Judging by the 90 to 10 vote that followed, many senators share Helms's acute sensitivity to charges that the United States is not carrying its share of the burden and to being compared unfavorably with one of the UN's smaller member states. National pride, it seems, is as close to the surface and as evocative in congressional debates about the UN in 1999 as in those about the League eighty years earlier. The ongoing controversy over funding for peacekeeping suggests, once again, that, for many members of Congress, the distance between ambivalence and antipathy toward the world body is not far at all. As the following chapter illustrates, this fine line can also be seen in the vocal and unceasing concerns of some in Congress for the reform of the world organization.

CHAPTER EIGHT

Reform for All Seasons

The economy of asking a dollar's value for a dollar spent is good. The economy of a narrowed vision is dangerous.

—*NEW YORK TIMES*, 1946

The people of our country are beginning to count dollars and cents and costs, and not without reason. They see the tremendous expenditures, and some are quite skeptical about whether or not those expenditures are producing value for value in terms of dollars and cents.

—REPRESENTATIVE THOMAS HALE BOGGS SR., 1949

We do the United Nations no favors by understating or neglecting its shortcomings.

—SENATOR JOHN F. KERRY, 1993

There is only one true constituency for reform at the U.N., and that is the United States Congress.

—REPRESENTATIVE HAROLD D. ROGERS, 1997

THE UNITED NATIONS is a remarkable institution: remarkably responsive to new programmatic opportunities, yet remarkably resistant to administrative reform. Burdened by an archaic and dysfunctional administrative structure, it still seeks and often manages to be at the cutting edge of the issues of the day. This discrepancy has not gone unnoticed. At least once a decade, a tide of management reform washes over the organization, only to leave its stubborn administrative and structural shortcomings still firmly in place. Despite its bureaucratic inertia, the world body readily adapts its substantive and programmatic priorities to incorporate the latest political challenge mandated by the member states, whether it be decolonization, human rights, peacekeeping, disarmament, humanitarian affairs, sustainable development, or democracy building. For all of the UN's substantive dynamism, however, one characteristic has endured: what it achieves is despite, not because of, its administrative procedures, personnel policies, fiscal rules, and management structure.

Historically, the UN has managed to get by as a politically agile and bureaucratically clumsy body. In recent years, however, poor management has itself become a political issue, sapping support for the world body's substantive work. In fact, if one counts the number of words expended, the biggest complaint of Americans across the political spectrum about the United Nations system these days concerns my seventh theme—the organization's management—rather than its politics or priorities, the big worries of much of the 1970s and 1980s. Indeed, although the peace and security issues addressed in the last two chapters underlay the congressional retreat from the UN in the mid-1990s, it is a sign of how low the relationship has sunk in the latter years of this decade that questions of reform and finance have come to dominate the U.S.-UN debate. These subjects are addressed in this chapter and the next.

The signs of U.S. government consternation about UN management shortcomings are plentiful. Since 1985, when it first voted to condition U.S. funding on UN reforms, Congress repeatedly has justified withholding legally assessed dues payments to the world body as leverage for compelling restrictions in its spending, budgeting processes, assessment scales, personnel, and administrative and financial oversight. The Clinton administration's proposals for UN reform, moreover, have focused not on its structure or its performance, but instead on financial and administrative matters. In 1996 the United States was willing to stand virtually alone in opposition to a second term for the organization's chief administrative officer, Secretary-General Boutros Boutros-Ghali, in part because he was seen as insufficiently energetic in pushing for significant management reform.[1]

The United States, of course, is not the only member state concerned about the way the UN conducts its members' collective business. The organization's chief funders have always kept a close and wary eye on how it spends their respective voters' and taxpayers' money. Each government has its own parliament looking over its shoulders for signs of waste and abuse. The degree to which the United States has come to focus on these concerns and the priority they have assumed in Washington's policymaking, however, are quite without precedent or parallel. Unlike more fundamental issues, such as collective security, international decisionmaking, and sovereignty, concerns about administration and finance have not always been at the top of U.S. government priorities vis-à-vis the world organization. Grumblings about these matters usually have been more pronounced during periods of U.S. public and official disappointment about developments relating to core political issues or to the political dynamics of the institution. Given the constitutional separation of powers in Washington, moreover, Congress has usually been more vocal and passionate about these concerns than has been the executive branch. This chapter begins with a look at the historical roots that help to explain what may seem to others as an American obsession with the administrative failings of the United Nations.

Unfinished Business in Planning the League and the UN

The founders of the League of Nations and the United Nations, who often spoke eloquently of great issues of war and peace, sovereignty and the brotherhood of man, rarely evinced even a passing interest in how their high-minded enterprises would be managed or funded. They felt that they had more important things to think about. The debates, quite properly, were on first-order issues: purposes, principles, and decisionmaking methods, not on ordinary and parochial concerns, such as who would be minding the store, how the costs would be divided, and how the inevitable bureaucracies would be organized. For America the first question to be addressed had to be whether it would take its proper place as a leading member state and, if so, what commitments and obligations this would entail. Once the principal statesmen and legislators had found satisfactory answers to these core questions, then others could be delegated to work out the details of just how the new organization would operate on a daily basis. After all, bureaucratic and financial matters would be of little concern to the United States if a failure to resolve the larger issues satisfactorily meant the nation would remain outside of the new body.

American critics of the League likewise wasted little breath on potential administrative and financial shortcomings. Besides, there would have been little reliable information available on such matters concerning an organization that did not yet exist. Bishop Thomas Benjamin Neely, in his 1919 tract chocked full of lurid visions of a League-based world government, was left to assert vaguely that "membership in the League of Nations would involve the United States in greatly increased expense." Lacking numbers or precedents, he nonetheless postulated that these costs "are likely to become heavier and heavier as the years go on."[2] In this, at least, he was prescient.

Though not a member of the League, the U.S. government joined the International Labor Organization in 1934 and regularly sent individuals or teams to observe League activities, and many U.S. citizens served on League committees as private experts. Through practical experience, U.S. officials came to appreciate the value of having the League secretariat and facilities available for arranging international conferences. In late 1933 President Franklin Roosevelt noted that, on nonpolitical matters, "the United States is cooperating more openly in the fuller utilization of the League of Nations machinery than ever before."[3] Greater familiarity, of course, does not always breed admiration. For example, A. Cressy Morrison reported that at the 1927 Geneva World Economic Conference, the League secretariat served as "a part of the steam roller designed to color the thought of the delegation." In his view, not only did the staff have a decidedly internationalist perspective, but the conference preparations were costly:

> All the documentary preparation for the economic conference was necessarily in the hands of the officials of the league. Their point of view being international, then the documents prepared are likely to be international, because they select sympathetic writers for the preparation and so the documentation of the economic conference, amounting to about 120 volumes, . . . costing approximately $100,000 of the league's money, had a strong international tendency.[4]

It should come as no surprise, of course, that the staff of an international organization believes in the value of international cooperation. Depending on their content and relevance—and the professional stature of League economists, as well as of UN statisticians, appears to have been quite high— the assembling of 120 volumes of preparatory papers could be an indication of either overly thorough staff work or a waste of time and paper. What is striking about Morrison's observations, however, is the degree to which they foreshadowed recent complaints about a UN secretariat that is said by its detractors to be out of control, politically skewed, and addicted to producing tons of useless papers.

At Dumbarton Oaks and San Francisco, questions about how the new world organization was to be administered and paid for were at best tertiary concerns.[5] According to former senator Claiborne Pell, "when we were in San Francisco, the whole emphasis was on security and peacekeeping. . . . [T]he Security Council is really what the U.N. was created to be all about."[6] Questions of administration and finance had been addressed very late in the State Department's planning process and had not been particularly controversial. There was a clear preference in Washington for an independent "international" civil service rather than a "national" one in which secretariat members would be seconded from member governments, as the Soviets

preferred. Roosevelt at one point proposed that the organization be headed
by a high-level president, who would chair intergovernmental meetings, but
in the end that idea was dropped as unrealistic for an intergovernmental
organization.[7]

On the whole, Washington's proposals were accepted at San Francisco
with little controversy. The Soviets questioned including language in the
charter about the need for the secretariat to be independent, but they readily acceded to the majority view. Likewise, their proposal to have four
deputy secretaries-general directly elected by the member states was also
not accepted (anymore than was their call in the early 1960s for a "troika" of
secretaries-general). Several smaller delegations tried, unsuccessfully, to
remove the requirement that all permanent members of the Security
Council would have to approve the nominee for the secretary-generalship.
Left for the General Assembly was the "technical" task of determining how
to apportion the organization's expenses among the member states. In retrospect, it is striking how soon these supposedly minor questions were to
produce major East-West and North-South fissures within the membership.

The charter produced at San Francisco offers only skeletal indications
of what the UN's administrative and financial arrangements should look
like. Article 100 clearly states the principle of independence for the staff,
and article 101 gives some sense of the qualities to be given priority in
selecting staff: "the highest standards of efficiency, competence, and
integrity" plus "due regard" to geographical distribution. The secretary-
general "shall be the chief administrative officer of the Organization," to be
"appointed by the General Assembly upon the recommendation of the
Security Council" (article 97). His duties, however, are described only in the
vaguest terms and nothing is said about the length of his term of office or
whether it should be renewable. The size and shape of the secretariat also
are left undefined. Article 17 leaves budgeting and financing questions to the
General Assembly, one of the few topics on which it can take binding decisions. Article 19, which has occasioned some sharp controversies, states that
a member state "in arrears in the payment of its financial contributions to
the Organization shall have no vote in the General Assembly if the amount
of its arrears equals or exceeds the amount of the contribution due from it
for the preceding two full years." This provision can be waived if the
Assembly "is satisfied that the failure to pay is due to conditions beyond the
control of the Member."

From this rough framework, it was left to the Assembly's first session in
London to fill in the all-important details of how the new organization

would function. The task of chairing the administrative and budgetary subcommittee was given to Arthur H. Vandenberg. Even then, the special interest of congressional Republicans in these matters was acknowledged. On February 27, 1946, Vandenberg proudly reported back to the Senate that "in 37 days the United Nations turned a blueprint into a going concern. It turned an ideal into a reality. . . . On January 10 we had a scrap of paper. In 37 days we gave it life." Noting that "fifty-one nations, spanning the gamut of race, color, language, and tradition, had to concur," he wondered "how long, and with what travail, it would have taken our own Congress to complete a comparable task."[8] Although at that point it sounded as though the U.S.-UN relationship was still in full bloom, the honeymoon turned out to be remarkably brief.

Penny Pinchers and Big Spenders: An Early Frost

Despite Senator Vandenberg's upbeat report on the degree of cooperation at the London session, congressional concerns about UN spending and the U.S. financial burden arrived early and never left. Vandenberg himself had worried in London about the "fancy" plans that some favored and warned against mistaking "pomp for power." Counseling his UN subcommittee on the need for administrative sobriety and financial solvency, he warned against permitting the UN's "aspirations to so far outrun its resources that any peace-loving nation would ever find it financially impossible to maintain its membership." For in his view, the UN "must never become a so-called 'rich man's club,' it must always remain the 'town meeting of the world.'"[9]

One of the first targets of congressional wrath was the UN Relief and Rehabilitation Administration (UNRRA), the UN's first humanitarian relief agency. Representative Charles W. Vursell, R-Ill., complained in February 1947 not only of the "high salaries and bonuses" of UNRRA officials, but of their "immunity from investigation," since "no committee of the Congress has the power of subpoena to bring them in before a committee for an investigation." This latter concern, stemming from Congress's inability to exercise direct oversight over the use of American contributions to international organizations, remains a core issue in U.S.-UN and congressional-executive relations today. As Vursell phrased it:

> When you give a little group of men at the top the protection of immunity
> from investigation by the Congress, when you give them the opportunity

without restraint to vote bonuses, establish provident funds, raise salaries without let or hindrance, you may be pretty certain that the horse will be taken from out of the barn before the door is locked.[10]

Fred E. Busbey, R-Ill., responded with another theme that has since become commonplace: that the relief funds for "downtrodden people" could have been handled with greater efficiency and fewer politics by private groups, such as the Red Cross.[11] Calls for partnership with civil society have had a long history, as have catcalls for the secretary-general. When the first secretary-general, Trygve Lie, stepped down, Representative H. R. Gross, R-Iowa, complained that his pension was "the fattest reward that anybody has come into for a long time for a trifling bit of work. . . . [The] U.N. may not have been of any use to anybody else, but it has certainly been a gold mine to Trygve."[12] Lie was, in the legislator's view, the "lucky dependent" of the American people.

In October 1947 the Senate Committee on Expenditures in Executive Departments, chaired by George D. Aiken of Vermont, appointed a three-member team, headed by Irving M. Ives, R-N.Y., "to investigate how the United Nations and other international organizations spend their funds and account for them." Aiken declared that, because the United States was the world body's largest contributor, American taxpayers "are entitled to assurance that these funds are being properly and economically administered."[13] Whether the parliaments of other member states should be accorded the same opportunity was not addressed, nor were the consequences should the results of the oversight efforts of Congress differ from those of the executive branch.

Nine months later, the Senate group issued a scathing preliminary report, whose conclusions have been echoed in scores of congressional complaints ever since. Lamenting the lack of "central program planning," the senators pointed to "overlapping and duplication of effort" and "a proliferation of bodies" caused by weak coordination both within the policymaking of national governments themselves and among the UN's independent specialized agencies—all endemic structural problems related to the decentralized architecture of the UN system. According to the perceptive and prescient Senate report, "whenever a particular project appears important at the moment, a new commission or committee is appointed to look into the matter. . . . Thus the Food and Agricultural Organization is presently working on 450 different projects, and at the United Nations Educational, Scientific and Cultural Organization Conference in Mexico City last fall 150 different projects were adopted." While acknowledging the need "to attract and keep the ablest of personnel," the report charged that UN staff were receiving "approximately nine different types of allowances in addition to miscellaneous travel allowances and six different types of welfare and insurance benefits." Overall, the group concluded that UN employees were receiving salaries "considerably out of line" with the compensation of U.S. nationals "doing similar work."[14]

At the fall 1946 session of the General Assembly, Senator Vandenberg warned that the UN and its specialized agencies were expanding too rapidly, complicating the coordination task of the Economic and Social Council (ECOSOC) and making it difficult for some member states to meet their assessed payments to them. The next spring, in May 1947, Chairman Vandenberg and other members of the Senate Foreign Relations Committee opposed President Truman's nomination of Francis Biddle, attorney general in the Roosevelt administration, to be U.S. representative to ECOSOC, in part because a "more cautious" man was needed to help "curb the expansion of the so-called specialized agencies affiliated with the council."[15] Two months later, the committee issued a unanimous report recommending U.S. participation in the World Health Organization but also expressing "vigorous disapproval of the loose budgetary arrangements existing between the United Nations and its various specialized agencies." Because each of the specialized agencies "has its own separate budget" and are "financially autonomous segments of the United Nations system," the result might be "overlapping and duplication" that could produce "very serious results," according to the report.[16]

This early committee report captured the essential ambivalence that has since characterized so much of the American attitude toward the UN: an affinity, even admiration, for its purposes coupled with profound doubts about its administration and efficiency. To the editors of the *New York Times,* however, all of the fuss about money and management missed the central point. A November 4, 1946, editorial opined that "with so many stupendous problems on its hands the United Nations cannot afford to get roiled up about its administrative budget." Quoting Daniel Burnham, the *Times* concluded: "'Make not little plans—they have no magic to stir men's blood.' It is magic that we now need to build peace, not little plans and penny-pinching."[17] This is the expansive and high-minded spirit that imbued the rhetoric, and perhaps even the thinking, of the UN's chief supporters at the preparatory meetings and conferences. In their minds, their first task was to convince the American people and their congressional representatives of the nobility and urgency of the UN's great purposes. The second task, which has proven far more difficult, has been to demonstrate convincingly that the organization is managed and structured in a way to accomplish these ends.

Since the UN's beginning, its boosters have been quick to point to the relatively modest budgets of the world organization, whether compared with the cost of war or of national (or even local) government. In 1953 Alexander Wiley, chairman of the Senate Foreign Relations Committee, observed that the 1953 regular budget of the UN, at $48.3 million, "is approximately the cost of a single destroyer" and "a reasonable figure when we consider the great goals to which the U.N. is dedicated."[18] Ambassador Warren R. Austin, in 1948 House hearings, pointed out that "there is a substantial inflow of funds from abroad to finance United Nations activities in New York" and that "this annual expenditure is likely to grow rather than diminish."[19] (For New York City merchants, at least, his assumptions about rising UN outlays had a silver lining; whether the representatives from the South and West, who tended to be more skeptical of the UN in principle as well as in practice, were convinced by his argument is doubtful.)[20] In any case, in 1949 Clyde Eagleton, of New York University and the American Association for the United Nations, told the House that "the peoples of the world give for the total budget of the great organization, which they expect to provide them with peace and security, far less money than New York City spends for cleaning the streets."[21] (Again, it was unclear whether representatives from other parts of the country took this to mean that New York City had unusually dirty streets or that the UN budget was too modest.)

For all of these comparisons and for all of the UN's noble purposes, it is also true that the devil is often in the details. Fewer and fewer members of Congress, in light of their fiduciary responsibilities to their constituents, were willing to overlook serious fiscal and administrative questions for the sake of high principles poorly realized. As the influential Representative Thomas Hale Boggs Sr., D-La., asserted in 1949, the American people "realize that we cannot continue to carry the burden alone."[22] Americans, it should be recalled, had traditionally been known both for their fondness for high principles and soaring visions and for their tightfistedness when it came to government expenditures. It could be argued, in fact, that this coexistence of idealism and practicality has served America remarkably well in a variety of fields and endeavors since its earliest days, fostering both forward-looking entrepreneurship and a hands-on style of management.[23] Both traits were evident in American policies and attitudes toward the UN during its infancy. A logical and productive combination in many ways, at times

these two impulses no doubt pulled policy in contradictory directions, making the United States appear, at least from a distance, to have doubts about
the organization it had done so much to create.

These initial controversies over how the world organization would be
funded and managed occurred when expectations about the UN's performance and potential were declining, not ascending, making the claims and
predictions of the organization's most fervent boosters ring all the more
hollow. In 1948, for example, Secretary of State George C. Marshall cautioned Congress that "basic human frailties cannot be overcome by Charter
provisions alone, for they exist in the behavior of men and governments."[24]
Nonetheless, Marshall assured them, "when the substance of the world situation improves, the United Nations will be able to function with full effectiveness." Yet these assurances could not have been very comforting at a time
when Americans were becoming increasingly bearish about the future of
relations with Moscow and about the prospects for peaceful cooperation.
For the UN's proponents, Marshall's line of reasoning, while perfectly sensible, created a circular dilemma: for one of the organization's prime selling
points was that it could help defuse tensions and prevent conflict, as well as
facilitate cooperative efforts to better the world situation. If the UN could
function only in the good times, then its substantive value as "a centre for
harmonizing the actions of nations" would be markedly diminished.
Likewise, it was hardly encouraging to hear that the proper functioning of
the UN's machinery would have to follow improvements in the world situation rather than vice versa. After all, if the UN's operations were plagued by
structural deficiencies, bureaucratic inertia, and the lack of fiscal accountability, then there was little reason to have confidence in its ability to handle
an increasingly complex and demanding international agenda.

Spinning Wheels: Barriers to Reform

Among the less-noticed casualties of the cold war was the UN reform
agenda. East-West divisions worked to freeze the shape and structure of the
secretariat as well as of the intergovernmental bodies. The Soviet Union and
its allies, outnumbered within the new body, became strict constructionists
from fear that innovations would be to their disadvantage. Bureaucratic
rigidities and redundancies were reinforced by the need to ensure that the
sensitive work of the organization could get done without interference by
extraneous political considerations.[25] To guarantee confidentiality and to
bolster western confidence in the secretariat's ability to handle peacekeeping

and related issues discreetly, eastern bloc nationals received posts in some sections of the organization and were largely excluded from others. To an auditor, these redundancies would appear to be inefficiencies. To a purist, they would appear to violate charter strictures on geographical balance in the secretariat. But they had the considerable virtue of allowing the body to play a constructive role in maintaining international peace and security, its first responsibility.

Over time the UN organization chart came to resemble less and less the way things actually got done. Horizontal lines of communication tended to get stunted because of the lack of trust on political issues, while vertical, hierarchical, and informal reporting lines flourished. Official bodies continued to meet regularly, but more and more of the decisionmaking was done through informal consultations and ad hoc channels, which gave greater weight to the big powers than the Assembly's one-nation, one-vote and sovereign equality rules would suggest.

Much of this flexibility and bending of management rules served to help the organization survive the political stresses caused by East-West and North-South differences. To the extent that the UN worked, it often did so despite, rather than because of, its formal structures and procedures. Yet the habit of loose and jury-rigged administration and financing persisted well beyond the end of the cold war. For example, the ad hoc practices adopted for hiring, promotion, and career tracks often seemed to defy professional management standards. Member states got into the habit of giving voluntary contributions to support their favorite programs, including some peacekeeping operations, further eroding financial discipline. Extra-budgetary spending came to exceed budgetary outlays, making planning that much more problematic. Moreover, time and again key member states made it clear that they were not seeking a reformer for the top job at the UN. For example, Kurt Waldheim, whose chief distinction was prudence and risk avoidance, was awarded two terms as secretary-general and, except for multiple Chinese vetoes, nearly won a third.[26]

A divided UN proved resistant to change, at least on the wide array of management questions that were politically controversial within the membership. During the cold war years, that at times seemed to encompass almost everything. The influx of scores of new member states largely served to add additional layers of political complexity to seemingly straightforward management questions. Matters of posts, promotions, budgets, and reporting lines took on political dimensions in this most political of organizations. They became the objects of North-South, as well as East-West, struggle. Every national mission to the UN, the U.S. mission not least among them, became engaged in a never-ending tug-of-war over who got which posts and how the organization's resources were to be divided among so many competing priorities (see chapter 4).

The UN's turf battles may have seemed petty relative to the sweeping rhetoric of the San Francisco conference. But questions concerning who oversaw which programs and how limited funds were to be utilized were hardly insubstantial questions, for they largely defined what the organization was and where it might make a difference. To their credit, from the UN's first days the more constructive congressional critics, in their emphasis on administrative and financial reform, understood this. After all, providing oversight of these unglamorous operational matters reflects one of the chief roles Congress plays within the federal government. Although some of the UN's boosters have sought to belittle the importance of these questions, American policymakers and legislators—like their counterparts from many other member states—have recognized that the way administrative, financial, and programmatic matters are handled may have important consequences for the organization's capacity to carry out its substantive work.

Political developments certainly complicated efforts to spruce up the UN's management, but they were hardly the only factors favoring the status quo. Bureaucratic inertia, the bane of so many organizations, took deep root within the UN system as well. The nature of international arrangements, moreover, has made this universal phenomenon particularly troublesome in the UN. For the United States, it has been more than a little awkward on the one hand to preach the principle of independence for the international civil service and on the other hand to appear to be trying to micromanage the secretariat. Management and financial issues cannot be neatly distinguished from their political and programmatic context. For example, the principle of geographical balance, as enshrined in the charter and championed by the developing countries, complicates judgments about performance and efficiency, especially when the very process of building international harmony is a prime purpose of the world body. Also, the huge size of the UN's board of directors—the 185 member states in the Assembly—permits any number of alliances between individual secretariat officials and specific countries on particular issues. In many cases, seasoned UN officials have the option of playing one group of countries off against another in debates about administrative and financial matters.

In addition to these political and bureaucratic causes of inertia, there have also been constitutional ones. The founders, uncertain of their future relationships and defensive of their prerogatives, made sure that altering the basic structure and decisionmaking processes established at San Francisco would be no easy task. Under article 108, charter amendments require adoption by two-thirds of the members of the General Assembly and ratification by their respective constitutional processes, including by all five permanent members of the Security Council. As a result the only amendments that have been approved have been to expand bodies—the Security Council from eleven to fifteen members in 1965 and the ECOSOC from eighteen to twenty-seven in 1965 and to fifty-four in 1973—as the UN's membership grew threefold. Some may argue that the tripling of the size of ECOSOC made it more representative, but few would contend that it has become a more effective instrument for carrying out the economic and social priorities of any group of member states. At the UN, larger may be more popular, but it may not always be better. For example, under the banner of "democratization," a large majority of member states are now pushing for a very substantial enlargement of Security Council membership, to twenty-five or more. Although such a large expansion might make the Council more representative and its actions more legitimate in the eyes of the developing world, it also could complicate the Council's ability to make decisions expeditiously and to act decisively in crisis situations.

In addition to institutional constraints, the decentralized structure of the UN system has also complicated efforts to promote greater management efficiency and programmatic effectiveness. In fact, much of the reform effort, beginning with the 1948 Senate review, has consciously or unconsciously sought to address the deficiencies of the structural model preferred by the United States and other western countries, which was loosely based on the functional theories of David Mitrany.[27] Under this approach, the specialized agencies, whose relationships to the central UN were to be negotiated individually by ECOSOC under the provisions of article 63, were left with considerable autonomy, so that they could pursue their "good works" at some distance from the politics of the center. To those, including many Americans, concerned about the dangers of politicization of the technical and humanitarian work of the world body, the benefits of decentralization clearly outweighed the administrative costs caused by overlap and lack of coordination, particularly during the cold war years when the specialized agencies and Bretton Woods institutions could be kept largely beyond the spheres of Soviet influence. With their own governing bodies, sources of funding, and appointment processes, most of these agencies and the Bretton Woods institutions have remained responsible to their own donors and member states rather than to the UN's principal organs. According to Robert Jackson, the Australian author of a famous 1969 study on how to increase the UN's capacity for carrying out major development programs, the surest way to reform the development side of the organization would be to centralize the budgets of all the specialized agencies. However, he cautioned, "then you really would see opposition to change! That battle was fought out when I was at Lake Success in the early days and the supporters of the sectoral approach won the day."[28]

The initial choice of a decentralized system has complicated the endemic problem of coordination in two ways. First, it has made systemwide reform next to impossible unless the key member states themselves can find common ground on a systemwide reform agenda and can pursue it in a persistent, concerted, and systemwide fashion. That is most unlikely when particular agencies and member state legislatures team up to oppose coordination or consolidation efforts, as UNICEF and Congress did in 1997 when they sought to discourage any consideration of merging UN development programs.[29] Second, the decentralized nature of the UN system has put a premium on the ability of each of the major member states to coordinate policymaking within its national capital. In the United States, for example, the interests of those government agencies focused on particular aspects of the UN's work have not always coincided with the broader policy and reform concerns of the State Department or of Congress. The former is likely to be more concerned with maximizing performance in "its" sectors and the latter with ensuring budgetary efficiency and excluding extraneous politics. These differences have surfaced more than once on reform questions.

Despite all of this, the UN has evolved in some remarkable ways over the years. Resistant to formal reform, the organization has nonetheless proved remarkably adaptable to changing circumstances and opportunities.[30] As it became clear that the UN's collective security machinery could rarely be used because of cold war divisions in the Security Council, the concept and practice of using military forces for consent-based peacekeeping operations to separate warring parties and to buy time for diplomacy to work—something never envisioned under the charter and with few historical precedents—became the centerpiece of the organization's efforts to maintain international peace and security. More recently, international political conditions changed sufficiently to permit the UN to adopt a whole new political and social agenda—democratization, election-monitoring, and the building of civil society—that was not contemplated, or even mentioned, in the charter. The organization has evolved into much more of a center for global norm setting, in areas as diverse as human rights, arms control and disarmament, population, humanitarian obligations, commerce, communications, decolonization, development, and the environment, than anyone had foreseen in its early years. In the process, the organization has both benefited from and contributed to a marked shift in common notions of the scope and limits of national sovereignty.

The United Nations, in short, has been good at adaptation and poor at reform. When political consensus has called for new directions, the organization has often been able to accommodate impressive changes in its programs and sense of purpose, yet these have been managed within a bureaucratic, financial, and institutional framework that has widely been characterized as stultifying, and that has largely stagnated. Not surprisingly, the world body has been much better at adding new programs to meet new or altered needs than at trimming or eliminating lower priority or outdated ones. Many of the member states have resisted efforts to require sunset provisions when new programs are launched.[31] Larger multilateral decision-making bodies, like the General Assembly, find it easier to accept everyone's programmatic priorities than to refuse anyone's, especially when working under consensus rules. It is no coincidence that the number of General Assembly agenda items multiplied—from 61 at its second session to 175 at its forty-eighth—as the number of member states tripled.[32] Setting clear priorities and making sharp choices among existing programs come much harder. In the abstract, every member state favors UN reform, but each has both its own view of what that means and its favorite activities that require protecting. Likewise, even a penny-wise Congress has as frequently called for new UN programs to handle the urgent need of the moment as it has proposed doing away with existing activities or agencies. As a result, the UN is usually asked to do more with less, to serve everyone's priorities but to keep overall posts and costs down. In the end, what has been produced is a UN system that is very broad in its ambitions and decidedly shallow in its resources for achieving them.

Muddling Through: Reform as a Way of Life

For an organization seemingly allergic to far-reaching management reform, the UN has been remarkably receptive to launching major reform campaigns—at least one per decade. Among these have been Jackson's *Study of the Capacity of the United Nations Development System* in 1969, noted earlier; the 1975 experts report on the UN's economic and social machinery rapporteured by Richard N. Gardner; the 1986 Group of Eighteen study that called for a raft of budgetary, personnel, and administrative adjustments; and the July 1997 report of Secretary-General Kofi Annan presenting a broad-based reform package. Internal auditors, the Office of Internal Oversight Services, the Joint Inspection Unit, the Efficiency Board, and the interagency Administrative Committee on Coordination (ACC), among others, offer a steady stream of in-house management proposals and critiques. Among the member states, oversight is provided by the Assembly's Fifth Committee (budgetary and administrative matters), the Advisory Committee on Administrative and Budgetary Questions (ACABQ), the Committee on Contributions, the Special Committee on the Charter of the UN and on the Strengthening of the Role of the Organization, the Board of Auditors, the International Civil Service Commission (ICSC), the Investments Committee, the Panel of External Auditors, the UN Administrative Tribunal, the UN Joint Staff Pension Fund, the Committee for Programmes and Coordination, a large number of intergovernmental bodies overseeing specific substantive areas, and, in recent years, a series of special General Assembly working groups on different aspects of the reform agenda.

The proliferation of oversight and reform bodies has demanded so much time from staff, as well as from delegations, that many insiders have suggested that simplifying and rationalizing these efforts would be a good place to start a true reform process. Reporting to multiple oversight bodies has become a major source of the excessive production of paper to which critics often point, and members of the secretariat complain that small as well as large member states are engaging in excessive micromanagement, reducing budgetary flexibility and programmatic initiative, as well as sapping staff morale. In his reform plan Secretary-General Annan diplomatically noted the need for "a well-defined division of functions between the General Assembly and the Secretary-General" and cautioned that "encroachment by either on the authority of the other undermines the efficiency and effective operation of the Organization." Because, in his view, the Assembly "has adopted resolutions and established practices, including in relation to high-level appointments, that have constrained the Secretary-General's ability to administer the Secretariat" and at other times "has provided insufficient guidance as to programme objectives and implementation," Annan urged "restoring the balance that was envisioned when the Organization was established."[33]

Member states have an obligation, as well as an unquenchable thirst, to exercise close oversight of how the UN is run and how their taxpayers' funds are spent. This is, moreover, an enduring responsibility without time limit. As Annan stressed not once, but twice, in his report, reform is a process, not an event.[34] It is, moreover, a perpetual process, because every successful organization needs to reappraise continually and regularly what it is doing and how it is trying to do it under changing conditions. There are certain management standards on which most of the membership can agree and which require some form of ongoing monitoring, such as fiscal prudence and integrity, cost controls, avoidance of overlap and duplication of effort, a rational personnel system that recognizes and encourages good work, coupled with effective recruitment and training programs; utilization of new communications technologies and information systems; and responsive, accountable, and transparent management at all levels. Some progress has been made in recent years on these fronts, much of it reflected in Annan's report, which pointed to a 25 percent contraction in secretariat posts since the mid-1980s, zero growth in the budget from the 1994–95 biennium to 1996–97, and negative growth in the proposed 1998–99 biennium program budget.[35] Yet the organization is still hampered by a byzantine personnel system, excessive red tape, and a bureaucratic culture that discourages initiative and entrepreneurship rather than rewarding them. Instead of slashing the number of top managers, particularly at the under-secretary-general level, as a number of reformers have urged, Annan instead has chosen to add one for each one eliminated, no doubt in part because of pressure from various member states seeking high-level posts for their nationals.

Annan further promised to reduce nonprogram costs from 38 percent of the regular budget to 25 percent over the next two bienniums and to turn the savings into a "dividend for development." But this dual commitment illustrates the fundamental dilemma of trying in a single reform package to serve two different masters with divergent objectives: those seeking to reduce UN spending (chiefly the United States, with sympathy from some other major donors) and those wanting the UN to do more to help the developing countries (the vast majority of member states, including many industrialized countries). During the reform debates in the General Assembly, a number of delegations characterized the interplay as a tug-of-war between those members trying to downsize the UN and those preferring to "right-size" it in relation to what it is trying to achieve. In essence, Annan has proposed steps to strengthen the management capacities of his office with the addition of a deputy, a senior management group, and executive committees for the major program sectors; to adopt results-based budgeting; and to make the organization more efficient, while applying any savings to development, the top priority of most member states. By gaining Assembly approval for most of his initial proposals, the secretary-general has achieved a political compromise between competing interests without undertaking any controversial or radical surgery on the shape or size of the organization.[36] Such half-steps and trade-offs are to be expected in multi-lateral decisionmaking, but it has been precisely this tendency to compromise that has led influential voices in Congress throughout this century to question whether U.S. interests are or can be fully served in such a multi-national decisionmaking process.

As in most things having to do with the UN, Washington's reactions to Annan's reform proposals have been all over the lot. Where one stands, as always, seems to depend on where one sits. President Clinton hailed the "most far-reaching reform of the United Nations in its history," but Senator Rod Grams, who chaired the International Operations Subcommittee and who had just served on the U.S. delegation to the UN, regretted that "this meager package represents nothing more than the status quo, and that is unacceptable." In his words, the "plan merely reshuffles the deck at a time when the number of cards needs to be reduced." Speaking for Senator Jesse Helms, aide Marc Thiessen complained that the plan "really doesn't do anything" and that the UN will "have to go a lot further than this."[37] Attitudes toward UN reform, it seems, act as a litmus test of broader perspectives on the world organization, as many member states would have objected if the secretary-general had tried to exceed his authority by terminating programs that had been mandated by intergovernmental bodies. With the next step—making tough choices among competing priorities—up to the member states, the prospects for major cuts, as always, are dubious.

In recent years the scope of unilateral demands placed by Congress on the UN in the name of reform is nothing short of staggering. The first major broadside was the Kassebaum-Solomon amendment of 1985, which required a 20 percent cut in U.S. contributions to the UN or any of its agencies that failed to adopt weighted voting, based on size of contributions, on budgetary matters.[38] The latter, of course, would have required an amendment to the UN charter and a rescinding of the one-nation, one-vote principle in the Assembly. In the end, the authors of the amendment accepted instead the UN's adoption of a consensus-based budgeting practice that has held now for more than a decade, plus cuts in the number of secretariat posts. So many legislative restrictions have been placed on the president's ability to authorize a U.S. vote in the Security Council for new peacekeeping operations that the world body is at risk of abandoning what had been one of its central and most promising lines of work. As of fiscal year 1996, Congress unilaterally declared that the United States would pay no more than 25 percent of UN peacekeeping costs, although the UN continues to assess the United States at the rate of about 31 percent, according to the formula agreed to by the United States and the other member states, adding each year to the massive U.S. arrears of some $1.6 billion to the world body. Among dozens of other UN reforms demanded by Congress under threat of further withholdings, one of the more successful and sensible was the call in 1994 for the appointment of an independent inspector general to ferret out cases of malfeasance or gross waste in the organization, a move that the member states were already considering.

The culmination of these twin trends—mounting arrears and expanding reform demands—has been an on-again, off-again effort by the Clinton administration and the congressional leadership to work out a "grand bargain" that would pair a far-reaching reform package with substantial arrears payments. As of mid-1999 it had not been possible to put all of the pieces together: in late 1997 Representative Christopher H. Smith, R-N.J., added conditions on the seemingly unrelated question of family planning and abortion that Congress approved but that President Clinton found unacceptable; Clinton vetoed the arrears-for-reform legislation in October 1998.[39] A revised version of the bill (S. 886) cleared both the Senate Foreign Relations Committee (April 1999) and the full Senate (June 1999) with a single negative vote. It was widely expected, however, that Representative Smith would again insist on his antiabortion amendment on the House side.[40] What is abundantly evident is that other member states will see even the streamlined conditions contained in the 1999 bill as unfair unilateral demands. The bill's two dozen reform provisions were worked out largely by Helms and Joseph R. Biden Jr., the chairman and ranking minority member, respectively, of the Senate Foreign Relations Committee, in consultation with the Clinton administration.[41] S. 886 includes detailed reporting requirements on UN peacekeeping operations and U.S. support costs and permits full payment of current regular budget obligations only if the UN has maintained a no-growth budget, respected the independence of the inspector general, and banned further global conferences (sec. 801). The legislation authorized the appropriation of about two-thirds of U.S. arrears over a three-year period, contingent on the reforms, with the remaining arrears to be placed in a "contested arrears account" that would not be counted toward the possible loss of the U.S. vote under article 19 (sec. 931). Among the reform "benchmarks," two of which the president can waive, are that U.S. sovereignty would be respected, that international fees and taxes (or even the promotion of such ideas) would be prohibited, that no effort would be made to establish a UN standing army, that American property rights would be safeguarded, that key UN management and financial reforms would be extended to other UN agencies, that the United States or the five major donors would be given permanent seats on the budget committee (ACABQ), that the U.S. General Accounting Office would be free to inspect the UN's books, that the UN would adopt a merit-based personnel system, and that U.S. assessments for the UN would be reduced from 25 percent to 22 percent in fiscal year 1999 and to 20 percent in fiscal year 2000 (secs. 921, 931, and 941). Perversely, the legislation conditions the payment of arrears to the UN on the achievement of several steps, including reducing U.S. assessments to 22 percent, in the ILO, FAO, and WHO, independent agencies with their own memberships and governing bodies.

These unilateral demands, not unexpectedly, have not been well received by the other member states, which resent such strong-armed tactics and the appearance of rewarding the United States for accumulating such large arrears by allowing it to use their payment as leverage over the membership as a whole. Others would characterize a number of the congressional benchmarks as unilateral favors to the United States, rather than as true UN reform. Why should reducing American assessments below its share of global GNP or its capacity to pay, for example, be considered a reform of the world organization? To guarantee seats for the United States and other major donors on the budget committee, some say, would be contrary to the movement in the UN today toward "democratization" and "transparency," that is, toward reducing the degree of control that a few delegations exert on the organization across the board. Many delegations have come to question the sincerity of the U.S. calls for reform and to wonder—tactfully in public and pointedly in private—whether there are deeper political motivations for American actions. Relatively few are convinced that the U.S. reform proposals as a whole either are intended to or will have the effect of strengthening the UN's capacity for doing its job. And none want to appear to be caving in to U.S. financial pressures.

Around Turtle Bay, tempers are short these days when questions of finance and reform surface. In response to a query about further reform steps at a December 1998 press conference, the normally unflappable secretary-general responded testily that "I think we should be allowed to focus on our work and not face constant harassment of reform, reform, reform. We have done enough. It is an ongoing process. We want to focus on our essential tasks."[42] Two weeks later, Ambassador Richard Sklar of the U.S. Mission to the UN used decidedly undiplomatic language to characterize the General Assembly negotiations that led to a slight increase in the UN budget outline for 2000–2001 after years of no growth. "It was a frustrating exercise dominated by those who don't pay and therefore don't care what we spend," he told a reporter, blaming four states by name, Algeria, Cuba, Pakistan, and Syria, which he labeled "four irrational, unreasonable . . . reactionary states that claim to represent the developing world and are only talking for themselves."[43]

All of this, naturally, has fueled speculation about whether the United States is seeking to downgrade the UN, to reexert control over it, or to distance itself from the world body. Some even ask whether the real objective is to reshuffle the organization's substantive priorities through bureaucratic and structural adjustments? Why, some wonder, would a great power like the United States give higher place to the efficiency of the organization than to its effectiveness and programmatic priorities, to how it works than to what it does? Does this mean that the United States now places so little value on the activities and programs of the world body that costs have become the controlling issue in U.S.-UN relations? Others ask, if the UN is seen in Washington to be doing the wrong things, pursuing purposes that do not serve American national interests, then why would the United States want it to do so more efficiently? Such circular and layered reasoning may sound to Americans like the stuff of political paranoia, but to others, U.S. policies have been inexplicable, at best.

Delegates from many developing countries appear convinced that the real U.S. objective is to trim the development side of the UN's work, while selectively boosting its peace and security operations when they serve American security interests. They also tend to have an exaggerated sense of U.S. power, especially over the office of secretary-general. They worry that the reform process could have an unforeseen and unfavorable impact on the balance of political power within the organization, leaving the developing countries in an even weaker position. These fears, which are pervasive among much of the UN secretariat as well, were expressed forthrightly by Iqbal Haji, a veteran international civil servant writing in 1997:

> The core of the US demand is this: cut the economic work of the UN . . . and transfer the resources to the "law and order" functions. Without a clear understanding of this issue of central importance to the US, there is no amount of restructuring the UN can undertake that will satisfy the sole super-

power. . . . The powers-that-be in the US . . . regard the developing world
either as basket cases (hence the emphasis on "humanitarian aid") or as competitors for global markets and hence a threat to their economic security.
Either way, helping the third world develop their economies makes less sense
to many in the West.[44]

What many defenders of the UN's development programs have failed to
acknowledge, however, is that the U.S. retreat from the UN's peacekeeping
ambitions came about even more sharply, so development has hardly been
the only place where the United States has questioned the effectiveness of
UN operations. Nor have Americans been alone in their concerns about the
effectiveness of UN development efforts. The Nordics, for example, have
long been in the forefront in both supporting and criticizing the UN approach toward development.[45]

Given the decades-old American interest in revitalizing the work of the
organization, it might well be asked instead why the United States has sought
so little in the successive waves of UN reform campaigns. When Rosemary
Righter of the *Times* of London asked a senior U.S. official in 1987 why the
U.S. reform proposals were essentially negative, she was told that "the problem with a positive agenda is that you can never tell in the UN what will
come out at the other end. The best proposal can have disastrous results. The
environment is not yet good enough to take major initiatives."[46] It would
appear, then, that the ambivalence that U.S. officials feel about the multilateral process itself has served to dampen American expectations about what
it is possible to achieve in the way of deep and durable reform in the world
body. Given these doubts, few policymakers or policy influentials in the
United States still harbor any expectations that they will be able to remold
the UN to conform neatly with American preferences and priorities.

Both American commentators and UN officials, moreover, have responded that the desire to see the UN well managed stems from a sincere
commitment to the world body's programs and purposes. As this author has
testified before Congress, those who value what the United Nations is seeking to achieve should take special care to see that its limited human and
material assets are used in as effective and focused a manner as possible.[47]
The organization's supporters should be—and figures such as Brian
Urquhart, Sadako Ogata, Elliot Richardson, Maurice Strong, Erskine
Childers, and Richard Stanley have been—in the vanguard of those seeking
deep and durable reform of its operations, bureaucracy, and procedures.[48]
Americans are hardly alone either in expressing such sentiments or in

putting forward creative and practical reform proposals. As Kofi Annan has put it, "an effective and efficient United Nations—a United Nations which is focused, coherent, responsive and cost-effective—is more needed than ever" given the "unprecedented demands and opportunities" it is facing.[49]

Some of the UN's strongest supporters in Congress, such as Senator John F. Kerry, have sounded this theme. In 1993 the Massachusetts Democrat contended that the UN "cannot succeed without what amounts to 'tough love' from the United States."[50] As then ambassador Madeleine K. Albright added, "with friendship comes responsibility. . . . I will continue to tell it like it is."[51] Three years later, in 1996, she asserted that "wasteful practices are neither inevitable nor tolerable. Given the nature of the UN's work, they literally take food from the mouths of the hungry and the means of survival from those in desperate need."[52]

From this perspective, those who look the other way when scarce resources are squandered are the ones showing a lack of commitment to the UN's core purposes. Having served for a year as under-secretary-general for administration and management under Boutros-Ghali, former U.S. attorney general Richard Thornburgh laments the "shoot the messenger rather than read the message mentality that infects much of the management bureaucracy within the U.N." (at that time, at least). Although he suggested that, in terms of "fraud, waste and abuse," the UN "is no different, and perhaps no better or no worse than agencies of the U.S. Government, our States, other nationalities," the problem in his view was that the UN had been doing "precious little" about it.[53] The harsher critics of the organization go further, contending that the management and accountability problems within the world body have become so acute and so pervasive as to compromise its effectiveness in terms of its capacity to perform even its priority functions. For example, Stefan Halper, a media commentator and official in the Nixon, Ford, and Reagan administrations, charges that "the United Nations has become a Kafkaesque bureaucracy beset by inefficiency, systemic corruption and misconceived programs." He concludes that unless the UN is "fundamentally reorganized . . . in a relatively short time, it may cease to exist."[54]

Whether one believes that these matters should be treated as determining factors in the U.S.-UN relationship, there is no doubt that they have come to contribute significantly to the depth and breadth of America's contemporary ambivalence toward the United Nations in particular and toward international organizations in general. Throughout the effort to attain a "grand bargain," the Clinton administration has been caught between a rock and a hard place, unable to deliver either the congressional or the UN side of the proposed bargain. Ironically and sadly, in terms of steps to improve UN performance significantly, neither the administration nor Congress has proposed anything that could even faintly qualify as grand. It is a great deal of fuss about rather little when viewed from the perspective either of the founders' high purposes or of the kind of deep and durable restructuring the organization really needs. Nevertheless, as the muddle thickens, the political stakes, for both the United States and the UN, appear to be rising along with the escalating congressional demands on the world body.

The Odd Couple: Congress and UN Reform

Congress' interest in UN reform is certainly understandable, at times even constructive and commendable, but the way it has been expressed over the past decade has tended to complicate an already difficult process. The UN is a collection of governments, not parliaments. The latter often play central roles in shaping national foreign policies and in appropriating funds for international activities, but it is governments that have standing to represent member states in intergovernmental forums and to negotiate bilaterally and multilaterally with other countries. The fact that Congress has been permitted to dominate U.S. relationships with the world body in recent years, in fact to use its power of the purse to define the terms of U.S. participation, has left the UN and its other member states in a perplexing position. They cannot afford either to ignore congressional mandates or to become embroiled in American domestic politics, whether between parties or between branches of government. Most officials and diplomats at the UN accept, however grudgingly, that the organization has little choice but to make accommodations to American power to some degree. And a number of delegations and UN officials appear to have more quiet sympathy with parts of the U.S. reform agenda than they care to express publicly. But even the process of accommodation becomes a puzzling proposition when the United States expresses itself with multiple voices that seem to have divergent agendas and when the reform goal posts are pushed back again and again.

None of this helps to build confidence in American motives or objectives. The distance between Turtle Bay and Capitol Hill in terms of reliable communications, shared values, and mutual trust could not be greater. In part this stems from the established practice of largely communicating through intermediaries—whether the executive branch, nongovernmental actors, or the media—in which neither side has full confidence. This, in turn, encourages stereotypes of irresponsible, spendthrift, aggrandizing UN bureaucrats and of ignorant, reactionary, isolationist members of Congress. Boutros-Ghali becomes a threat to American sovereignty, Kofi Annan enjoys a remarkably brief honeymoon, and Jesse Helms is caricatured as the source of all that ails the U.S.-UN relationship, as if these problems are of recent vintage. Under such circumstances, it comes as no surprise that the UN community on the whole has greeted congressional reform initiatives with a degree of suspicion about ulterior motives matched only by the skepticism with which initial UN reform measures have been greeted on Capitol Hill.

In this sense, the recent reform campaign at the UN, though unprecedented in scope and ambition, opened on a sour note. Congress said "reform or else," making it seem like a punishment for bad behavior and a concession to American power. Other delegations had little faith that Congress would appropriate the arrears even if all of its demands were met in full. Nor was there any assurance that Washington would not come up with a new set of benchmarks a year or two down the road, since Congress was already asking for much more than the Clinton administration initially had and some legislators were arguing that the "grand bargain" did not go nearly far enough in trimming the world body. Both sides of the U.S.-UN tug-of-war have long memories, a fact that gives scant reason for confidence or optimism either about the UN's capacity to reform or about Congress' willingness to meets its financial obligations. Credibility and trust have been in short supply on all sides.

Like other levers of national power, financial threats appear to be most credible and effective when used selectively, targeted carefully, and, if possible, coupled with some incentives. The secretary-general has always been more susceptible to financial pressures than are other sovereign member states. Financial threats, therefore, have been most productive when directed to those largely administrative matters over which the office of the secretary-general has some control rather than to those questions requiring broad cooperation from the rest of the membership, such as shifts in assessment scales, program mandates, or decisionmaking procedures. In a multilateral body like the UN, moreover, multinational appeals are generally given more weight and have greater influence than those undertaken unilaterally. Wherever possible, it is helpful to recruit partners, preferably from several parts of the world, before launching new initiatives that will require action by any of the large intergovernmental bodies. At the very least, it makes it easier for other countries to save face rather than appearing to bend to unilateral U.S. demands.

These rules for effective UN diplomacy may reflect the lessons of experience, but they still prove problematic for UN critics on Capitol Hill. Congress, quite simply, is not organized, equipped, or legally competent to conduct multilateral diplomacy. That is the province of the executive branch, which readily includes members of Congress in U.S. delegations to international bodies but which would hardly encourage Congress either to conduct its own foreign policy or to develop independent alliances with legislators in other countries in order to put forward a transnational and parliamentary united front in the world body. The unilateral manipulation of dues payments by Congress has already crippled U.S. relations with the UN. American legislators have been determined to send a message both to the UN and to the White House, with full recognition that withholdings are a blunt and often ineffective instrument that undermines efforts to fine-tune U.S. foreign policy or to put U.S.-UN relations on an even keel and a predictable course.

Some members of Congress, of course, are still willing to speak up for the need to fulfill U.S. financial obligations to the UN and to question whether further withholdings will forward the UN reform agenda.[55] But their numbers appear to be dwindling. Although their sentiments reflect long-standing tenets about the need to meet America's international commitments, they contrast sharply with the deep sense of mistrust of multilateral arrangements and agreements that has been voiced with growing frequency in congressional commentary of recent years. Contending that "none of the arrears will be paid if reforms are not achieved," Senator Grams asserted that even though such a position had not been well received by other member states, "being a leader means doing what is right, even when it is not popular."[56] Such unilateralist sentiments, it appears, are becoming mainstream on Capitol Hill these days.[57]

The prevalent view on the Hill was succinctly summarized by Representative Smith, who said that the UN "is too big, it spends too much, and many of its programs and specialized agencies truly are out of control. And, yes, we Americans have been paying for more than our share of U.N. expenses."[58] Few legislators would question these conclusions, although some express doubt about whether financial withholding is the way to deal with them. There is a spectrum of views, as well, on the question of whether protecting U.S. sovereignty should be a major concern of reform efforts (see chapter 3).[59]

In recent years, the drive on Capitol Hill to reform the UN has been led by those who to begin with were the most skeptical of what the organization does and stands for. It is as if the foxes have decided to remodel the chicken coop. Internationalists have joined the chorus at times and on particular issues, but rarely have they been in the lead.[60] The reform issue, moreover, has been cast largely along partisan lines, with Republican ardor on the Hill for perfecting the UN having risen precipitously with the arrival of a Democrat in the White House. At times, especially in the area of peace-keeping, the critics appear to be using the UN as a front for attacks aimed ultimately at the president's conduct of foreign and security policy. The paucity of accurate and timely information on these questions in Wash-ington, moreover, has contributed to what often appears to be a disconnect between reform progress at the UN and attitudes on the Hill. All of this, nat-urally, has fed the pervasive skepticism at the UN and in other countries about congressional sincerity about making the UN a more effective instru-ment for achieving its charter principles.

Doubts about the depth of Washington's commitment to real UN reform, of course, are not directed solely at Capitol Hill. The Clinton administration, due to its own tardiness in making appointments as well as to Senate delays in their confirmation, has rarely been in a position to field its first team when planning or pursuing its reform agenda in UN forums. These gaps were especially glaring during Clinton's first term, when con-gressional attitudes toward the world organization took a decisive turn for the worse. For half of these first four years, the key post of assistant secretary of state for international organization affairs was vacant. And for more than half of this period, the newly created position of U.S. representative to the UN for management and reform—the point person for moving the reform agenda forward in diplomatic circles and at the UN—went unfilled. During the most critical year of reform negotiations at the UN, from the spring of 1996 to the spring of 1997, both posts were vacant. Senator Grams has pointedly complained, moreover, that Ambassador Richard Sklar, the U.S. representative at the UN on these matters, missed many of the key negoti-ating sessions on UN budget guidelines for 2000–2001 during the fall of 1998 because the State Department had also assigned him to assist with reconstruction work for Bosnia.[61] As of June 1999, the United States had gone almost a year without a permanent envoy to the UN (although Richard Holbrooke's nomination appeared to be close to gaining Senate confirmation). True, a certain amount of turnover is inevitable, and the Senate Foreign Relations Committee has hardly been expeditious in its han-dling of the president's foreign affairs appointments across the board. Yet the repeated failure of the Clinton administration to keep its UN team at full strength has reinforced the prevalent impression at the UN and on Capitol Hill that this issue holds a relatively low priority in its plans and policies.

The core questions, in any case, remain: is Congress willing to live with the ups and downs, the trade-offs and compromises that characterize truly multilateral organizations? And do members of Congress care about the work of the UN as much as they desire to lower its costs, and the U.S. share of them? If they are uncomfortable with multilateral decisionmaking, indifferent to the activities of the organization, and doubtful about whether these programs serve U.S. national interests, then the UN will remain extremely vulnerable to further withholdings or other strictures emanating from Congress at any time and with little notice, reform or no reform. No senator has devoted more time and effort to the question of reforming, or taming, the world body than Jesse Helms. It was hardly reassuring, therefore, to hear the chairman of the Senate Foreign Relations Committee comment in a 1996 hearing that "passage of the Kassebaum-Solomon bill . . . sent a clear message if ever there was one to the United Nations either to reform or die. . . . The United Nations has neither reformed nor has it died. The time has come for it to do one or the other. You could flip a coin as far as I am concerned."[62] His "flip" throwaway line suggests that it matters little to him whether the organization is rejuvenated or eliminated, hardly an encouraging attitude for someone poised "to save the UN," as the title to his 1996 *Foreign Affairs* article proclaims. Furthermore, if reform could accomplish so little, because the organization is so insignificant, then why did the senior senator from North Carolina devote so much effort during the following two years to reaching a "grand bargain" with the Clinton administration? Would the savings be so large, or is the threat to American values and sovereignty so great? Or do the answers have more to do with his role, track record, and legacy as committee chairman? Whatever the reasons, Helms's characteristic candor reveals much of the pervasive ambivalence, even indifference, of many influential members of Congress to the fate of the United Nations. For these reasons, as the following chapter details, questions of finance have come to the fore in debates about U.S. participation in the UN far more than in debates about other more expensive aspects of foreign policy given a higher place among national priorities.

CHAPTER NINE

Who Should Pay for the UN?

Rarely have so many important people taken so much time to spend so little.

—SENATE SUBCOMMITTEE
ON THE UNITED NATIONS CHARTER, 1954

Perhaps this House cannot take us out of the United Nations, but through its control of the purse strings of America we can starve it to death.

—REPRESENTATIVE JOHN T. WOOD, 1952

The payment record of many U.N. members is so shameful that they could not get credit at a 5 and 10 cent store.

—REPRESENTATIVE EDGAR W. HEISTAND, 1962

Nothing is more important to our foreign policy at this moment than paying our UN dues and regaining our credibility and leadership abroad.

—REPRESENTATIVE JOHN E. PORTER, 1998

IT IS PROBABLY a good thing that the preparatory conferences at Bretton Woods and San Francisco did not attempt to tackle the question of who would pay what portion of the costs of the grand new experiment in international cooperation: the delegates might still be squabbling. Given how thorny this issue has been ever since, and the way it has repeatedly brought out the narrowest and most combative instincts of the member states, the UN's high-minded founders might have become discouraged about the prospects for cooperation among nations on the much larger political, economic, and security issues of the day. Attention to financial details, moreover, might well have distracted them from their higher calling of designing the core institutional framework for the postwar world. Finances, like the reform issues considered in the previous chapter, have since consumed an inordinate amount of time and attention both in the United Nations and in the halls of Congress.[1]

From the UN's earliest days, U.S. legislators have asked why other member states, if they shared the U.S. enthusiasm for the new body, were not readier to make greater financial sacrifices for its realization. (Such comments, of course, were reciprocated by representatives of other countries offended by U.S. "penny-pinching.") Despite the difficult postwar conditions, it should have been possible for other members to do more, said the Americans, to support this relatively modest but supposedly essential cornerstone of peace. Then, as now, there was little evidence that congressional concerns about UN spending and the U.S. share of UN dues stemmed from strong public sentiment. A 1943 public opinion survey, for example, found that roughly two out of three Americans said that they would be willing to "pay more taxes for a few years while the new union was being organized even if people in the other countries couldn't afford to pay much." In a January 1951 poll, only 2 percent cited costs of the U.S. share of the financial burden as a reason to consider withdrawing from the UN.[2] Apparently the gap between congressional and public sentiment on funding issues was as large in the 1940s as it is in the 1990s (for survey data, see chapter 10).

During the 1945 debate on the ratification of the UN charter, which more resembled a testimonial than an open inquiry, several senators questioned the scope and size of likely U.S. financial commitments. Henrik Shipstead, one of only two senators to vote against ratification, warned that America was "involved in a financial race with disaster" and that "if the United States, as the world's milk cow, should run dry, not only these novel international experiments would die for lack of nourishment, but so would men's hopes that they should see any such things as the 'four freedoms' extended to supply their most desperate necessities."[3] Although he favored the charter, Senator Howard A. Smith, R-N.J., stressed his strong opposition "to the United States acting in the role of Santa Claus for the rest of the world, and above all, for trying in any way to establish ill-advised WPA's [Work Projects Administrations] throughout foreign countries." Elaborating on these traditional Republican and anti–New Deal views, he concluded that "the worst thing we could do for the world would be to let the impression get abroad that we are expecting to pay the bills. We cannot help individuals or nations by doing for them what they very definitely must do for themselves."[4]

The United States was not the only country seeking international organization on the cheap. Few, if any, of the member states seemed in any rush to pay for the new body, despite all of the grand statements about its central role in establishing a new era of peace and harmony. In his report to Congress on the opening General Assembly session in London, Senator Arthur Vandenberg commented that America's "provisional share is 25 percent. In other words, the United States will spend for peace, on this account far less

per annum than it spent per hour on war."[5] Unfortunately, his upbeat summary was premature. When the General Assembly's Committee on
Contributions—a group of experts asked to determine the relative capacity
to pay of the various member states—reported its initial findings to the next
Assembly session in the fall of 1946, the United States was asked to pay
about half of the bill (49.89 percent, to be precise).[6] Reportedly the U.S. delegation was alarmed that other delegations favored "the imposition of what
amounts to 'international taxation.'"[7] This would be resented by the
American public, it was said, and might make Congress "unwilling to
appropriate the necessary funds, jeopardizing American participation in the
United Nations."

Taking, as usual, a higher road in public, Vandenberg assured the other
UN delegates that the United States was not seeking to save money, despite
its historic concern about "taxation without representation," but rather "to
save the United Nations from an unwholesome fiscal climate in which our
united and common judgments—our sovereign equalities—are not calculated to thrive." In his view, a 25 percent ceiling would be low enough so that
the largest donor would not be able to exert "fiscal control" over the new
organization, which he apparently was willing to forgo for the sake of larger
principles. If "the total burden would fall on a few states and . . . the size of
the budget would be inconsequential to many states," he cautioned, then
"the few, in sheer self-defense, would probably insist upon special rights of
audit and control which are at variance with the 'sovereign equality' to
which we are indispensably devoted."[8] Today, the UN's financial structure
has indeed come to resemble the highly asymmetrical situation that
Vandenberg warned against. A scant ten months after Vandenberg's statement, moreover, the Senate sent a three-member team to investigate the
world body's financial dealings, thereby exercising a degree of unilateral
financial and administrative oversight of the world body. Apparently other
legislators saw nothing improper in attempting to exercise some degree of
"fiscal control."

The United States, recognizing the postwar dislocations in much of the
rest of the world, agreed to pay up to one-third of the UN's costs, plus an
additional amount for a single year. The final agreement for 1947 was
39.84 percent. In the ensuing years, the United States managed to negotiate
one reduction after another, but resistance to lowering the ceiling was so
strong that it was not until 1973, more than a quarter century later, that
Vandenberg's "provisional" figure of 25 percent was attained. It even took
seven years of hard bargaining before the United States was able to shed the

"one year only" premium and get down to the agreed 33.3 percent figure. As Dean Acheson commented, the issue was especially heated in 1952, because "both Assembly and Congress were deeply interested in the proportion of UN budget expenses to be assessed against the United States, but for opposite reasons—the Assembly to keep it up, the Congress to get it down." The product, in his words, was "acrimonious debate," followed by eventual compromise.[9]

The unpleasant and at times unproductive flavor of the discussion among the member states on adjusting the assessment scale also can be seen in excerpts from a December 1951 statement of Representative John M. Vorys, R-Ohio, before the General Assembly's Fifth (administrative and budgeting) Committee:

> The organization is based on the sovereign equality of all members. Does this mean equality of rights but inequality in obligations? . . . I doubt whether any state would submit overlong to overtaxation and underrepresentation in an international organization. I also doubt whether this organization should be overdependent overlong upon any nation or small group of nations because of the size of their contribution or contributions. . . . Everyone nearly who has spoken has complained about having to pay his share of the bill, and that is certainly a normal situation.[10]

Despite these pleas and veiled threats, plus complaints about America's heavy human and financial sacrifices for the "UN's war" in Korea, the U.S. share was reduced that year only from 38.92 to 36.90 percent.

Vorys's experience in the Fifth Committee, which was all too typical, raises questions about the U.S. practice of assigning congressional delegates to that Assembly committee. Although a natural fit with Congress' fiscal responsibilities, this practice has reinforced the tendency on the Hill to see the UN through a financial and administrative prism, hardly a flattering way to view the organization. American legislators have had far less experience visiting or examining UN operations in the field. As a result they often have seemed to be much better informed about what the UN spends than about what it does. At times this perspective may provide a healthy antidote to the enthusiasms of U.S. or UN policymakers pushing for expanded UN programs in areas of particular interest. But it also helps to explain the differences in executive branch and congressional attitudes that have so often made it difficult for the United States to speak with a single voice and to pursue a coherent and consistent strategy within international bodies.

These differences in priorities and perspectives, moreover, have constituted a prime source for America's inconsistent and ambivalent policies toward international organizations.

Burden Sharing and Legal Obligations

As is abundantly evident even by this brief account, congressional unhappiness with the financial practices of the United Nations has deep roots. Before the infant UN had even reached its second birthday, some members of Congress were already incensed by the long list of member states in arrears on their dues payments.[11] Although most legislators accepted the necessity for the United States to meet its financial obligations to the world body, a vocal and often vitriolic group of southern Democrats and conservative Republicans repeatedly questioned the equity of the U.S. burden throughout the UN's first decade. Among their favored themes were that the United States was being "suckered" by the other member states, that U.S. foreign aid was underwriting the dues payments of others, that U.S. taxpayers were subsidizing communist propaganda through the UN, that it was unhealthy for any international body to be so dependent on the financial support of one member state, and that Congress has a constitutional responsibility to decide and oversee how taxpayers' funds are spent.[12]

Other than venting their anger and pressuring the executive branch to convince other member states to change the rules and assessment scale, however, what could members of Congress do about all of this? This was, and remains, a frustrating dilemma for many on Capitol Hill. On the one hand, Representative Frederic R. Coudert Jr., R-N.Y., emphasized in a key 1953 debate that "this House at this time has no choice but to accept these appropriations, to vote them, so that the United States may carry out its elementary conventional obligations on an international plane."[13] Such appeals to the legal and treaty requirements of membership apparently fell then, as they so often seem to today, on deaf ears. Both the House and the Senate, in nonbinding resolutions, voted to limit U.S. funding to international organizations, as of 1953, to no more than one-third of their budgets (the base agreed to in 1946).[14] In doing so, Congress put itself on record that although it still supported the principle of collective financial responsibility in theory, it should be able to decide unilaterally the ceiling to be placed on the U.S. portion of the burden. Then, as now, it was widely believed on Capitol Hill that such unilateral actions or threats were required to persuade other nations to carry their fair share of the collective financial bargain.

Even though frustration with the multilateral process for apportioning dues had led Congress to unilaterally impose a ceiling on American contributions, U.S. representatives at the UN continued to invoke Vandenberg's argument as the ultimate purpose of this effort to lower U.S. dues. According to their circular logic, the goal was to use unilateral financial leverage to the point at which America's share of the finances would be so low as to prevent it from using this tool any longer, that is, to make financial power a waning asset.

This strategy fell short not only on logical and legal grounds, but also because it was based on static assumptions about the behavior of other member states. American threats to withhold contributions and its actions to lower the ceiling on its payments were aimed largely at getting others to carry more of the burden, not at crippling the organization's programs and activities. Matters got a good deal more complicated in the late 1950s and the early 1960s, when Washington wanted the UN to do more, especially in keeping the peace in the Middle East and the Congo, that would entail higher costs and experiments with new methods of financing. This proved to be a particularly inauspicious period for expanding horizons: a time of withholdings by scores of countries, including the Soviet Union and France, two of the five permanent members of the Security Council, and of the most serious constitutional and financial crisis in the organization's history.

This challenge to the resiliency and integrity of the world body began with the dispatch of two peacekeeping operations that initially engaged broad support from the membership: the United Nations Emergency Force (UNEF I) to monitor the cease-fire between Egypt and Israel in late 1956 and the United Nations Operation in the Congo (UNOC) in July 1960 to assist the newborn government of the Republic of the Congo.[15] In both cases, several member states objected to making assessments for peacekeeping operations compulsory. The Congo operation, moreover, ran into changing conditions on the ground and growing East-West differences in New York, leaving the UN forces in the middle of a cold war struggle for influence in the region. A number of countries that had maintained solid payment records to the organization began to withhold payments linked to these two missions, plunging the world body into an increasingly severe financial and political crisis.

By the end of 1961 the United Nations had accumulated a deficit of $114 million, largely from the two peacekeeping missions, $74.7 million in the Congo account and $26.4 million for the Middle East.[16] Some seventy member states, about two-thirds of the membership, had failed to pay their share of one or both missions.[17] The General Assembly sought an advisory opinion from the International Court of Justice. In a split decision on July 20, 1962, the world court held that peacekeeping expenditures "constituted 'expenses of the Organization' within the meaning of Article 17, paragraph 2 of the Charter," which states that they "shall be borne by the Members as apportioned by the General Assembly."[18] Five months later, the Assembly passed, largely along East-West lines, a resolution accepting the court's advisory opinion. Two urgent questions remained: How would the immediate UN financial crisis be handled? And would article 19—which stipulates that when a member state falls two years behind in its payments to the world body, it loses its vote in the Assembly—be enforced? In the end, neither question received a satisfactory answer, and the legally and politically ambivalent results of the financial crisis of the early 1960s laid the groundwork for the subsequent ones of the mid-1980s and late 1990s.

Meeting the Immediate Crisis: UN Bonds

In an effort to meet the urgent financial crisis, the General Assembly in late 1961 authorized the secretary-general to issue interest-bearing bonds of up to $200 million, with the principal to be repaid through the regular budget over twenty-five years.[19] Eventually about 85 percent of the available bonds were sold, enough to provide short-term financial solvency for the world body but not enough either to show solid political support from the membership as a whole or to reassure increasingly skeptical members of Congress. Moreover, in the years that followed, several member states withheld that portion of their annual dues equivalent to the amount of the principal to be repaid each year, creating a long-term, if modest, deficit in UN accounts.

During the 1962 congressional debate on the UN bonds, four principal strands of argument emerged. President Kennedy, his foreign policy team, and their supporters in Congress posed the issue as a test of faith in the world organization, as a way to overcome Soviet obstructionism, and as a financially prudent means of exerting American leadership in the world. Skeptics argued that once again the United States was being asked to carry most of the burden while other member states shirked their full responsibilities. A smaller group concurred that something needed to be done to help the UN but said that the proposed stopgap measure was not the best way to go about building a dependable and durable financial foundation for the beleaguered body. A fourth theme, from a broader perspective, stressed that the real problems facing the UN were political and structural, not financial.

President Kennedy, in a message sent to the House on January 30, 1962, painted UN dues as a bargain for national security and underlined that "members that participate in the privilege of membership should participate also in its obligations." Moreover, he wrote, "failure to act would serve the interests of the Soviet Union, which has been particularly opposed to the operation in the Congo and which voted against this plan as part of the consistent Communist effort to undermine the United Nations and undercut its new Secretary General."[20] Most of the vocal supporters, as in the past, came from the Democratic side of the aisle. Senator John J. Sparkman, D-Ala., the acting chairman of the Senate Foreign Relations Committee, calling this "a crucial moment of confidence and support" for the UN, noted that "although we may be disappointed in the response of others the United Nations is too important to us for this country to waver now in its support."[21]

There were plenty of doubters in Congress, including some wavering Democrats, and the purchase of bonds was only accepted after much debate and significant modifications in the initial plan.[22] Several Republicans fretted that Uncle Sam once again was being played for a sucker. Speaking in favor of a compromise bill, which eventually was accepted, to peg U.S. bond purchases to those of others, Senator Winston L. Prouty, R-Vt., asserted that it would "make it unmistakably clear that we are willing to help put the United Nations house in order, but that we are not ready to pay anyone's back rent." The basic problem, in his view, was that "in the General Assembly there is a parity of power without parity of responsibility."[23]

To many legislators, the worsening crisis raised doubts about the political viability, as well as the financial health, of the world body. "Isn't it rather discouraging to feel that the United Nations are so uncooperative," commented Senator Homer E. Capehart, R-Ind. "[D]oes it mean that the United Nations are falling apart, or they can't get together?" Noting that he had voted for every UN appropriation in his eight years in the House, Representative John F. Baldwin Jr., R-Calif., announced that he would not support the bond issue because "we will never solve this problem by 'picking up the check' every time there is a deficit." Echoing one of Vandenberg's favorite themes, Senator Bourke B. Hickenlooper, R-Iowa, questioned whether the bond issue "wouldn't . . . turn the United Nations pretty much into a U.S. organization?" This was not a test of faith in the UN, argued Senator Aiken of Vermont, but "a question of financial ethics." According to Representative

Thomas M. Pelly, R-Wash., "a regular assessment is the only answer if the United Nations is to succeed. . . . Otherwise as an effective organization I would say it is doomed."[24]

The bond package did offer some temporary financial relief for the world organization, but the broad-ranging debate it engendered in Congress also marked a turning point in the nature and sources of criticism of the UN. "There was a time when the United Nations was criticized solely by its enemies," Aiken remarked. "I think it is perfectly proper for the old, longtime friends of the U.N. to insist that it so conduct its affairs that it may live and be effective far into the future." Reasserting Congress' oversight responsibilities, he contended that if the UN survives "it will be because some people have had the courage to insist that it carry on its operations as a sound, solvent, and efficient organization; and we cannot do that without opening the door and looking inside to see what is going on"—something Congress was to do with increasing frequency in the years ahead.[25]

One of those newly critical friends of the UN was Senator Mike Mansfield, D-Mont., who had just served on the U.S. delegation to the General Assembly. "It is not finances which are at the heart of the United Nations' problems," he stressed, "it is the procedural distortion between the power to make decisions and the power, the will, and responsibility to carry out decisions which has produced these difficulties in the United Nations." The result, in his view, was "the air of detachment from reality," while Soviet vetoes had turned the Security Council into a "center for exacerbating" great power tensions. The United States had then further distorted the organization's structure, he argued, by "seeking to shift to the General Assembly the influence, the authority, and the responsibility in political questions which were assigned by the charter to the Security Council." And, he continued:

> The General Assembly has receded from its original paramount charter function of an international forum from whence the moral force of the world could thunder on the great issues of world peace and progress. . . . The thunder grows fainter as the Assembly tends to evolve into the steps of the local courthouse, for the transaction—on a vast and international scale—of trivial politics.[26]

These were not the shrill charges of the far right, which had long had a hollow ring, but the much more telling and credible concerns of one who feared that the UN was becoming its own worst enemy.

Paradise Lost: The Article 19 Crisis

In the polarized atmosphere of the early 1960s, key delegations treated the question of how to finance peacekeeping missions as a matter both of high principle and of high politics. Yet the result of the ensuing political struggle was a compromise that fudged the fundamental principles involved and that planted the seeds for further financial turmoil down the road. Although the World Court opinion and subsequent General Assembly vote convinced several smaller countries to meet their peacekeeping obligations in full, the major holdouts, including the Soviet Union and France, adamantly refused to budge from their interpretation of principle. By the time the General Assembly was to meet in the fall of 1964, Moscow's total withholdings were expected to surpass the equivalent "of the contributions due from it for the preceding two full years," thus potentially triggering the article 19 penalty of loss of vote in the Assembly. France would find itself in a similar position a year later. This created a dilemma never before faced by the organization: what to do if a key founding member, a superpower and a permanent member of the Security Council no less, refused to meet its financial obligations. By the end of the confrontation, both the UN and the United States had blinked, but not before Congress, speaking with one voice from both sides of the aisle, had its say.

Edgar F. Foreman, R-Tex., reflecting the prevailing mood on the Hill, declared that "there is a simple policy: 'No money, no vote'—let the U.N. enforce it." During the summer of 1964, members of both parties offered a series of amendments to the foreign aid bill designed to encourage delinquent member states to pay their UN bills. Representative Charles E. Bennett, D-Fla., proposed that the United States should withhold payments for any UN "program or activity which is contrary to the policies of the United States." Another amendment in the House would have barred U.S. funding of more than one-third of any UN program. A Senate amendment would have prohibited any foreign aid, unless the president requested a waiver, to any government that was more than a year behind in its payment to the UN for the regular budget or for peacekeeping and security operations. William Fulbright, the chairman of the Senate Foreign Relations Committee, opposed the amendment, cautioning that it could complicate America's "continuous diplomatic offensive" aimed at getting article 19 penalties enforced against "Soviet bloc countries" at the upcoming Assembly.[27]

None of these amendments passed, but a week later, on August 17, 1964, a concurrent sense of Congress resolution urging the enforcement of the provisions of article 19 was approved without opposition. Representative Gerald R. Ford, R-Mich., urged that the United States "be very hard and tough. There is no room for compromise." The House sponsor of the legislation, Edna F. Kelly, D-N.Y., pointing out that "some 15 member countries are more than 2 years behind in paying their assessments," repeated what had by then become a familiar congressional refrain that "there should be 'no representation without taxation' at the U.N." William S. Mailliard, R-Calif., emphasized that the Kennedy administration, in pushing for approval of the bond issue two years earlier, had "made a commitment to the Members of Congress that we would do this bailing out only with the understanding that Article 19 of the charter was fully enforced so far as the United States could enforce it." The purpose of the resolution, according to Dante Fascell, D-Fla., chairman of the House Subcommittee on International Organizations and Movements, was to "have a salutary effect in prompting the delinquent U.N. members to pay up their dues."[28]

In retrospect, several of the points voiced during the House debate sound as ironic as they were prophetic now that the tables are turned and it is the United States that is refusing to fulfill its obligations to the UN. Silvio Conte, R-Mass., worried about the impressions that withholdings by some member states would have on "a new nation coming into the organization." He fretted that "since these nations—many of them—are comparatively poorer, they might feel justified in avoiding these obligations. They might, in fact, point to certain richer nations as an example." In the words of Edmond A. Edmondson, D-Okla., "membership in the United Nations is not a one-way street, to be traveled only when things are going your own way. With participation goes responsibility." Finally, Robert B. Duncan, D-Ore., reminded his colleagues that "in passing this resolution, we must not forget that the day may come when the United States may disagree with the actions of the United Nations, to the support of which this same article 19 will commit us." Those rainy days did come, perhaps sooner than he expected, but few representatives would recall either his words or the ardor with which this resolution was cheered at the time.[29]

As the opening of the 1964 Assembly session approached, the signs of confrontation became more and more ominous. Nikita Khrushchev, the Soviet premier, told visiting UN secretary-general U Thant that Moscow "will walk out of the General Assembly and perhaps quit the United Nations altogether if its vote is taken away for nonpayment of bills."[30] France also refused to budge.[31] Wary of the growing "game of brinkmanship," a *New York Times* editorial called for a "compromise" that could "bridge the contradictory positions."[32] But rather than exploding, the Assembly session in essence imploded. Some U.S. officials continued to maintain that a consistently tough stance would have the dual advantage of easing congressional concerns and of firming support for the UN's financial integrity among other member states, thus making it more likely that when push came to shove, Moscow would have accepted a face-saving way out that would not have undermined the principle of collective responsibility embodied in articles 17 and 19.[33] Others in the Johnson administration preferred a less confrontational, if more ambiguous, course: to avoid voting altogether rather than to press the issue of whether the Soviets and others would be permitted to vote. In the end Ambassador Stevenson, reportedly on his own initiative, raised this option with his Soviet counterparts, who agreed that this would be a good way to postpone a clash that could seriously damage the world body.[34]

As a result of this shift in U.S. policy, the 1964–65 Assembly session managed—other than one vote to abandon voting—to act by consensus or to decide through unofficial balloting in the office of the President of the Assembly.[35] A Special Committee on Peacekeeping Operations was established to work through the political impasse, as well as to find a basis for future peacekeeping operations. On the last day of August 1965, the special committee reached a three-part consensus agreement that read as follows:

—That the General Assembly will carry on its work normally in accordance with its rules of procedure;

—That the question of the applicability of Article 19 of the charter will not be raised with regard to the United Nations Emergency Force and the United Nations Operation in the Congo;

—That the financial difficulties of the organization should be solved through voluntary contributions by Member States, with the highly developed countries making substantial contributions.[36]

In other words, Soviet and French peacekeeping arrears were set aside so that they would not count against their overall arrears under article 19. In this context, it is striking that the UN's two most serious financial crises—in the 1960s and 1990s—on the surface revolved around disputes among key member states about the oversight and financing of peacekeeping operations, which in turn stemmed from more fundamental struggles over power and authority in the world organization.

In his inaugural speech at the UN in August 1965, the new U.S. envoy to the UN, Ambassador Arthur Goldberg, confirmed the American view "that the concept of collective financial responsibility adopted by the United Nations in 1945 is a sound principle and a landmark in the practice of international organizations," that article 17 "is impeccably clear," and article 19 "clear beyond question." He went on to underline that the United States "cannot abandon our adherence to positions which we firmly believe to be constitutionally, legally, procedurally and administratively correct," although "the time is now for the General Assembly to get on with its heavy agenda, which is indeed the unfinished business of mankind." And, he issued his famous reservation: ". . . we must make it crystal clear that if any Member can insist on making an exception to the principle of collective financial responsibility with respect to certain activities of the Organization, the United States reserves the same option to make exceptions if, in our view, strong and compelling reasons exist for doing so. There can be no double standard among the Members of the Organization."[37] In the end, the United States continued to proclaim inviolable principle, while accepting something far less from others and asserting its own right to violate the same principles when expedient. At best, the outcome could inspire ambivalence.

In some ways, the muddled course of events should not have been so surprising. Leaving a degree of ambiguity was characteristic both of multilateral diplomacy in general and of the UN's traditional approach to conflict resolution, even within its own house. As Harlan Cleveland, then assistant secretary of state for international organization affairs, aptly put it, most member states had a "passionate determination to avoid a decision."[38] (The UN's passion for being indecisive, of course, contributes to the ambivalence of an American public looking for vision and clear-cut answers to tough questions.) There were practical reasons as well for opting for the less risky course. Everyone understood that a world organization without either one of the superpowers would soon come to resemble the League of Nations. In a world fraught with dangerous confrontations, the last thing one needed would be the break-up of the one organization assigned the task of trying to defuse existing or potential crises throughout the world. In the short run, at least, to high-level policymakers the costs to the UN's financial integrity must have seemed a price worth paying.[39] In terms of immediate political concerns, the precipitating event—the controversial Congo operation—had been completed, much to Washington's satisfaction, in mid-1964 in any case.

In the eyes of the public and its representatives in Congress, who had been led to believe that important principles were at stake, however, the arti-

cle 19 crisis was enormously damaging to what little integrity and pre-
dictability UN financing still retained. The principle of collective responsibility was left in limbo by the actions of three of the five permanent members
(and the Republic of China had itself accumulated substantial arrears by that
time). The Goldberg reservation, as well as the set-asides granted Moscow
and Paris, left the window to future selective withholdings wide open for
Congress or for other countries seeking to exercise unilateral financial leverage from time to time. Congress, given its budgetary responsibilities under the
Constitution, might well decide that it was as well positioned as the executive
to determine whether there were "strong and compelling reasons" for withholding funds from the UN. In light of the current financial crisis, it is worth
noting that a June 1998 report to Congress by the U.S. General Accounting
Office reminds the legislators of the Goldberg reservation and points out that
the Soviet and French arrears stemming from the 1964 crisis "are still counted
in the total unpaid contributions owed, but are not included in calculations
for article 19."[40] The GAO report also notes, however, that thirty-nine member states lost their vote under article 19 in early 1998, as those provisions
have been enforced with greater regularity in recent years.

The way the article 19 crisis was handled, moreover, particularly the
rapid retreat from principle by the Johnson administration, did nothing to
boost congressional and public confidence either in the United Nations or
in the executive branch. Not only was the financial integrity of the world
organization threatened, but much of the meaning and force of the notion
of an international legal obligation was lost, slipping from the firm ground
of absolute principle to the soft, shifting, and gray terrain of declarations of
national interest. As an October 1964 memorandum from the United States
to the UN missions of all other member states declared:

> It is not only that Article 19 means what it says—that the Member shall have
> no vote—it is that failure to apply the Article would be a violation of the
> Charter which would have far-reaching consequences.

> Failure to apply the Article would break faith with the overwhelming major-
> ity of Members who are paying their peacekeeping assessments—often at great
> sacrifice—as obligations binding under the Charter.

> Failure to apply the Article would be a repudiation of the International Court
> of Justice and of that rule of international law whose continued growth is vital
> for progress toward peace and disarmament.[41]

All of this has since come back to haunt U.S.-UN financial dealings and to help sour the overall relationship. For a time thirty-five years ago, at least, the United States had it right.

Legal Relativity and the Withholding Habit

Once the legal barriers to selective withholdings of payments to the UN began to crumble, the floodgates to further congressional questioning of U.S. obligations began to open wider and wider. What had started as a trickle in the early 1950s with efforts to set the ceiling on U.S. payments unilaterally had by the 1970s become a favorite tool of legislators seeking to shape American foreign policy choices, to record their disgruntlement about UN actions, or to score points with particular constituencies at home. Except in those cases where the administration was willing to make a strong legal and political case for full payments, the debates in Congress came to revolve more and more around issues of relativity and practicality: Would withholdings achieve the desired result? What were other member states doing? Were there better options? Political questions came to overshadow completely the legal considerations. As UN forums became less friendly environments in which to conduct U.S. foreign policy, the administration's case for the requirement of full, prompt, and unconditional payments became harder to make. The practical effect of asserting these standards and the primacy of international legal obligations—after all—was necessarily to limit congressional leverage and to stifle its voice in policymaking toward international organizations. From a political perspective, therefore, congressional questioning of these legal standards was understandable, if not justified.

The critical decade for the shift from legal to political factors in U.S. funding of the UN was the 1970s. During these years Beijing assumed China's UN seat, the United States cast its first vetoes in the Security Council, the Assembly equated Zionism with racism, and the nonaligned majority tried repeatedly to use the General Assembly and other UN forums to legislate sweeping changes in the substance of North-South relationships in ways detrimental to U.S. national interests and, in some cases, contrary to American values. In 1970 the United States refused for the first time to vote for the UN budget because of what Secretary of State William Rogers called "its unusually large increase of 14 percent, including an 8 percent pay increase for professionals in the Secretariat."[42] By the time that Ronald Reagan, the first American president openly skeptical about the value of international organization, was elected in 1980, the congressional habit of expressing displeasure with UN actions through threats of financial with-holdings was already well established.

The starkest sign of Congress' unwillingness to play by the old rules was the August 1985 Kassebaum-Solomon amendment, which required the withholding of one-fifth of U.S. dues payments until financially weighted voting in the General Assembly and the specialized agencies was achieved. No longer was Congress content with grumbling about UN financial and management questions, while largely acceding to executive authority for carrying out U.S. policies at the UN, including the negotiation with the other member states of legally binding assessment rates. The amendment was a departure not only because of its content, but also because of its co-sponsorship by Senator Nancy Landon Kassebaum. Her mainstream Kansas Republican lineage, moderate voice, and internationalist outlook had made her a popular and widely respected figure on Capitol Hill, and her amend-ment swept the Senate by a 71 to 13 margin.[43] Although later a bit sheepish about her choice of tactics, Kassebaum resolutely defended the need to take sharp, unilateral action to attract the attention of other member states to long-standing U.S. complaints about UN mismanagement and spending habits. Richard Lugar, chairman of the Senate Foreign Relations Committee and another moderate internationalist Republican, asserted that the action was needed "to send a signal to the United Nations" and to spur a process of negotiation concerning "proportionality with regard to our contribution."[44] Stunned by the unilateralism embodied in the congressional action, the twelve member states of the European Community protested to Secretary of State George P. Shultz on March 14, 1986, that the failure of the United States to meet its financial obligations to the world body "could lead to seri-ous political consequences." America's "selective adherence" to international law, they underlined, "erodes the very foundation of the international order."

As detailed earlier, this was hardly the first time that Congress had tried to legislate restrictions on U.S. payments to the UN, but in this case the executive branch responded in a new way. Rather than unequivocally assert-ing the nation's obligation to meet its agreed dues payments to the world organization as previous presidents had, the Reagan administration appeared to welcome the Kassebaum-Solomon amendment. Vernon Walters, then the U.S. envoy to the UN, told the Senate Foreign Relations Committee that the American delegation and its allies had been able to employ the congressional action "to restore the United Nations, not to destroy it."[45] Alan Keyes, then assistant secretary of state for international organization affairs, was unstinting in his praise for the legislation, which he saw as crucial to persuading other member states to accept the consensus rule in UN budgeting, something he considered to be a major breakthrough in the effort to protect the financial interests of the major donors. Referring to the consensus rule and other reforms adopted by the forty-first General Assembly, he told the House that:

> Nothing would have been accomplished absent the pressure generated by Congressionally mandated cutbacks in the U.S. contribution to the UN. Thanks to this pressure, the reform issue dominated the General Assembly's agenda. Thanks to this pressure, all recognized that credible results were essential. Thanks to this pressure, delegations reached an agreement incorporating the consensus principle.[46]

This striking shift in the executive branch stance on withholdings provided more than ample encouragement to hard-line UN skeptics on Capitol Hill to believe that it was high season for legislative assaults on the world body.

At the same time, Keyes argued that indiscriminate withholdings could be counterproductive, that funding should be turned off and on depending on the progress the UN was making toward U.S. objectives. Writing in the *New York Times* in September 1986, he commended "the leverage that our country gained with last year's constructive congressional restrictions on contributions," but he cautioned against further cutbacks that could undermine the reform effort.[47] Apparently some legislators had gotten in the habit of withholding and were reluctant to turn the financial spigot back on so quickly. In his view, the lesson was about the need to coordinate executive and congressional actions, about tactics not legality: "we have to appreciate how to use leverage responsibly." Through "a consolidation of effective leverage," he told the Senate Foreign Relations Committee, the United States would be "buying an institutional, structural change" at the world organization.[48]

Ironically it was President Reagan who, in the waning days of his second term, signaled that with some significant UN reforms in hand, it was time to place U.S.-UN relations on a more normal and positive footing. Senator Daniel Patrick Moynihan caricatured the turnabout as that of a lame-duck administration finally recognizing "that international law and international order is after all something in which the United States has an interest." He noted wryly that "a deathbed conversion is better than no conversion, and I believe in the salvation of souls."[49] In his final speech to the General Assembly, President Reagan commended the UN for its substantive work on terrorism, AIDs, and narcotics and for its enactment of "sweeping measures affecting personnel reductions, budgeting by consensus, and the establishment of programme priorities." Calling these steps "extremely important," Reagan stated that this reform progress "has allowed me to release funds withheld under congressional restrictions. I expect that the reform programme will continue and that further funds will be released in our new fiscal year."[50]

Before Reagan's final trip to the UN, the White House announced on September 13, 1988, that it had mandated an interagency study to "work out a multi-year plan to pay our arrearages to the United Nations," in which National Security Advisor General Colin Powell was to play a major part.[51] Congressional Democrats were quick to welcome what they termed an overdue action by the administration.[52] The task of actually fulfilling this commitment, and providing these carrots, of course, fell to Reagan's successor, President George Bush, as well as to Congress. Bush, who had represented the United States at the UN in the early 1970s and felt comfortable in its halls, was known as an ardent internationalist, despite his attacks during the campaign on the Democratic nominee, Michael Dukakis, for being soft on the UN and a weak-kneed multilateralist. During the second and third years of the Bush administration, Congress did consent to partial payments to the UN of U.S. arrears, before its attitudes toward the UN again soured and its penchant for withholdings returned.

The ebb and flow pattern of U.S. payments to the UN is likely to persist as long as influential members of Congress question whether the nation is legally obligated to meet its assessed dues, whether for the regular budget or for peacekeeping. During the autumn of 1997, the Senate Foreign Relations Committee, in a novel interpretation, decided that the UN charter "in no way creates a 'legal obligation' on the United States Congress to authorize and appropriate" dues payments. In its view, "the United States Constitution places the authority to tax United States citizens and to authorize and appropriate those funds solely in the power of the United States Congress."[53] John Bolton asserted at about the same time that it was "flatly incorrect" to say that the United States had incurred legal obligations to pay its dues when it ratified the UN charter. In his view, "treaties have no special or higher status than other acts of Congress, . . . treaties are simply 'political' obligations, . . . treaty obligations can be unilaterally modified or terminated by congressional action, . . . [and] America's constitutional requirements override 'international law.'" From this line of argument, he concluded "that the U.S. shall meet its commitments when it is in its interests to do so and when others are meeting their obligations as well."[54] During the Reagan administration, a senior official argued in private sessions that the charter itself permits nonpayment of dues, because it does not invoke any penalties until a member state is a full two years delinquent in its obligations.

This perspective is not accepted by most American legal experts or by many in the Clinton administration, but it has proven popular with legislators seeking a legal rationale for exerting unilateral financial leverage and for reasserting Congress' control over payments to the UN. The statements of the Senate Foreign Relations Committee "reflect a dangerous misunderstanding of the relations between international law and domestic law," contends Richard N. Gardner, a professor of international law and organization at Columbia University. "If Congress exercises its constitutional right to violate a treaty," he noted, "the United States still has a legal obligation to other countries; and our refusal to live up to our commitments can have legal consequences," as affirmed by the decision of the International Court of Justice in the article 19 crisis.[55] The United States, of course, retains the right to withdraw from the world body at any point, although public opinion surveys have consistently suggested that this would be a markedly unpopular step. In 1945 Congress was not obligated to consent to ratification of the charter or to pass the UN Participation Act of 1945, which confirms U.S. obligations. In doing so, however, Congress agreed to play by the rules and to assume the financial obligations associated with membership.

At the same time, it should be acknowledged that the assessment scales, means of financing, and the manner in which they are determined are not set in stone. There is always room for improvement and for adaptation to changing circumstances. In stipulating that "the expenses of the Organization shall be borne by the Members as apportioned by the General Assembly," article 17 simply leaves these inherently political matters up to the member states to decide. The United States can, and has, exercised substantial leverage in shaping the way in which these matters are determined by the Assembly. When it fails to get its way, the United States has the option of withdrawing its membership. But no member state can have it both ways: to keep the full benefits of membership while deciding unilaterally when, to what degree, and under what circumstances it will meet its financial obligations to the world body. In a March 1998 statement on the Senate floor, Patrick Leahy, D-Vt., put it well:

If we want to get out of the United Nations, then let us vote to do that. If we want to say we will never spend another cent in the United Nations, let us vote to do that. But to first give our word that we will pay what we contractually owe and then on the day we desperately are pushing the United Nations to back us in Iraq, to say we break our word, we can't do that.[56]

There would be utter chaos in the management and financing of the UN if each of 185 member states, or even if each of the major donors, was free to set its own dues levels and payment schedules, to decide how the funds were to be used, and to assert a series of conditions that would have to be met before payment would be made. Absent the principle of collective financial responsibility, it is hard to see how such a broad-based and complex organization could be viable.

Taken to its logical conclusion, the arguments put forward by the Senate Foreign Relations Committee and John Bolton raise very serious dilemmas for larger American interests as well. As Professor Gardner points out, "if America does not live up to its obligations, then any nation would be free to violate any commitment made to us."[57] Although international law is usually not directly enforceable—at least in the same way as domestic law—it is generally observed both because nations (not least the United States) derive important benefits from a law-based international system and because reciprocity holds to the degree that other countries may take actions in one field or another to penalize the violator of agreements, norms, or treaties or to gain compensation for any harm they have suffered. To the extent that any parliament or government declares itself free to ignore international law at will, the United States will have that much harder a time making the case that agreements that matter to us—whether in trade, arms control, rights of passage, environment, intellectual property, or human rights—should be considered inviolate and enforceable under international law. For a power with worldwide interests in an era of global communications and economic ties, a predictable and stable legal order is an indispensable asset. As Representative Lee H. Hamilton, D-Ind., put it, a world in which "any nation is free to violate any commitment made to the United States or to any other nation . . . is not a world in which we should want to live."[58]

The Withholding Debate

On Capitol Hill the often partisan debate over the wisdom of further withholding has addressed both its legal and its tactical implications. In recent

years, the focus has tended to shift from the former to the latter. For example, in a 1993 hearing, when the Democrats controlled Congress,
Republican Senator Larry Pressler, S. Dak., found little support from his
colleagues when he expressed frustration over how to propel UN reform, "I
do not know what a Senator does. . . . There is a frustration level. That is
why we sponsor some of these arrearages." And he asked "how will those
people who appropriate the funds put pressure on the U.N., unless they
threaten not to appropriate the funds?"[59] At that point, several Democratic
senators spoke to U.S. legal obligations and asserted that America's capacity
to influence these questions in international arenas had in fact been hampered by the nation's growing arrears to the UN.[60]

The circle of legislators advocating withholdings appears, however, to
have expanded significantly in recent years.[61] According to Representative
Harold D. Rogers, R-Ky., "there appears to be one thing and one thing only
that captures the attention of the U.N., and that is money."[62] Along similar
lines, Senator Rod Grams, R-Minn., emphasized in a 1997 speech that "the
U.S. did not simply accumulate its arrears arbitrarily, but often withheld its
contributions to the U.N. for the specific purpose of encouraging certain
reforms. Although the results have so far been modest, it is clear that even
minor reforms would not have been achieved without this financial leverage." Repayments, he continued, should "be used as a 'carrot' for achieving
similar results."[63] Joining the largely Republican chorus for withholdings
has been Democrat Alan B. Mollohan, W. Va., who commended his House
colleagues for "trying to effect reforms in the United Nations through the
only way really the United States Congress can effectively do that, through
the appropriations process. We have been extremely effective at doing that,
I think, and ratcheting up the pain on the United Nations to the point that
we have seen a lot of good responsiveness from them."[64] (The largest portion of U.S. arrears to that point, however, actually had resulted from legislation—Public Law 103-236, signed by President Clinton on April 30,
1994—that unilaterally placed a 25 percent ceiling on U.S. peacekeeping
payments, rather than from cuts aimed to bring about management
reform.)

As the chorus on Capitol Hill in favor of withholdings has grown, so
too has the number willing to speak in favor of paying off America's debt to
the UN. Among the themes favored by UN supporters have been the need
to fund its efforts to bring peace to troubled regions, to restore U.S. leadership and leverage in the world body, and to shed America's embarrassing
"deadbeat" status.[65] Although most of those calling for payment of arrears

have been Democrats, two of the UN's most articulate supporters have been Republican representatives John E. Porter, Ill., and James A. Leach, Iowa.

They are not the only prominent Republicans beginning to question the effectiveness of the withholding tool. Before retiring from the Senate, in 1996 Kassebaum explained to her colleagues that "I was an early advocate of the reform-for-funding concept in the mid-1980s, although I tend to think that approach has reached the limits of its usefulness."[66] Former UN envoy Jeane Kirkpatrick had concluded by 1996 that "the discussion of U.S. arrearages has become embarrassing and dysfunctional."[67] As early as 1971 William F. Buckley Jr. had cautioned that withholding funds from the UN would be "interpretable as an act of petulance."[68] Even Senator Helms, while not the least bashful about the legal implications of conditioning U.S. payments to the UN, has come to question the effectiveness of this tactic. In 1996 he told a Senate hearing that "withholding contributions has not worked. We have tried that. We have been there."[69] Perhaps most telling was a comment in March 1998 by Benjamin Gilman, chairman of the House International Relations Committee. "According to a February GAO report on the U.N. financial status," he noted, "our unpaid arrears have impeded progress in reducing our Nation's assessment rate and in encouraging other countries to pay their fair share of the costs of running this international organization."[70] Unilateral withholding, in other words, was proving dysfunctional.

Both sides of this cause-and-effect debate about the relationship between U.S. withholdings and UN reform face some problems of logic and circular reasoning. For those favoring full funding, the claim that the UN has made substantial reform progress and therefore deserves support leads to the counterclaim that the reforms only prove the persuasiveness of U.S. withholdings. This conclusion, in turn, might simply encourage further cuts down the road keyed to further "reforms," a worry that has led some delegations at the UN to resist additional reform steps that might be interpreted as a reward for what they deem to be bad behavior on the part of the United States. It is illogical, however, to attest both that the withholdings have been effective and that United Nations has not achieved any significant reform. Critics who disparage UN management and claim that all of the reform measures to date have been a charade and that the United States is the only reform-minded member state are pulling the rug out from under the rationale for unilaterally cutting funding to force change in the organization.[71]

It seems, in fact, that through the years Congress has withheld payments to the UN so many times for so many reasons that the effect has been blunted over time. Other member states are well aware that repeated surveys suggest that most Americans are uncomfortable with the tactic of with-holding legally assessed dues and that every postwar president has called for full payment of these obligations. According to former UN secretary-general Javier Pérez de Cuéllar, in June 1990 President Bush told him "of the great embarrassment I feel about the money the United States owes to the United Nations. . . . Great nations, like great men, should keep their word." Reportedly, the president then advised the secretary-general that in conver-sations with members of Congress, "the harder you can come down on the need for the United States to keep its commitment, the better."[72]

The tenor of the current debate in the UN also suggests that the more the United States has resorted to withholdings, the less impact this tactic has had on the organization. Other member states are digging in their heels on some questions, such as the assessments scale and U.S. representation on a key budget committee, in the face of unrelenting American pressure, saying the United States should get current in its payments first (see chapter 8). And if the United States gets its way on having its assessments lowered to 20 percent for the regular budget (less than Japan by the year 2000) and 25 percent for peacekeeping, then its financial leverage will become a dwin-dling asset, literally and figuratively. The opening of this Pandora's box may also encourage others to adopt similar tactics to compel changes in the world body to their liking. In March 1999, for example, Liberal Democratic party legislators in Japan proposed cutting their nation's voluntary contri-butions to the UN by 10 percent annually until Japan is given a permanent seat on the Security Council.[73]

To the consternation of its severest critics, the UN not only has with-stood these financial challenges, it has largely retained its popularity with the American public and with other member states. At the same time, the withholdings have made the United States look weak in three ways: First, such unilateral actions would not be needed if there was broad support among the member states for most of the U.S. reform agenda. Second, the resort to withholdings suggests that the United States, which has histori-cally stressed the importance of paying assessed dues and meeting treaty obligations, could not get its way through more traditional and subtle expressions of power within the organization. And third, withholdings have tended to highlight the disarray in Washington policymaking, especially between Congress and the executive, and the more fundamental uncertainty of U.S. policymakers about America's place in the post–cold war world.

These tactics have had an additional unintended consequence: they have distracted international attention from the substance and purposes of reform and shifted it to the legality and equity of the withholdings themselves.[74] In the process, the choice of tactics has undermined the strategic purposes for which they were invoked in the first place. As Secretary of State Madeleine Albright asserted in January 1999, U.S. nonpayment of arrears is "more than embarrassing, it makes it impossible for us to get what we want at the UN."[75] Similarly, in 1998 Princeton N. Lyman, assistant secretary of state for international organization affairs, declared that:

> Anecdotal evidence from the staff at the U.S. Mission in New York indicates that at every possible opportunity, other member states use the arrears to skewer U.S. negotiating positions, whether the topic is related to arrears or not. The arrears situation has seriously eroded our influence on reform. Many of the reforms achieved this year in the UN were spearheaded by the U.S.— zero nominal growth across the UN system, consolidation of several departments, introduction of results-based budgeting, a code of conduct for employees, reduction of personnel ceilings. But there was an expectation in the UN that these reforms would produce a U.S. commitment to paying arrears. With the U.S. failure to do so, U.S. support for reform is now resented and our advocacy can actually be a disadvantage in the UN Secretary-General's further reform agenda.[76]

Lyman then cited a series of management questions, including the use of gratis personnel for peacekeeping, UN procurement from U.S. vendors, and budget discipline, that were moving in an unfavorable direction because of resentment about the arrears situation. The possible loss of vote in the General Assembly due to nonpayment of arrears "would be a stunning embarrassment for the US," Ambassador Lyman said, and "would lead to further pressures to reduce our influence in the Security Council, and all other fora."

As a result of these developments, a growing portion of the intergovernmental debate in the UN has been about U.S. tactics and policies, rather than about UN shortcomings that need to be corrected. As Lee Hamilton cautioned his House colleagues in March 1998, "*the United States* is already being called into question in the United Nations. We have already lost our position on the Committee on the Budget [ACABQ] . . . and . . . we could lose our vote in the General Assembly."[77] According to Ambassador Richard

Sklar, who spearheads reform and management questions for the United States in the UN, "our influence is plummeting through the floor every day." In response to his calls for further economies, he reported that other delegates say, "what right do you have to talk to us? You're a deadbeat."[78] Bureaucratic and political inertia has been legitimized, at least in the minds of some delegations, as an answer to what is seen as financial blackmail by the wealthiest and most powerful member state. Rather than building on the common concerns of many member states about UN performance, the United States has adopted a course of action guaranteed to emphasize its differences with the rest of the body, leaving its allies in a particularly awkward and disgruntled state.

For these and other reasons, several prominent Republicans have urged going beyond withholding tactics in the effort to seek more fundamental changes in the world body. Each sees the key in shifting the basis of most funding from assessed dues to voluntary payments. Jesse Helms has advocated slashing the UN's bureaucracy in half, shrinking the portion of UN spending to be covered by assessed contributions to a core budget of $250 million, and making all other funding voluntary. By imposing such a "market test," he wrote in 1996, "each country would decide the value of programs by how much they were willing to pay. Those programs that are really vital will continue to receive support, while those championed only by the bureaucracy will die of malnutrition." Rather than just withholding assessed dues to the UN, Helms would raise the ante, by having the United States "deliver an ultimatum" that it will withdraw unless the UN reforms "quickly and dramatically." "I am convinced," he declared, "that without the threat of American withdrawal, nothing will change."[79]

Jeane Kirkpatrick has suggested that "the United States should try to make a deal with the United Nations" on arrears, because she questions whether reductions in U.S. funding required by American legislation can properly be considered arrears. "I do not think we should keep accumulating arrearages either," she has said, and "perhaps we can agree to pay arrearages with monies we might otherwise spend for voluntary contributions." Moreover, in her words, "perhaps we can deal with the United Nations on moving some activities out of the assessed category, as John Bolton had suggested, into the voluntary category."[80] According to Bolton's analysis, one of the shortcomings of an assessment system is that "although the sheer size of the U.S. contribution gives us considerable bargaining leverage, the 'inevitability' of the ultimate American payments substantially undercuts that leverage." He called for "a system of completely voluntary contributions," including for peacekeeping, and has pointed out that "some of the best-run agencies in the U.N. system are currently funded by voluntary contributions."[81]

There is some surface appeal to the notion of shifting more and more UN funding to a voluntary basis, although it is not evident that voluntary financing would be sufficient, especially over time, to cover major costs, such as those incurred in large-scale peacekeeping operations.[82] On the whole, Congress has tended to be somewhat more responsive to voluntary appeals than to assessed obligations, perhaps in part because it feels more in control of the former than the latter. It is, however, instructive, though not entirely reassuring, to recall an exchange from a 1988 hearing on appropriations for voluntary UN programs. In his prepared testimony, Richard S. Williamson, the assistant secretary of state for international organization affairs, acknowledged that the Reagan administration was only requesting 3 percent more than the year before, which was considerably less than Congress had then appropriated, to show "sensitivity" to congressional priorities without affecting the overall budget targets worked out between Congress and the administration. The administration, in other words, was leaving it to Congress to find cuts in other programs if it wanted to maintain the UN voluntary funding levels. From the perspective of the subcommittee chairman, Daniel K. Inouye, Democrat of Hawaii, "it appears that once again this subcommittee will have to come to the rescue of these organizations so that both they and U.S. foreign policy interests round the globe may remain on a sound footing."[83]

In recent years, however, both the voluntary and the assessed accounts have been squeezed by the Republican majority on Capitol Hill. Although a voluntary system would ease the arrears problem, the UN and its agencies have also had some difficulties in collecting voluntary pledges. The ultimate goal, moreover, is not to handle the arrearage debacle, but to put the organization on a sound and durable financial foundation. No doubt some aspects of the UN's work would prove financially more popular than others, as is the case today, yet this pattern of choice might correspond more closely to who is best at public relations rather than to who does the best or most urgent work or to those program areas in which the organization has a comparative advantage. Who would fund the unexciting but essential core administrative costs of the organization, for instance? Under such a scheme, the UN would confront this dilemma perennially just as hundreds of nonprofit organizations do. There is no assurance, in any case, that the U.S. share of UN funding under a voluntary scheme would be so much less than at present, since the United States traditionally has provided more than 20 percent of voluntary contributions to the UN system (excluding peace-keeping-related support).

Whether a voluntary payment system would help or hinder UN management—presumably a key reform goal—is not clear. Bolton contends that voluntarily funded agencies tend to have strong performance records and that a replenishment system, such as that employed by the International Fund for Agricultural Development and others, could provide some financial assurances for forward-planning purposes.[84] Still, agencies dependent on voluntary contributions often need to develop or encourage the formation of public and parliamentary constituencies within key donor countries to press for their appropriations, as in the case of UNICEF and UNHCR. As advocacy groups, moreover, they may be more concerned with securing funding than with encouraging transparency or pushing for management reform within the agencies themselves. Whatever the implications for the administration of individual programs or agencies, there is ample evidence that the management of the UN system as a whole, the effort to achieve coordination and unity of purpose, has been seriously hampered by the fact that separately funded agencies, each with its own set of member state donors and public constituencies, have little incentive to work together as a team.

How a wholesale shift from assessed to voluntary funding would be accomplished is not apparent in any case. At the very least, the General Assembly, according to the provisions of article 17, would have to approve. Most member states would perceive this—and properly so—as an effort by major donor countries to exert greater control over the programs and priorities of the organization. At this point, the mood in the Assembly cuts in just the opposite direction. In all probability, article 17, paragraph 2, which stipulates that "the expenses of the Organization shall be borne by the Members as apportioned by the General Assembly," would need to be amended if all of the core expenses were to be covered on a voluntary basis. This would appear to be an insurmountable obstacle to undertaking a wholesale shift to voluntary funding at this point or anytime in the foreseeable future.

Layers of Mistrust

The financial imbroglio is exacerbated by the lack of trust on all sides: among the UN secretariat, other member states, the executive branch, and

Congress. No one seems to have much confidence either in the figures provided by or the intentions and interests of the other parties to the dispute. Each expects, and tends to see, the worst motivations in the actions of the others. The situation is complicated, moreover, because the doubts among nations on this score are replicated domestically by the lack of confidence between the administration and Congress.

In a 1988 *Washington Post* op-ed piece, written after he left government, Alan Keyes charged that "high-level policy officials at the State Department, working with the U.S. mission in New York, are pushing for premature certification on U.N. reform" and, by reopening "the funding spigots," were sending "a clear signal to the officials and delegates in New York: they can safely continue with business as usual."[85] His charges found substantial resonance on the Hill.[86] Going further, Senator Pressler suggested in a 1993 hearing:

> I have a feeling our State Department is whispering in the ear of people up at the U.N. that the Department will give this [UN reform] a lot of lip service, the Department will tell Senators that they are going to do it, but nothing is going to happen. We are going to pay our dues, and there is nothing that is going to change. These Senators are just making some noises down there.[87]

"It is no secret," remarked Senator Grams in 1996, "that Congress has often been unhappy with the lack of emphasis that past and present administrations have placed on specific reform proposals."[88] According to Senator Helms, "the Clinton Administration has undertaken no serious effort to cut or reduce this massive, wasteful international bureaucracy. If anything, the administration is continuing to acquiesce to the growth of this United Nations."[89]

Clearly the key legislators pushing for further UN "reforms," including a reduction in U.S. assessments, evince little faith in the executive branch's willingness or ability to move this agenda forward at the UN. In fact, from their perspective American diplomats and diplomats from other countries appear to have more in common than do U.S. officials from different branches of government. State Department officials, as well as U.S. diplomats, are charged with managing relationships with other countries and asserting American values and interests in the world. Therefore, they are more likely to be directed outward and to be more influenced by external factors than are members of Congress, who are bound to be more focused inward toward their constituents, their parties, and their fiscal responsibilities. This predisposition to see the world differently has, in recent years,

been compounded by partisanship; constitutional issues relating to the separation of powers; the weakening of the committee structure, seniority, and
leadership in both chambers; the influx of large numbers of new members
of Congress with little interest or experience in foreign affairs; and the lack
of compelling foreign policy goals or visions since the end of the cold war.
Splits within the Republican party and the rise of single-interest constituencies have also contributed to Congress' increasingly narrow and inward
perspectives.

All of this, of course, has made reliable communications between Turtle
Bay and Capitol Hill that much more difficult. The UN's task in any case is
to be responsible to governments, not parliaments. When a serious split
develops between the administration and Congress, and the latter has little
confidence in the former either to transmit its concerns to New York faith-
fully and fully or to negotiate with other member states forcefully, then a
sense of mutual confidence is very hard to develop. As noted in chapter 8, all
of this is further complicated by the distinct visions Congress and the
administration have of what constitutes a desirable reform agenda. Congress, moreover, is in the enviable position of being able to complain about
all sorts of things without the capacity or responsibility of trying to negotiate with 184 sovereign member states with their own interests, constituencies, and parliaments.

Yet for all of the headaches caused by different perspectives, communication gaps, and imperfect transparency and credibility, the heart of the
problem today is the same as it was more than fifty years ago: everyone
wants to pay less for but have more say within the organization. Although
the sums of money are not large compared with those expended for other
national purposes, the political stakes are considerable. In October 1997,
the U.S. envoy to the UN, Bill Richardson, told the Fifth Committee that
"the failure to revise the scale of assessments for U.N. member states could
seriously damage the U.S. relationship with the United Nations."[90]
Reportedly his written text went even further, stating that it could lead to
"the process of America's disengagement" from the United Nations.[91]
Despite this stern warning, the changes in the assessment scale adopted two
months later by the General Assembly were hardly what the United States
was seeking.[92] According to the president's annual report to the Congress,
United States Participation in the United Nations, "some UN member states,
especially the members of the European Union, indicated that any reopening of the scale negotiations would be contingent upon the U.S. ability to
secure an acceptable funding package for payment of its UN arrears."[93]

Although the Assembly left the door open to a review of the dues scales for 1999 and 2000 rather than waiting for the normal three-year interval, it decided to keep the United States at 25 percent, to lower the floor for the poorest eighty-six member countries to below 0.01 percent, to reduce thirty-four of these to a minuscule 0.001 percent, and to permit China, with its massive and growing economy, to remain under 1 percent through 2000. By lowering the floor, the Assembly decided that more than one-sixth of the UN's membership need only pay $13,000 annually for full membership privileges.[94] In effect, it determined that the gap in dues requirements among the members should be widened to a ratio of 25,000 to 1, with seven countries paying more than 75 percent of the budget and one hundred only 0.43 percent. Despite the very real financial difficulties of some member states, it would be hard to justify the Assembly action in terms either of fiscal responsibility or sovereign equality or of the one-nation, one-vote principle. Surely it should not cost a nation less to belong to the UN than an individual to go to college or to buy a car.

While the standoff between U.S. pressure and the resistance being displayed by other member states is understandable, even predictable, for all of the tactical and political reasons cited above, it is hardly healthy for the reputation and effectiveness either of the world body or of its most influential member. The amount of time, effort, and political capital being expended on the dues tug-of-war is wildly disproportionate to the funds involved. It looks more and more to outside observers as if all sides—developing countries, the other industrialized countries (with a few exceptions), and the United States—want the benefits of the UN on the cheap. The current lack of vision and commitment is so pervasive that the founders would despair at how low their high expectations and noble purposes have fallen. The persistence of financial turmoil within the organization suggests that the time is fast approaching when a fundamental reshaping of assumptions about voting rights and financial responsibilities will be as inevitable as it is overdue. The UN's financial crisis is reflective of a more pervasive uneasiness about the decisionmaking processes of multilateral institutions. American ambivalence, in that regard, may well prove to be only the tip of the iceberg. Judging from the political dynamics considered in the next chapter, altering course to avoid a crisis of immense and possibly fatal proportions will be no easy matter.

CHAPTER TEN

The Political Landscape

When we get to the borders of the United States we are neither Republicans nor Democrats.

—PRESIDENT WOODROW WILSON, 1919

I find myself somewhat suspicious of the unanimity with which the charter is apparently received by this body. Practically no measure of real importance has been accepted with such docility by the opposition.

—SENATOR WILLIAM FULBRIGHT, 1945

America's foreign policy will not be written in the eloquent language of the United Nations Charter. . . . It will be written, it will finally be controlled, by the deeply imbedded, underlying directing forces of our domestic policies.

—SENATOR WALTER GEORGE, 1948

EVEN A CURSORY review of the eight themes discussed in the preceding chapters makes two conclusions abundantly clear: the sources for American ambivalence toward international institutions and undertakings are ample and varied; and the key to understanding the peculiarities of U.S.-UN relations lies in the dynamics of American domestic politics. If one seeks to influence the course of U.S. policies toward international organizations, then it is to the forces that shape domestic policies and politics that one must look.

For many observers, the journey to understand the complexities and subtleties of American attitudes begins with the apparent contradiction between the disdain that many members of Congress express toward the United Nations and the seemingly broad public support for the world body, as evidenced in surveys of public opinion. Why, it is asked, is there such a glaring disconnect between the attitudes of the public and of those elected to represent them in the nation's capital? There are several plausible explanations, including that both caricatures—of implacable congressional antagonism and of ardent public support—tend to be exaggerated by the proponents of opposing viewpoints. As argued in this chapter, neither congressional nor public viewpoints are so simplistic or so uniform, and the gap may not be as large as it appears to be on the surface. Aggregate poll numbers, moreover, may not tell as much as do demographic breakdowns. And neither set of numbers reveals how deeply the respondents feel about the question. The debate about the UN and about U.S. payments to it can better be understood, as well, as a rather small piece of a much more complex political mosaic in a period of considerable flux and uncertainty in domestic politics. Moreover, the UN itself is not always the issue. At times, relations with the world body serve as a convenient symbol in intractable and indeterminate political struggles over the formation and direction of U.S. foreign policy.

This chapter seeks to shed some light on the domestic political forces that have shaped these apparent paradoxes in American policies toward the United Nations. As previous chapters have suggested, there was a lot of unfinished business after the founding conference in San Francisco and, tellingly, after Senate consideration of the charter and then the UN Participation Act. This chapter opens with a brief look at why this was so and how these unresolved questions and unhealed divisions still hinder the development of a durable foundation for U.S.-UN relations. It then turns to the public side of the political equation, examining poll data in some detail, including demographic patterns and public attitudes toward financial and burden-sharing questions. In conclusion, it returns to core issues of presidential leadership, partisanship, and relations between the executive and legislative branches of government.

Debate Postponed, Issues Unresolved

Eight decades after the Senate considered membership in the League of Nations, the ambivalent effects of its treatment of the League can still be felt in congressional discourse about the United Nations and the U.S. place in it. This enduring, if crippling, legacy stems, paradoxically, from both the indeterminate nature of the substantive debate and the seemingly decisive nature of the outcome. Then, as now, most senators favored U.S. participation in the international organization of the day. At the same time, most favored accepting the reservations, primarily related to sovereignty, proposed by Senator Henry Cabot Lodge. This bipartisan group, however, fell seven votes shy of the required two-thirds majority in the second vote on March 19, 1920, in part because President Woodrow Wilson opposed compromise on what he, like Lodge, saw as matters of high principle. The debate, in essence, remained unresolved; neither side could claim a substantive victory. Yet for reasons of tactics and personality, the result was decisive: no U.S. participation in the first great experiment in international organization of this century.

American opinion leaders and scholars derived a variety of conclusions from the fateful collision between the League and the Senate. Some of the more insightful lessons, which have an uncanny relevance today, were drawn by a high-level study group convened by the Council on Foreign Relations in 1935. The results of their deliberations, as captured by the group's rapporteur, Columbia law professor Philip C. Jessup, included the following observations:

> It was the League as a superstate which was opposed so violently in the United States. Such a league was a ghostly spectre which never had any existence in fact but the superstition strongly persists in American thought.
>
> There is a hostility deep-rooted in large sections of American opinion toward the acceptance of any obligation which would compel the United States to participate in any international repressive or punitive measures as a result of an engagement made in advance of the event.
>
> There is a rather unreasoning and beclouded devotion to the Monroe Doctrine (the meaning of which is obscure to most), but a devotion which stems from a traditional attachment almost religious in its fervor.
>
> There is a potent unwillingness in the Senate to entrust broad authority in international affairs to the executive. . . .
>
> Except in times of national emergency, there is little adherence to the assertion of Daniel Webster that politics stop at the water's edge. While an unpopular foreign policy is a vulnerable point of attack for a party's political opponents, few votes are gained by even the most successful ventures in foreign affairs. This attitude of the American electorate tends to discourage politicians from supporting new departures in foreign policy and helps to explain the success of such attacks as those on the League of Nations and the World Court.
>
> There is a very considerable body of idealistic opinion which, however, is only occasionally translated into effective political action.[1]

Jessup and the council study group added another finding of enduring importance concerning the Senate's failure to consent to adherence to the World Court, which also lacked seven votes for the required two-thirds majority on January 29, 1935. According to their analysis, "at least some

Senators realized that the militant minority opposed to the Court would punish a vote for the treaty whereas the well-intentioned majority would not reward it."[2] Then, as now, political influence stemmed not only from numbers, but from how one played the game.

The Japanese attack on Pearl Harbor, however, served to shake up the domestic political dynamics, at least temporarily. As the human and material costs of the war mounted, a single painful lesson of the Senate's seeming rejection of the League came to be accepted as gospel by larger and larger numbers of Americans: the League had failed to prevent the Second World War because it had been fatally weakened by U.S. nonparticipation. To give a veneer of permanence to participation in the new United Nations, its founders did not include a withdrawal clause in the charter and called the UN's five leading powers "permanent members" of the Security Council. As documented later in this chapter, public approval for creating a stronger international organization with full U.S. participation grew with the mounting human costs of the conflict, until the sentiment was overwhelming by war's end. The successful results of the UN's founding conference in San Francisco and the prominent role played by American delegates there simply served to reinforce public enthusiasm. With such fertile political soil to till, the Truman administration's vigorous public relations campaign for the new organization was bound to be fruitful.

The Senate knew what it was expected to do, and to do quickly: join the chorus with as little hesitation as possible. Allen J. Ellender, D-La., remarked that "so far I have received but one letter from my State expressing opposition to ratification of the Charter." Another supporter, Scott W. Lucas, D-Ill., commented that no one should vote for the charter solely "because he believes it politically dangerous to do otherwise." Claude D. Pepper, D-Fla., challenged a reluctant supporter of the charter, Burton K. Wheeler, D-Mont., about whether he had seen any public opinion polls that were not highly favorable and pointedly noted that Wheeler "is coming around to support the Charter before the next election in his State."[3] The Senate debate was conducted with such decorum and firmness, in fact, that public critics of the new world body complained that the whole ratification process had been staged and orchestrated by the administration to ensure no repeat of the 1919–20 fiasco.[4] According to Thomas Franck, a noted New York University law professor, the administration-organized campaign to gain Senate support for the United Nations was "surely one of the most dramatic examples of hard-sell huckstering in twentieth century American politics."[5] Senator Wheeler complained of "polls based upon the propaganda which floods the country" and of similar "fake polls." In his view, "the people of the United States and their elected representatives in this Senate body have been maneuvered into a position where they are not going to be able to do anything more than acquiesce in an ultimatum. . . . They have been told they must accept this instrument or nothing."[6]

Although most likely just the tip of the proverbial iceberg, the comments of the charter's advocates on the floor of the Senate gave a sense of the nature and degree of peer pressure that was marshaled in support of the charter. Senator Lucas was blunt about the lessons of history:

> The world still remembers what the Senate failed to do when the League of Nations was before it for ratification. It still looks upon this legislative body with doubt and skepticism and well it might, in view of what happened 25 years ago. The opportunity is now before this legislative body to correct the mistake that was committed at that time. We can regain for the United States Senate the confidence of the Allied Nations by demonstrating now that we are a group of forward-looking Americans who believe firmly in world cooperation.[7]

Calling the charter "possibly the most momentous document ever produced by man," Senator John L. McClellan, D-Ark., noted that ratification was "a foregone conclusion" and that "there can hardly be real necessity for debate or argument in this Chamber in support of its ratification." In his view, "we dare not procrastinate and unduly delay our entering upon this great enterprise— this highest and noblest of experiments upon which governments and human society have ever engaged or undertaken." Contending that "the United States Senate committed a tragic error in failing to ratify the League of Nations," he stressed that "we cannot, we must not, fail again."[8]

Alben W. Barkley, D-Ky., the future vice president, complimented his colleagues on the "high order" of their addresses. "The debate on the Charter has proceeded today in good order," he commented, "probably I should not say 'debate,' because it is not really a debate." He said that he saw no need to describe or define the charter in any greater detail, despite the complaints of one or two senators, because "we all understand its purposes, as set out in the preamble."[9]

The twin concerns prevailing in the Senate—to avoid another wrenching experience like the League controversy and to minimize the possibility of a public backlash—were certainly understandable. But was it appropriate or responsible for a body that claims to be one of the world's great debating, as well as legislating, bodies to rush to judgment about what was said to be the most ambitious experiment in international cooperation ever attempted? And if the need to overcome America's isolationist strains was so apparent and urgent, then might it not have been better, in the long run, to have encouraged a more open and thorough national debate over participation in the new world body at that point, when the internationalist forces were clearly in the ascendancy and a proper burial for isolationism could have been arranged? A handful of senators apparently thought so. William Fulbright, D-Ark., a strong advocate of international organization, commended senators Tom Connally and Arthur Vandenberg for their leadership, but he wryly noted that "sometimes I wish that they had not been quite so persuasive. A little more spirited debate, a little more opposition on the floor might serve to sharpen our understanding and our appreciation of the true significance of this agreement."[10] Presciently, in all of the backslapping and self-congratulations, he apparently found cause to worry.

Perhaps the most prophetic comments, in the midst of an enormous outpouring of lofty rhetoric, came from Francis J. Myers, D-Pa. Myers said that he "would hate to see a repetition of the disaster of 1919," but he underlined that "there is room here for a fight" between internationalists and isolationists. He expressed "disappointment that opponents of the theory of international joint action for peace are not flying their battle flags now, but are instead apparently waiting for future opportunities to make flank attacks when their purposes will be less obviously—but perhaps more effectively served."[11] Indeed, as the preceding chapters have chronicled, in the intervening years there have been many propitious opportunities for such assaults on the UN's vulnerable flanks and these have often been carried out with considerable success. In this sense, the stress on unanimity and bipartisanship in 1945 created a false impression that America's commitment to the UN rested on far broader and deeper political foundations than was the case. In retrospect, this period was just the calm before (as well as after) the storm.

Highly outnumbered and politically incorrect for the times, senators with serious reservations about the wisdom of the charter tended to be low key, circumspect, or conditional in their comments.[12] Henrik Shipstead, R-Minn., was an exception, the only senator to express at length his reasons for opposing the charter. He complained of being labeled a "perfectionist," which he described as "a new word [that] has been invented to throw at those who insist on examining the various specious remedies recommended for the world's diseases." Contending that the debate between isolationists and internationalists "was ended in 1941," he argued that "the question at issue is whether this charter is real or 'phony'; whether it is in truth an instrument to secure international peace and justice, or a cynical imposture bred by hypocrisy out of power politics." [13] Half a century later, many skeptics about the UN are still complaining about being called isolationists and insisting that they might feel differently about an international organization that could really perform as promised.

By seizing the moment, Roosevelt and Truman made certain that 1945 bore little resemblance to 1919. Buoyed by the sea change in public attitudes, they were able to throw U.S. political weight solidly behind the efforts to build a much stronger successor generation of international institutions out of the ashes of the League. They rallied bipartisan support in Congress through the involvement of key congressional Republicans in postwar planning and, critically, at the San Francisco conference, building on the Senate's eagerness to escape its own history. These astute tactics, which starkly contrasted with President Wilson's stubborn fumbling, ensured that the UN would not be stillborn. Yet over time it became increasingly apparent that things had not changed so fundamentally on the strategic level. As noted in the preceding chapters, several crucial issues were left unresolved at the UN's founding. A number of key State Department officials privately remained skeptical about the prospects for the new organization. Dean Acheson, who handled the charter's review by the Senate Foreign Relations Committee as assistant secretary of state and who was to become President Truman's secretary of state in 1949, had long been wary of Wilsonian idealism and of placing too much dependence on international institutions. As he later wrote, the charter's "presentation to the American people as almost holy writ and with the evangelical enthusiasm of a major advertising campaign seemed to me to raise popular hopes which could only lead to bitter disappointment." [14] The rush to judgment in the Senate, moreover, left the opposition both sore and unsatisfied. Aptly, Shipstead questioned "whether the end we seek can be accomplished blindfolded or by obscuring the real issues." [15] In the end, however, the public (not to mention other member states) was left with the dual impression that both UN capacities and the U.S. government's commitment to making the organization work were a lot more solid than they turned out to be when the going got tough.

Broad Measures of Support

Whatever tribulations it has faced on Capitol Hill, the United Nations has traditionally been held in a position of esteem and respect by the bulk of

Table 10-1. *Question: Would you say your overall opinion of the United Nations is favorable, mostly favorable, mostly unfavorable, or very unfavorable?*
Percent

Question	Very favorable	Mostly favorable	Mostly unfavorable	Very unfavorable
May 1990 (Pew)	15	55	13	6
Jan. 1993 (*Time*/CNN)	22	55	14	5
May 1993 (Pew)	21	52	13	4
July 1994 (Pew)	21	55	14	5
Feb. 1995 (Pew)	13	49	18	8
June 1995 (Pew)	14	53	20	8
Feb. 1996 (Pew)	19	46	20	9
Feb. 1997 (*Time*/CNN)	21	52	16	8
Sept. 1997 (Pew)	11	53	19	9
Dec. 1998–Jan. 1999 (Zogby)	18	53 (somewhat)	18 (somewhat)	9

Source: The Pew figures can be found in the Pew Research Center for the People and the Press, *America's Place in the World II* (Washington, D.C.: Oct. 1997), 91, the two *Time*/CNN polls were conducted by Yankelovich Partners, Washington, D.C., on Jan. 22–25, 1993 and Feb. 5–6, 1997. For Zogby International results, see its press release of Jan. 4, 1999, http://www.zogby.com/news/home.htm., and UN Press Release SG/2050, Jan. 4, 1999.

the American people. This holds true today. Throughout the 1990s, as table 10-1 details, survey respondents by more than a 2-to-1 margin have said that their "overall opinion" of the world organization is favorable. In a December 1998–January 1999 poll by Zogby International, the margin was 70 to 27 percent. As with other general assessments of the UN, the levels of support rose a bit after the 1991 Gulf War and sagged slightly in the following years. The overall picture, however, has not changed significantly during the decade.

Responses to the statement that "the United States should cooperate fully with the United Nations" have followed a similar pattern in the 1990s: rising after Desert Storm and fading some since. The volatility in the 1970s and 1980s was much greater, however, as reflected in table 10-2. The biggest dip, as evidenced in other questions about American attitudes toward the UN, came after the 1975 Zionism-racism resolution, with another, smaller, decline during the rancorous early years of the Reagan administration.

There has never been much popular support for either side of the "get the U.S. out of the UN and the UN out of the U.S." slogan. This has been

Table 10-2. *Question: Please tell me whether you agree or disagree with the following statement: The United States should cooperate fully with the United Nations*

Percent

	Agree	Disagree
1964	72	16
1968	72	21
1972	63	28
1976	46	41
1980	59	28
1985	56	35
1991	77	17
April 1993	71	22
Oct. 1993	64	28
Feb. 1995	65	29
June 1995	62	30
Sept. 1997	59	30

Source: The Pew Research Center for the People and the Press, *America's Place in the World II*, 106, utilizing data from polls by Potomac Associates, the Gallup Organization, and the Institute for International Social Research.

particularly evident during the 1990s, despite—or perhaps because of—the rising volume of congressional attacks on the United Nations. In the latest poll to ask the question (November 1997, CNN/*USA Today*), Americans rejected the idea of withdrawing from the world body by almost a 10-to-1 margin. At the peak of anti-UN feelings, following the November 1975 Zionism-racism resolution, fewer than one-sixth of respondents called for the United States to "give up" its UN membership, as indicated by table 10-3. Despite the occasional mutterings in Congress and by other UN critics about the possible salutary effect of moving the headquarters of the world body to another country with fewer amenities, the notion has never had much popular support. By a 75-to-14 percent margin, Americans said in the November 1997 poll that they preferred the UN to "stay in the US."[16]

These findings suggest that the American people are far from abandoning the world organization, despite some signs of a slight softening of approval ratings in recent years. The UN is apparently seen as one of the basic building blocks of the international system in this era of globalization and interdependence. Most Americans appear to accept global engagement, whatever its downsides, as a fact of life for the United States. Participation in the UN, which remains a respected institution for all of its flaws, is one

Table 10-3. *Question: Do you think the United States should give up its membership in the United Nations, or not?*
Percent

	Yes	No
May 1951	12	75
Nov. 1951	11	73
Jan. 1962	5	90
Nov. 1963	8	79
July 1967	10	85
Feb. 1975	11	75
Nov. 1975	16	74
June 1982	12	79
Oct. 1983	12	79
Aug. 1985	11	81
Oct. 1990	8	88
Oct. 1995	9	84
Nov. 1997	9	88

Source: The data from 1951 through 1990 are from Gallup surveys; see *The Gallup Poll Monthly,* Oct. 1990, p. 16, while the October 1995 and November 1997 polls were for CNN/*USA Today.* For the past three decades, the National Opinion Research Center has asked whether "our government should continue to belong to the United Nations, or should we pull out of it now?" and has obtained similar results.

way of expressing this engagement and of seeking to advance U.S. principles and interests. Based on an intensive five-year study of public attitudes on international issues, Steven Kull, I. M. Destler, and Clay Ramsay of the Program on International Policy Attitudes (PIPA) of the University of Maryland concluded in October 1997 that "despite the pervasiveness of the assumption that the US public favors international disengagement in the wake of the Cold War, there is a striking lack of evidence for this view."[17] In another major October 1997 study, the Pew Research Center for the People and the Press found "no greater degree of isolationism . . . in the public today than in 1993" and concluded that isolationism, though still "a large minority sentiment," had "stabilized in recent years."[18] Similar conclusions have been reached by the Chicago Council on Foreign Relations through its 1994 and 1998 surveys, in which historically high and growing numbers of Americans see the United States playing an increasingly important leadership role in the world.[19] The 1998 poll confirmed as well the public's preference for multilateralism, its willingness to participate in UN peacekeeping, and its support for the payment of U.S. arrears to the world body.

The American people's respect for what the UN stands for and their acceptance of its place as part of the fabric of international life, however, does not imply either that they know much about what the world body does or that they approve of what they have heard about its operations. Acceptance does not assume affection. And esteem does not exempt the UN from criticism. Americans' lack of knowledge about the UN, moreover, is legendary. When asked by a 1998–99 Zogby International survey to name something the UN is involved in other than peacekeeping, 49 percent could not think of anything.[20] Fewer than half (49 percent) of those queried in an October 1990 Gallup Poll could identify the city in which UN headquarters is located, despite the calls for moving it out of New York and the publicity then surrounding the Security Council meetings on Iraq's invasion of Kuwait.[21] Younger people tend to be more favorable toward the UN, but only 28 percent of 18- to 29-year-olds gave the correct answer. Likewise, in a 1985 Gallup Poll only one in five could name a single UN agency.[22] When the United States withdrew from UNESCO a few years earlier, private contributions to the U.S. Committee for UNICEF, the most popular and widely known agency, suffered because a number of donors confused it with UNESCO. Three-quarters of the respondents to a September 1996 PIPA survey "believed that the UN budget was four or more times its actual size."[23]

Compared with the more consistently positive responses to the general questions cited above, public assessments of the UN's job performance have been mixed and variable. Through the years, Gallup and several other polling firms have periodically asked respondents whether in general they "think the United Nations is doing a good job or a poor job in trying to solve the problems it has had to face?" As table 10-4 indicates, the "good job" ratings have ranged from a low of 24 percent in 1951 to a high of 64 percent in 1959, and the "poor job" responses from 7 percent in 1959 and 1963 to 56 percent in 1995. Several conclusions are suggested by these results. There has been no consistent historical trend; some of the lowest approval ratings occurred in the early 1950s, and the 1990s has been a particularly volatile decade. In the 1960s "good" ratings consistently exceeded "poor" responses, while the opposite was true in the 1980s. During the 1950s, 1970s, and 1990s, there were both "good" and "poor" years. Negative responses exceeded 50 percent for the first time after the 1975 Zionism-racism resolution, and a gradual decline in UN approval ratings over several years was reversed in 1990 as the Bush administration began to use the Security Council as a vehicle for rallying international support for the effort to reverse the Iraqi invasion of Kuwait.

Table 10-4. *Question: In general, do you think the United Nation is doing a good job or a poor job in trying to solve the problems it has had to face?*[a]
Percent

	Good	Fair	Poor
Dec. 1950 (Gallup)	27	30	36
May 1951 (Gallup)	24	30	36
Aug. 1953 (Gallup)	30	36	22
Dec. 1953 (Gallup)	55	NA	30
July 1954 (Gallup)	58	NA	25
Nov. 1956 (Gallup)	51	26	11
Dec. 1959 (Gallup)	64	23	7
Oct. 1960 (Gallup)	57	23	9
June 1961 (Gallup)	54	25	11
June 1962 (Gallup)	49	29	14
Nov. 1962 (Gallup)	50	29	12
Nov. 1963 (Gallup)	54	29	7
July 1964 (Gallup)	49	26	16
July 1967 (Gallup)	50	NA	35
Sept. 1970 (Gallup)	44	NA	40
Nov. 1971 (Gallup)	35	NA	43
Nov. 1975 (Gallup)	33	NA	51
Feb. 1978 (Gallup)	40	NA	39
Sept. 1980 (Gallup)	31	NA	53
Jun. 1982 (Gallup)	36	NA	49
Oct. 1983 (Gallup)	36	NA	51
Feb. 1985 (Gallup)	38	NA	44
Aug. 1985 (Gallup)	28	NA	54
Oct. 1990 (Gallup)	54	NA	34
March 1993 (CNN/*USA Today*)	52	NA	44
June 1993 (Gallup)	46	NA	41
June 1995 (CBS News)	42	NA	46
Aug. 1995 (CNN/*USA Today*)	35	NA	56
Oct. 1995 (CNN/*USA Today*)	36	NA	49
Feb. 1996 (CNN/*USA Today*)	46	NA	46

Source: The 1950 through 1990 figures are from *The Gallup Poll Monthly,* Oct. 1990, p. 16; the CNN/*USA Today* polls were conducted by the Gallup Organization (March 29–31, 1993, Aug. 28–30, 1995, Oct. 19–23, 1995, and Feb. 23–25, 1996); and CBS News conducted its survey June 4–6, 1995.

a. In 1989, 1992, 1995, 1996, and 1998, the Wirthlin Group asked this same question on behalf of the United Nations Association. These results can be found at www.unausa.org/programs/poll95 and www.unausa.org/programs/topline. They are not included here since they were in most cases significantly more positive than those achieved by other pollsters and they cover only the past decade and therefore are less useful for tracking purposes.

None of this provides fuel for the prevalent misimpression that the American people have suddenly and inexorably lost enthusiasm for the world organization. Their assessments of the performance of the UN have fluctuated with the course of international events and with their perceptions of the relevance and fairness of actions within the world body. The UN has received poor marks when it appears to have veered from core principles, as in the case of the Zionism-racism resolution. When it has seemed to be fulfilling its founding purpose of rallying the collective will to resist aggression, as in the case of the Iraqi invasion of Kuwait, support has soared. The rest of the time, when the UN is out of the headlines, attitudes are more mixed, with apathy and ambivalence more abundant.

Public perceptions no doubt have been influenced by the stances taken by members of Congress; prominent commentators, including the U.S. representative to the UN; and, particularly, the president. The low ratings in the early 1980s may well reflect both the negative attitude of the first Reagan administration and the frustrations accumulated from the political beating the United States and its friends had taken in the General Assembly on a number of North-South issues in the 1970s. Given a lag in public perceptions, the more consensual climate in the UN of the late 1980s was not reflected in an upturn in approval ratings until the early 1990s, with the end of the cold war and the beginning of the UN role in the Gulf War. More recently, the virulent attacks on the UN by members of Congress and by most Republican presidential candidates may have sparked some slippage of support. On the whole, however, the public has been remarkably practical and realistic about the world body, with their evaluations of the UN's performance revolving more on how U.S. interests and values are being served than on ideological or idealistic assumptions.

It is also important to keep current public misgivings in historical perspective. The high points in America's attitudes toward the UN were not very high and did not last very long. The best run was in the late 1950s and early 1960s, followed by a substantial rise in negative ratings in the late 1960s.[24] This shift coincided with the growth in numbers of developing countries in the organization and with the increasing militancy of the nonaligned movement on several contentious issues. For all of the euphoria generated at the founding conference in San Francisco, moreover, the public's honeymoon with the world organization was remarkably short-lived. The looming cold war soon overshadowed the dream of a more cooperative world order, and its effects on domestic politics in the late 1940s and early 1950s were both chilling and polarizing.

The searing experience of World War II had galvanized support for joining a postwar world organization. In a series of polls in January and September 1943 and February 1944, the National Opinion Research Center queried: "If a union of nations is formed after the war, do you think it would be a good idea for the United States to join it?" The response was overwhelmingly positive: 70 to 16 percent, 88 to 11 percent, and 71 to 13 percent, respectively.[25] Yet once the new organization was created, expectations soon cooled. More than half (52 to 34 percent) of the respondents to a February 1946 survey by the American Institute of Public Opinion (AIPO) of the Gallup Organization doubted that the UN would "be able to prevent another world war during the next 25 years."[26] The decline in expectations about the preventive value of the new body was reflected in two State Department polls, taken in 1945 and 1947, that asked "in general, what chance do you think the UN Organization has to prevent wars between big nations—good, fair, or no chance at all?" During those two years, the number responding "no chance at all" doubled from 11 to 23 percent, while those seeing a "good chance" fell from 36 to 22 percent. The public was evenly divided, moreover, when AIPO in May 1946 asked whether respondents were "satisfied or dissatisfied with the progress that the United Nations has made to date."[27] Foreshadowing future patterns, Republicans and veterans tended to be less satisfied, and Democrats more satisfied, with UN performance. The dissatisfied usually outnumbered the satisfied when AIPO repeated the same question in surveys over the next three years.[28]

For all of their purported idealism, most Americans did not cling long to any illusions about the UN's capacity to remake the world or to do away with national interests. Rather, they have proved to be consistently hardheaded and somewhat nationalistic in their views about UN performance. They remain largely faithful to the founding conception of what a world organization ought to be and to the need for U.S. engagement and leadership. At many points, however, they have found reason to fault the way in which the UN has gone about its work. Americans, by and large, are not ambivalent about the existence of the UN or about U.S. participation. These are, to most people, givens. Americans, however, are today, as they have been since the UN's founding, sharply divided about the organization's operations and performance. Americans are far more accepting of the UN as a necessary part of the fabric of international relations than they are of its failings and shortcomings. They want the United States to be in the UN, but, at the same time, they expect their representatives to push hard for improvements in the way the UN goes about its important work.

To observers from other nations, this dual attitude may at times appear inconsistent or even duplicitous. Most Americans, however, see nothing wrong with being counted both among the UN's strongest supporters and among its strongest critics.

Demographics:
Who Are the Believers, Skeptics, and Opponents?

Americans as a whole appear ambivalent about the UN in part because different groups of citizens have quite distinct views. Within each of these groups, however, the degree of support or opposition to the world body has tended to be fairly consistent through the years. The consistency and distinctiveness of these perspectives, in fact, have made it more difficult to produce a nationwide consensus. Since the days of the League of Nations—which was closely and personally associated with President Wilson—Democrats in general have been more supportive of international organization than Republicans; liberals and moderates more than conservatives; younger more than older people; and women more than men. But socioeconomic, educational, ethnic, and geographical factors have also played a part.

A closer look at the demographic breakdowns for the Pew Research Center surveys of September 1997, February 1996, and June 1995 will give a clearer sense of who is most and least favorably disposed toward the United Nations. Focusing on the core question of whether a respondent's opinion of the world body is very favorable, mostly favorable, mostly unfavorable, or very unfavorable, the historic trends noted above appear to be holding up consistently.[29] In the 1997 survey, 42 percent more women saw the UN favorably than unfavorably, while the figure for men was 28 percent. Among 18- to 29-year-olds, the same favorable margin was 44 percent, while for those 65 or older it was 27 percent. The difference was 52 percent for Democrats and only 19 percent for Republicans. The disparities between those who voted for Clinton in 1996 and those who voted for Bob Dole were even wider, with Dole voters twice as likely to have unfavorable views and almost three times as likely to have very unfavorable opinions of the UN. This provides further evidence of what has become painfully obvious in congressional debates: UN issues are evoking increasingly partisan responses in the domestic political discourse.

The 1997 results also appeared to confirm, as have many earlier polls, that education and income levels matter. College graduates once again were the most favorable, and those with less than a high school education the least positive. In fact, those who had not completed high school were twice as likely to have a "very unfavorable" view of the UN than college graduates. (In a number of surveys through the years, the best educated respondents have been the most committed to staying in the organization, but they have also tended to be relatively critical of UN performance and desirous of seeing it improved.) In the 1997 Pew poll those with family incomes above $75,000 were the most favorable, and those under $20,000 the least. The differences among geographic regions were not large, but as in most polls, those from the East and Midwest tended to be a bit more positive than those from the South and West. The South had the most "very unfavorable" responses, although overall southerners were slightly more positive than westerners.

As in past polls, in the 1997 Pew survey Jews were the most supportive of the UN among religious groups, with 72 percent rating the UN favorably and only 23 percent unfavorably. Jewish attitudes toward the UN were even more positive in the December 1998–January 1999 Zogby International poll: 85 percent favorable and 8 percent unfavorable. Given the legacy of the Zionism-racism resolution and Israel's relatively isolated position in the General Assembly (it alone belongs to no regional group), it is remarkable that Jewish Americans have remained so favorably disposed toward the world organization—a fact that few diplomats at the UN seem to understand or appreciate. These results underline just how distorted is the canard that is still sometimes heard in diplomatic circles that Jewish influence is somehow behind American disillusionment with the UN. In both polls Catholics and nonevangelical Protestants also had favorable opinions of the UN, while evangelicals and born-again Christians gave the UN somewhat lower marks than the national average, as one might expect. Hispanics and Asian Americans, as usual, saw the UN in a relatively positive light in both surveys. Among racial and ethnic groups, they tend to be the most consistently supportive of the UN. In the Zogby poll, African Americans were more favorable to the UN than were non-Hispanic whites, as has historically been the pattern, but the opposite held true in the 1997 survey.[30] (On the question of full payment of UN dues, however, African Americans have been more supportive than whites with some regularity.)

Who has the least favorable views of the UN? Who are the hard-core opponents of multilateral cooperation? In the recent Zogby survey those with the highest proportion of "very unfavorable" responses were born-again Christians (16.6 percent) and Republicans (16.2 percent), while in 1997 they were male veterans over 57 years old (17.6 percent). A year earlier, in the February 1996 poll, they were supporters of Pat Buchanan (22.1 percent) and "regular" listeners to talk radio (17.8 percent). When asked which news story they followed very closely, those viewing the UN "very unfavorably" were most likely to cite the Republican primary in New Hampshire and new legislation to ease regulations on telecommunications. They were also the least likely to follow the ups and downs of the stock market. Those with a dim view of the UN, in other words, may tend to fit the profile of GOP activists concerned about government regulation of private enterprise yet not sufficiently affluent to be heavily invested in the stock market.

The results of the February 1996 Pew survey pointed to a major cleavage within the GOP on UN issues in the midst of the presidential primary season. Sixty-four percent of nonevangelical Republicans gave the UN "favorable" ratings, only 1 percent below the national average and 3 percent less than independents gave the world body. Evangelical Republicans, in contrast, rated the UN favorably only 43 percent of the time, a full 21 percent less than other Republicans. These results confirm the split discussed earlier between the traditionally internationalist wing of the party, prominently represented by President Bush, and those more populist party activists who are deeply suspicious of international organizations as potential threats to American values and sovereignty. On domestic issues the former tend to be economic conservatives or libertarians and the latter to focus heavily on social or moral issues. This cleavage, in turn, has greatly complicated efforts in recent years to enunciate a coherent U.S. strategy toward the UN or to develop bipartisan support in Congress for international policy initiatives.

International organizations, therefore, find themselves caught between two camps in Republican party politics: those who believe in free trade, asserting U.S. global leadership, respecting international commitments, and building international law and institutions, yet are critical of UN managerial and operational deficiencies;[31] and those who are protectionist, suspicious of international entanglements, concerned about degradations of national sovereignty, and wary that participation in multilateral processes and institutions could do lasting harm to American values and interests. The former tend to be wealthier, better educated, and more likely to believe that they benefit from free trade and the globalization of the economy. The latter are generally less affluent, less educated, and much less able to defend their jobs and communities from the ravages of global economic competition. Feeling disenfranchised and marginalized by the internationalist instincts of more traditional Democratic and Republican leaders alike, many of these people have turned to Pat Buchanan's brand of populism, with its strong anti-UN rhetoric.

This split within Republican ranks can be seen most starkly in congressional debates about the World Trade Organization, the World Bank, and the International Monetary Fund. Although the UN itself has little impact on transnational economic developments, it symbolizes much that the first group espouses and the second group dreads. Both camps, however, can agree that the UN is ineffective and needs a major overhaul, so pushing for deep UN reform is a platform with which Republican legislators can appeal to both wings of the party, despite their intractable differences about ultimate purposes. In this way, and through deeper commitment and superior political organizing, those who lack the material and educational advantages that would normally translate into political power have had a disproportionately influential voice on UN-related issues on the Hill, where it is usually easier to block something you do not like than to build support for something that you do.

Reaching Congress: A Mission Impossible?

Questions about apparent discrepancies in the attitudes of the general populace toward international organization and those of their representatives in Congress have persisted throughout this century. Why, for example, has the apparently widespread pro-UN public sentiment not been felt more directly and forcefully in congressional debates? According to Kull and Destler, based on the extensive PIPA study at the University of Maryland, "on no topic do policy practitioners misread the U.S. public more than on the subject of the United Nations."[32] Although a June 1996 PIPA poll found a 2-to-1 majority (58 to 29 percent) of public respondents favoring "the US paying its UN dues in full," when PIPA at the same time asked elites from Congress, the executive branch, media, and NGOs about their perceptions of public attitudes on this issue, the response was radically different. Among the sample of policymakers and policy influentials, "a plurality (48 percent) of all respondents, and an overwhelming majority (82 percent) of members of Congress and 63 percent of journalists said that Americans generally held a negative view of paying UN dues."[33] PIPA discovered similar misperceptions on a wide range of foreign policy issues, with policy elites consistently assuming that the public is much less internationalist than in fact polls would suggest.

Clearly sentiments that are more supportive of the UN have not been articulated and delivered in a politically effective manner. Poll results are a poor substitute for political action. In part, it appears that some UN advocates have become discouraged by the meager results their repeated appeals have achieved on Capitol Hill. They fret that their case is not getting a fair hearing and that key congressional leaders have a closed mind on these questions. UN supporters also tend to correspond or meet with the more supportive members of Congress, which tends to be a considerably more pleasant experience than confronting those ideologically opposed to the world organization. And, not surprisingly, in many cases UN supporters are not well organized in the congressional districts of those representatives who are most skeptical of the UN. As the historical record makes all too clear, pro-UN groups—lacking consistent leadership, effective organization, and a compelling message—have failed miserably in their efforts to translate public sentiment into political capital.[34] Fairly or not, sympathetic members of Congress have complained for years that neither they nor their less sympathetic colleagues receive many letters, calls, or visits urging support for UN funding or programs. An exasperated Senator Richard G. Lugar, R-Ind., who championed the need to meet U.S. financial obligations to the UN, commented in 1998 that constituents were not "beating down the doors for the United States to pay for its share at the U.N. There's even grudging toleration of it."[35]

There is reason to believe, as well, that support for the UN among the American people may be as shallow as it is wide. In its 1990 and 1994 surveys, the Chicago Council on Foreign Relations asked public and elite respondents whether each of sixteen issues "should be a very important foreign policy goal of the United States." For the public "strengthening the United Nations" ranked tenth and for the elites eleventh of the sixteen in 1994. From 1990 to 1994 "support for strengthening the United Nations has increased among the public from 44 percent to 51 percent, but has declined among the leaders, a reversal of previous trends."[36] According to the September 1997 Pew survey, 30 percent of the public cited "strengthening the United Nations" as a "top priority," down from 36 percent in June 1995 and 41 percent in September 1993. Likewise, support for making "strengthening the United Nations" a top priority fell from 1993 to 1997 within every elite group interviewed by Pew, most to a level lower than the general public.[37] Whereas 33 percent of labor leaders said it should be a top priority, only 13 percent of policy staff on Capitol Hill agreed, illustrating once again the sharp difference between Democratic and Republican attitudes. All of this suggests that political elites do not hear much public demand for strengthening U.S. relations with the UN for two reasons. First, the elites themselves, as a whole, are not favorably disposed to taking up such a thorny issue and hence are not prone to listen for it. Second, the general public gives the matter a low, and declining, priority in any case.

Because the U.S. relationship with the UN is not considered a top priority by either the public or policy elites, it has hardly been a make-or-break issue in congressional elections. A 1998 survey commissioned by the United Nations Association found that a majority of Americans claimed they would be less likely to vote for a candidate who favors withdrawing from the UN or not paying UN dues, but in reality these have never been significant issues in congressional elections.[38] Other than in times of war, domestic questions almost always are decisive. Besides, incumbents usually win re-election handily unless the electorate is deeply dissatisfied with the national state of affairs. For example, more than 98 percent of House members running for reelection in November 1998 won, regardless of party or ideology, much less of whether they had pro- or anti-UN voting records.

In this regard, a compilation of key House votes relating to the UN during the 105th Congress (1997–98) is instructive. The Emergency Coalition for U.S. Financial Support of the United Nations identified nine important votes concerning UN funding, peacekeeping, UNESCO-sponsored programs, and withdrawal from the organization. Of the House members, 38 voted consistently on the anti-UN side (36 Republicans and 2 Democrats) and 124 (117 Democrats, 6 Republicans, and 1 independent) voted consistently for the UN. All 148 of these representatives who ran for reelection (14 did not) won, regardless of whether they could be labeled as knee-jerk UN supporters or opponents. It is also worth noting, given the prevalent characterization of the House as being unremittingly hostile toward international organization, that those voting consistently for funding and participation in UN programs actually outnumbered those consistently opposed by more than a 3-to-1 margin.

These findings suggest that the difficulties UN funding bills have confronted in Congress cannot be blamed entirely on the body's alleged ideological disposition against the UN in particular and international organization in general. Public attitudes toward UN funding, moreover, are not as uniformly positive as UN support groups have tended to claim. For example, when asked, Americans are likely to say, as do their representatives in Congress, that the United States pays too large a share of the UN's costs. In an October 1990 Gallup Poll, at a high point in UN popularity, 40 percent responded that the U.S. contribution was "too much," 5 percent "too little," and 31 percent "about right."[39] According to the results of a June 1995 Times Mirror survey, 60 percent thought that the United States paid more than its "fair share" compared with "other major countries," 4 percent less, and 28 percent just its fair share.[40] When asked by CBS News in June 1995 whether U.S. financial support for the UN should be "increased, decreased, or kept the same," the responses were 11, 28, and 54 percent, respectively. As noted above, whatever their impressions and perceptions, most respondents do not have even the vaguest notion of what the United States actually is supposed to pay, either in absolute or percentage terms.

The November 1997 CNN/USA Today poll therefore approached this issue in two different ways. When asked with no preliminary explanation whether "the amount of money the United States currently contributes to the United Nations' budget is too much, too little, or about the right amount," 42 percent said "too much," 5 percent "too little," and 32 percent "about the right amount." Ironically, the results were even more negative when the pollster first explained the UN's assessment formula, noted that the United States paid 25 percent because of its share of the world economy and ability to pay, and pointed out that current U.S. dues for the regular budget were $312 million. Knowing these basic facts, 52 percent responded "too much," 3 percent "too little," and 38 percent "about right." As often happens when large dollar figures are cited in poll questions, the negative results may be attributable in part to the mention of the specific amount, which would have appeared large to many people when not seen in context, especially to fiscal conservatives, African Americans, and people with low income and educational levels, as was the case here. There was little difference, however, in the responses of Democrats, Republicans, and independents to these questions, suggesting that concerns over the size and share of U.S. payments to the UN are well distributed over much of the political spectrum.

Two PIPA surveys, in February 1994 and June 1996, also sought to delve deeper into attitudes toward U.S. payments to the UN by addressing the question from two different angles. In the earlier poll, 34 percent said they thought U.S. peacekeeping assessments were "too high," 14 percent "too low," and 32 percent "about right."[41] After the assessment formula was described in a positive way, 33 percent still said that the amount was "too high," the number saying it was "too low" dropped to 4 percent, and those choosing "about right" rose sharply to 58 percent. It is striking that, even after the explanation, one-third of the respondents insisted that the United

THE POLITICAL LANDSCAPE 275

States was paying too much—apparently additional information was not going to dissuade them—and that the growth in the "about right" category came almost entirely from those who had thought the United States had been paying too little and from those who had been undecided or unsure of how to respond. In 1996, 50 percent of those interviewed replied that the U.S. dues assessment was "more than its fair share" compared with "other countries," 4 percent thought it was too little, and 31 percent believed it was "about right." When told that "the US is assessed 25 percent because that is its share of the world economy," 37 percent still declared it "unfair," while 56 percent thought the method "fair." Again, more than one-third were not moved by this oversimplified explanation of the logic of the UN methodology, which also takes per capita income into account to relieve the burden on poorer countries.

In 1994 and 1995, PIPA included a series of questions in its polls designed to illicit the public's views on the magnitude of U.S. peacekeeping payments to the UN. Respondents were asked about peacekeeping outlays, as a percentage of the defense budget and in comparison to other areas of federal spending, and about the level of per capita taxes going to cover peacekeeping operations. In each case, as one would expect, respondents had a wildly inflated view of what was actually being expended for these tasks; 61 percent in the April 1995 survey believed "the amount of money the US spends on peacekeeping is probably too much."[42] Although PIPA found considerable support for raising U.S. payments for UN peacekeeping once the respondents had received more information on the actual percentages and outlays involved, the politically salient fact is that most Americans today perceive—rightly or wrongly—that both absolute expenditures on the UN and the U.S. share of the burden are much too high. Facts aside, these perceptions fuel and shape the American political debate, especially in Congress, on relations with the UN and with the other member states.

But what of illegal withholdings of assessed dues payments to the UN? Surely there is little public support for such strong-armed tactics? Actually, the picture is mixed, with more support for withholdings than one might expect given the widespread public commitment to maintaining the world body and the U.S. role in it. In February 1997, *Time*/CNN posed the following question:

As you may know, the United States currently owes the United Nations approximately one billion dollars in back dues. Do you think the United States should: Pay the U.N. now what it owes in back dues because it is the U.S.'s

obligation to pay its share of the U.N. budget, or not pay back dues to the U.N.
until it carries out reforms that the U.S. has requested?

Despite the use of phrases such as "owes back dues" and "obligation to pay
its share," a plurality of 47 percent responded that payment should not be
made until reforms are carried out, while 41 percent said the United States
should pay now. As usual, those who felt strongest about the need to pay
promptly included Jews (73 percent), those with a post-graduate education
(55 percent), blacks (52 percent), and 18- to 29-year-olds (47 percent).
There was virtually no difference between men and women or among
Democrats, Republicans, and independents, all of whom showed a plurality
for continuing to withhold until reforms are accomplished.[43]

The support for withholding was even stronger in the November 1997
CNN/USA Today poll, which employed different wording. Noting that the
United States "has withheld more than 1 billion dollars in dues over the past
few years to force the UN (United Nations) to change its financial practices," the pollsters then asked "do you favor or oppose this decision by the
US?" When seen as a question of reversing U.S. policy and when linked to
changes in the UN's "financial practices," the public favored the decision to
withhold by more than a 2-to-1 margin (63 to 26 percent). In this case
Republicans (70 to 21 percent) were somewhat more favorable to maintaining the withholding policy than were Democrats (61 to 28 percent) and
independents (60 to 29 percent). Regardless of party affiliation, however, the
ratio was still more than 2 to 1. The responses from moderates (66 to
26 percent) and conservatives (66 to 23 percent) were almost uniform.
These results are particularly significant because the survey was undertaken
when the legislative arrears-for-reform package was being debated in the
House of Representatives. Given the wording of the question, the sharp
response suggests that if this issue is cast as a U.S.-versus-the-world question, then there is no doubt about where the public would stand.[44]

As a general matter, however, Americans do believe that the United
States, as other member states, should pay its dues to the world organization. This is a different and more abstract question, it should be emphasized, than whether there is support for the existing withholding policy.
A series of polls over the past five years has found a large majority of
Americans—usually by a 2-to-1 ratio—favoring the United States paying
its "dues" or "back dues" to the UN in full.[45] A December 1995 Wirthlin
poll for UNA-USA and a September 1996 PIPA survey both found that
congressional candidates who favored paying UN dues would receive more

support than those who did not.[46] In the Wirthlin survey, however, while 30 percent said they would be less likely and 13 percent more likely to reelect a member of Congress who "voted against paying America's dues to the United Nations," a full 46 percent—more than the other two responses combined—said that this issue would "not affect" their voting. Withholding dues from the UN may not win legislators large numbers of votes, but the political costs are unlikely to be very large either.

None of these poll results, of course, should be seen in a political or institutional vacuum. Congress takes its budgetary prerogatives very seriously. The public also tends to look to Congress for fiscal responsibility. For example, half of the respondents to a May 1993 CBS News survey said that they trusted Congress more than the president to make decisions about the U.S. budget (although both branches were in Democratic hands at that point). People, moreover, expect the executive and congressional branches to work together on major policy challenges. When surveyed, pluralities usually respond that the role of Congress in the making of foreign policy is about right.[47]

More vigorous presidential leadership on these questions could make a difference. In theory, the breadth of public sympathy for the world body should make it possible to rally greater public and even congressional support for the payment of arrears. Championing the payment of UN arrears in a more visible and concerted manner would seem to entail relatively modest political risks; the hard-core opponents are not going to support the president in any case. But such a step also would promise few political dividends in light of the shallow and diffuse character of public support for the UN. F. Chris Garcia, a political science professor at the University of New Mexico, made a telling comment in May 1998 when asked why Ambassador Bill Richardson was preparing to move within President Clinton's cabinet from the post of permanent representative to the UN to secretary of energy. "The energy position is so important, particularly to New Mexico, that if he's looking to run in a statewide race, this would certainly help him in a very tangible way," Garcia said. "The United Nations position is more symbolic."[48] The United Nations is for the president, as for the people, a matter of priorities. In January 1998, for the first time President Clinton included payment of America's debt to the UN as one of many legislative goals articulated in his State of the Union message, a plea he repeated the next year. Yet the issue remains a largely symbolic one, devoid of politically meaningful content. It is still hardly at the top of his— or the public's—political agenda, permitting congressional adversaries to force the president's hand by tying UN payments to other, more politically salient, issues.

A prime example was the move by Representative Smith to attach antiabortion language to the 1998 reform-for-arrears bill that would have both reorganized the State Department and appropriated much of the U.S. arrears to the UN in return for deeper reforms and a larger congressional voice in U.S. policies toward the world body. Specifically, Smith's amendment would have prohibited U.S. aid to international organizations that lobby foreign governments to ease their policies restricting abortions. Although the 1998 wording worked out in a House-Senate conference report was a somewhat watered-down version of what Smith had sought in past years, the president vetoed the legislation in October 1998 because of its anti-abortion content.[49] This, in turn, doomed prospects for resolving the U.S. debt to the UN and for revising its assessment scale. As noted in chapter 9, the fallout has already included the Assembly's rebuff of the U.S. candidate for its prime budgetary oversight body. Unless unexpected funds are appropriated for the UN in late 1999, the next step could be a move in January 2000 to deny the United States its vote in the General Assembly, triggering a confrontation that could make the article 19 crisis of the early 1960s appear tame in comparison.

According to Smith, who supports other UN programs, "if President Clinton is serious about the problems looming before the United States, he needs to reconsider his *own* priorities."[50] To Senate Majority Leader Trent Lott, R-Miss., the president's veto threat indicated that he "apparently doesn't care" about paying the dues. Putting it more bluntly, as usual, Senator Helms, whose arrears-for-reform package was at risk, suggested in April 1998 that for the president "this is show-and-tell day. Put up or shut up." But as Joseph R. Biden Jr., D-Del., Helms's cosponsor of the UN package, acknowledged, as a political issue, "abortion is in a league of its own. . . . This is a big deal for the Administration." Apparently so, because the president made no reference to the arrears in his 1998 speech to the General Assembly. Suggesting that "Chris Smith and Bill Clinton deserve each other on this one," a Democratic Senate staffer ruefully commented that "they're playing chicken. But what they don't care about is the U.N."[51] This cynicism would appear to be justified: just four years earlier the president decided to sign the fiscal year 1994–95 State Department authorization bill despite its inclusion of the unilateral 25 percent cap on peacekeeping payments and other withholdings of assessed dues, which he declared "could place the United States in violation of its international treaty obligations."[52] He complained, but he signed. The lesson is clear: in terms of domestic politics, abortion matters, international commitments do not.

In contrast, it should be recalled that the last time a president took on a hostile Congress over the fate of an international organization was Woodrow Wilson's futile defense of the League of Nations eighty years ago. It was not an encouraging precedent. A Democratic president with considerable oratorical skills sought to go over the heads of a Republican Congress in a direct and heartfelt appeal to the American people. "I am convinced, after crossing the continent," declared Wilson, "that there is no sort of doubt that eighty percent of the people of the United States are for the League of Nations." Furthermore, he charged that "all the elements that tended toward disloyalty [in World War I] are against the League."[53] Having persuaded himself of his project's popularity, having demonized his political adversaries, and having assured himself of the moral righteousness of his cause, Wilson was in no mood for reaching out to the Senate reservationists or for compromising what he viewed as points of high principle.[54] According to Harold Evans, when Senator Lodge and Theodore Roosevelt met in December 1918 to map their opposing strategy, "both men realized Wilson's league was so popular it could not be defeated outright. They agreed it would have to be nibbled to death."[55] Their tactics succeeded then, as they have so often since, despite the impressive continuity of American public support for international organization.

Presidents Roosevelt and Truman, determined not to repeat Wilson's mistakes, co-opted the Republican legislators and got them on board early in the process. In his first term Clinton, unsure of himself both in foreign affairs and in dealing with Congress, was slow to learn this lesson. And relatively few Republican legislators still paid homage to the Vandenberg school of statesmanship and bipartisanship. As a result enormous damage has been done to U.S.-UN relations. In trying to revive and restructure this relationship it should be understood that public opinion polls, citations of international obligations, and inspiring rhetoric will not convince Congress to move on issues, particularly financial ones, when it feels that fundamental principles of congressional-executive relations are at stake. As outlined in the next chapter, the only answer, and the one that Washington has been stumbling toward in recent years, is to bring Congress into the U.S. decisionmaking process as a full partner in the reshaping of policies toward international organization. It won't be easy, but the easy answers have been tried and found lacking.

CHAPTER ELEVEN

Old Realities, New Opportunities

AS THE PRECEDING CHAPTERS make abundantly and painfully clear, the roots of American ambivalence toward international organization are many and deep. They stem from the nation's political culture, from the structure of its institutions of government, and from its place in the hierarchy of nations, as well as from the values and attitudes of its people. Most Americans have viewed international institutions with more doubt and disappointment than hostility, with more unfulfilled idealism than unremitting cynicism. As a result the political mainstream no longer expects much or fears much from international bodies. The debate has been left to the internationalist and unilateralist flanks, both firmly anchored in the local political soil and with a distinctively American character. Drawing on deep wells of idealism and humanitarianism, internationalist political values and policy prescriptions continue to thrive in the nation's academic, nonprofit, and religious institutions. They have helped to shape American responses to the crises in Kosovo, Haiti, Kuwait, and, initially, Somalia. But in defining U.S. relations with international bodies, it has been the hard-core opponents of international organization who have been the most highly charged emotionally and ideologically. The intensity of their feelings and the depth of their animosity have permitted them to exercise political influence out of all proportion to their numbers. Given the stubbornness of this rift, these two unbending and diametrically opposed schools of thought have coexisted with remarkably little interaction or discernible convergence for decade after decade, leaving little room for creativity or flexibility in policymaking.

Buffeted by these two seemingly irreconcilable impulses, U.S. policy-makers have found it next to impossible to speak with a strong and consistent voice in global political forums. On the one hand, this century has produced, often with far-sighted U.S. leadership, a far broader and more diverse set of multilateral institutions than had ever before been imagined. On the other hand, Americans have been more persistently divided about international institutions and their nation's proper place in them than about any other foreign policy issue. These fissures, moreover, are increasingly evident these days as the tide toward globalization and multilateralism begins to appear irreversible.

It seems ages ago when, at a turning point in world history and with dynamic and determined presidential leadership, these differences were muted temporarily during the latter stages of World War II, permitting at least the appearance of a national consensus behind the founding of the United Nations in 1945. Yet, even at this most creative moment, the world organization that was produced was itself a compromise, a modest structure charged with fulfilling great ambitions. And, as chronicled in previous chapters, several problematic matters were left unsettled, only to fuel controversies years later. The United Nations, in short, was the product of ambivalence. Ironically, at its founding other countries appeared more cautious and doubtful about the organization's prospects than was the United States. The unusually propitious conditions that permitted the establishment of the United Nations, moreover, wilted quickly in the face of the unfolding cold war.

Since the heady days of San Francisco and the remarkably brief honeymoon that followed, domestic divisions over how the United States should interact with the outside world have given American policies toward the world body an inconsistent, patchwork look. Allies and adversaries alike have been puzzled both about the sources of American ambivalence and about how to deal with its policy consequences. Surely some times have been better than others, and the organization has managed to expand and diversify its programs over the years. During the cold war era, successive administrations in Washington—Democratic and Republican alike—found ways to keep congressional complaints in check, in part because neither end of Pennsylvania Avenue could risk letting the bottom fall out of U.S. relations with the UN, despite an assortment of tensions and crises along the way.

Yet the sense of bipartisan national commitment, the spirit of confident internationalism, and the optimism about the prospects for broad-based international cooperation that permeated the founding conference have not been replicated over the intervening half century. The United Nations, like the proverbial man in the middle, has attracted flack from both political flanks. As detailed in the preceding chapter, the middle has held, but its enthusiasm and sense of assurance, both already tempered, have begun to sag ominously. Created, moreover, at a time when the can-do spirit of New Dealism still lingered in the nation's capital and people thought that government still had most of the answers for a brighter future, the United Nations has found it hard to adjust to an era of declining confidence in government, of shrinking budgets, and of expanding roles for civil society and for all sorts of nonstate actors. In turn, as chapter 3 underlined, the UN has come to appear to some as a relic from an earlier age of big government and statist solutions.

The roots of ambivalence, in sum, have been nourished by key themes from America's history, geography, ideology, values, and political culture, as well as by its geopolitical position and the course of international events. Attempts to bring these divergent threads together have been hampered by the nature and structure of the U.S. political system, with its emphasis on the separation of powers, single-issue domestic constituencies, two competing political parties, and an assertive media and private sector. Treated by all sides as an essentially symbolic issue, relations with the UN, the ultimate political football, have gotten kicked around Washington year after year. As if the structural impediments were not debilitating enough, relations with the world body have been complicated by America's notion of its own exceptionalism, described in chapter 2, and by its special sense of idealism, independence, and individuality coupled with the exercise of raw political, economic, and military power.

Further compounding these underlying factors are the anomalies of the current strategic and political situation. Almost a decade after the fall of communism, U.S. foreign policy is still struggling to find its way in the messy post–cold war world. Lacking a compelling strategic rationale to galvanize bipartisan public support for international involvements, U.S. policymaking has tended, even more than usual, to be reactive and based on short-term perspectives. Longer-range goals, such as reinforcing the structures and redirecting the course of the postwar system of international institutions, have consequently been shunted aside in favor of coping with the day's emergencies. The executive branch continues to articulate, often quite eloquently, the case for meeting America's international obligations. But, as chapter 10 pointed out, its sporadic efforts have not been backed by the kind of major investment of political capital that could persuade a recalcitrant and partisan Congress.

Reflexively seeking the middle ground, President Clinton—like his political adversaries—at times has acted as if support for international institutions is a "liberal," or interventionist, stance rather than a mainstream pillar of the postwar foreign policy consensus. Partly because of its failure to make a convincing positive case for why the nation would benefit from a strengthened international system in the twenty-first century, the Clinton administration has been put on the defensive both on Capitol Hill and in the halls of the UN. Trapped between these two irreconcilable poles, neither of which it can control, the administration—like the UN itself—has failed to meet either's expectations. The most painful example was the president's decision in October 1998 to veto the bill containing the UN arrears package because of language on abortion he found politically unacceptable, not because of its long list of unilateral demands on the UN and the other member states.[1]

If the Clinton administration has been hesitant and half-hearted, then the Republican majority in Congress has been irresponsible and short-sighted, again and again disregarding America's legal and financial obligations when they proved inconvenient. Correctly sensing that the president's strength and confidence in domestic affairs were matched by uncertainty and hesitancy in the international arena, congressional leaders have repeatedly challenged his authority over the conduct of foreign policy, most recently in Kosovo. As chapters 7, 8, and 9 assiduously chronicle, no target has been more tempting than Clinton's handling of relations with and funding of the UN and its peacekeeping operations. For those hard-core skeptics on the political right, international organization, feared as a stepping stone toward world government, has been a red-flag issue throughout this century. As in Wilson's days, the sight of a Democratic president with internationalist leanings once again has triggered the most nationalistic and jingoistic impulses of some of the more independent-minded legislators in the Republican-controlled Congress. Add to this Clinton's tendency in his early years, like Wilson before him, to consult too little and too late with congressional leaders on questions relating to international institutions, and the result is a crippling combination of executive-legislative gridlock, of weak congressional leadership, and of strident partisanship on a host of matters relating to international law and organization.

No Shortcuts or Easy Solutions

None of this will be easy to mend, and no miracle cures are in sight. The United States is on a collision course with other member states. Even if the Helms-Biden arrears-for-reform legislation is approved by Congress and signed by the president—with or without Representative Smith's antiabortion rider—there would not be enough money in the first year's payments to the UN to reduce the U.S. arrears below the level that would trigger an automatic loss of vote in the General Assembly under the provisions of article 19. Such a step, in turn, could spark either deeper soul searching at the UN as well as in Washington or a nasty confrontation between the United States and other member states. Ominously, some congressional Republicans apparently would welcome such a confrontation.[2] From the UN's perspective, the Helms-Biden legislation is at best a mixed blessing. A step forward in some respects, the arrears-for-reform measure would repay only about two-thirds of what the UN says it is owed, while requiring that the remainder be placed in a contested arrears account that could not be counted in future article 19 calculations. As chapter 8 related, the legislation contains a large number of unilateral demands or benchmarks that other member states would find excruciatingly hard to swallow. Meanwhile, the coming U.S. presidential election year is bound to generate more than its share of simplistic and partisan commentary on the UN. There is nothing in the legislation, moreover, that would prevent another round of congressional recriminations and demands a few years down the road. Efforts to implement the many conditions attached to this legislation are bound to touch off further controversy in Washington as well as at the UN. Alternatively, at some point in the future pressures might be eased with a different president, a different Congress, and a different chairman of the Senate Foreign Relations Committee. Yet even such an optimistic scenario would not solve any of the underlying strategic, political, and cultural issues that set America apart from the other member states and from the international secretariats.

Doubts about international organization are deeply embedded in the American political culture. They cannot be wished away or addressed with bandage "solutions." They are not just going to fade away as if they were some sort of a passing fad or aberration. It does not help, moreover, to dismiss these complaints as simply the products of American arrogance, paranoia, ignorance, or xenophobia, or to grandly assert the primacy of international obligations and commitments over the demands of domestic politics. For any country, foreign policy initiatives and arrangements that do not have broad public and parliamentary support will be vulnerable over the long run. It is sobering, in this regard, to note that congressional discomfort with international organization has persisted throughout this century despite public opinion surveys year after year suggesting that the people were more supportive than their representatives. Clearly, neither sending legislators copies of poll results nor conducting education and public relations campaigns is the answer. As noted in chapter 10, there is no evidence that the voting records on UN issues of members of Congress affected the outcome of any of their races for reelection in November 1998.

Surely some of the congressional concerns lack substance, balance, and gravity, yet others raise important and legitimate questions both about how foreign policy is made in the United States and about how it is executed within international organizations. As chapter 9 documented, questions about burden sharing and about how America fits into universal bodies are older than the UN itself. Most were left unresolved at San Francisco, and satisfactory answers have yet to be found. There is nothing sacrosanct about the organization's existing financial and burden-sharing arrangements, most of which are not charter-based. Certainly U.S. representatives have sometimes dressed up narrow matters of national interest—such as financial assessments—as grand questions of principle, but what delegation has not done that on occasion? More important, through the years U.S. representatives have also been among the first to articulate the need for constructive change in the UN and other world bodies even when others were quite comfortable with the status quo, with maintaining the symbolism of multilateral cooperation even when its substance waned, and with sweeping problems under the rug.

That the United States has remained a leading participant in the United Nations for more than half a century is, under the circumstances, a remarkable accomplishment. It attests to the consummate political skills of Roosevelt and Truman, to the strength of the internationalist establishment until it imploded over Vietnam, to the persistence of the idealistic strain in the American public, and to the utility of the world organization in strategic, as well as functional and humanitarian terms, during the four decades of the cold war. The United States suffered more than its share of political setbacks in UN forums over these years, but, as chapter 5 relates, although its commitment wavered, it never broke. The current crisis of confidence between the United States and the UN, however, is more generic and therefore that much more worrisome. It stems from a cumulative process of disaffection (on both sides of this equation), from a creeping concern about the implications of globalization, and from a core American dissatisfaction with the rules of the game as they were defined more than five decades ago for a smaller and tamer UN.

Since the collapse of communism, the United States on the whole (despite some recent slippage) has done better on political, as well as administrative, issues in the UN than in earlier years when its full-hearted participation was less in doubt. Today, there is no single critical crisis to be overcome, flaw to be corrected, or wrong to be righted. The seemingly existential angst stems instead from a general uneasiness with America's place in the UN and with the UN's place in the world. Chapter 10 points out that this affliction has certainly not affected the citizenry evenly and that most Americans remain both supportive and respectful of the world body—if only in a vague sort of way.

The fact that this White House, with its well-honed political instincts, has not chosen to make a more impassioned and concerted effort to rally public and congressional support for the beleaguered UN, however, attests to a pervasive sense among Democratic as well as Republican political elites that, at least at this point in time, this is not a winning cause. A lame duck president with high job approval ratings could well afford to take a few political risks by exercising more than rhetorical leadership on questions like this that could affect his place in history, but Clinton apparently sees little political rationale for doing so. The task for UN supporters, then, is not so much to make the case for the value of the world organization as to help build the kind of political operation that would convince the president and congressional leaders that there are solid domestic political reasons, and not just legal and strategic ones, for giving a higher priority to the UN and other international organizations.[3] If bashing the UN and forsaking international commitments remain cost free at the ballot box, then members of Congress will have little incentive to take more responsible positions.

Toward a New Domestic Compact

Given the sorry history related in the foregoing chapters, it will require nothing less than a new domestic compact among competing political factions to rearrange the terms and dynamics of the political tug-of-war within the United States on UN issues. A good place to start would be for the two opposing schools of thought, or at least the more centrist elements within them, to begin to talk to each other on a serious and sustained basis. Neither the UN nor its critics are going away any time soon. No one is going to win this stale and Pyrrhic struggle. In fact there is so little public debate on U.S.-UN issues these days, and the quality of what exists is so poor, that it is little wonder that most Americans are disinterested. At the same time, the polarization, at least among policy influentials, on these questions is both remarkable and remarkably counterproductive. It produces and perpetuates the ambivalence that too often has characterized U.S. policies, sapping the national will as well as undermining America's leadership potential.

Some UN advocates would do well to shed their purist instincts, accept that nationalism need not be the root of all evil, and stop caricaturing those with opposing views as isolationists, neanderthals, or paranoids.[4] UN skeptics, on the other hand, should recognize that there is nothing un-American about the desire to strengthen international cooperation and organization, that neither conservatives nor Americans are alone in their commitment to making the UN work better and more transparently, and that going it alone is no way either to preserve sovereignty or to advance national interests.[5] Advocates have been good at preaching—especially to the converted—but astonishingly poor at organizing effective political action. Skeptics, who have the ear of influential legislators if not the public, are good at identifying what they do not like about the UN and quick to call for further conditions on U.S. payments, but stunningly shy and uncreative about articulating a positive and realistic agenda. At this rate, neither side has much chance of winning the hearts and minds of the American people or of slowing the uncertain drift in UN policymaking. Their feud has become as dysfunctional as it is shrill. Both sides should do more listening and less shouting.

What might advocates and skeptics talk about? They could usefully compare their respective visions about what kind of international organization is needed to forward the interests that America is likely to share with other nations in the new century. For either group to clarify its notion of the national interest would in itself be a step forward.[6] The broader the scope of agreement on ultimate goals, the greater the likelihood that there could be some meeting of the minds about the best route to get there. At this point, however, neither side of the debate has brought much clarity to these fundamental, and presumably a priori, questions.

As underlined at several junctures in this volume, however, there is also a pressing need to get beyond symbolic and rhetorical arguments and down to specifics. Five areas suggest themselves for such a dialogue:

—First, the participants could assess whether existing international institutions have the capacity to achieve the kinds of goals they have jointly identified. By comparing their respective visions with what exists in terms of established international arrangements, it should be possible to identify gaps and obstacles that would need to be overcome. Such an exercise would provide a reality check, as well as a way to gauge whether there is any prospect for convergence even within the United States on the shape and contents of the next stage of the UN reform agenda. Is there, for example, an American consensus on international burden-sharing and decisionmaking procedures, particularly regarding conflict prevention and peacekeeping operations? Of the many options for UN reform being debated in New York, which conform most closely to the preferences and priorities of the American people?

—Second, remarkably little public debate has been focused on the dozens of benchmarks attached to the reform-for-arrears bill. As discussed in chapter 8, these provisions seek to impose a wide range of unilateral conditions that would alter the character of U.S.-UN relations in exchange for partial payment of U.S. arrears. Negotiated behind closed doors by the Clinton administration and the leadership of the Senate Foreign Relations Committee and presented to the American public and to the other UN members as a fait accompli, this package has never been subjected to rigorous and free-ranging public scrutiny.

—Third, American opinion leaders from a variety of perspectives should seek to forge a consensus on how to finance future international endeavors. What costs should be funded through voluntary payments, and which through assessed dues? How should the financial and material burdens be distributed among the member states? Under what conditions, if any, should unilateral withholdings of assessed dues be considered? As chapter 9 noted, Republicans and Democrats alike have a range of views on these questions.

—Fourth, there needs to be a more candid and more public discussion of the changing nature of sovereignty. This has been a lively topic in academic and theoretical literature for some time, but the public discourse has been polarized, rhetorical, and sparse. Internationalists have tended to be too dismissive of the issue and of the concerns that generated it. Conversely, some critics from the right, as noted in chapter 3, have suggested that participation in multilateral bodies entails ceding a freedom of action that in fact long ago ceased to exist. Their scenarios may be far-fetched, but the skeptics do have a point: traditional notions of sovereignty, long under siege from a variety of directions in a rapidly evolving environment, do need refashioning through a fuller review in public and policy circles.

—Fifth, a dialogue between supporters and skeptics could consider ways of easing the recurrent recriminations between Congress and the executive about how commitments to the UN are made, implemented, and monitored. Since its first term, the Clinton administration has improved its consultations with Capitol Hill. In peacekeeping, however, the cost has been to preclude timely and effective UN action in crisis after crisis. Nevertheless, congressional mistrust of both the UN and the administration has not abated. Much more needs to be done, for example, through enhanced communications, a closer oversight role for Congress and its research arms, and a heightened effort to get members of Congress to visit UN operations in the field.

Over time, such a dialogue might be able to flesh out some elements of a national strategy toward international organization that could, for once, command broad bipartisan support.[7]

In considering who might constructively participate in such a dialogue, it should be recalled that the policy debate to date has largely revolved around two different sets of questions: the degree of American involvement in the world (internationalists versus isolationists), and the degree to which the United States should be engaged through unilateral or multilateral undertakings (unilateralists versus multilateralists). It would clarify matters to distinguish between these two dimensions of the argument. Those who are both suspicious of international institutions and eager to minimize America's role in the world (unilateral isolationists) are least likely to join any conceivable national consensus. There may be real possibilities, however, for bringing the other three groups together on a broad national platform that recognizes the need to employ both unilateral and multilateral policy options as practical and appropriate in each situation. Such a platform would also be nondoctrinaire about the degree of American involvement, approaching this question on a pragmatic, case-by-case basis, with a clear understanding that full participation in international organizations does not obligate the United States to become overextended or overly ambitious by reaching beyond a widely acceptable definition of the national interest. One can be constructively engaged in the world, even exercise selective leadership, without offering an unlimited commitment of U.S. funds and forces. The veto, after all, should assure that possibility on the international level, just as the checks and balances of the political structure do on the national level.

Paradoxically, the very intensity of recent attacks on the UN as a threat to sovereignty suggests that they are a defensive, if misguided, reaction to what apparently is perceived to be an almost inevitable tide toward multilateralism and globalization. As discussed in chapter 4, the political class warfare championed by Pat Buchanan has the air of desperation about it. To be a unilateralist and an isolationist on the eve of the millennium requires more than a little denial, for it entails harking back to an era of American history that never was, accepting a minority and marginal place in the U.S. political spectrum, and bucking present-day economic, technological, and geopolitical realities. Caught in this bind, it is understandable that those political figures and commentators with such views will shout the loudest, paint the most dire scenarios, and seek to identify villains—such as the UN—to blame for the course of events.

Long ago interdependence was elevated from the status of a catch phrase of internationalists to a generally accepted, if not wholly welcomed, fact of life. There is no alternative to the global economy; to the flow of people and ideas; to restraints on arms, human rights abuses, and environmental destruction; or to the strengthening of international law and organization. Given these dynamics, it is hardly surprising that norm-building among states, through the codification, accumulation, and dissemination of international law, of both the hard and the soft varieties, is proceeding at a breathtaking pace in field after field. Yet even if the expansion of international law and organization is an inevitable by-product of the nation state system in a period of extraordinary transnational technological, economic, and cultural change—and the nativist protestors are only crying against the prevailing wind—it does not necessarily follow that *this* world organization or *this* set of rules will represent the wave of the future. Although often couched in more prosaic terms, the gathering debate—and we have only seen the preliminary rounds to date—will not be about *whether* the twenty-first century should be a period of international and transnational institution building. That is a given. Rather, it will be about the terms and the blueprints that will guide the construction of the next generation of organizations and arrangements.

These times, therefore, demand that the proponents of international organization stretch their vision as well. Clinging to every timeworn procedure and custom of UN organs, as if they were sacrosanct, is no way to prepare for the challenges ahead. In this regard, the stultifying sense of inertia that pervaded the intergovernmental reform debates at the UN contrasted most unfavorably with the sweeping rhetoric of change with which both governments and commentators greeted the reform process. Defending the UN as it is, after all, is not the way to go about strengthening its capacities and improving its performance. There is every reason to expect that the UN will remain controversial in the United States for years to come. In fact, should the U.S. vote in the General Assembly be denied or seriously challenged in January 2000, then questions relating to the legitimacy of UN procedures and structures will quickly come to a head.

Even if such an acute confrontation is avoided or postponed, American critics and supporters alike will be watching how well and how far the UN member states are willing to go to recast this mid-twentieth-century intergovernmental organ so that it can function usefully in the very different world of the twenty-first century. Although many of the domestic sources for U.S. discontent with the UN in particular and with international organization in general are beyond the reach and influence of other countries, in this area an interactive process appears to be under way between the domestic and international levels of the reform and financing debate. As chapters 8 and 9 documented, there is good reason to believe that congressional recalcitrance on arrears payments has made some member states less willing to move forward on the reform agenda. At the same time, much of the discussion in Washington about reform, finance, and arrears has revolved around perceptions of the course of events in New York as conditioned by the member states. So far the interactive process has largely been a negative one, as the layers of mistrust on these questions have been compounded by critical information gaps and lags. The international community, through its actions, could do a great deal more to reinforce the position of American supporters of the UN. To this end, the new domestic compact should be bolstered and matched by a new international compact before the current downward spiral becomes irreversible.

Toward a New International Compact

This new compact between the United States and the other member states should be based on the answers to two deceptively simple questions. One, what kind of a UN does the United States want: a weak one or a strong one? Two, what kind of a United States do the other UN members want: a follower or a leader? A candid discussion of these questions is long overdue. The old modus vivendi seems to be breaking down. The United States, given its long-running dissatisfaction with the established rules of the game, is asking for, indeed demanding, special treatment. Many Americans believe that their nation gets more respect and deference in the real world outside the world body than within it. The tone is set primarily by the other member states and secondarily by the secretary-general and the secretariat, although both could do more to make the UN a more hospitable place for the exercise of U.S. diplomacy. Formal structural reform of the UN's principal organs is unlikely to provide the answer. The modest results of the intergovernmental reform deliberations to date make clear that the prospects at this point are bleak for rewriting the charter or for changing decisionmaking procedures in a way more favorable to U.S. interests. The political winds, at least in the General Assembly, are blowing in the opposite direction. America's relations with the other member states are hardly an appropriate subject for formal agreements, in any case. They are an apt topic, however, for the kinds of informal consultations, nonpapers, and even nonmeetings for which the UN community is well known, not to mention for nongovernmental dialogues and for the inner reflections of individual delegations and regional groupings. Given the centrality of the United States to the world organization's future, the paucity of serious research, dialogue, and commentary on the subject is both surprising and worrisome.

The first step toward bridging the divide is to recognize that the United States, for all of its claims to exceptionalism, is not the problem, or at least not the whole problem. It should be, and often has been, a big part of the solution. The UN needs an in-house critic, an influential member state pushing for performance improvements, if its considerable institutional inertia is to be surmounted. Although damaging in many ways, the crisis with the United States can be, and to some extent already has been, used productively by the secretary-general—if not by the member states—to spur changes, however modest, that will improve UN administration and operations to everyone's ultimate benefit. Congress has been wrong to condition the payment of assessed dues and arrears on the UN's implementation of various unilateral demands, and the U.S. reform agenda has been far too narrow, but it would be counterproductive to hold up needed UN reforms until the United States makes good on its debts and pledges. There is a dangerous temptation, fed by those most resistant to change in the first place, to shift attention from controversial and challenging questions on the reform agenda to criticizing the United States for its withholdings (something on which it is easy for everyone else to agree).

As underlined in chapter 8, modifying UN structures and procedures to improve its performance can forward the interests of all member states. Such changes should not be seen as a favor to the loudest advocates of reform. Over time these steps can bolster the credibility of the institution, making it more likely that larger, as well as smaller, states will bring important matters to the institution and will treat its decisions and actions with respect. All members should favor greater accountability in the use of funds; more efficient deployment of personnel; more consistent application of charter principles on the recruitment, hiring, utilization, and promotion of staff at all levels; less duplication and greater coordination of effort; continued budgetary discipline; and fuller accountability and transparency throughout the UN system, all combined with sufficient managerial flexibility to permit some shifting of resources to meet changing needs and new opportunities. In terms of increasing transparency and ferreting out cases of waste or abuse, the establishment of the Office of Internal Oversight Services, in essence an inspector general, has been a step forward, although it would have been better if the member states could have acted on this before congressional pressure was brought to bear. The resistance in the General Assembly to adopting the secretary-general's proposal to include "sunset" provisions in new initiatives—setting a time limit, to be followed by a review before any renewal by the Assembly—is discouraging, however.[8]

Not all of the U.S. reform proposals, of course, are designed solely to make the organization work better and be more responsive. Other member states should not find it difficult to distinguish those of general benefit from those—such as discounts on arrears or assessments—that are for unilateral advantage. Likewise, it should be easier to build a consensus to accelerate progress on measures to boost efficiency, effectiveness, and coordination, such as those put forward by Secretary-General Annan in his July 1997 plan, than to get general agreement on how to rearrange the name plates around the table in the Security Council or other intergovernmental organs. If blockages on the latter continue to retard progress on the former, then skeptics will be justified in calling the reform campaign a major disappointment that has done more to illuminate what is wrong with the organization than what its potential could be.

It is certainly understandable that America's allies and partners are particularly chagrined by its apparent retreat from multilateralism and from its obligations under the existing international legal and institutional order. They have a lot to lose if the United States abandons the UN as it once did the League. Yet they should realize that when they call out for U.S. leadership, it is inconsistent to then prescribe how this must be defined and expressed tactically, programmatically, and strategically. An activist America may well have its own agenda that is not wholly congruent with those of its friends. For example, it is hard to deny that Ambassadors Moynihan and Kirkpatrick played leading, albeit controversial, roles in the evolution of the UN, although hardly on the terms or in the directions contemplated by U.S. partners. Certainly it is fair to ask the United States for early and full consultations, a reasonable degree of consistency, observance of agreed rules, and a careful hearing of allied viewpoints. But it is neither realistic nor reasonable to expect the United States to lead from behind.

Likewise, if others see one of the functions of international organization to be to entangle American initiatives in a web of multilateralism, so as to limit its unilateral ambitions and instincts, then even moderate U.S. political figures would have little enthusiasm for such an enterprise. It has been said too often in UN corridors that with the collapse of the Soviet Union there is no one left to counterbalance American power. From a U.S. perspective, the purpose of the UN is to augment national policy options, not to limit them. At the same time, it serves everyone's interests to see the UN and other international institutions as places where common interests and projects can be identified and defined in such a way that the United States will *want* to harness its capacities, along with those of the other member states, to joint undertakings of mutual interest. If the U.S. relationship with the world body is cast primarily in terms of obligations, rather than of incentives and benefits, then it is bound to be a somewhat reluctant and limited one, instead of a true partnership.

What is good for Europe, Japan, Canada, or Australia is not automatically good for the United States. As the continuing crises in the Balkans and Iraq have underscored, allies have a broad range of common interests, but they are not clones. At the moment, moreover, the United States and its allies each face a different mix of domestic pressures, which need to be taken into account in seeking common policies in multilateral forums and negotiations. Officials and commentators from other countries should make a greater effort both to understand the often perplexing domestic forces that shape and condition U.S. policies and to reach out to skeptical American groups in a more sustained and deeper dialogue on these questions than has been the pattern in the past. Both sides of such a discussion would benefit. Likewise, in seeking to define common goals and priorities for policies toward international institutions, it would be helpful to try to take into account the perspectives of both sides of America's unresolved domestic struggle. Although it may be more agreeable to talk to American internationalists, these days they all too often cannot deliver on their encouraging and sympathetic words.

On several subjects, Congress is forcing the administration to think small and to avoid costly new engagements and more intrusive international arrangements, but many allies are pushing in quite the opposite direction. In this context, the tendency of ad hoc alliances between western middle powers and transnational nongovernmental organizations—many of them U.S.-based—to push forward multilateral negotiations on important questions, such as land mines and an international criminal court, at a faster pace than U.S. domestic politics can accommodate may have troubling implications for the U.S. relationship with the UN and other international institutions. In these cases, it would be helpful if U.S. partners would make a greater effort to take congressional attitudes into account in the process, timing, and substance of negotiations. These are worthwhile, even historic endeavors, and one need not cede substantive veto power to Senator Helms, but in the long run it could well prove counterproductive to rush to the conclusion of agreements that the U.S. government cannot sign or ratify. Like the League of Nations, an international order without U.S. participation loses much of its meaning and tends to encourage unilateralist tendencies within the American body politic.

The representatives of some of America's closest allies also might reconsider the self-righteous tone that they, Secretary-General Annan, and so many UN supporters in the United States (including this author at times) have adopted concerning the U.S. arrears. Annan, for example, remarked in late 1998 that "we feel deceived" by the U.S. failure to pay its arrears despite his reform efforts. "We see this as a moral as well as a contractual obligation," he underlined.[9] Their anger and frustration are understandable, and Congress should be made aware of their disappointment and reminded of how the withholdings are damaging western interests as a whole. It should be recalled, however, that for much of the UN's first decade, the United States carried an extra financial burden due to difficult conditions in Europe and elsewhere, that two of the five permanent members of the Security Council had their debts set aside even after the International Court of Justice decided against them in the article 19 crisis, that a third permanent member as a developing country had its assessment drastically reduced and its arrears placed in a special account, that many member states are behind in their payments at any given time, and that, while America's overall support and contributions to the UN and other international agencies have slipped, they remain substantial.

If pressed too hard by foreign governments, members of Congress and many citizens are likely to get their patriotic backs up. They need little encouragement to launch another round of argument about who won the cold war, who has carried the biggest burden for the collective defense for the latter half of this century, or whose armed forces are expected to convince the likes of Saddam Hussein and Slobodan Milosevic to pay attention to the Security Council's edicts. Americans, even many of those committed to international cooperation, have a nationalistic streak or two. In the abstract the public by large margins favors paying our dues, but as chapter 10 also pointed out, the people seem much less receptive to the notion that existing withholding policy should be reversed before progress is made on UN reform. In that regard, the General Assembly's decisions in late 1998 to raise the budget planned for 2000–2001 and to reject a second American's candidacy for its chief budgetary oversight body, the ACABQ, do not bode well for improving communications or building confidence on finance issues.[10] Traditionally it was assumed that the UN's largest contributor would naturally be represented on this committee, but it is beginning to appear that U.S. candidates are being voted down precisely because of their nationality. Both the 1998 and the 1999 versions of the Helms-Biden reform-for-arrears bill, moreover, condition full payment of U.S. arrears on some form of permanent U.S. representation on this committee. It is more than a little perverse that the ACABQ, an obscure committee that few members of Congress had heard of before the United States was denied a seat, has become a key battleground in the tug of war between the United States and other member states over which comes first: reform or arrears. Hopefully a way can be found to make simultaneous progress on both fronts, step by step.

On this and a host of larger questions, the developing country majority in the UN should take care not to repeat the mistakes of the 1970s, some of which were traced in chapter 5, when an earlier generation of diplomats and political figures sought to accomplish things in the UN that were unfeasible in the real world outside. As noted in chapter 9, the General Assembly's decision in late 1997 to lower the floor on UN assessments, so that some thirty countries will now only have to pay $13,000 annually—1/25,000 of the U.S. share—to retain full voting rights in the organization appears remarkably short-sighted. Should the United States lose its vote in the Assembly for being two years in arrears, American critics will rush to cite this step as a prime example of the organization's fiscal irresponsibility, even hypocrisy, and of the surreal quality of the one-nation, one-vote rule. More ominously, these days several developing countries seem intent on feeding the worst fears of American skeptics by using the reform process, based on superior numbers in the Assembly, to frustrate U.S. initiatives, to put the

United States on the defensive, or to propose limits on its power and prerogatives in the organization.

Nowhere is this clash of interests more explosive than in the charged debate over Security Council reform. Many developing countries, along with several industrialized countries, have called for eliminating the veto rights of the five permanent members. This is not going to happen, given that any of the five can veto proposed amendments to the charter, but even such talk feeds congressional anxieties. For the first time, Americans neither sit on the ACABQ nor head the UN's largest development program, the UNDP. All of this suggests that U.S. influence in the UN is ebbing, that the UN is becoming a less friendly place for the exercise of American power, and that America's existing rights in the world body are becoming increasingly difficult to maintain. Some delegations go so far as to assert that the membership of the Security Council should be doubled or that each region should have at least one permanent seat on the Council with full veto power, steps that would make it even more difficult and time-consuming for the Council to act in crisis situations. When equity seems to matter more than effectiveness to many member states, the process of Security Council reform begins to resemble a scramble to reserve more deck chairs even as the ship is sinking. Likewise, it should be asked whether the key to enhancing the legitimacy and credibility of the Council lies in expanding the number of countries around the table or in improving the quality of its decisions and in implementing and enforcing them more fully and consistently.

Over the past decade, the overall trend in the developing world has been toward more pragmatic, more moderate, and less authoritarian regimes. These encouraging developments had, until the sharp worsening in U.S.-UN relations during the past few years, been reflected in the more constructive tenor of North-South discourse in the world body. Voting coincidence in the General Assembly between the United States and other member states more than tripled between 1988 and 1995.[11] Now these hard-won gains are in danger of slipping away. After seven years of solid gains, voting coincidence in the Assembly has fallen off, so far modestly, over the past three years.[12] Too often, the more extreme and confrontational voices in nonaligned and G-77 caucuses—as in Congress—seem to be the loudest, blocking forward movement on feasible reform steps and bolstering maximalist positions. Congressional demands on the UN, coupled with cutbacks in foreign assistance, have served, in turn, to reinforce the fears of some developing countries about American priorities and about the dangers of unfettered U.S. power in the world organization.

In this volatile atmosphere, it would strengthen the UN immeasurably if individual developing countries would seek to avoid a pack mentality while searching for ways of building more reliable North-South bridges. It would help, as well, if developing countries would recognize that they already have a greater voice inside than outside the UN and that the chief goal of UN reform should be to strengthen its capacities, which requires engaging the United States fully in its activities, rather than to shift further the balance of power within the organization from one bloc to another. Given the current political context, the UN in some ways is more fragile and vulnerable today than it was during the turbulent 1970s. Without careful handling, the one goal presumably shared by all members—the preservation and strengthening of the institution itself—could be jeopardized. It is no longer unimaginable that the UN could suffer the same fate as the League if relationships on all sides are not handled carefully. Although member states will play the leading roles in writing and acting the next stages in this drama, two nonstate actors—the secretary-general and civil society—will play important supporting roles that are yet to be fully scripted.

The Office of the Secretary-General: Catalyst or Lightning Rod?

By his style as well as his substance, Kofi Annan is a far more reassuring and engaging figure for most Americans than his predecessor. This is one of the more encouraging signs at a time when U.S.-UN relations are so troubled. According to an August 1998 public opinion survey conducted by Wirthlin Worldwide for the United Nations Association of the USA, 53 percent of respondents approved of the job Annan was doing, 14 percent disapproved, and 25 percent had never heard of him. These are far better marks than the 30 percent approval, 22 percent disapproval, ratings received by Boutros Boutros-Ghali three years before. Apparently Annan's nonthreatening personality just does not fit the image of a power-hungry empire builder, and his statements regarding the role of the UN have been appropriately modest and sensible, recognizing the need for transparency, accountability, and partnerships with nongovernmental organizations, academia, the private sector, and regional organizations. His July 1997 reform package had the dual distinction of being both sensible and comprehensive, but, in light of the lack of a substantial degree of political consensus among the member states, it did not reach very far or very deep. With the caution of three decades of experience in the secretariat, this secretary-general would seem an unlikely candidate for getting too far out front of the member states. As he told the *Economist*, "the UN is not a house in which revolutionaries flourish."[13]

Yet even cautious and polished diplomats can get burned dealing with highly contentious security issues—such as Iraq and Kosovo—in which the big powers believe they have big stakes and the five permanent members are divided. For Kofi Annan, Iraq has been a politically painful case in point. Undertaken at the behest of the Security Council, his February 1998 journey to Baghdad won high marks, and favorable press coverage, for personal courage and diplomatic skill. Yet, by negotiating an agreement with Saddam Hussein to permit UN arms inspectors to continue their work in return for forestalling a western military strike, the secretary-general in essence placed his office between a rock and a hard place, between an unrepentant and untrustworthy rogue dictator and U.S. freedom of action on a sensitive strategic issue. Subsequently, the credibility of both Secretary-General Annan and President Clinton suffered when they appeared to equivocate once Saddam Hussein decided six months later to test the UN's mettle yet again by defying the right of UNSCOM (the Security Council's UN Special Commission) inspectors to carry out unfettered searches for weapons of mass destruction.[14] During the next round in the recurrent crisis, in November, the secretary-general found lower-profile ways of helping to defuse the tensions for the moment. And, while voicing concerns over civilian losses and the use of force, he wisely remained on the sidelines during the American and British bombing of Iraqi military targets in December 1998. But, in terms of U.S.-UN relations, the worst was yet to come.

In early January 1999, a front-page story appeared in the *Washington Post* quoting several anonymous "confidantes" of the secretary-general to the effect that he was concerned about reports that the United States had inappropriately used intelligence gathered by the UNSCOM operation in Iraq for its own purposes.[15] Although the secretary-general was quick to distance himself from these statements,[16] which no doubt were welcomed in Baghdad and by those on the Council pressing for a softening of its sanctions on Iraq, the resulting furor in Washington and in the editorial columns of leading newspapers showed how tender relations remain between the United States and the UN. The next day, a *Washington Post* editorial accused the secretary-general and his team of employing "pernicious tactics" in "their gutless ploy" to undermine the UNSCOM operation and its head, Ambassador Richard Butler of Australia. "It may not be surprising that the United Nations veers toward appeasement," the editorial concluded, "but it's a dangerous game."[17] Republican Senator Frank Murkowski criticized the Clinton administration for having "relied on Kofi Annan and the Iraq appeasers to sign meaningless deals with Saddam Hussein regarding inspections that were useless from the moment they were signed."[18] Others echoed the appeasement theme, even though Annan did his best to explain that "the Secretary General's office will have the potential to advance the interests of all states only so long as it does not appear to serve the narrow interests of any one state or group of states."[19]

These reactions should not have been too surprising to UN officials, given the typically mixed responses of Americans to the secretary-general's trip to Baghdad almost a year earlier. True, Annan had received largely positive press coverage, and it appeared as if the American public had taken to the soft-spoken UN leader who had the energy and enthusiasm to tackle the task of global trouble shooting.[20] In Washington, however, while the executive branch may have been relieved at being taken off the hook in a messy situation, UN skeptics in Congress were anything but pleased. Republican Representative Gerald Solomon went so far as to suggest that the secretary-general "ought to be horse whipped" for some of his comments on the mission to Baghdad.[21] Calling the secretary-general's assertion that the United States ought to consult with other members of the Security Council before launching military strikes against Iraq "disturbing," Senator John Ashcroft, R-Mo., declared that Annan's statements were "indicative of U.N. arrogance and disrespect for U.S. sovereignty."[22]

At its core, this episode was not about press relations, intra-UN intrigues, or trying to please implacable foes in Congress, for it raised a number of the fundamental dilemmas addressed in chapters 6 and 7 about the respective security roles of the United Nations and the United States. Beyond the questions about who said or did what to whom is the basic dilemma of how to handle a threatening rogue state like Iraq. The members of the Security Council appear to be deeply divided over what mix of sticks and carrots should be employed, and the secretary-general, in essence, has allowed his office to be put in the middle of the struggle. The three schools of thought introduced in chapter 6, coalescing around the respective notions that the problem is war, the unilateral use of force, or justice, may help illuminate why Iraq is proving to be such a dilemma for both Annan and the Council. Although many in the UN community seem to believe that the priority should be on preventing war and discouraging the unilateral use of force, for many Americans the problem with Iraq is achieving a just and secure peace, even if it requires the unilateral or bilateral use of force without a specific Council mandate.

When he returned from Baghdad in February 1998, the secretary-general acknowledged that diplomacy can be aided by threats of force, but, like other secretaries-general before him, Annan has emphasized the charter's prescription that, other than in self-defense under article 51, member states are to attempt to settle their differences peacefully.[23] In his reform plan, moreover, Annan candidly pointed out that the world body currently lacks the capacity to organize and carry out even charter-authorized military enforcement operations. All of this leads to a quandary that is likely to plague U.S.-UN relations for the foreseeable future: the political culture of the UN and the politics of the Security Council at this point virtually preclude the use of multilateral force under its auspices, yet it also discourages its unilateral or ad hoc employment outside of the Council's supervision, except possibly to repel a rogue state aggressor.[24] Economic sanctions, as noted earlier, are coming into growing disrepute within the UN community as well, leaving the organization with little more than pacific means to handle those who flaunt international norms. The UN needs more tools, not fewer, at a time when the security situation around the world is becoming increasingly fluid and fragmented by transborder and intrastate conflict, humanitarian emergencies, terrorism, and the proliferation of weapons of mass destruction. And the January 1999 flap over the uses of arms inspectors and intelligence in Iraq will cast a cold shadow over the prospects for a major UN role in the monitoring of the expanding range of international arms control and disarmament agreements.

Stripped of many of the tools to do the job, and enveloped in a political culture that is at best ambivalent toward security matters, the UN appears to have been relegated—or to have relegated itself in some cases—to the sidelines on many of the security challenges of greatest interest to the American people. The UN's harshest critics, of course, will not regret this outcome, nor will those on the left who opposed the Security Council's authorization of the use of force to expel Iraqi forces from Kuwait in the first place. But what of those mainstream Americans who are only vaguely supportive of the institution: those who boost the organization's favorable poll results but do not feel strongly enough to translate their fuzzy feelings into any form of political action? How are they to be convinced that the UN is doing enough to maintain international peace and security—its primary founding purpose—when it is retreating from its most visible roles, including peacekeeping, peace enforcement, and arms monitoring?

The crisis in Kosovo has shed further light on these dilemmas, even as it has posed other ones more starkly. The secretary-general has played a less central but more productive role in facilitating the end of full-scale hostilities and the return of the Kosovar refugees than he did in Iraq. Because he has not had to negotiate directly with Slobodan Milosevic, the president of the Federal Republic of Yugoslavia and now an indicted war criminal, Annan has been able to be outspoken in his condemnations of the massive ethnic cleansing in Kosovo and in his defense of international human rights and humanitarian norms.[25] Although never endorsing the use of force by NATO without authorization from the Security Council, the secretary-general repeatedly stressed that the world must not stand idly by when faced with genocide of the scale the Serbs were committing in Kosovo.

On the day that a deeply divided Security Council met to debate the launch of NATO airstrikes against Yugoslavia, the secretary-general "deeply regretted that, despite all efforts by the international community, the Yugoslav authorities had rejected a political settlement which would have halted the bloodshed in Kosovo and secured an equitable peace for the population there." While underlining the Security Council's "primary responsibility for maintaining international peace and security," he asserted that "it is indeed tragic that diplomacy had failed, but there are times when the use of force may be legitimate in the pursuit of peace."[26] The secretary-general, in other words, appears to be identifying with the third school of thought noted earlier: that in Kosovo, at least, there can be no peace without a measure of justice. And although it would be best to pursue these ends under the direct authority of the UN, at times the Council's inability to agree on a course of action to uphold the world body's principles leaves concerned member states little choice but to act through regional arrangements, preferably under chapter 8 of the charter.

In Kosovo in 1999, as in Iraq in 1991, the role of the UN appears once again to be moving to center stage only as the fighting begins to ease. In the words of Annan's aide, Shashi Tharoor, it "was a NATO war; the peace will be a United Nations peace."[27] On those matters in which the UN and its agencies have a comparative advantage over a military alliance like NATO—such as refugee return, humanitarian relief, postwar reconstruction, election monitoring, and civil administration—they will be mandated to take the lead during the healing process. To America's NATO partners, as well as to the larger community of nations, the more inclusive membership of the UN makes the Security Council a politically more palatable and legally more legitimate umbrella for authorizing the terms of the settlement process as well.

In Kosovo, the UN and NATO are playing complementary roles in some respects, but several troubling dilemmas for the world have also been highlighted. As long as the UN lacks the will or the capacity, or both, to use military force, it can exercise relatively little influence, oversight, or effective authority over the ways others employ force in the name of its principles. Some Council members, most notably China, continue to be reluctant to provide political or legal blank checks for those member states that are militarily powerful or willful, as was done in the case of Iraqi aggression against Kuwait in 1990. Yet the increasing embrace of humanitarian norms as justification for the use of force—a trend the secretary-general says he welcomes—implies an activist and interventionist philosophy for the Council that runs counter to the reluctance of the militarily most powerful Council members to engage in enforcement action outside Europe and the Persian Gulf or to entrust such responsibilities to the UN.[28] Also, developments in Kosovo, including the anomaly that governance and sovereignty are to be divorced under the terms of the settlement, have further eroded and muddled the notion of sovereignty, worrying Chinese communists and American conservatives alike.

These are matters, of course, that must ultimately be determined by the member states, not by the secretary-general. Yet only the office of the secretary-general contains the bully pulpit for enunciating the organization's multilateral purposes, above the interests and perspectives of individual member states. In Kofi Annan, the organization has a leader who is both articulate and experienced in issues of peacekeeping and security. He cannot be expected to have simple answers to these profound dilemmas and contradictions, but it is both his responsibility and his opportunity to begin to set forth his vision of the UN's security roles and priorities for the new century. He cannot and should not try to develop a formula that would appeal to all factions of American thinking on these matters. But unless he clarifies his own vision of the UN's place in emerging security structures, his future actions—as in Iraq—will be open to constant misinterpretation. Ambivalence in the office of the secretary-general will only be magnified several fold among the American people and their leaders.

Civil Society: The Key to Opening or Locking the Door?

Ironically, as chapters 5 and 10 noted, the growing involvement of all sorts of nonstate actors in UN programs and deliberations in recent years has made American conservatives, despite their antistatist and antibureaucratic predilections, even less comfortable and more alienated from the world body and its important norm-setting functions. To be on the conservative side of the political spectrum within what is widely regarded as one of the more conservative member states places one in a distinct minority position to begin with in UN forums. Undoubtedly a range of perspectives is represented among the almost three thousand nongovernmental organizations that have status at the UN, but it is also evident that conservative groups and perspectives are underrepresented.[29] In part, that is because participation tends to be somewhat of a self-selecting process, since those NGOs at the world body naturally tend to be interested in and supportive of UN activities in one area or another. Many of them play an operational role in helping to carry out UN-mandated programs in the field. NGOs seeking status at the world organization, moreover, need some international affiliation. With the vocal exception of the National Rifle Association and a few others, only a handful of conservative U.S.-based NGOs have applied for or received NGO status at the UN.

The world conferences convened in the late 1980s and early 1990s to address various economic, environmental, and social issues generally were open to a broader range of organizations, often through parallel public forums. But because they also became global gatherings for each particular batch of transnational single-issue advocacy groups, they often produced, especially from the public assemblies, long lists of extra programs and responsibilities for states, the UN, and other international organizations, with implications both for finance and for sovereignty. At times, in fact, NGO assemblies have resembled caricatures of some of the less attractive characteristics of the General Assembly itself. In this way, the input of non-state actors paradoxically has often added impetus to statist solutions to transnational problems. Americans skeptical of international organization, moreover, tend to be equally concerned about the implications for national identity and interests of the growing bonds among professional, business, and advocacy groups that transcend national boundaries. Pat Buchanan has been particularly vocal about the threats posed to American national interests by such transnational elites, even as the secretary-general has sought to build ties with the private sector, something that would have been inconceivable a quarter century ago.[30]

Because American conservatives are unlikely to support an organization in which they cannot find a way to have an influential voice, the question of how civil society will be defined, selected, and allowed to participate in the UN of the twenty-first century is taking on added political import. Perversely, this is a subject that gives pause both to conservative Americans and to delegates from some of the more autocratic governments represented in the world body. The larger question of how to take into account the views and operational capacities of nonstate actors in the deliberations and programs of this intergovernmental institution has proven to be one of the most sensitive, intractable, and conceptually difficult issues on the current UN reform agenda.[31] Although the secretariat largely welcomes the active participation of civil society—seeing in it potential boosters—the trend is disturbing to many delegations, which question the place of nongovernmental entities in decisionmaking and governance bodies. After all, is it not the role of governments to represent all shades of civil society in the global body? This could well turn out to be a defining question for the future of international organization, as well as for the nature and extent of American participation, be it governmental or nongovernmental.

The growing extent to which both the UN system and nation states are dependent on nongovernmental entities, including the private sector, to implement policy mandates may well point to the likely course for future evolution of international organization: toward practical, task-oriented arrangements, which have less formal decisionmaking structures and less of a statist orientation than the postwar UN model. Embryonic forms of this new generation of transnational arrangements, mixing governmental and nonstate actors as needed, can be seen in a wide range of financial, trade, environmental, humanitarian, human rights, judicial, and arms control regimes. A number of these appear to be prospering, or at least holding their own, even as the central and more established political bodies face a wave of political and financial challenges. Americans, of course, are often more comfortable with flexible, task-oriented arrangements than with the rigidities of formal intergovernmental mechanisms with strict voting rules and universal memberships. Clearly this is the direction in which international organization has been evolving: toward a proliferation of the pieces and an erosion of the center. The UN system is in danger of becoming a vast and undisciplined solar system, populated by dozens of planets and with a declining sun at its center attempting to hold the pieces together in a coherent whole. The growing role of civil society could well accelerate this trend, while further complicating the decisionmaking process.

The founders of both the League of Nations and the United Nations, however, had something far more ambitious and substantial in mind. They did not envision their creations as simply global meeting places from which most important tasks would be delegated or spun off so that others would oversee their implementation. Certainly they recognized the utility of functional and technical cooperation. Even functionalists, however, did not consider functional bodies to be the highest level in the evolution of international organization.[32] They were to serve either as a stepping stone toward or as a supplement for more central political instruments designed to make the world a safer and more secure place. This dream has not died, despite the prevailing doubts about the capacity of international organization to perform core political and security tasks, but it has been put on hold for the indefinite future. The best minds of the twentieth century have been unable to conceptualize, much less design, the political bridge between broad-based functional cooperation and a reliable international security system.

In 1999, as in 1919, the first step toward making this vision a reality lies in the United States and in solving its domestic political riddle. In a number of ways noted above, however, the international community can make this process of domestic convergence easier or harder, quicker or slower. As with so many other matters, President Harry Truman put it simply and well. On October 23, 1946, he assured the General Assembly that the United States would "support the United Nations with all the resources we possess . . . not as a temporary expedient but as a permanent partnership." Quoting these lines, he told Congress the next year that:

> That policy—in season and out—in the face of temporary failure as well as in moments of success—has the support of the overwhelming majority of the American people. It must continue to have this support if the United States is to play its appointed role in the United Nations, if the United Nations is to fulfill its purposes and if our land is to be preserved from the disaster of another and far more terrible war.[33]

Perhaps sensing the troubled times ahead, he went on to underline, for the benefit of the legislators, that at the United Nations "our representatives have spoken for the whole Nation." Too often in the half-century since, such an assertion could not be made with confidence. For our country has been divided, time and again, in the very meeting halls designed to bring the nations and peoples of the world together. Until these domestic rifts are healed, America cannot hope either to bring to international organizations the depth of commitment and the steadfastness of purpose that President Truman so aptly identified as essential to their success or to maximize within their halls the attainment of our national interests and values. In the next century, as in the last, foreign policy will begin at home.

Notes

Chapter One

1. The level of U.S. arrears varies over the course of the fiscal year, depending on billing and payment cycles. During most of 1998, the UN calculated U.S. arrears to be about $1.5 billion. Over the years, the United States has announced its decision not to pay for certain items in the UN budget, leaving about $400 million of the arrears in dispute. See press briefings by UN Under-Secretary-General for Management Joseph Connor on Oct. 7, 1998, Nov. 4, 1998, and March 18, 1999, http://www.un.org/news/briefings; and www.un.org/news/ossg/finance.

2. "United States Pays $197 Million to the United Nations Regular Budget," USUN Press Release 196 (98), Nov. 4, 1998, http:www.undp.org/missions/usa/98_196.htm; and U.S. General Accounting Office, *United Nations: Financial Issues and U.S. Arrears,* June 1998, GAO/NSIAD-98-201BR, p. 5. Also see Christopher S. Wren, "Unpaid Dues at the U.N. Could Cost U.S. Its Vote," *New York Times,* June 28, 1998.

3. "Fifth Committee Recommends Costa Rica, Pakistan, India, United Kingdom, Italy and Japan for Election to ACABQ," UN Press Release GA/AB/3257, Nov. 6, 1998. Tellingly, the candidate from China, which pays less than 1 percent of the UN budget, was also rejected. The United States is not the only large dues-payer without a seat on the Advisory Committee on Administrative and Budgetary Questions (ACABQ). Germany, with the third largest assessment, was also denied a seat in the latest round of voting.

4. Betsy Pisik, "U.N. Budget Plan Angers U.S.," *Washington Times,* Dec. 29, 1998. Also see USUN Press Release 240 (98), Dec. 21, 1998, for a related U.S. statement in the General Assembly.

5. For an account of the major internationalist movements in the United States up to the Senate's rejection of the League of Nations in 1920, see Warren F. Kuehl, *Seeking World Order: The United States and International Organization to 1920* (Vanderbilt University Press, 1969).

6. David Stout, "Clinton Vetoes Measure to Pay $1 Billion in Late U.N. Dues," *New York Times*, Oct. 21, 1998.

7. For an earlier discussion of this seeming paradox by this author, see "The United Nations, Multilateralism, and U.S. Interests," in *U.S. Foreign Policy and the United Nations System*, ed. Charles William Maynes and Richard S. Williamson (W. W. Norton for the American Assembly, 1996), 27–53.

8. The activities and evolution of these internationalist groups are thoroughly chronicled in Ruhl J. Bartlett, *The League to Enforce Peace* (University of North Carolina Press, 1944) and in Robert A. Divine, *Second Chance: The Triumph of Internationalism in America During World War II* (New York: Atheneum, 1967). Around 1900, prominent Americans preferring a more isolationist course also formed private organizations, such as the Anti-Imperialist League, to promote their views to policymakers, the media, and the public. For a discussion of the activities of the Anti-Imperialist League, see Eric A. Nordlinger, *Isolationism Reconfigured: American Foreign Policy for a New Century* (Princeton University Press, 1995), 52–53 and 187, and Robert L. Beisner, *Twelve Against Empire: The Anti-Imperialists, 1898–1900* (McGraw-Hill, 1968), 218–38.

9. Letter from Chairman of the Senate Foreign Relations Committee, Jesse Helms, to U.S. Secretary of State Madeleine K. Albright, March 26, 1998.

Chapter 2

The Truman quote is from his State of the Union message to Congress, delivered on Jan. 14, 1946, *Documents on American Foreign Relations*, ed. Raymond Dennett and Robert K. Turner (Princeton University Press, 1948), 8: 16. The Keyes quote is from an op-ed column "Why Imperil U.N. Reform?" *New York Times*, Sept. 25, 1986. The Weston quote is from "U.S. Debt Called 'Indefensible'; Weston Says It's Catch-22," *Diplomatic World Bulletin*, 28 (April–May 1997): 1.

1. *Congressional Record*, 79th Cong., 1st sess., July 23, 1945, 91, pt. 6: 7964.

2. Wilson speech of Sept. 20, 1919, in Los Angeles, *Public Papers of Woodrow Wilson, War and Peace, Presidential Messages, Addresses and Public Papers (1917–1924)*, ed. Ray Stannard and William E. Dodd (Harper and Brothers, 1927), 2: 308.

3. This prevalent sense of national pride, of course, has long been a prime target of social critics, especially from the political left. For a provocative recent commentary on the role and place of national pride, see Richard Rorty, *Achieving Our Country: Leftist Thought in Twentieth Century America* (Harvard University Press, 1998), esp.1–38.

4. Seymour Martin Lipset, *American Exceptionalism: A Double-Edged Sword* (W. W. Norton, 1996), 51–52.

5. See, for example, Robert Kagan, "The Benevolent Empire," *Foreign Policy* 111 (summer 1998): 24–35. For a thoughtful critique of these themes, see Charles William Maynes, "The Perils of (and for) an Imperial America," *Foreign Policy* 111 (summer 1998): 36–48.

6. David Rothkopf, "In Praise of Cultural Imperialism?" *Foreign Policy* 107 (summer 1997): 48–49, 51.

7. Walter A. McDougal divides the American "bible of foreign affairs" into old and new testaments, with the 1890s the demarcation point. According to his analysis, the old testament was about "being and becoming" and keeping the outside world out, whereas the new testament has sought "to nurture democracy and economic growth around the world." See McDougal, *Promised Land, Crusader State: The American Encounter with the World Since 1776* (Houghton Mifflin, 1997).

8. Wilson address of Sept. 20, 1919, in Los Angeles, *Public Papers*, 2: 323.

9. Senator William E. Borah, R-Idaho, one of the sixteen "irreconcilables" opposing the League in the Senate stressed that he and other so-called "isolationists" had never been isolationist on matters of trade, commerce, finance, and humanitarian assistance, "but in all matters political, in all commitments of any nature or kind, which encroach in the slightest upon the free and unembarrassed action of our people or which circumscribe their discretion and judgement, we have been free, we have been independent, we have been isolationist." McDougal, *Promised Land,* 149.

10. Senate Committee on Foreign Relations, *Purchase of United Nations Bond* (S. 2768), Hearings, Feb. 6, 7, 9, 19, 1962, 87th Cong., 2d sess. (Government Printing Office, 1962), 60.

11. John R. Bolton, assistant secretary of state for international organization affairs in the Bush administration, has suggested that "skepticism about the United Nations is another aspect of what scholars have termed 'American exceptionalism,' the idea that the United States is, simply stated, different from other countries." Bolton, "America's Skepticism about the United Nations," *U.S. Foreign Policy Journal,* USIA Electronic Journal 2 (May 1997): 1, http://www.usis.usemb.se/journals/itps/0597/ijpelpj2bolt.htm.

12. For a recent defense of isolationism, or strategic nonengagement, as the basis for future as well as past U.S. foreign policy, see Eric A. Nordlinger, *Isolationism Reconfigured: American Foreign Policy for a New Century* (Princeton University Press, 1995), esp. 50–62. Noting that most historians have concluded that isolationism served the United States well until the late nineteenth century, Nordlinger questions the prevailing view that a more internationalist and interventionist strategy was needed after that point as the United States gained the characteristics of a great power. In his view, the major changes under way in the world at that time "did not require or justify the rejection of strategic isolationism. The new realities did not put America's strategic immunity at risk."

13. Commentators have endlessly criticized Wilsonian idealism as a basis for U.S. foreign policy. It should be recognized, however, that isolationism, although initially a realistic strategy for a weak and divided young nation, was itself an expression of American idealism and exceptionalism. Nordlinger, *Isolationism Reconfigured,* 186–93.

14. Dean Acheson, *Present at the Creation: My Years in the State Department* (W. W. Norton, 1969), 6.

15. *Congressional Record,* 79th Cong., 1st sess., July 24, 1945, 91, pt. 6: 8001.

16. Department of State, *The United States and the United Nations, Report by the President to the Congress for the Year 1946* (Government Printing Office, 1947), viii.

17. House Committee on Foreign Affairs, *Structure of the United Nations and the Relations of the United States to the United Nations,* Hearings, May 4–7, 11–14, 1948, 80th Cong., 2d sess. (Government Printing Office, 1948), 84.

18. Adlai E. Stevenson, *Looking Outward: Years of Crisis at the United Nations,* ed. Robert L. and Selma Schiffer (Harper & Row, 1963), 128–29.

19. Nicholas Murray Butler, "An American View," in *The Nations and the League,* ed. George Paish (London: T. Fisher Unwin Ltd., 1920), 143.

20. Wilson address of Sept. 23, 1919, in Salt Lake City, *Public Papers,* 2: 353–54.

21. Wilson Jackson Day message of Jan. 8, 1920, *Public Papers,* 2: 454.

22. William Howard Taft and William Jennings Bryan, *World Peace: A Written Debate between William Howard Taft and William Jennings Bryan* (New York: George H. Doran Co., 1917), 93–94.

23. John H. Clarke, a former justice of the U.S. Supreme Court, and A. Lawrence Lowell, the president of Harvard University, made similar arguments. See John H. Clarke, *America and World Peace* (Henry Holt, 1925), 39–40; and Edith M. Phelps, ed., *Selected Articles on a League of Nations,* 4th ed. (New York: H. W. Wilson Co., 1919), 353.

24. Thomas Benjamin Neely, *The League: the Nation's Danger* (Philadelphia: E. A. Yeakel, 1919), 201, 211.

25. Taft and Bryan, *A Written Debate,* 103.

26. Wilson address of Sept. 25, 1919, in Pueblo, Colo., *Public Papers,* 2: 399–416.

27. Philip C. Jessup, *Elihu Root* (Dodd, Mead & Co., 1938), 2: 381, 388.

28. Phelps, *Selected Articles,* 330, 332.

29. Ibid., 343.

30. James F. Byrnes address of Nov. 16, 1945, in Charleston, S.C., *Documents on American Foreign Relations,* ed. Raymond Dennett and Robert K. Turner (Princeton University Press, 1948), 8: 12.

31. House Committee on Foreign Affairs, *Structure of the United Nations,* 55.

32. Lipset, *American Exceptionalism,* 292.

33. House Committee on Foreign Affairs, *Structure of the United Nations,* 62.

34. John Gerard Ruggie, "The Past as Prologue? Interest, Identity, and American Foreign Policy," *International Security* 21 (spring 1997): 120.

35. United Nations, General Assembly, A/40/PV.48, Oct. 24, 1985, 52.

36. Annan address to the Danish Foreign Policy Society, Copenhagen, Sept.1, 1997, UN Press Release, SG/SM/6310, Sept. 2, 1997, 1.

37. "Pope Kofi's Unruly Flock," *Economist,* Aug. 8, 1998, U.S. ed., 19–22.

38. "U.S. Debt Called 'Indefensible,'" *Diplomatic World Bulletin,* 1.

39. "Assembly President Stresses Importance of Sole Remaining Super-Power Pursuing 'Global Leader Role' as 'Predictable Player'," UN Press Release, GA/9219, Feb. 26, 1997, 3.

40. Robert Kagan develops similar themes but to somewhat different conclusions, in "The Benevolent Empire."

41. "Rebuilding the International Civil Service," *UN Staff Report* 21 (Nov. 1996): 15.

42. Barbara Crossette, "Aid from Rich Nations to Poor Fell in 1996," *New York Times,* Oct. 17, 1997.

43. United Nations, *World Economic and Social Survey 1997* (New York: 1997), table A.32, p. 268.

44. United Nations, *World Economic Survey 1992,* table A32, p. 221; *World Economic Survey 1993,* table A31, p. 244; *World Economic and Social Survey 1994,* table A31, p. 294; *World Economic and Social Survey 1995,* table A32, p. 332; *World Economic and Social Survey 1996,* table A32, p. 340; and *World Economic and Social Survey 1997,* table A32, p. 268. According to OECD figures, U.S. ODA disbursements rose modestly in 1996, but its totals still trailed those of Japan ($9.377 to $9.439 billion, respectively). See United Nations Development Program (UNDP), *Human Development Report 1998* (Oxford University Press, 1998), 196.

45. UNDP, *Human Development Report 1998,* 196.

46. Dartmouth College, "United States and United Nations: Problems and Prospects, A Discussion with Dennis Goodman and Edward Luck," *World Outlook* (winter 1987): 74.

47. Richard Holbrooke, *To End a War* (Random House, 1998), 202.

48. Barbara Crossette, "Boutros-Ghali vs. 'Goliath': His Account," *New York Times,* Nov. 20, 1996.

49. As early as 1915, the editors of the *New Republic* flagged "the problem of representation, of the large and populous state as against the small ones, of the 'satisfied powers' against the 'unsatisfied.'" "A League of Peace," *New Republic* (June 26, 1915): 190–91.

50. As Dennis Goodman, then senior deputy assistant secretary of state for international organization affairs, candidly commented in 1987, "we can take initiatives, but it is very hard to control them outside of the Security Council. Once you put them on the table, people can start amending them, and in the end you may find that you can't support your own proposal because it has been changed beyond recognition." Dartmouth College, "United States and United Nations," 75.

51. Acheson, *Present at the Creation,* 112.

52. *Congressional Record,* 94th Cong., 1st sess., Nov. 11, 1975, 121, pt. 28: 35954.

53. Senate Foreign Relations Subcommittee on International Operations, *United Nations Reform,* Hearings, Sept, 11, 1996, 104th Cong., 2d sess. (Government Printing Office, 1996), 12.

54. "Assembly President Stresses Importance," UN Press Release, 3.

55. Byrnes, address of Oct. 31, 1945, *Documents on American Foreign Relations* 8: 9.

56. Jesse Helms, "Saving the U.N.: A Challenge to the Next Secretary-General," *Foreign Affairs* 74 (Sept.–Oct. 1996): 5.

57. Winston Churchill, address of July 31, 1957, reprinted in *American Bar Association Journal* 43 (October 1957): 915.

58. Henry Cabot Lodge, *As It Was: An Inside View of Politics and Power in the '50s and '60s* (W. W. Norton, 1976),184, 185. Americans were not the only ones to worry

about how the asymmetries in the Assembly had been exacerbated by the rapid growth in UN membership and the inclusion of dozens of ministates. In his annual report for 1966–67, Secretary-General U Thant also floated the idea of creating an associate member category: "it may be opportune for the competent organs to undertake a thorough and comprehensive study of the criteria for membership in the UN, with a view to laying down the necessary limitations on full membership, while defining other forms of association which would benefit both the 'micro States' and the UN." Georges Abi-Saab, "Membership and Voting in the United Nations,"in *The Changing Constitution of the United Nations,* ed. Hazel Fox (London: British Institute of International and Comparative Law, 1997), 28. According to Abi-Saab, a noted Egyptian legal scholar based in Geneva, "as history teaches us, excess democracy leads to oligarchy or autocracy, and has led to a great concentration and opacity of power within the UN," which he believes is focused in the Security Council.

59. *Congressional Record,* 92d Cong., 1st sess., Nov. 2, 1971, 117, pt. 30: 38702.

60. *Congressional Record,* 94th Cong., 1st sess., Nov. 11, 1975, 121, pt. 28: 35933.

61. Burton Yale Pines, ed., *A World Without a U.N.: What Would Happen If the United Nations Shut Down* (Washington, D.C.: Heritage Foundation, 1984), xvi.

62. Patrick J. Buchanan, "Have the Globalists Over-Reached?" *The American Cause,* July 28, 1998, http://www.theamericancause.org/pjb-98-0728.html., p. 3.

63. See chapter 10 and Ole R. Holsti, *Public Opinion and American Foreign Policy* (University of Michigan Press, 1996), 150. As Holsti notes, "Republicans tend to favor a leadership role consistent with American superpower status, whereas Democrats are more supportive of a U.S. role as a 'normal nation' that pursues its interests in conjunction with others, including through the United Nations. Stated somewhat differently, members of the GOP appear more inclined to favor unilateral action in the pursuit of national interests, whereas multilateralism finds stronger support among Democrats."

64. For a somewhat shrill critique of "double standards" in the U.S. approach to human rights and the codification and application of international law, see Amnesty International, *Rights for All,* chap. 7, http://www.rightsforall-usa.org/info/action/index.html. For a column by a leading American legal scholar lamenting recent steps by Congress, the executive branch, and the Supreme Court that would appear to undermine the international legal order, see Thomas M. Franck, "Notes from the President," *ASIL Newsletter,* American Society of International Law, May–June 1998, http://asil.org/newsletter/may-june98/home.htm.

65. Indeed, from time to time congressional critics of the United Nations complain that it is a godless organization, which—like public schools in the United States—does not open its sessions with prayer and therefore lacks divine guidance. See, for example, the comments of the following House members: Edward H. Rees, R-Kan., *Congressional Record,* 80th Cong., 1st sess., Dec. 16, 1947, 93, pt. 9: 11489–90; Joseph R. Bryson, D-S.C., *Congressional Record,* 81st Cong., 2d sess., Dec. 19, 1950, 96, pt. 12: 16758; Lawrence H. Smith, R-Wis., *Congressional Record,* 82d Cong., 2d sess., July 1, 1952, 98, pt. 11:

A4208–09; and John T. Wood, R-Idaho, *Congressional Record*, 82d Cong., 2d sess., Feb. 25, 1952, 98, pt. 8: A1157, A1158.

66. Martin Kreisberg, "Dark Areas of Ignorance," in *Public Opinion and Foreign Policy,* Lester Markel, ed. (Harper and Brothers for the Council on Foreign Relations, 1949), 57.

67. Hadley Cantril, ed., *Public Opinion 1935–1946* (Princeton University Press, 1951), pp. 910, 914, 916, 917.

68. Gallup International Inc., *Gallup Opinion Index* (66, Princeton, N. J., Dec. 1970).

69. Gallup International Research Institutes, "Rating the United Nations," *Index to International Public Opinion 1984–1985* (New York: Greenwood Press, 1986), 748.

70. In a Zogby/GfK survey conducted in early 1999, the United Kingdom had the lowest percentage of favorable responses (50 percent) among the eight NATO countries and the second highest portion of unfavorables (22 percent), giving it, on balance, the most negative response of the eight. See Zogby International/GfK Global Poll, "United Nations Global Opinion Poll of Thirteen Countries" (Utica, N.Y.: Zogby International, April 22, 1999); and UN Press Briefing, "World Perception of United Nations," April 27, 1999, www.un.org/news/briefing/docs/1999/19990427.unpoll.html.

71. Ibid. Italy, at 73 percent had the most "favorable" response among NATO respondents. Mexico and Brazil, both at 77 percent, topped the overall list.

72. The United Kingdom came next with 22 percent unfavorable and then Italy with 20 percent.

73. For a fuller analysis of the results, see Steven Greenhouse, "Poll Shows 4 Nations Differ on the Main Threat to Peace," *New York Times,* April 2, 1994.

74. World survey conducted by *Yomiuri Shimbun,* in *Index to International Public Opinion 1992–1993* (New York: Greenwood Press, 1994), 681.

75. Multinational survey conducted by *Yomiuri Shimbun,* in *Index to International Public Opinion 1995–1996* (New York: Greenwood Press, 1997), 672.

Chapter 3

The Lodge quote is from Edith M. Phelps, ed., *Selected Articles on a League of Nations,* 4th ed. (New York: H. W. Wilson Co, 1919), 359. The Kennedy quote is from his remarks to the UN General Assembly, A/PV.1209, Sept. 20, 1963, 7. See also *Public Papers of the Presidents, John F. Kennedy, 1963* (Government Printing Office, 1964), 698. The Dole quote is from his article "Shaping America's Global Future," *Foreign Policy* 98 (spring 1995), 36.

1. Anne-Marie Burley has emphasized the regulatory role of the state as a New Deal characteristic that was projected onto the postwar order. See Anne-Marie Burley, "Regulating the World: Multilateralism, International Law, and the Projection of the New Deal Regulatory State," in *Multilateral Matters: The Theory and Praxis of an Institutional Form,* ed. John Gerard Ruggie (Columbia University Press, 1993), 125–56.

2. For a detailed analysis of U.S. public attitudes toward government, see Pew Research Center Poll, *Deconstructing Distrust: How Americans View Government* (Princeton, N.J.: Princeton Survey Research Associates, March 10, 1998).

3. John R. Bolton, "America's Skepticism About the United Nations," *U.S. Foreign Policy Journal,* USIA Electronic Journal 2 (May 1997): 1, http://www.usis.usemb.se/journals/itps/0597/ijpelpj2bolt.htm.

4. Seymour Martin Lipset, *American Exceptionalism: A Double-Edged Sword* (W. W. Norton, 1996), 281–83.

5. In an October 1997 poll, 57 percent responded that they did not trust government, compared with 39 percent who did; see Alexis Sinendinger, "Of the People, for the People," *National Journal,* April 18, 1998, 851. According to a January 1998 survey for CNN and *USA Today,* 58 percent said that the federal government was too big, 31 percent responded that it was about the right size, and only 6 percent felt that it had been cut too much; see CNN/*USA Today* Poll (Princeton, N.J.: Gallup Organization, Jan. 6, 1998). In a Pew poll of September-October 1997, 37 percent agreed that the federal government needs major reform and 58 percent called for some reform, while only 4 percent saw little need for change; see Pew Research Center Poll (Princeton, N.J.: Princeton Survey Research Associates, Sept. 25, 1997). Fifty-two percent agreed with the assertion that "the federal government has become so large and powerful that it poses a threat to the rights and freedoms of ordinary citizens" in an April 1995 survey for *Time* and CNN, while 44 percent disagreed; see *Time*/CNN Poll (Washington, D.C.: Yankelovich Partners Inc., April 27, 1995). A March 1995 poll for the Council for Excellence in Government found Americans by a 72 percent to 21 percent margin concurring that the federal government "creates more problems than it solves"; see Council for Excellence in Government Poll (Washington, D.C.: Hart and Teeter Research Companies, March 16, 1995).

6. See, for example, Lipset, *American Exceptionalism,* 289–90.

7. In a CNN/*USA Today* Poll (Princeton, N.J.: Gallup Organization, Oct. 22, 1994), 75 percent said most members of Congress were out of touch and 58 percent that they were more focused on the needs of special interests than on those of their constituents; in a *Time*/CNN Poll (Washington, D.C.: Yankelovich Partners Inc., June 2, 1994), 70 percent stated that Congress was doing a poor job maintaining ethical standards. According to polls conducted before the congressional election in November 1996, 62 percent declared that their representative deserved to be reelected, and 61 percent approved of his or her job performance. See, respectively, Pew Research Center Poll (Princeton, N.J.: Princeton Survey Research Associates, Oct. 14, 1996) and CBS/*New York Times* Poll (New York: Oct.17, 1996). In the November 1998 election, more than 98 percent of House members seeking another term were reelected.

8. See the results of a June 1995 survey and a June 1996 survey, both cited in Steven Kull, I. M. Destler, and Clay Ramsay, *The Foreign Policy Gap: How Policymakers Misread the Public* (University of Maryland, Center for International and Security Studies,1997), 52. Also, in a 1996 article, British journalist Martin Walker cites poll data showing a

sharp decline from the 1960s to the 1990s in the percentage of Americans expressing confidence that their government did "the right thing most of the time." He also refers to a 1995 survey by Stanley Greenberg, a pollster for President Clinton, in which fewer than 20 percent said that "their government could be trusted to do the right thing," while 58 percent expressed "confidence in the United Nations to do the right thing most of the time." Martin Walker, "The New American Hegemony," *World Policy Journal* 13 (summer 1996): 19. Regarding parallel declines in public confidence in both the federal government and international institutions after the Watergate scandal, see Charles William Maynes, "The United Nations: Out of Control or Out of Touch?" *The Year Book of World Affairs 1977* (Boulder, Colo.: Westview Press for the London Institute of World Affairs, 1977), 105–06.

9. For example, in a January 1994 survey, 56 percent said that state legislatures would be more efficient in the "use of taxpayers money" compared with 17 percent for Congress, by a 52 percent to 30 percent margin state legislatures were said to get more done than Congress, and by an even wider 64 percent to 16 percent gap, state legislatures were said to care more about the respondent than did Congress. *Time*/CNN Poll (Washington, D.C.: Yankelovich Partners, Jan. 17, 1994). Likewise, by a three-to-one ratio in a January 1995 poll asking whether local or federal government "should be most responsible for people's well-being," people preferred the local level; see NBC News Poll (New York: Jan. 25, 1995). Respondents to a November–December 1995 survey, by a 61 percent to 24 percent margin, said that state government could be trusted "to do a better job running things" than the federal government. Henry J. Kaiser Family Foundation/Harvard University/*Washington Post* Poll (Princeton, N.J.: Princeton Survey Research Associates, Nov. 28–Dec. 4, 1995).

10. *Congressional Record,* 92d Cong., 1st sess., Oct. 27, 1971, 117, pt. 29: 37890.

11. Paul introduced the latest version, the American Sovereignty Restoration Act of 1999 (HR 11461), on March 17, 1999, on behalf of nine cosponsors.

12. *Congressional Record,* 105th Cong., 2d sess., March 26, 1998, 144, no. 36: H1597 (Paul), H1599 (Calvert).

13. Testimony of Ralph Nader on the Uruguay Round of the General Agreement on Tariffs and Trade before the Senate Foreign Relations Committee, June 14, 1994, Federal News Service, Washington, D.C., 1, 6, 8.

14. José Alvarez, "Who's Afraid of the New World Order?" *Law Quadrangle Notes* 39 (spring 1996): 43, 44.

15. Patrick J. Buchanan, "Have the Globalists Over-Reached?" *The American Cause,* July 28, 1998, http://www.theamericancause.org/pjb-98-0728.html, p. 2.

16. Jesse Helms, "Saving the U.N.: A Challenge to the Next Secretary-General," *Foreign Affairs* 74 (Sept./Oct. 1996): 4.

17. Ibid., 3, 4.

18. During the 1994 debate over the implementation of the Uruguay Round of the General Agreement on Tariffs and Trade and the establishment of the World Trade

Organization, the attorneys general of forty-two states wrote to President Clinton seeking a summit meeting to review their concerns that the WTO and its dispute resolution panels might find against the laws and regulations of individual states, which would not have standing to participate directly in the defense of their laws and practices. For the text of the letter and list of signatories, see the *Congressional Record,* 103d Cong., 2d sess., July 13, 1994, 140, no. 90: 8853–54.

19. See, for example, Alvarez, "Who's Afraid of the New World Order?" 41.

20. Kofi A. Annan, *Renewing the United Nations: A Programme for Reform,* United Nations, General Assembly, A/51/950, July 14, 1997, 6, 21.

21. See, for example, Michael J. Glennon, "The New Interventionism: The Search for a Just International Law," *Foreign Affairs* 78 (May–June 1999): 2–7.

22. Alvarez, "Who's Afraid of the New World Order?" 41.

23. Helms, "Saving the U.N.," 5.

24. University of North Carolina, University Extension Division, *The League of Nations* (1921), 10–14.

25. Spencer, Borah, and King are quoted in Elmer Bendiner, *A Time for Angels: The Tragicomic History of the League of Nations* (Alfred A. Knopf, 1975), 100.

26. Phelps, *Selected Articles,* 337.

27. Wilson speech of Sept. 25, 1919, in Pueblo, Colo., *Public Papers of Woodrow Wilson: War and Peace, Presidential Messages, Addresses, and Public Papers (1917–1924),* ed. Ray Stannard Baker and William E. Dodd (Harper & Publishers, 1927), 2: 402.

28. Charles Nagel, *The League of Nations,* May 30, 1919 (np), 4–5.

29. Editors, "The Return," *The Nation* 109 (July 12, 1919): 30.

30. Elmer Bendiner, *A Time for Angels,* 100.

31. Phelps, *Selected Articles,* 345.

32. United Nations, General Assembly Resolution A/53/202, Dec. 17, 1998.

33. Gene M. Lyons and Michael Mastanduno, "State Sovereignty and International Intervention: Reflections on the Present and Prospects for the Future," in *Beyond Westphalia? State Sovereignty and International Intervention,* ed. Gene M. Lyons and Michael Mastanduno (Johns Hopkins University Press, 1995), 251.

34. William Howard Taft and William Jennings Bryan, *World Peace: A Written Debate Between William Howard Taft and William Jennings Bryan* (New York: George H. Doran Company, 1917), 49.

35. United Nations Association of the USA, *Crisis and Reform in United Nations Financing* (New York: 1997), 57–58.

36. Taft and Bryan, *World Peace,* 49.

37. *Congressional Record,* 82d Cong., 2d sess., April 4, 1952, 98, pt. 3: 3514.

38. Daniel Gouré, "Should the United Nations Have the Authority to Levy Taxes?" in *Delusions of Grandeur,* ed. Ted Galen Carpenter (Washington, D.C.: Cato Institute, 1997), 140.

39. Ibid., 140, 142.

40. John M. Goshko, "Talk of Tax by U.N. Draws Fire in U.S.; Lawmakers Offer Bill to Bar Levies," *Washington Post,* Jan. 23, 1996.

41. For a compilation of proposals for independent funding sources for the United Nations, see Harlan Cleveland, Hazel Henderson, and Inge Kaul, eds., *The United Nations: Policy and Financing Alternatives, Innovative Proposals by Visionary Leaders* (Washington, D.C.: Global Commission to Fund the United Nations, 1995). When Senator Hubert H. Humphrey in the early 1960s floated the idea of independent revenues as a solution to the UN's periodic insolvency, his was a lonely voice in the Capitol that has had few echoes since. He argued that the only long-term answer to unreliable payment of dues by member states would be for the United Nations to "seek new sources of revenue independent of contributions of its members." In his view, "the real test of American leadership is our determination to put U.N. finances on a long-range self-financing basis." He suggested UN "tax rights" on areas currently beyond national tax jurisdiction, such as "space traffic and communications rights, ocean resources, and polar resources." *Congressional Record,* 87th Cong., 2d sess., April 2, 1962, 108, pt. 4: 5674.

42. Bob Dole, letter to the editor, *Washington Post,* Feb. 1, 1996.

43. For the latter, see Thomas P. Sheehy, "The U.N. Tax: Not Now, Not Ever," *Heritage Foundation Executive Memorandum* 445 (Feb. 9, 1996): 2; John R. Bolton, "The Creation, Fall, Rise, and Fall of the United Nations," in *Delusions of Grandeur,* ed. Ted Galen Carpenter (Washington, D.C.: Cato Institute, 1997), 57; and Ted Galen Carpenter, "The Mirage of Global Collective Security," in *Delusions of Grandeur,* 26.

44. John M. Goshko, "Talk of Tax."

45. *Congressional Record,* 105th Cong., 2d sess., March 26, 1998, 144, no. 36: H1581.

46. Pat Robertson, *The New World Order* (Dallas: Word Publishing, 1991), 207. Among other unlikely developments, Robertson envisions a radically new UN voting system based on population, giving the United States little voice, and a United States that has been disarmed by the UN so that it has no choice but to "acquiesce" to the UN's financial demands. He further contends that "the Third World in the United Nations has already voted to take away by decree the wealth of Europe and America and give it to themselves" by approving a 1974 General Assembly resolution on a new international economic order.

47. Editorial, "Report on Foreign Aid," *New York Times,* March 12, 1970.

48. United Nations, General Assembly Resolution 2626 (25) ("International Development Strategy for the Second United Nations Development Decade"), Oct. 24, 1970, para. 43.

49. See, for example, the U.S. explanation of vote on the consensus resolution on the Seventh Special Session, 3362 (S-7), Sept. 16, 1975, in Department of State, *U.S. Participation in the United Nations, 1975, Report of the President to Congress* (Government Printing Office, 1976), 103–04.

50. Samuel Huntington, letter to the editor, *New York Times,* March 29, 1970.

51. United Nations, General Assembly, A/50/PV.40, Oct. 24, 1995, 39.

52. United Nations, General Assembly, A/50/PV.15, Oct. 2, 1995, 15–16.

53. United Nations, General Assembly, A/50/PV.12, Sept. 29, 1995, 4.

54. Henry Cabot Lodge, *The Senate and the League of Nations* (Charles Scribner's Sons, 1925), 237.

55. *Congressional Record,* 70th Cong., 1st sess., May 8, 1928, 69, pt. 8: 8069–73.

56. *Congressional Record,* 82d Cong., 2d sess., April 4, 1952, 98, pt. 3: 3514.

57. Nicholas Murray Butler, "An American View," in *The Nations and the League,* ed. George Paish (London: T. Fischer Unwin, Ltd., 1920), 139–40, 145.

58. Norman Cousins, "As 1960 Sees US: Two Stories, Two Endings," *Saturday Review of Literature,* Aug. 5, 1950, 13.

59. Senate Committee on Foreign Relations, *Purchase of United Nations Bonds* (S. 2768), Hearings, Feb. 6, 7, 9, 19, 1962, 87th Cong., 2d sess. (Government Printing Office, 1962), 229.

60. "A League of Peace," *New Republic,* June 26, 1915, 191.

61. Philip C. Jessup, *The International Problem of Governing Mankind* (Claremont College, 1947), 4, 6, 56.

62. Cousins, "As 1960 Sees US," 13.

63. James F. Byrnes, *Documents on American Foreign Relations,* ed. Raymond Dennett and Robert K. Turner (Princeton University Press), 8: 22.

64. Senate Committee on Foreign Relations, *Purchase of United Nations Bonds,* 60, 61.

65. House Foreign Affairs Subcommittee on Human Rights and International Organizations, *Foreign Assistance Legislation for FY 1988-89,* Hearings, Feb. 25, March 6, 12, 1987, 100th Cong., 1st sess. (Government Printing Office, 1987), pt. 4: 68. Emphasis added.

66. Jeffrey R. Gerlach, "A U.N. Army for the New World Order?" *Orbis* (spring 1993): 233.

67. Gerlach, in fact, cites an article by Robert C. Johansen of the Institute for International Peace Studies at the University of Notre Dame that makes such a case for greater enforcement power for the Security Council. Robert C. Johansen, "Lessons for Collective Security," *World Policy Journal* (summer 1991): 569–70.

68. Senate Committee on Foreign Relations, *United Nations Charter Amendments,* Hearings, April 28–29, 1965, 89th Cong., 1st sess. (Government Printing Office, 1965), 32.

69. Ibid., 32–33.

70. It is widely accepted across much of the political spectrum that there are times and circumstances under which these advantages of multilateral approaches should be controlling. As a general proposition, however, relatively few American commentators believe that U.S. foreign policy choices should be limited or determined by multilateral decisionmaking processes on a consistent basis. For example, in offering his isolationist strategy for future U.S. foreign policy, Eric Nordlinger does not reject participation in the

UN and other multilateral instruments. Indeed, he cites the burden-sharing and legal advantages of multilateral initiatives in some cases, such as in economic sanctions and in undertaking military action abroad, as in Iraq. Yet in the end, his fundamental preference is for "an independent foreign policy," for "the free hand of unilateralism," and for "not permitting others to define what is and is not in our interest." Eric A. Nordlinger, *Isolationism Reconfigured: American Foreign Policy for a New Century* (Princeton University Press, 1995), 278.

71. George Bush and Brent Scowcroft, *A World Transformed* (Alfred A. Knopf, 1998), 415.

72. "Statement on the UN and US Policy by Senator John Ashcroft," March 9, 1998, http://www.globalpolicy.org/security/issues/ashcroft.htm.

73. Phelps, *Selected Articles,* 359.

74. Ibid., 326, 328, 331.

75. In his debate with Senator Lodge, for example, A. Lawrence Lowell readily acknowledged the drafting of the plan for the League was "very defective." Phelps, *Selected Articles,* 336–37.

76. According to Shotwell and Salvin, "the history of these past years, however, has by no means justified this theory, for the more definite the text the harder it is to fit it into all the varied and unforeseen circumstances in the vast range of international relations, and the easier it is for a legalistic minority to object. This problem of the rigid text is only too well known now because of the emphasis upon it of the Union of Soviet Socialist Republics. . . . [A]t San Francisco we did not expect that a veto would be used in any but a few rare instances where the vital interests of a nation were at stake." James T. Shotwell and Marina Salvin, *Lessons on Security and Disarmament from the History of the League of Nations* (New York: King's Crown Press for the Carnegie Endowment for International Peace, 1949), 1.

77. Ibid.

78. *Congressional Record,* 81st Cong., 2d sess., Sept. 22, 1950, 96, pt.11: 15640.

79. *Congressional Record,* 70th Cong, 1st sess., May 8, 1928, 69, pt. 8: 8069–73.

80. Burton Yale Pines, ed., *A World Without a U.N.* (Washington, D.C.: Heritage Foundation, 1984), ix.

81. Alan L. Keyes, "Alan Keyes: On the United Nations," Alan Keyes for President 1996, http://sandh.com/keyes/un.html.

82. In the late 1960s, Stanley Hoffmann identified this as one of the "contradictions" of U.S. policymaking. Stanley Hoffmann, *Gulliver's Troubles, Or the Setting of American Foreign Policy* (McGraw-Hill for the Council on Foreign Relations, 1968), 75.

83. *Congressional Record,* 87th Cong., 2d sess., April 4, 1962, 108, pt. 5: 5910.

84. Dole, "Shaping America's Global Future," 36, 37.

85. On a stridently partisan note, John Bolton has charged that the Clinton administration "scorned traditional definitions of the national interest, welcomed the watering down of American influence that UN-centric diplomacy entailed, and ignored the loss of American independence and flexibility caused by becoming wrapped around the UN

axle"; see Bolton, "The Creation, Fall, Rise, and Fall of the United Nations," 45. Ted Carpenter advocates a policy of "cautious unilateralism or strategic independence" that would "include a restrained and somewhat skeptical relationship with the United Nations"; see Carpenter, "The Mirage of Collective Security," 24–25. Citing statistics concerning the relatively low "overall voting coincidence by U.N. members with the United States" in the General Assembly, Jeffrey Gerlach warns that "a U.N. security system would require every state to cede in some degree its right to make independent security decisions based on its own national interest. To those concerned with the U.S. national interest, it is thus among the most disconnecting outcomes of collective internationalism to wonder how often the U.S. view would and would not prevail in the international system"; see Gerlach, "A U.N. Army for the New World Order?" 233. The statistical base for his position, of course, would be much less impressive, but much more relevant, if it reflected outcomes from the Security Council, with its selective membership and voting procedures, as well as from the General Assembly.

86. Bureau of International Organization Affairs, *Voting Practices in the United Nations* (Washington, D.C.: Department of State, annual). The annual statistics from 1985 through 1997 are cited in an endnote to chapter 5. From a high point in 1995 of 50.6 percent, voting coincidence declined to 44.2 percent in 1998.

87. Bush and Scowcroft, *A World Transformed,* 491.

88. *Congressional Record,* 65th Cong., 3d sess., Feb. 21, 1919, 57, no. 73: 3913–15.

89. Thomas Benjamin Neely, *The League, the Nation's Danger* (Philadelphia: E. A. Yeakel, 1919), 137.

90. William Howard Taft, *Taft Papers on League of Nations,* ed. Theodore Marbury and Horace E. Flack (Macmillan, 1920), 259.

91. Minutes of League of Nations Commission, March 26, 1919, *Papers of Woodrow Wilson,* ed. Arthur S. Link (Princeton University Press, 1987), 56: 303.

92. Phelps, *Selected Articles,* 344.

93. Harry S Truman on the State of the Union, Jan. 14, 1946, *Documents on American Foreign Relations,* 8: 14.

94. Phelps, *Selected Articles,* 344, 348.

95. F. R. Clow, *The Executive in a League of Nations* (Madison, Wis.: Normal Schools of Wisconsin, June 1919, 4 in a series of pamphlets), 16.

96. Patrick J. Buchanan, *The Great Betrayal: How American Sovereignty and Social Justice Are Being Sacrificed to the Gods of the Global Economy* (Little, Brown, 1998), 107.

97. Ibid., esp. 6–7.

98. Helms, "Saving the U.N.," 3.

99. There is an abundant literature on the evolving nature of sovereignty. Among those works that are especially relevant to this discussion are Lyons and Mastanduno, *Beyond Westphalia?*; Abram Chayes and Antonia Chandler Chayes, *The New Sovereignty: Compliance with International Regulatory Agreements* (Harvard University Press, 1995); Jessica T. Mathews, "Power Shift," *Foreign Affairs* 76 (Jan.–Feb. 1997): 50–66; and Anne-Marie Slaughter, "The Real New World Order," *Foreign Affairs* 76 (Sept.–Oct. 1997): 183–97.

100. *Congressional Record,* 79th Cong., 1st sess., July 24, 1945, 91, pt. 6: 7971.

101. For example, in a 1993 critique of "collective internationalism" and of recent UN actions that "have served to erode the concept of sovereignty," such as authorizing assistance to "the Kurdish population within Iraqi borders," Jeffrey Gerlach takes issue with conservative commentators, such as Charles Krauthammer, William Safire, and John R. Bolton, along with more liberal writers, such as David J. Scheffer, Indar Jit Rikhye, and Alan K. Henrickson. All are guilty, in Gerlach's view, of putting the United States on "the slippery slope" of "blurring the distinction between international and primarily domestic affairs" or of suggesting that "collective security ranges beyond the issues of political and economic oppression." Contending that "a more benign world must come gradually, from the grass-roots level," Gerlach concludes that "the United States does not need a United Nations with the broad mission of imposing its vision of peace and prosperity on the world." Gerlach, "A U.N. Army for the New World Order?" 230, 231, 236.

102. Judith Miller, "Soros to Donate Millions More to Help Russia," *New York Times,* Oct. 20, 1997.

103. Lawrence K. Altman, "Gates Giving $100 Million to Fight Childhood Disease," *New York Times,* Dec. 2, 1998.

104. Richard W. Stevenson, "The Chief Banker for the Nations at the Bottom of the Heap," *New York Times,* Sept. 14, 1997.

105. Wolfgang H. Reinicke has made useful distinctions between de jure, or legal, sovereignty and de facto, or operational, sovereignty and between internal and external sovereignty. In his view, it is in the quadrant of the operational aspects of internal sovereignty that the sharpest political challenges lie. See, especially, chap. 2 of his recent book, *Global Public Policy: Governing without Government?* (Brookings, 1998), 52–74.

106. As John Foster Dulles commented during a 1948 radio broadcast, "Woodrow Wilson was right when he preached the folly of attempting to be isolationist in a world that had become interdependent. We took Wilson's advice after we had paid the penalty for not taking that advice when first it was given." Frances Farmer, ed., *The Wilson Reader* (New York: Oceana Publications, 1956), 258.

107. Fareed Zakaria, *From Wealth to Power: The Unusual Origins of America's World Role* (Princeton University Press, 1998), 191–92.

108. Kofi A. Annan, *Renewal Amid Transition, Annual Report on the Work of the Organization, 1997* (New York: United Nations Department of Public Information, 1997), 1.

Chapter 4

The Morrison quote was cited by Senator Jesse H. Metcalf, *Congressional Record,* 70th Cong., 1st sess., May 8, 1928, 69, pt. 8:8069; the Malone quote is from the *Congressional Record,* 81st Cong., 2d sess., May 1, 1950, 96, pt. 5: 6065; the Rusk quote is from

Senate Foreign Relations Committee, *United Nations Charter Amendments,* Hearings, April 28–29, 1965, 89th Cong., 1st sess. (Government Printing Office, 1965), 13; and the Buchanan quote is from his article "Have the Globalists Over-Reached?" *The American Cause,* July 28, 1998, http://www.theamericancause.org/pjb-98-0728.html, p. 2.

1. See, for example, Todd M. Davis, ed., *Open Doors 1995/96: Report on International Educational Exchange* (New York: Institute of International Education, 1996), and "More U.S. College Students Are Studying Abroad," *New York Times,* Dec. 1, 1996.

2. Frances Farmer, *The Wilson Reader* (New York: Oceana Publications, 1956), 259.

3. For a lucid discussion of the context and origins of Washington's Farewell Address, see Walter A. McDougal, *Promised Land, Crusader State: The American Encounter with the World Since 1776* (Houghton Mifflin, 1997), 44–48.

4. During World War II Walter Lippmann argued strongly against the narrow interpretation of Washington's words, noting that "surely it is clear that while Washington was opposed to permanent alliances which would involve the United States in the disputes *within Europe,* he took it for granted that where American interests were at stake, temporary alliances with European powers were desirable." Lippmann considered this misinterpretation to have been one of a series of "mirages" that prevented the United States from building the kinds of alliances and military posture that could have deterred the war. Walter Lippmann, *U.S. Foreign Policy: Shield of the Republic* (Little, Brown, 1943), 62; see also ch. 5.

5. For an interpretation of the Farewell Address as a "realistic" and "self-confident" basis for American foreign policy, see Eric A. Nordlinger, *Isolationism Reconfigured: American Foreign Policy for a New Century* (Princeton University Press, 1995), 50–51.

6. For an insightful interpretation of America's embrace of world power during these years, see Fareed Zakaria, *From Wealth to Power: The Unusual Origins of America's World Role* (Princeton University Press, 1998).

7. See, for example, Calvin De Armond Davis, *The United States and the First Hague Peace Conference* (Cornell University Press for the American Historical Association, 1962), and Joseph H. Choate, *The Two Hague Conferences* (Princeton University Press, 1913).

8. William Howard Taft address of Feb. 22, 1919, in Salt Lake City, *Taft Papers on League of Nations,* ed. Theodore Marbury and Horace E. Flack (Macmillan, 1920), 252.

9. Wilson address of Sept. 20, 1919, in Los Angeles, *Public Papers of Woodrow Wilson, War and Peace, Presidential Messages, Addresses and Public Papers (1917–1924),* ed. Ray Stannard and William E. Dodd (Harper and Brothers, 1927), 2: 309. Wilson suggested, in fact, that the League would permit the realization of Washington's vision.

10. Elmer Bendiner, *A Time for Angels: The Tragicomic History of the League of Nations* (Alfred A. Knopf, 1975), 102.

11. A generation later, in the midst of the Second World War, Walter Lippmann pointed out that "if in fact the League outlawed alliances, and still sought to enforce

peace, then it was an unlimited commitment supported by no clear means of fulfilling it. Thus the League was attacked both as a concealed alliance and as a utopian pipe dream. The dilemma was presented because Wilson was trying to establish collective security without forming an alliance. He wanted the omelet. He rejected the idea of cooking the eggs." Lippmann, *U.S. Foreign Policy,* 75–76.

12. Wilson address of Sept. 25, 1919, in Pueblo, Colo., *Public Papers,* 2: 401.

13. Wilson letter of March 8, 1920, to Senator Gilbert M. Hitchcock, *Papers of Woodrow Wilson,* ed. Arthur S. Link (Princeton University Press, 1991), 65: 69.

14. Wilson letter of March 15, 1920, to Frank L. Polk, *Papers of Woodrow Wilson,* 65: 87.

15. Elmer Bendiner, *A Time for Angels,* 100.

16. William Howard Taft and William Jennings Bryan, *World Peace: A Written Debate Between William Howard Taft and William Jennings Bryan* (New York: George H. Doran Company, 1917), 89.

17. Charles Nagel, *The League of Nations* (np, 1919), 11, 18.

18. Thomas Benjamin Neely, *The League, the Nation's Danger* (Philadelphia: E. A. Yeakel, 1919), 136–37.

19. Philip C. Jessup, *International Security: The American Role in Collective Action for Peace* (New York: Council on Foreign Relations, 1935), 13.

20. *Congressional Record,* 80th Cong., 1st sess., Dec. 2, 1947, 93, pt.13: A4459.

21. Martin Kreisberg, "Dark Areas of Ignorance," in *Public Opinion and Foreign Policy,* ed. Lester Markel (Harper and Brothers, for the Council on Foreign Relations, 1949), 57.

22. Pat Robertson, *The New World Order* (Dallas: Word Publishing, 1991), 259.

23. For a perceptive and entertaining commentary by a German journalist on America's global dominance, see Josef Joffe, "America the Inescapable," *New York Times Magazine,* June 8, 1997, 38, 41, 43.

24. Patrick J. Buchanan, *The Great Betrayal: How American Sovereignty and Social Justice Are Being Sacrificed to the Gods of the Global Economy* (Little, Brown, 1998), 113.

25. Richard Hofstadter, "The Pseudo-Conservative Revolt—1954," in *The Paranoid Style in American Politics and Other Essays,* ed. Richard Hofstadter (Harvard University Press, 1996), 62.

26. Dean Acheson, *Present at the Creation: My Years in the State Department* (W. W. Norton, 1969), 358. For a fuller account of the McCarthy period from his perspective, see 358–70, 250–53, 698, 713–14.

27. Senate Judiciary Subcommittee to Investigate the Administration of the Internal Security Act and Other Internal Security Laws, *Activities of United States Citizens Employed by the United Nations,* Hearings, Oct. 13–15, 23–24, Nov. 11–12, Dec. 1–2, 10–11, 17, 1952, 82d Cong., 2d sess. (Government Printing Office, 1952), 16.

28. Acheson, *Present at the Creation,* 698.

29. For a detailed telling of the Hiss case and related developments, see Sam Tanenhaus, *Whittaker Chambers: A Biography* (Random House, 1997).

30. *Congressional* Record, 82d Cong., 2d sess., April 4, 1952, 98, pt. 3: 3519.

31. For Acheson's account of this episode, see *Present at the Creation*, 250–53.

32. Robertson, *The New World Order*, 52.

33. Buchanan, *The Great Betrayal*, 24.

34. *Congressional Record*, 92d Cong., 1st sess., Nov. 2, 1971, 117, pt. 30: 38703.

35. *Congressional Record*, 83d Cong., 1st sess., Feb. 18, 1953, 99, pt. 1: 1162.

36. Acheson, *Present at the Creation*, 698.

37. Shirley Hazzard, *Defeat of an Ideal: A Study of the Self-Destruction of the United Nations* (Little, Brown, 1973), particularly ch. 2.

38. Javier Pérez de Cuéllar, *Pilgrimage for Peace: A Secretary-General's Memoir* (St. Martin's Press, 1997), 7, ix.

39. Acheson, *Present at the Creation*, 369, 370.

40. Rosemary Righter, *Utopia Lost: The United Nations and World Order* (New York: The Twentieth Century Fund Press, 1995), 283. For a hard-hitting critique of the inadequacies of the UN's personnel system and bureaucratic practices, see 177–83, 280–89.

41. Kofi A. Annan, *Renewing the United Nations: A Programme for Reform*, A/51/950, July 14, 1997, 20–21.

42. Traditionally, Americans held the top posts in six UN agencies (UNICEF, UNDP, UPU, WFP, WIPO, and IOM) and the World Bank, in addition to the top management position in the UN proper. In April 1999, a non-American, Mark Malloch Brown of the United Kingdom, was appointed head of the UNDP. In terms of the percentage of professional and senior staff positions, Americans held 12.8 percent in the UN secretariat, 9.0 percent in UN subsidiary bodies, and 9.1 percent in UN specialized agencies and the IAEA, as of December 31, 1997. Department of State, *United States Participation in the United Nations: Report by the President to the Congress for the Year 1997* (July 1998), 82. For Jeane Kirkpatrick's comments on Soviet and third world efforts to keep Americans out of top secretariat positions, see George Archibald, "Americans Shut Out of Crucial U.N. Posts," *Washington Times*, Jan. 5, 1999.

43. Wilson address of Sept. 22, 1919, in Reno, Nev., *Public Papers*, 2: 336.

44. George Wharton Pepper, *America and the League of Nations* (London: Society of Comparative Legislation, 1920), 6, 13.

45. August Heckscher reports that, during the summer of 1919, "severe race riots broke out; lynchings occurred across the country. In Washington that July the Secretary of War, after consulting with the President, called up troops to maintain civil peace, and the imposition of martial law was narrowly averted. Popular passions that were to ignite the red scare and the wholesale arrests of aliens were already smoldering." August Heckscher, *Woodrow Wilson* (Collier Books, 1993), 591.

46. Henry Cabot Lodge, *The Senate and the League of Nations* (Charles Scribner's Sons, 1925), 236, 394–95, 293 (emphasis added).

47. For examples, see Ruhl J. Bartlett, *The League to Enforce Peace* (University of North Carolina Press, 1944), 79–80.

48. *Congressional Record*, 66th Cong., 1st sess., May 26, 1919, 58, pt. 1: 236, 237.

49. According to Heckscher, President Wilson believed that Republican concern about League interference in domestic affairs was largely focused on immigration policies and that "prejudice against Orientals was, in some quarters, as strong as he had found it in the first days of his administration, and he did not want to offend Japan by bringing it to the surface." Heckscher, *Woodrow Wilson*, 552.

50. *Congressional Record*, 66th Cong., 1st sess., May 26, 1919, 58, pt. 1: 243.

51. Neely, *The League, the Nation's Danger*, 154–57, 165.

52. *Congressional Record*, 66th Cong., 1st sess., May 26, 1919, 58, pt. 1: 238 (Hitchcock), 239 (Knox).

53. Ralph Stone, *The Irreconcilables: The Fight Against the League of Nations* (Lexington: University Press of Kentucky, 1970), 100–07.

54. Senate Committee on Foreign Relations, *The Charter of the United Nations, Hearings*, July 10, 1945, 79th Cong., 1st sess. (Government Printing Office, 1945), pt. 2: 177–78.

55. *Congressional Record*, 81st Cong., 2d sess., May 1, 1950, 96, pt. 5: 6065.

56. Although his statement assumed that Anglo Saxons somehow had not been "transplanted" to "our" shores like other nonnative Americans, the tone was certainly an improvement over the ugly use of the race card during the League debate. *Congressional Record*, 79th Cong., 1st sess., July 27, 1945, 91, pt. 6: 8111.

57. *Congressional Record*, 79th Cong., 1st sess., July 23, 1945, 91, pt. 6: 7964.

58. Acheson, *Present at the Creation*, 112.

59. For further discussion of this point, see Peter F. Cowhey, "Elect Locally—Order Globally: Domestic Politics and Multilateral Cooperation," in *Multilateralism Matters: The Theory and Praxis of an Institutional Form*, ed. John Gerard Ruggie (Columbia University Press, 1993), 168–69.

60. John Gerard Ruggie, "The Past as Prologue? Interests, Identity, and American Foreign Policy," *International Security* 21 (spring 1997): 112, 116.

61. It should be noted, however, that the gender gap—with women more positive toward the UN than men—tends to be even more pronounced.

62. Steven Kull, I. M. Destler, and Clay Ramsay, *The Foreign Policy Gap: How Policymakers Misread the Public* (University of Maryland, Center for International and Security Studies, October 1997), 185–88.

63. Carnegie Endowment for International Peace, *The United States Public and the United Nations: Report on a Study of American Attitudes on the U.N. and the Communication of Information to the U.S. Public* (New York: Carnegie Endowment for International Peace, 1958), 11.

64. *Congressional Record*, 81st Cong., 1st sess., July 18, 1949, 95, pt. 7: 9631.

65. Ibid.

66. For an extended colloquy on this point, see the *Congressional Record*, 81st Cong., 2d sess., April 28, 1950, 96, pt. 4: 5993–6000.

67. James Reston, "Senators to Hear Biddle on U.N. Job," *New York Times*, May 13, 1947.

68. *Congressional Record,* 92d Cong., 1st sess., Oct. 26, 1971, 117, pt. 29: 37558.

69. *Congressional Record,* 80th Cong., 2d sess., Jan. 15, 1948, 94, pt. 9: 204.

70. Robertson, *The New World Order,* 256.

71. Ibid., 208.

72. Buchanan, "Have the Globalists Over-Reached?" 3.

73. *Congressional Record,* 105th Cong., 2d sess., March 26, 1998, 144, no. 36: H1581.

74. Ali A. Mazrui, "The New Dynamics of Security: The United Nations and Africa," *World Policy Journal* 12 (summer 1996): 42.

75. *Congressional Record,* 87th Cong., 2d sess., July 31, 1962, 108, pt. 11: 15115.

76. *Congressional Record,* 87th Cong., 2d sess., April 4, 1962, 108, pt. 5: 5909–10.

77. *Congressional Record,* 92d Cong., 1st sess., Oct. 27, 1971, 117, pt. 29: 37753.

78. Acheson, *Present at the Creation,* 112.

79. Burton Yale Pines, *A World Without a U.N.: What Would Happen If the United Nations Shut Down* (Washington, D.C.: Heritage Foundation, 1984), xvi–xvii.

80. Alan Tonelson, "What Is the National Interest? Intervention vs. Minding Our Own Business: Charting a New American Foreign Policy," *Atlantic Monthly* 268 (July 1991): 51.

81. Steven Erlanger, "After the Attacks: The Diplomacy; Missile Strikes Are Seen As New Strategy for U.S.," *New York Times,* Aug. 23, 1998.

82. Robertson, *The New World Order,* 42.

83. Jesse Helms, "Saving the U.N.: A Challenge to the Next Secretary-General," *Foreign Affairs* 74 (Sept.–Oct. 1996), 7.

84. Senate Committee on Foreign Relations, *Purchase of United Nations Bonds* (S. 2768), Hearings, Feb. 6, 7, 9, 19, 1962, 87th Cong., 2d sess. (Government Printing Office, 1962), 64.

85. Ibid., 8.

86. Buchanan, *The Great Betrayal,* 6, 113.

87. Ibid., 291, 292.

88. Ruggie, "The Past as Prologue?" 110.

89. Ibid., 114.

Chapter 5

The Ribicoff and Humphrey quotes are from the *Congressional Record,* 94th Cong., 1st sess., Nov. 11, 1975, 121, pt. 28: 35774, 35775; the Goodman quote is from Dartmouth College, "United States and United Nations: Problems and Prospects, a Discussion with Dennis Goodman and Edward Luck," *World Outlook* (winter 1987): 84; and the Thiessen quote is from John M. Goshko, "U.N. Panel Calls on U.S. to Halt Death Penalty," *Washington Post,* April 4, 1998.

1. John Lewis Gaddis, *We Now Know: Rethinking Cold War History* (Clarendon Press, Oxford University Press, 1997), 36.

2. House Committee on Foreign Affairs, *The Structure of the United Nations and the Relations of the United States to the United Nations,* Hearings, May 4–7, 11–14, 1948, 80th Cong., 2d sess. (Government Printing Office, 1948), 281.

3. Dean Acheson, *Present at the Creation: My Years in the State Department* (W. W. Norton, 1969), 699.

4. Adlai E. Stevenson, *Looking Outward: Years of Crisis at the United Nations,* ed. Robert L. and Selma Schiffer (Harper & Row, 1963), 134, 136.

5. Senate Committee on Foreign Relations, *Purchase of United Nations Bonds* (S. 2768), Hearings, Feb. 6, 7, 9, 19, 1962, 87th Cong., 2d sess. (Government Printing Office,1962), 65.

6. See, for example, Stanley Hoffmann, *Gulliver's Troubles, or the Setting of American Foreign Policy* (McGraw-Hill for the Council on Foreign Relations, 1968), 57.

7. The strength of anti-American sentiment in the world body, even during the difficult years of the late 1970s and early 1980s, is debatable. For an assessment of the situation, see Edward C. Luck and Peter Fromuth, "Anti-Americanism at the United Nations: Perception or Reality?" in *Anti-Americanism in the Third World,* ed. Alvin Z. Rubinstein and Donald E. Smith (Praeger Publishers, 1985).

8. Daniel Patrick Moynihan, *A Dangerous Place* (Little, Brown, 1978), 59.

9. Ibid., 225.

10. Godfrey Hodgson, "The Establishment," *Foreign Policy* 10 (spring 1973): 8, 14–15, 11.

11. Daniel Patrick Moynihan, "The United States in Opposition," *Commentary* 59 (March 1975): 31, 35, 40, 42.

12. *Congressional Record,* 92d Cong., 1st sess., Oct. 26, 1971, 117, pt. 29: 37457 (Fisher); 37482 (Byrd); 37483 (Goldwater); 37518 (Fannin).

13. Martin E. Nolan, "Pax Americana Tumbles Down," *Boston Globe,* Nov. 2, 1971.

14. *Gallup Poll Monthly* 301 (Princeton, N.J., Oct. 1990), 16.

15. *Gallup Opinion Index* 72 (Princeton, N. J., June 1971), 16–18.

16. *Congressional Record,* 92d Cong., 1st sess., Oct. 28, 1971, 117, pt. 29: 38132.

17. Introduced by Senator Peter H. Dominick, R-Colo., on behalf of senators James E. Buckley, Cons-N.Y., Barry Goldwater, R-Ariz., and Edward J. Gurney, R-Fla. *Congressional Record,* 92d Cong., 1st sess., Oct. 28, 1971, 117, pt. 29: 37908.

18. Leon Gordenker, "'Pernicious Symbolism' at the U.N.," *Washington Post,* July 6, 1974.

19. United Nations, General Assembly, A/PV. 2400, Nov. 10, 1975, 152–56, 162.

20. *Congressional Record,* 94th Cong., 1st sess., Nov. 11, 1975, vol. 121, pt. 28: 35776.

21. Ibid., 35949.

22. Ibid., 35949 (Bauman), 35952 (Biaggi), 35934 (Frenzel), 35932 (Downey).

23. Ibid., 35949 (Yates), 35951 (Riegle), 35952 (Rinaldo), 35955 (Nix).

24. Ibid., 35775 (Packwood), 35878 (Glenn), 35779 (Mathias, Biden, Taft).

25. Ibid., 35784 (Kennedy), 35774 (Ribicoff).

26. For a fuller analysis of this question, see Edward C. Luck, "The Impact of the Zionism-Racism Resolution on the Standing of the United Nations in the United States," *Israel Yearbook on Human Rights* (Dordrecht: Martinus Nijhoff Publishers, 1987), 17: 95–119.

27. *Congressional Record,* 94th Cong., 1st sess., Nov. 11, 1975, 121, pt. 28: 35878.

28. Ibid., 35932 (Flowers); 35918 (Allen).

29. "Secretary-General Says It Is Essential for Israel and Her Adversaries to Commit Themselves to Comprehensive Peace," UN Press Release, SG/SM/6504, March 25, 1998, 4.

30. *Congressional Record,* 79th Cong., 1st sess., July 24, 1945, 91, pt. 6: 7985.

31. *Congressional Record,* 84th Cong., 1st sess., Jan. 27, 1955, 101, pt. 1: 832.

32. *Congressional Record,* 94th Cong., 1st sess., Nov. 11, 1975, 121, pt. 28: 35774.

33. Alan L. Keyes, "Fixing the UN," *The National Interest* (summer 1986): 16.

34. See, for example, John R. Bolton, "The Creation, Fall, Rise, and Fall of the United Nations," in *Delusions of Grandeur: The United Nations and Global Intervention,* ed. Ted Galen Carpenter (Washington, D.C.: Cato Institute, 1997), 46; Charles M. Lichenstein, "We Aren't the World: An Exit Strategy from U.N. Peacekeeping," *Policy Review* (spring 1995): 66; Burton Yale Pines, ed., *A World Without a U.N.: What Would Happen If the United Nations Shut Down* (Washington, D.C.: Heritage Foundation, 1984), xvii; and Pat Robertson, *The New World Order* (Dallas: Word Publishing, 1991), 56.

35. Ralph Nader, testimony to the Senate Foreign Relations Committee on the Uruguay Round of the General Agreement on Tariffs and Trade, Federal News Service, Federal Information Systems Corp., June 14, 1994, 2, 4, 8.

36. For an instructive and sobering account of how some relatively obscure non-governmental organizations helped to derail the intergovernmental negotiations for a Multilateral Agreement on Investment (MAI), see Stephen J. Kobrin, "The MAI and the Clash of Globalization," *Foreign Policy* 112 (fall 1998): 97–109.

37. For a critique of UN population programs and objectives, see Sheldon Richman, "The United Nations and the Myth of Overpopulation," in *Delusions of Grandeur: The United Nations and Global Intervention,* ed. Ted Galen Carpenter (Washington, D.C.: The Cato Institute, 1997), 161–70.

38. For more information and commentary on the rocky NRA-UN relationship, and the stormier relationship between the NRA and the Japanese government, see Katharine Q. Seelye, "National Rifle Association Is Turning to World Stage to Fight Gun Control," *New York Times,* April 2, 1997; and Raymond Bonner, "U.N. Panel May Approve Limit on Guns Despite N.R.A. Pleas," *New York Times,* April 30, 1998.

39. Tanya K. Metaksa, "Global Gun Control Is On the March," Aug. 1997, http://www.nra.org/politics96/0897tar.html.

40. United Nations, Report of the Secretary-General, *Criminal Justice and Strengthening of Legal Institutions: Measures to Regulate Firearms,* Economic and Social Council, E/CN.15/1998/4, March 11, 1998.

41. Alan L. Keyes, "Alan Keyes: On the United Nations," 1996, http://sandh.com/keyes/un.html.

42. Robertson, *The New World Order*, 222–23.

43. In March 1999 the UN Human Rights Commission received reports critical of practices in the United States on these latter two issues. On religious intolerance, see the Reuters story, "UN Expert Hits U.S. on Muslims, Native Americans." March 17, 1999, http://abcnew.go.com/wire/world/Reuters19990317_1387.html. On women in prison, see Elizabeth Olson, "U.N. Panel Is Told of Rights Violations at U.S. Women's Prisons," *New York Times*, March 31, 1999; and UN Economic and Social Council, Commission on Human Rights, Report of the Mission to the United States of America on the Issue of Violence Against Women in State and Federal Prisons, E/CN.4/1999/60/add.2, Jan. 4, 1999. These were two of a long list of contentious issues addressed in a rather shrill Amnesty International report prepared for its USA Campaign and released in October 1998, *Rights for All*, http://www.rightsforall-usa.org/info/action/index.html.

44. Barbara Crossette, "U.N. Monitor Investigates American Use of the Death Penalty," *New York Times*, Sept. 30, 1997.

45. John M. Goshko, "Helms Calls Death Row Probe 'Absurd U.N. Charade,'" *Washington Post*, Oct. 8, 1997.

46. *Congressional Record*, 105th Cong., 1st sess., June 17, 1997, 143, no. 84: S5740.

47. *Congressional Record*, 105th Cong., 1st sess., Oct. 7, 1997, 143, no. 138: H8539–40 (Young), H8540 (Chenoweth), H8558 (Riggs).

48. Ibid., H8539 (Vento), H8541 (Farr), H8542 (Hinchey, Miller).

49. Senate Subcommittee of the Committee on Appropriations, *Foreign Assistance and Related Programs Appropriations for Fiscal Year 1989*, Hearings, March 30, April 12, 14, 1988, 100th Cong., 2d sess., (Government Printing Office, 1988), 176.

50. With 120 cosponsors, Representative Young reintroduced the bill on March 1, 1999 (HR 883). For a discussion of the bill, see United Nations Association of the USA, *Washington Report*, March 5, 1999, http://www.unausa.org/dc/info/publands2.htm.

51. Neil A. Lewis, "House Tweaks Clinton over Creation of National Monuments," *New York Times*, Oct. 8, 1997.

52. For a more detailed discussion of the growth of NGOs represented at the UN, see ch. 11 in this volume and Kofi A. Annan, *Arrangements and Practices for the Interaction of Non-Governmental Organizations in All Activities of the United Nations System*, A/53/170, July 10, 1998, 2.

53. Dartmouth College, "United States and United Nations," 83, 84.

54. Soon after stepping down from the post of permanent representative, Jeane Kirkpatrick told a Senate committee that in the 1960s and 1970s the United States and other democracies had allowed "to develop around us a political system in which we are a permanent minority. . . . We almost permitted the bullies to take control of the playground." Senate Committee on Governmental Affairs, *U.S. Financial and Political Involvement in the United Nations*, Hearings, May 9, 1985, 99th Cong., 1st sess. (Government Printing Office, 1985), 5.

55. According to the State Department, since 1985 the voting coincidence between the United States and other member states has been as follows: 1985, 22.5 percent; 1986,

23.7 percent; 1987, 18.6 percent; 1988, 15.4 percent; 1989, 16.9 percent; 1990, 21.3 percent; 1991, 27.8 percent; 1992, 31.0 percent; 1993, 36.8 percent; 1994, 48.6 percent; 1995, 50.6. percent; 1996, 49.4 percent; 1997, 46.7 percent; and 1998, 44.2 percent. These statistics are from the annual publication of the Bureau of International Organization Affairs, *Voting Practices in the United Nations* (Washington, D.C.: Department of State). The State Department also points out that three-quarters of all General Assembly resolutions since 1994 were adopted by consensus and that efforts to rationalize the Assembly's agenda have resulted in a decrease in the number of resolutions produced each of the last several years. See *Voting Practices in the United Nations 1998*, 1.

56. See, for example, Luck and Fromuth, "Anti-Americanism at the United Nations."

Chapter 6

The Fulbright quote is from the *Congressional Record*, 79th Cong., 1st sess., July 23, 1945, 91, pt. 6: 7964; the Burdick quote is from the *Congressional Record*, 81st Cong., 2d sess., Sept. 20, 1950, 96, pt. 11: 15304; and the Lodge quote is from *As It Was: An Inside View of Politics and Power in the '50s and '60s* (W. W. Norton, 1976), 184.

1. For example, Michael J. Glennon, a California law professor and former legal counsel to the Senate Foreign Relations Committee, recently dismissed the UN as being fundamentally anti-interventionist. Michael J. Glennon, "The New Interventionism: The Search for a Just International Law," *Foreign Affairs* 78 (May–June, 1999): 2–7. For responses, see Thomas M. Franck, "Break It, Don't Fake It," and Edward C. Luck, "A Road to Nowhere," *Foreign Affairs* 78 (July–Aug., 1999):116–19.

2. *Congressional Record*, 79th Cong., 1st sess., July 24, 1945, 91, pt. 6: 8003.

3. See the results of 1989 and 1992 Roper polls conducted for the United Nations Association of the USA (UNA-USA), as analyzed in Jeffrey Laurenti, *Directions and Dilemmas in Collective Security: Reflections from a Global Roundtable* (New York: UNA-USA, 1992), 18–19.

4. House Committee on Foreign Affairs, *To Seek Development of the United Nations into a World Federation (H. Con. Res. 64)*, Hearings, Oct. 12–13, 1949, 81st Cong, 1st sess. (Government Printing Office, 1950), 221.

5. Ibid., 230.

6. "A League of Peace," *New Republic*, June 26, 1915.

7. William Howard Taft and William Jennings Bryan, *World Peace: A Written Debate Between William Howard Taft and William Jennings Bryan* (New York: George H. Doran Company, 1917), 88.

8. Oscar Newfang, *The United States of the World: A Comparison between the League of Nations and the United States of America* (G. P. Putnam's Sons, 1930), 200.

9. Edith M. Phelps, ed., *Selected Articles on a League of Nations* (New York: H. W. Wilson Co., 4th ed., 1919), 322, 326.

10. Ibid., 338.

11. Ruhl J. Bartlett, *The League to Enforce Peace* (University of North Carolina Press, 1944), 50–51. In fact, much of the league's initial leadership came from internationalist Republican circles (56–58).

12. Newfang, *The United States of the World*, 215.

13. Ibid., 217, 218.

14. Taft and Bryan, *World Peace*, 20–21.

15. House Committee on Foreign Affairs, *The Structure of the United Nations and the Relations of the United States to the United Nations*, Hearings, May 4–7, 11–14, 1948, 80th Cong., 2d sess. (Government Printing Office, 1948), 279.

16. Ibid., 281.

17. For an argument in favor of confederation as a model for global organization, in which the UN system is interpreted as a confederal arrangement, see Daniel J. Elazar, *Constitutionalizing Globalization: The Postmodern Revival of Confederal Arrangements* (Lanham, Md.: Rowman and Littlefield Publishers, 1998), esp. 164–70.

18. Scott Nearing, *Labor and the League of Nations* (New York: Rand School of Social Science, 1919), 10–11.

19. Thomas Benjamin Neely, *The League, the Nation's Danger* (Philadelphia: E. A. Yeakel, 1919), 128.

20. *Congressional Record,* 79th Cong., 1st sess., July 23, 1945, 91, pt. 6: 7965.

21. Ibid., 8003.

22. In this regard, the political dilemmas faced by intergovernmental organizations are distinct from those confronted by national governments. Officials in democratic societies are used to getting criticism from all sides. In trying to serve the needs and views of the majority of citizens in the political center, national leaders are bound to attract—and may even welcome—political attacks from the extreme flanks. National governments, however, have alternative ways of satisfying, co-opting, or segregating different constituencies that are rarely available to international organizations. Withholding dues or threatening to withdraw from a multilateral body, moreover, is easier to contemplate than refusing to pay taxes or threatening secession from a national union.

23. Defenders of the new World Trade Organization, despite its more focused mandate, faced a similar too-weak, too-strong dilemma in presenting their case to Congress. The tactical ambivalence of Clinton administration officials in describing the WTO to the Senate Foreign Relations Committee in 1994 left at least one senator, normally sympathetic to international organization, exasperated. Senator Russell Feingold, D-Wis., commented that,

> As I try to explain this agreement to my constituents in Wisconsin I believe that they will in effect say to me, "Isn't this really kind of like creating a United Nations of trade?" And they are going to want to know whether this thing has teeth or not, very similarly to questions that have been raised about the United Nations throughout its history. The sense I get here is that some of the defense of this agreement wants to say sometimes that it has teeth, but whenever it

impacts negatively on the United States it really won't have any teeth. And
that's not going to be very easy for me to get them to believe.

On the other side, Ambassador Rufus Yerxa, the deputy U.S. trade representative
attempting to sell the new organization to the Senate, sounded equally perplexed. "You
can understand a little bit of frustration on my part," he lamented to the Senators,
"because on the one hand I've heard people argue, 'Gee, there's no Security Council in
which we have a veto,' and I've heard that we're turning the WTO into a U.N. for trade,
so I'm not quite sure whether people wanted us to follow that precedent or not." Indeed,
this uncertainty within the executive branch about how capable an international system
the American people really want has never been fully resolved. At the same time, Senator
Feingold is right to object that this ambivalence has been fostered, in part, by the dual
messages so often heard from the White House and State Department: in the abstract
these organizations are of great importance, but operationally, when American interests
might be in jeopardy, their actions are said to carry little weight. Senate Foreign Relations
Committee Hearing on the World Trade Organization, June 14, 1994, Federal News
Service, Federal Information System Corp., 1994, 31, 35.

24. For a discussion of this dilemma in the report of a high-level international task
force headed by Lord Carrington and Moeen Qureshi, see International Task Force on
the Enforcement of U.N. Security Council Resolutions, *Words to Deeds: Strengthening the
U.N.'s Enforcement Capabilities* (New York: United Nations Association of the USA,
Dec. 1997), esp. sec. 1.

25. In UN circles, prevention has been a favored topic of study and policy initiatives
since the end of the cold war. If prevention fails, however, then all of the dilemmas asso-
ciated with the enforcement of collective security would return. See, for example,
Secretary-General Boutros Boutros-Ghali, *An Agenda for Peace: Preventive Diplomacy,
Peacemaking and Peace-keeping*, A/47/277, June 17, 1992; Carnegie Commission on
Preventing Deadly Conflict, *Preventing Deadly Conflict* (New York: Carnegie Corpora-
tion of New York, 1997); and Kofi A. Annan, "Achievement of Effective Prevention Is
Testament to Succeeding Generations 'That Ours Had the Will to Save Them from the
Scourge of War,'" UN Press Release, SG/SM/6454, Feb. 5, 1998.

26. Alan Tonelson, "Beyond Left and Right," *The National Interest* (winter
1993–94): 14.

27. "A League of Peace," *New Republic*, March 20, 1915.

28. F. S. Northedge, *The League of Nations: Its Life and Times 1920–1946* (Leicester
University Press, 1986), 26. For a detailed history of the American counterpart, see
Bartlett, *The League to Enforce Peace*.

29. Taft and Bryan, *World Peace*, xii–xiii, 22, 23.

30. William Howard Taft, *Taft Papers on League of Nations*, ed. Theodore Marbury
and Horace E. Flack (Macmillan, 1920), 242.

31. John H. Clarke, *America and World Peace* (Henry Holt and Co., 1925), 37.

32. For a contemporary assessment of the halting efforts at U.S.-League coopera-tion on issues of peace and security, see Philip C. Jessup, *International Security: The American Role in Collective Action for Peace* (New York: Council on Foreign Relations, 1935), 17–19.

33. George Wharton Pepper, *America and the League of Nations* (London: Society of Comparative Legislation, 1920), 3, 5, 7, 13.

34. Phelps, *Selected Articles,* 352–53.

35. Taft and Bryan, *World Peace,* 27, 28, 30, 39.

36. Walter A. McDougal, *Promised Land, Crusader State: The American Encounter with the World Since 1776* (Houghton Mifflin, 1997), 141.

37. Charles Nagel, *The League of Nations* (n.p., May 30, 1919), 5–6.

38. Taft and Bryan, *World Peace,* 34.

39. Taft was so disappointed with Wilson's handling of the League question before the Senate that he vowed to vote for Harding instead in the 1920 presidential election. See Taft, *Taft Papers,* foreword.

40. Nagel, *The League of Nations,* 5.

41. Elmer Bendiner, *A Time for Angels: The Tragicomic History of the League of Nations* (Alfred A. Knopf, 1975), 99.

42. Ibid., 98, 100.

43. Northedge, *The League of Nations,* 2.

44. Walter Lippmann, *U.S. Foreign Policy: Shield of the Republic* (Little, Brown, 1943), 31.

45. Bob Dole, "Shaping America's Global Future," *Foreign Policy* 98 (spring 1995), 39.

46. *Congressional Record,* 105th Cong., 2d sess., March 25, 1998, 144, no. 35: S2543.

47. Senate Committee on Foreign Relations, *The Charter of the United Nations,* Hearings, July 10, 1945, 79th Cong., 1st sess. (Government Printing Office, 1945), pt. 2: 154.

48. Arthur H. Vandenberg Jr., ed., *The Private Papers of Senator Vandenberg* (Houghton-Mifflin, 1952), 200.

49. McDougal, *Promised Land, Crusader State,* 139.

50. White House, "Key Elements of the Clinton Administration's Policy on Reforming Multilateral Peace Operations," May 3, 1994, 1.

51. Commission on America's National Interests, *America's National Interests* (Harvard University, Center for Science and International Affairs, July 1996), 6.

52. Senate Committee on Foreign Relations, *The Purchase of United Nations Bonds,* (S. 2768), Hearings, Feb 6, 7, 9, 19, 1962, 87th Cong., 2d sess. (Government Printing Office, 1962), 188.

53. *Congressional Record,* 87th Cong., 2d sess., April 4, 1962, 108, pt. 4: 5910.

54. Richard Holbrooke, *To End a War* (Random House, 1998), 88, 202, 360.

55. Kofi A. Annan, *Renewing the United Nations: A Programme for Reform,* United Nations, General Assembly, A/51/950, July 14, 1997, 36.

56. Jeane J. Kirkpatrick, *Security Challenges in the Post–Cold War World,* Russell Symposium, 1995 Proceedings (Center for International Trade and Security, University of Georgia, 1996), 11.

57. Phelps, *Selected Articles,* 329.

58. Neely, *The League,* 150–53.

59. Phelps, *Selected Articles,* 349–50.

60. For an extensive discussion of wartime planning for the United Nations, see Townsend Hoopes and Douglas Brinkley, *FDR and the Creation of the U.N.* (Yale University Press, 1997).

61. James B. Reston, "Votes and Vetoes," *Foreign Affairs* 25 (Oct. 1946): 13.

62. Hoopes and Brinkley, *FDR and the Creation of the U.N.,* 126. Also see 116–17.

63. *Congressional Record,* 79th Cong., 1st sess., July 25, 1945, 91, pt. 6: 8017.

64. Henry Cabot Lodge, *The Storm Has Many Eyes: A Personal Narrative* (W. W. Norton, 1973), 251.

65. House Committee on Foreign Affairs, *Structure of the United Nations,* 57.

66. Ibid., 59.

67. Ibid., 61.

68. Reston, "Votes and Vetoes," 20.

69. House Committee on Foreign Affairs, *To Seek Development of the United Nations,* 214 (Smith), 218 (Fulton).

70. American Institute of Public Opinion, "Changing Opinions: A 50-Year Retrospective," *Index to International Public Opinion, 1992–1993* (New York: Greenwood Press, 1994), 706.

71. H. Schuyler Foster, *Activism Replaces Isolationism: U.S. Public Attitudes, 1940–1975* (Washington, D.C.: Foxhall Press, 1983), 81.

72. Robert C. Hilderbrand, *Dumbarton Oaks: The Origins of the United Nations and the Search for Postwar Security* (University of North Carolina Press, 1990), 254.

73. *Congressional Record,* 81st Cong., 2d sess., Sept. 20, 1950, 96, pt. 11: 15304.

74. *Congressional Record,* 80th Cong., 2d sess., May 10, 1948, 94, pt. 10: A2871.

75. *Congressional Record,* 79th Cong., 1st sess., July 24, 1945, 91, pt. 6: 8003.

76. *Congressional Record,* 80th Cong., 2d sess., May 5, 1948, 94, pt. 10: A.2747.

77. *Congressional Record,* 80th Cong., 1st sess., July 24, 1947, 93, pt. 12: A3784.

78. James B. Reston, "UN Held a Poor Scapegoat in Debating New United States Policy," *New York Times,* March 18, 1947.

79. Sumner Welles, "Abolishing the Veto—Would This Make UN a Reality?" *Washington Post,* July 22, 1947.

80. United Nations, General Assembly, Special Committee on Peace-Keeping Operations, A/AC.121/PV.15, Aug. 16, 1965, 11.

81. For a detailed account of the Five-Power discussion on the veto at the San Francisco founding conference, see Ruth B. Russell, *History of the United Nations Charter: The Role of the United States 1940–1945* (Brookings, 1958), 719–35. For the dif-

ficult deliberations at Dumbarton Oaks on the veto and Security Council decisionmaking, see Hilderbrand, *Dumbarton Oaks,* esp. 183–208.

82. Hoopes and Brinkley, *FDR and the Creation of the U.N.,* 148, 150.

83. George C. Marshall, address before the United Nations General Assembly, Sept. 17, 1947, excerpted in *Documents on American Foreign Relations* (Jan. 1–Dec. 31, 1947), ed. Raymond Dennett and Robert K. Turner (Princeton University Press for the World Peace Foundation, 1949), 9: 320. Also see statement by John Foster Dulles explaining this policy initiative in greater detail. Ibid., 9: 320–24.

84. House Committee on Foreign Affairs, *Structure of the United Nations,* 70. Also see testimony of George C. Marshall, 45, 54.

85. House Committee on Foreign Affairs, *To Seek Development of the United Nations,* 237–38.

86. As described in Hoopes and Brinkley, *FDR and the Creation of the U.N.,* 56.

87. House Committee on Foreign Affairs, *Structure of the United Nations,* 280.

88. In this context, it should be recalled that many American conservatives and libertarians had traditionally been uncomfortable with the notion of a massive standing national security apparatus, of which the United Nations was (and is) only a small part. Although isolationism was no longer a major political force by the end of the war, the architecture of the appropriate postwar national security structure was not obvious to most Americans. For a useful account of this debate, see Michael H. Hogan, *A Cross of Iron: Harry S Truman and the Origins of the National Security State, 1945–1954* (Cambridge University Press, 1998).

89. Reston, "Votes and Vetoes," p. 22.

Chapter 7

The Lodge quote is from Edith M. Phelps, ed., *Selected Articles on a League of Nations* (New York: H. W. Wilson Co., 4th ed., 1919), 332–33; the Wheeler quote is from the *Congressional Record,* 79th Cong., 1st sess., July 24, 1945, 91, pt. 6: 7989; and the Connally quote is from the Senate Committee on Foreign Relations, *The Charter of the United Nations,* Hearings, 79th Cong. 1st sess., July 10, 1945, pt. 2: 125.

1. *Congressional Record,* 79th Cong., 1st sess., July 27, 1945, 91, pt. 6: 8122.

2. Wilson speech of Sept. 22, 1919, in Reno, *Public Papers of Woodrow Wilson, War and Peace, Presidential Messages, Addresses, and Public Papers (1917–1924),* ed. Ray Stannard Baker and William E. Dodd (Harper and Brothers Publishers, 1927), 2: 333.

3. Philip C. Jessup, *Elihu Root, 1905–1937* (Dodd, Mead & Co., 1938), 2: 378.

4. Philip C. Jessup, *International Security: The American Role in Collective Action for Peace* (New York: Council on Foreign Relations, 1935), 6. Ruhl J. Bartlett, an advocate of the League, complained in 1944 that its opponents had greatly exaggerated the obligations it imposed. Bartlett, *The League to Enforce Peace* (University of North Carolina Press, 1944), 193.

5. Wilson, *Public Papers,* 2: 332.

6. Jessup, *Elihu Root,* 2: 393.

7. As August Heckscher has noted, "disappointed by the treaty's failure to follow more narrowly the Fourteen Points, they maintained that the League would have the effect of solidifying and guaranteeing a basically unjust order. Article X of the charter, protecting the territorial integrity of its member states, was as strongly opposed by them on the ground that it would prevent change, as it was opposed, for quite different reasons, by isolationist senators." Heckscher, *Woodrow Wilson* (New York: Collier Books, Macmillan, 1991), 589.

8. "A League of Peace," *New Republic,* March 20, 1915.

9. Wilson letter of March 8, 1920, to Senator Gilbert M. Hitchcock, *Papers of Woodrow Wilson,* ed. Arthur S. Link (Princeton University Press, 1991), 65: 69.

10. "Harding Demands Republican Senate," *New York Times,* Oct. 29, 1920.

11. Phelps, *Selected Articles,* 333.

12. Ibid., 332.

13. John Chalmers Vinson, *Referendum for Isolation: Defeat of Article Ten of the League of Nations Covenant* (University of Georgia Press, 1961), 74.

14. Jessup, *Elihu Root,* 2: 399.

15. Phelps, *Selected Articles,* 332–33.

16. Wilson, *Public Papers,* 2: 351. Three years later, on September 27, 1922, the assembly of the League expressed the opinion that "the obligation to render assistance to a country attacked shall be limited in principle to those countries situated in the same part of the globe." See Hamilton Foley, ed., *Woodrow Wilson's Case for the League of Nations* (Princeton University Press, 1923), 249.

17. To meet some of the concerns of Senate critics, article 21 of the covenant underlined that "nothing in this Covenant shall be deemed to affect the validity of international engagements, such as treaties of arbitration or regional understandings like the Monroe doctrine, for securing the maintenance of peace."

18. Phelps, *Selected Articles,* 335, 336.

19. Vinson, *Referendum for Isolation,* 103–04.

20. William Howard Taft, *Taft Papers on League of Nations,* ed. Horace E. Flack and Theodore Marbury (Macmillan, 1920), 320 (reprint from the *Public Ledger,* April 30, 1919).

21. Ibid.

22. *Congressional Record,* 79th Cong., 1st sess., July 24, 1945, 91, pt. 6: 7989.

23. *Congressional Record,* 83d Cong., 1st sess., May 5, 1953, 99, pt. 4: 4533.

24. The question of what conditions are likely to contribute to or detract from the likelihood that a UN peacekeeping operation will be successful in its own terms (assuming, of course, that the assent of the five permanent members of the Council indicates that they consider the mission to be in their interest) has received substantial study both by the Lessons Learned Unit of the UN's Department of Peacekeeping Operations and by outside authors. For a good example of the latter, see Michael W. Doyle, Ian

Johnstone, and Robert C. Orr, eds., *Keeping the Peace: Multidimensional UN Operations in Cambodia and El Salvador* (Cambridge University Press, 1997).

25. White House, "Executive Summary: The Clinton Administration's Policy on Reforming Multilateral Peace Operations," May 3, 1994, 1.

26. White House, "Key Elements of the Clinton Administration's Policy on Reforming Multilateral Peace Operations," May 3, 1994, 1.

27. Bob Dole, "Shaping America's Global Future," *Foreign Policy* 98 (spring 1995): 46.

28. Ted Galen Carpenter, "The Mirage of Global Collective Security," in *Delusions of Grandeur: The United Nations and Global Intervention*, ed. Ted Galen Carpenter (Washington, D.C.: Cato Institute, 1997), 26.

29. Jeffrey R. Gerlach, "A U.N. Army for the New World Order?" *Orbis* (spring 1993): 226.

30. Alan Tonelson, "What Is the National Interest? Interventionism versus Minding Our Own Business: Charting a New American Foreign Policy," *Atlantic Monthly* 268 (July 1991): 49. In his view, "the importance of the Third World to the United States has been shrinking steadily. America's internationalist foreign policy perversely has sought to reverse this process, and to bind America's future ever more closely to these generally woebegone lands and their desperate problems."

31. Christopher Layne, "Minding Our Own Business: The Case for American Non-Participation in International Peacekeeping/Peacemaking Operations," in *Beyond Traditional Peacekeeping*, ed. Donald C. F. Daniel and Bradd C. Hayes (St. Martin's Press, 1995), 92. Citing Somalia and Bosnia as examples, Doug Bandow of the Cato Institute has asserted that "UN operations also draw nations, particularly the United States, into irrelevant conflicts around the globe" and that "the UN has, at times, put Washington back into areas from which it had only recently disengaged after years of meddling." See Bandow, "UN Military Missions as a Snare for America," in *Delusions of Grandeur: The United Nations and Global Intervention*, ed. Ted Galen Carpenter (Washington, D.C.: Cato Institute, 1997), 77.

32. Alan Tonelson, "Beyond Left and Right," *The National Interest* (winter 1993–94): 14.

33. "Alan Keyes: On the United Nations," Alan Keyes for President 1996, http://sandh.com/keyes/un.html.

34. See, for example, Carpenter, "The Mirage of Global Collective Security," 21–22, and Bandow, "UN Military Missions," 76.

35. See Gerlach, "A U.N. Army for the New World Order?" 231; and Carpenter, "The Mirage of Global Collective Security," 16.

36. See Layne, "Minding Our Own Business," 96–97; and Alan Tonelson, "Superpower Without a Sword," *Foreign Affairs* 72 (summer 1993): 178.

37. Senate Committee on Foreign Relations, *The Purchase of United Nations Bonds* (S. 2768), Hearings, Feb. 6, 7, 9, 19, 1962, 87th Cong., 2d sess. (Government Printing Office, 1962), 2.

38. Ibid., 57–58.

39. White House, "Key Elements," 1, 6–7.

40. Charles M. Lichenstein, "We Aren't the World: An Exit Strategy from U.N. Peacekeeping," *Policy Review* 72 (spring 1995): 62–63.

41. Jesse Helms, "Saving the U.N.: A Challenge to the Next Secretary-General," *Foreign Affairs* 74 (Sept.–Oct. 1996): 6.

42. For example, House member John M. Vorys, R-Ohio, representing the United States before the Assembly's Administrative and Budgetary Committee in 1951, complained that the United States had undertaken the defense of Korea "at the request of the Security Council and with the publicly announced support of 53 member nations. The people in my country, whose sons are fighting and dying in this struggle, along with men of other nations, know that we are bearing not one-third of the burden, but far more than two-thirds of the burden of the United Nations in support of the principles of the Charter in Korea." Reprinted in the *Congressional Record*, 82d Cong., 2d sess., April 4, 1952, 98, pt. 3: 3516.

43. See, for example, the statements of representatives Clare E. Hoffman of Michigan, *Congressional Record*, 81st Cong., 2d sess., Sept. 22, 1950, 96, pt. 11: 15640 and Burdick of North Dakota, *Congressional Record*, 81st Cong., 2d sess., Sept. 20, 1950, 96, pt. 11: 15304.

44. For an analysis of the constitutional issues involved, from the perspective of a former legal counsel to the Senate Foreign Relations Committee and an advocate of a more active congressional and judicial role in U.S. foreign policy, see Michael J. Glennon, *Constitutional Diplomacy* (Princeton University Press, 1990).

45. White House, "Executive Summary," 14–15.

46. The efforts to translate the provisions of the "Contract with America" into legislation focused on the Peace Powers Act (S. 5) in the Senate and the National Security Revitalization Act (H.R. 7) in the House. Hearings were held by the House Committee on National Security on Jan. 19, 25, and 27, 1995; by the House Committee on International Relations on Jan. 24, 27, 30, and 31, 1995; and by the Senate Committee on Foreign Relations on March 21, 1995.

47. Lichenstein, "We Aren't the World," 64.

48. William Howard Taft and William Jennings Bryan, *World Peace: A Written Debate Between William Howard Taft and William Jennings Bryan* (New York: George H. Doran Company, 1917), 36–37.

49. Vinson, *Referendum for Isolation*, 71.

50. Thomas Benjamin Neely, *The League, the Nation's Danger* (Philadelphia: E. A. Yeakel, 1919), 171.

51. Charles Nagel, *The League of Nations* (n.p., May 30, 1919), 7, 8.

52. Phelps, *Selected Articles*, 350–52.

53. Vinson, *Referendum for Isolation*, 101.

54. To some extent, however, this tactic may also have served to postpone serious debate on these matters until many years later (see chapter 10).

55. In a 1947 colloquy on the House floor, for example, Estes Kefauver, D-Tenn., suggested that "the fact that our Secretaries of State and the President have seen fit to designate Members of the Senate, both Democratic and Republican, and also Members of the House to serve in representative capacities at the San Francisco Conference and other meetings where the peace structure has been discussed and decided upon, has aided greatly in having the results of those meetings accepted by the American people and by Congress." Concurring fully, Representative William W. Courtney, D-Tenn., asserted that "this time our foreign policy is neither Democratic nor Republican. It was forged by the Executive, by and with the aid, counsel, and advice of leaders of both parties, and it is being administered by able representatives chosen from both parties, and so is as nearly a nonpartisan approach as can be attained." *Congressional Record,* 80th Cong., 1st sess., Feb. 10, 1947, 93, pt. 1: 956.

56. Senate Committee on Foreign Relations, *Hearings on the Charter of the United Nations,* 124.

57. Ibid., 125.

58. Ibid., 125–26.

59. Ibid., 127.

60. *Congressional Record,* 79th Cong., 1st sess., July 25, 1945, 91, pt. 6: 8019.

61. Statement of Professor Robert F. Turner, House Committee on Government Operations Subcommittee on Legislation and National Security, *United Nations Peacekeeping: The Effectiveness of the Legal Framework,* Hearing, March 3, 1994, 103d Cong., 2d sess. (Government Printing Office, 1994), 150.

62. *Congressional Record,* 79th Cong., 1st sess., July 24, 1945, 91, pt. 6: 7988.

63. Ibid., 8122.

64. For a recent critique of the resulting tendency toward an "imperial presidency," see Alan Tonelson, "UN Military Missions and the Imperial Presidency: Internationalism by the Back Door," in *Delusions of Grandeur,* ed. Ted Galen Carpenter (Washington, D.C.: Cato Institute, 1997), 97–110.

65. White House, "Executive Summary," 1.

66. Fulbright has since written that it was the 1965 U.S. military intervention in the Dominican Republic, not the Vietnam War, that marked "the turning point" in his thinking about the need for greater congressional oversight. See his foreword to Glennon, *Constitutional Diplomacy,* xii.

67. For the mandate of the UNAMET operation in East Timor, see UN Security Council Resolution, S/RES 1246, June 11, 1999.

68. UN Press Release, SG/2050, Jan. 4, 1999, and Zogby International Press Release, Jan. 4, 1999, http://www.zogby.com/news/home.htm.

69. For a critique of the Council's performance in these matters and its effect on the UN's credibility, see International Task Force on the Enforcement of U.N. Security Council Resolutions, *Words to Deeds: Strengthening the U.N.'s Enforcement Capabilities* (New York: United Nations Association of the USA, 1997), esp. sections 1 and 2. For the decision adopted at the Assembly of Heads of State and Government of the Organization

of African Unity, held in Ouagadougou, Burkina Faso, June 8–10, 1998, see a British Broadcasting Corporation (BBC) broadcast of June 11, 1998; Gus Constantine, "U.N. Travel Ban on Libya Collapsing; Egypt's Mubarak Latest African Dignitary to Visit Gadhafi," *Washington Times*, July 10, 1998; and Africa News Online, U.S. Department of State, "Rubin Statement: OAU Resolution on Libya," June 16, 1998, http:/www. africanews.org/north/libya/stories/19980616_feat1.html.

70. For fuller accounts of this story, see Marc Fisher, "War and Peacekeeping: Battle Rages Over the GI Who Said No to U.N. Insignia," *Washington Post*, March 4, 1996, and Rowan Scarborough, "New's Father: Pride, No Regrets: Place in History is 'A Privilege,'" *Washington Times*, April 19, 1996.

71. Fisher, "War and Peacekeeping."

72. Ibid.

73. *Congressional Record*, 104th Cong., 2d sess., Sept. 5, 1996, 142, no. 120: H10067.

74. Ibid.

75. Scarborough, "New's Father."

76. *Congressional Record*, 104th Cong., 2d sess., Sept. 5, 1996, 142, no. 120: H10067.

77. Ibid.

78. Pat Robertson, *The New World Order* (Dallas: Word Publishing, 1991), 208.

79. See, for example, Steven Kull, I. M. Destler, and Clay Ramsay, *The Foreign Policy Gap: How Policymakers Misread the Public* (University of Maryland, Center for International and Security Studies, 1997), 93–94; and Jeffrey Laurenti, *Directions and Dilemmas in Collective Security* (New York: United Nations Association of the USA, 1992), 25, 29.

80. Fisher, "War and Peacekeeping."

81. Tonelson, "Beyond Left and Right," 15.

82. Taft and Bryan, *World Peace*, 30, 50.

83. George Wharton Pepper, *America and the League of Nations* (London: Society of Comparative Legislation, 1920, reprinted from the *Journal of Comparative Legislation and International Law*), 5–6.

84. Wilson letter of March 22, 1918, to Edward M. House, *Papers of Woodrow Wilson*, 47: 105.

85. Minutes of a Meeting of the Commission of the League of Nations, February 11, 1919, *Papers of Woodrow Wilson*, 55: 76.

86. Taft, *Taft Papers on League of Nations*, 215–16.

87. Ruth B. Russell, *History of the United Nations Charter: The Role of the United States 1940–1945* (Brookings, 1958), 677.

88. Townsend Hoopes and Douglas Brinkley, *FDR and the Creation of the U.N.* (Yale University Press, 1997), 117–18. For a discussion of the constitutional issues raised by article 43, see Michael J. Glennon and Allison J. Hayward, "Collective Security and the Constitution: Can the Commander in Chief Power Be Delegated to the United Nations?" *Georgetown Law Journal* 82 (4, April 1994): 1573–603.

89. For example, see the remarks on the Senate floor by George W. Malone, a Nevada Republican, in December 1950. *Congressional Record,* 81st Cong, 2d sess., Dec. 22, 1950, 96, pt. 12: 16983–84.

90. For a vivid account of the ill-fated Ranger raid in Mogadishu, see Mark Bowden, *Black Hawk Down: A Story of Modern War* (Atlantic Monthly Press, 1999).

91. For an account of U.S.-UN political relationships during the Somali crisis, see Stanley Meisler, "Dateline U.N.: A New Hammarskjöld?" *Foreign Policy* 98 (spring 1995): 189–91.

92. For a fuller explanation of the Somali operation, see Robert B. Oakley, "Using the United Nations to Advance U.S. Interests," in *Delusions of Grandeur,* ed. Ted Galen Carpenter (Washington, D.C.: Cato Institute, 1997); Robert Oakley and John Hirsch, *Somalia and Operation Restore Hope* (Washington, D.C.: U.S. Institute for Peace, 1995); and Senate Armed Services Committee, *U.S. Military Operations in Somalia,* Hearings, May 12, 1994, 103d Cong., 2d sess. (Government Printing Office, 1994).

93. Elaine Sciolino with Paul Lewis, "Mission in Somalia: Secretary Besieged," *New York Times,* Oct. 16, 1993.

94. Richard Holbrooke, *To End a War* (Random House, 1998), 202.

95. Meisler, "Dateline U.N.," 193.

96. See, for example, James Phillips, "Needed at the UN: More Secretary, Less General," Executive Memorandum 455, Heritage Foundation, Washington, D.C., June 24, 1996, 1; Bandow, "UN Military Missions," 76; and Gerlach, "A U.N. Army for the New World Order?" 227. For Boutros-Ghali's perspective, see his account of his years at the UN: *Unvanquished: A US-UN Saga* (Random House, 1999).

97. John R. Bolton, "The Creation, Fall, Rise, and Fall of the United Nations," in *Delusions of Grandeur,* ed. Ted Galen Carpenter (Washington, D.C.: Cato Institute, 1997), 55.

98. Meisler, "Dateline U.N.," 181.

99. House Committee on International Relations, *National Security Revitalization Act (H.R. 7),* Hearings and markup, Jan. 24, 1995, 104th Cong., 1st sess. (Government Printing Office, 1995), 4. See also her subsequent testimony before the Senate Foreign Relations Subcommittee on International Operations, *United Nations Reform,* Hearings, Sept. 11, 1996, 104th Cong., 2d sess. (Government Printing Office, 1996), 13.

100. "Alan Keyes: Position on Spc. Michael New," excerpt from Oct. 21, 1995, Keyes Rally in Temeculah, California, Alan Keyes for President 1996, http://sandh.com/keyes/mikenew.html.

101. White House, "Key Elements," 10.

102. Senate Subcommittee on International Operations, *United Nations Reform,* 13.

103. Barbara Crossette, "Squabble Over Mystery Letters in U.N. Mailbag," *New York Times,* Dec. 25, 1997.

104. George Bush and Brent Scowcroft, *A World Transformed* (Alfred A. Knopf, 1998), 491.

105. This is one of many conditions, or benchmarks, contained in the so-called Helms-Biden arrears for reform package, negotiated with the Clinton administration, as addressed in greater detail in chapter 8. See sec. 921(4), Title IX of the Foreign Relations Authorization Act, FY 2000–2001 (S. 886 and S. Report 106-43, April 27, 1999).

106. *Congressional Record,* 105th Cong., 2d sess., March 25, 1998, 144, no. 35: S2544.

107. *Congressional Record,* 105th Cong., 1st sess., Sept. 25, 1997, 143, no. 130: H7900.

108. Rod Grams remarks to Hearst Newspaper editors and publishers, New York, Oct. 20, 1997, 4, http://www.usia.gov/topical/pol/usandun/grams.

109. See, for example, the comments of representatives Constance Morella, R-Md., and Alan B. Mollohan, D-W.Va., *Congressional Record,* 105th Cong., 1st sess., Sept. 25, 1997, 143, no. 130: H7903 and H7902, respectively.

110. *Congressional Record,* 105th Cong., 2d sess., March 25, 1998, 144, no. 35: S2543. Ironically, the quote about Fiji that Helms attributed to Annan was not in the secretary-general's text, but in a call-out printed in the midst of the text. Such call-outs are usually added by the editor, not by the author. See Annan, "The Unpaid Bill That's Crippling the U.N.," *New York Times,* March 9, 1998.

Chapter 8

The editorial appeared in the *New York Times* of Nov. 4, 1946; the Boggs quote is from House Committee on Foreign Affairs, *To Seek Development of the United Nations into a World Federation,* Hearings, Oct. 12–13, 1949, 81st Cong., 1st sess. (Government Printing Office, 1950), 89; the Kerry quote is from Senate Foreign Relations Subcommittee on Terrorism, Narcotics, and International Operations, *Fiscal Year 1994 Foreign Relations Authorization Act: Budget Requests,* Hearings, May 12, June 9, 17, 1993, 103d Cong., 1st sess. (Government Printing Office, 1993), 64; and the Rogers quote is from *Congressional Record,* 105th Cong., 1st sess., Sept. 25, 1997, 143, no. 130: H7901.

1. Initially more optimistic, Madeleine K. Albright, then U.S. envoy to the UN, had assured Congress in 1993 that Boutros-Ghali was "a ringmaster determined to prod this elephantine bureaucracy into action." Senate Subcommittee on Terrorism, *FY 1994 Foreign Relations Authorization Act,* 70.

2. Thomas Benjamin Neely, *The League, the Nation's Danger* (Philadelphia: E. A. Yeakel, 1919), 159.

3. Philip C. Jessup, *International Security: The American Role in Collective Action for Peace* (New York: Council on Foreign Relations, 1935), 21. For a 1935 perspective on the development of U.S.-League relationships, see 11–23.

4. *Congressional Record,* 70th Cong., 1st sess., May 8, 1928, 69, pt. 8: 8069–73.

5. Apparently these issues caused hardly a ripple at the Dumbarton Oaks preparatory conferences. See Robert C. Hilderbrand, *Dumbarton Oaks: The Origins of the United Nations and the Search for Postwar Security* (University of North Carolina Press, 1990), 93, 106. For a discussion of how financial questions were addressed in U.S. planning and

in the UN's early sessions, see J. David Singer, *Financing International Organization: The United Nations Budget Process* (The Hague: Martinus Nijhoff, 1961), 1–29.

6. Senate Subcommittee on Terrorism, *FY 1994 Foreign Relations Authorization Act,* 89–90.

7. For a discussion of this proposal and others considered in U.S. planning, see Ruth B. Russell, *A History of the United Nations Charter: The Role of the United States 1940–1945* (Brookings, 1958), 369–78; for reactions to U.S. proposals at the San Francisco conference, see 854–63.

8. *Congressional Record,* 79th Cong., 2d sess., Feb. 27, 1946, 92, pt. 2: 1693.

9. Arthur H. Vandenberg Jr., ed., *The Private Papers of Senator Vandenberg* (Houghton Mifflin, 1952), 238, 239.

10. *Congressional Record,* 80th Cong., 1st sess., Feb. 26, 1947, 93, pt. 2: 1474, 1475.

11. Ibid., 1475.

12. *Congressional Record,* 83d Cong., 1st sess., May 26, 1953, 99, pt. 11: A2943. Also see comments by Representative Hamer H. Budge, R-Idaho, and an article from the *Washington Evening Star,* both in ibid., A2818–19.

13. "To Survey U.N. Costs: Senate Group Is Named to Study International Bodies," *New York Times,* Oct. 13, 1947.

14. William S. White, "U.N. Expenditures Called Excessive," *New York Times,* July 10, 1948.

15. James Reston, "Senators to Hear Biddle on U.N. Job," *New York Times,* May 13, 1947.

16. "Senators Warn on U.N. Budgets," *New York Times,* July 3, 1947.

17. Editorial, "U.N. and Penny-Pinching," *New York Times,* Nov. 4, 1946.

18. *Congressional Record,* 83d Cong., 1st sess., Feb. 13, 1953, 99, pt. 1: 1161.

19. House Committee on Foreign Affairs, *Structure of the United Nations and Relations of the United States to the United Nations,* Hearings, May 4–7, 11–14, 1948, 80th Cong., 2d sess. (Government Printing Office, 1948), 97.

20. Not everyone, of course, has been impressed by the repeated arguments about how much spending the UN pumps into the New York City economy. Years later, for example, Shirley Hazzard lamented that such "paltry and irrelevant arguments" served only to highlight "the absence of more cogent reasons for the United Nations' continuance." Shirley Hazzard, *Defeat of an Ideal: A Study of the Self-Destruction of the United Nations* (Little, Brown, 1973), 86.

21. House Committee on Foreign Affairs, *To Seek Development of the United Nations into a World Federation,* 231.

22. Ibid., 89.

23. For a series of stories illustrating the related question of Americans' penchant both for making money and for putting it to use for the common good, see Patricia O'Toole, *Money and Morals: A History* (New York: Clarkson Potter, 1998).

24. House Committee on Foreign Affairs, *Structure of the United Nations,* 43.

25. For example, former secretary-general Javier Pérez de Cuéllar has acknowledged that "as long as the Cold War continued, Soviet staff members, whether KGB or not, owed their first loyalty to Moscow rather than to the United Nations. It was expected that any information they obtained would be reported to the Soviet Mission. As a result, and to their understandable frustration, the Soviet nationals in my office were excluded from sensitive functions." Javier Pérez de Cuéllar, *Pilgrimage for Peace: A Secretary-General's Memoir* (St. Martin's Press, 1997), 8.

26. See, for example, Seymour Maxwell Finger and Arnold A. Saltzman, *Bending with the Winds: Kurt Waldheim and the United Nations* (Praeger, 1990).

27. David Mitrany, "The Functional Approach to International Organization," *International Affairs* 24 (July 1948): 350–63, and *The Progress of International Government* (Yale University Press, 1933).

28. Robert Jackson, *A Study of the Capacity of the United Nations Development System*, vol. 1, DP/5 (Geneva: United Nations, 1969), vi.

29. For conference report on H.R. 2159, the Foreign Operations Appropriations bill for FY 1998, see *Congressional Record*, 105th Cong., 1st sess., Nov. 12, 1997, 143, no. 159: H10602–29.

30. As Ralph Zacklin noted in 1968, the more difficult formal constitutional reform proves to be, the more likely pressure will build for informal modification of the organization's procedures. Zacklin and other observers in the 1950s and 1960s believed that the world body already had proved remarkably adaptable "to the changing circumstances wrought by a dynamic international society." See Ralph Zacklin, *The Amendment of the Constitutive Instruments of the United Nations and Specialized Agencies* (Leyden, Netherlands: A.W. Sijthoff, 1968), 172. For more recent comments along this line, see those of Carl-August Fleischhauer, former UN legal counsel, in Hazel Fox, ed., *The Changing Constitution of the United Nations* (London: British Institute of International and Comparative Law, 1997), xv–xix.

31. At this point, the General Assembly seems to have shelved the secretary-general's initiative in this regard. See Kofi A. Annan, *Renewing the United Nations: A Programme for Reform*, United Nations, General Assembly, A/51/950, July 14, 1997, 19; and Note by the Secretary-General, *United Nations Reform: Measures and Proposals—Time Limits of New Initiatives ("sunset provisions")*, A/52/81, March 31, 1998.

32. See official records of the U.N. General Assembly, Plenary Meetings, vol. 1 (New York: United Nations, annual).

33. Annan, *Renewing the United Nations*, 19.

34. Ibid., 14.

35. Ibid., 15–16.

36. United Nations General Assembly Resolution A/52/12, *Renewing the United Nations: A Programme for Reform*, pt. A, Nov. 12, 1997; pt. B, Dec. 19, 1997.

37. Clinton's remarks are from his speech to the 52d Session of the UN General Assembly, Sept, 22, 1997: *United States Participation in the United Nations, A Report by the President to the Congress for the Year 1997* (Washington, D.C.: State Department, 1998),

103–08; Grams and Thiessen were quoted in Barbara Crossette, "U.N. Chief Promises to Overhaul Organization from the Top Down," *New York Times,* July 17, 1997. A few months later, Grams offered a more nuanced evaluation: "I commend the Secretary-General for his efforts and for many of the changes he proposed to consolidate functions and improve the management structure of the U.N. But the fact that he didn't eliminate a single program or a single function is a testament to the power of the primary opponents of reform—the entrenched U.N. bureaucracy and those member states that clearly benefit from the current system." Remarks to Hearst Newspaper editors and publishers, New York, Oct. 20, 1997, http://www.usia.gov/topical/pol/usandun/grams.htm.

38. Section 143 of the Foreign Relations Authorization Act for FY 1986 and FY 1987, Public Law 99-93 (H.R. 2068), Aug. 16, 1985.

39. David Stout, "Clinton Vetoes Measure to Pay $1 Billion in Late U.N. Dues," *New York Times,* Oct. 21, 1998.

40. Tom Carter and George Archibald, "Senate OKs U.N. Funds with Strings Attached," *Washington Times,* June 23, 1999; and Norman Kempster, "Senate OKs Back Dues of U.N.—With a Hitch," *Los Angeles Times,* June 23, 1999.

41. See S. 886, the Foreign Relations Authorization Act, FY 2000–2001 (S. Rept. 106-43, 106th Cong., 1st sess., April 27, 1999), Title VIII, secs. 801 and 821, and Title IX, secs. 911, 912, 913, 921, 931, and 941. For a summary, see United Nations Association of the USA, *Washington Report,* May 6, 1999, http://www.unausa.org/dc/info/sreport10643.html. For a brief history and legislative summary of the vetoed bill, see United Nations Association of the USA, *Washington Weekly Report* 23–18, 19, June 19, 1997, pp. 1–4, at http://www.unausa.org/publications/wwr231819.htm.

42. "Transcript of Press Conference by Secretary-General Kofi Annan at Head-quarters," UN Press Release SG/SM/6837, Dec. 14, 1998.

43. Betsy Pisik, "U.N. Budget Plan Angers U.S.," *Washington Times,* Dec. 29, 1998. Also see USUN Press Release 240 (98), Dec. 21, 1998, for a related U.S. statement in the General Assembly.

44. Iqbal Haji, "What Does the United States Really Want?" *UN Staff Report* 22 (March 1997): 4.

45. For the latest in a series of Nordic UN reform reports, see *The United Nations in Development—Strengthening the UN through Change: Fulfilling Its Economic and Social Mandate* (Oslo: Nordic UN Reform Project, 1996).

46. Rosemary Righter, *Utopia Lost: The United Nations and World Order* (New York: Twentieth Century Fund Press, 1995), 72.

47. See, for example, statements before the House Subcommittee on International Security, International Organizations and Human Rights, *Management and Mismanagement at the United Nations,* Hearings, March 5, 1993, 103d Cong., 1st sess. (Government Printing Office, 1993), 60–67; and the Senate Subcommittee on Terrorism, *FY 1994 Foreign Relations Authorization Act,* 156–61.

48. See, for example, Erksine Childers and Brian Urquhart, *Renewing the United Nations System* (New York: Ford Foundation, 1994); Erskine Childers and Brian

Urquhart, *A World in Need of Leadership: Tomorrow's United Nations* (New York: Ford Foundation, 1996); and Peter Fromuth, ed., *A Successor Vision: The United Nations of Tomorrow* (Lanham, Md.: University Press of America, Inc., 1988).

49. "Secretary-General Pledges 'Quiet Revolution' in United Nations, Presents Reform Proposals to General Assembly," UN Press Release GA/9282/Rev. 2, July 16, 1997.

50. Senate Subcommittee on Terrorism, *FY 1994 Foreign Relations Authorization Act*, 64.

51. Ibid., 71, 73.

52. Letter from Madeleine K. Albright, to Professor Freitas do Amaral, Chairman of the High-Level Working Group on Strengthening the UN System, U.S. Mission to the UN, Feb. 21, 1996, p. 2.

53. Senate Subcommittee on Terrorism, *FY 1994 Foreign Relations Authorization Act*, 150, 151.

54. Stefan Halper, "Systemic Corruption at the United Nations," in *Delusions of Grandeur: The United Nations and Global Intervention*, ed. Ted Galen Carpenter (Washington, D.C.: Cato Institute, 1997), 127.

55. During the September 1997 House debate on the appropriations bill, for example, Nita M. Lowey, D-N.Y., warned against "irresponsible, haphazard" acts that could set back the UN reform efforts. Declaring that every member of the House favored further UN reform, she cautioned that "our outstanding debt to the U.N. is draining our power in the organization and has created a climate of resistance to U.S. proposals." Although "the U.N. has historically served U.S. interests," she continued, "our debt is making it hard for the organization to carry out the very activities that serve these interests." Constance Morella, R-Md., pointed out that "it is highly unlikely that the nations of the General Assembly are going to allow us to impose reforms when we are not paying our share, and even our allies, Britain, Germany and Japan, have indicated they will not support our reforms if we are not paying our arrears." Benjamin Gilman, R-N.Y., who chaired the House International Relations Committee, has justified withholding dues to compel UN reform, but he resisted what he termed "pennywise and pound-foolish" proposals to delay the initial arrears payment called for in the 'grand bargain' negotiated between the administration and Congress. Such a step, he cautioned, "would only ensure that our Nation has no influence or role in the ongoing effort to downsize and streamline the oversized U.N. bureaucracy." *Congressional Record*, 105th Cong., 1st sess., Sept. 25, 1997, 143, no. 130: E1879, H7903, and H7902, respectively.

56. Grams, remarks to the Hearst Newspaper editors and publishers.

57. Accusing the UN of backsliding on previous reform commitments, Representative Vincent Snowbarger, R-Ill., contended that once the U.S. administration had certified forward movement, "the UN promptly ceased its progress, and did its best to undermine efforts at reform." Therefore, in his view, "we should not put the cart before the horse by providing the money before the reform package is fully in place." In support of his 1997 amendment to delay the initial arrearage payment under the "grand bar-

gain," Representative Roscoe Bartlett, R-Md., suggested that "we are trying to bribe the UN into making reforms. If we reward them for reforms that might happen, bribing them is not going to happen." Taken literally, his comments imply that the United States should make payments to the world organization only to "bribe" or compel it to do something specific for the United States. *Congressional Record*, 105th Cong., 1st sess., Sept. 25, 1997, 143, no. 130: H7903.

58. Ibid., H7902.

59. In this regard, Senator Helms has contended that "successful reform would achieve the twin goals of arresting U.N. encroachment on the sovereignty of nation-states while harnessing a dramatically downsized United Nations to help sovereign nations cope with some cross-border problems." Jesse Helms, "Saving the U.N.: A Challenge to the Next Secretary-General," *Foreign Affairs* 74 (Sept.–Oct., 1996): 5. Representative Snowbarger pointed out that, while "the United Nations is a group of sovereign states; it is not sovereign itself. The people who work there must be made to understand that." He further contended that "we must put the officials at the UN on notice that much of what they call reform is not seen as such in America. Moves designed to eventually eliminate the United States' veto in the Security Council or provide an independent source of revenue for the organization should be utterly unacceptable to this Congress." *Congressional Record*, 105th Cong., 1st sess., Sept. 25, 1997, 143, no. 130: H7903.

60. An exception was a short-lived effort by Senator Nancy Kassebaum, R-Kan., and Representative Lee Hamilton, D-Ind., to float a tough, but bipartisan, set of reform proposals. See their op-ed, "Fix the U.N.," *Washington Post*, June 25, 1995.

61. George Archibald, "UN Reform: US Senator Says US Mission Undermines Effort," *Washington Times*, Jan. 19, 1999; George Archibald, "Embattled U.S. Envoy Cuts Trip to Bosnia," *Washington Times*, Jan. 27, 1999.

62. Senate Subcommittee on International Operations, *United Nations Reform*, Hearing, Sept. 11, 1996, 104th Cong., 2d sess. (Government Printing Office, 1996), 2.

Chapter 9

The Senate subcommittee quote is from staff study 6, quoted in J. David Singer, *Financing International Organization, the United Nations Budget Process* (The Hague: Martinus Nijhoff, 1961), 177; the Wood quote is from the *Congressional Record*, 82d Cong., 2d sess., April 4, 1952, 98, pt. 3: 3514; the Heistand quote is from the *Congressional Record*, 87th Cong., 2d sess., Jan. 23, 1962, 108, pt. 1:791–92; and the Porter quote is from the *Congressional Record*, 105th Cong., 2d sess., March 26, 1998, 144, no. 36: H1599.

1. In commenting on the results of the Bretton Woods preparatory meetings, J. David Singer noted that "by omitting any Charter reference to a specific method of calculating national assessments, the conferees spared the United Nations a dilemma which had threatened the League's financial integrity for five years, while attempts to amend the

Covenant had been unsuccessful; in this particular regard, they learned from the past." He also quoted a Venezuelan delegate at the San Francisco conference as cautioning that apportionment of expenses had proven to be "one of the most delicate and debated questions in international organization." Singer, *Financing International Organization,* 4–5, 6.

2. William A. Scott and Stephen B. Withey, *The United States and the United Nations: The Public View, 1945–1955* (New York: Manhattan Publishing Company for the Carnegie Endowment for International Peace, 1958), 12–14, 17.

3. *Congressional Record,* 79th Cong., 1st sess., July 27, 1945, 91, pt. 6: 8119. Shipstead claimed, moreover, that the United States had provided "the great bulk of resources which made victory possible" and that "the bulk of the resources required to start and maintain these immense undertakings on their careers must be furnished by the United States."

4. Ibid., 8033.

5. *Congressional Record,* 79th Cong., 1st sess., Feb. 27, 1946, 92, pt. 2: 1693.

6. Frank S. Adams, "U.S. Opposes Paying 50% of U.N. Budget; Favors 25% Limit," *New York Times,* Nov. 2, 1946. For a discussion of the contentious debates within the Committee on Contributions and the Fifth Committee, see Singer, *Financing International Organization,* 124–27.

7. "U.S. Willing to Pay U.N. a Third for Time," *New York Times,* Nov. 15, 1946.

8. Adams, "U.S. Opposes Paying 50% of U.N. Budget."

9. Dean Acheson, *Present at the Creation: My Years at the State Department* (W. W. Norton, 1969), 697, 698.

10. Reprinted in the *Congressional Record,* 82d Cong., 2d sess., April 4, 1952, 98, pt. 3: 3515–17.

11. In May 1947 Representative Frank B. Keefe, R-Wis., presented to his colleagues an already sizable list of member states in arrears to the world organization. To ensure that the UN can "effectively deal with the international problems and be an effective deterrent to another world war," as well as to make sure that "Uncle Sam may not be called upon as the years go on to bear the entire or a large portion" of its expenses, Keefe underlined the necessity of each member state meeting "without question and without stint . . . its full and complete obligation each year." He added that he hoped the long list of nations already in arrears did not demonstrate "a lack of interest on the part of these nations." *Congressional Record,* 80th Cong., 1st sess., May 2, 1947, 93, pt. 4: 4466.

12. See, for example, the comments of Representative John B. Williams, D-Miss., *Congressional Record,* 82d Cong., 2d sess., July 4, 1952, 98, pt. 7: 9443; Representative Clarence J. Brown, R-Ohio, *Congressional Record,* 82d Cong., 2d sess., April 4, 1952, 98, pt. 3: 3519; Senator Alexander Wiley, R-Wis., *Congressional Record,* 83d Cong., 1st sess., Feb. 18, 1953, 99, pt. 1: 1161; Senator William Langer, R-N.D., and Senator George W. Malone, R-Nev., *Congressional Record,* 84th Cong., 1st sess., Jan. 27, 1955, 101, pt. 1: 833.

13. *Congressional Record,* 83d Cong., 1st sess., May 5, 1953, 99, pt. 4: 4533.

14. Several House members wanted to go further, calling for the withholding of all U.S. payments to the UN or for drastic cuts in U.S. assessments. For example, H. R.

Gross, R-Iowa, offered an amendment in 1953 that "would cut 90 percent out of this contribution to the United Nations [based on the portion of costs allegedly paid by the United States in Korea] and would put other members of the organization on the same basis as their fractional contribution to the fighting and dying in Korea." Ibid., 4533. In a still more sweeping gesture, John B. Williams, D-Miss., drew up a bill in 1952 to "withdraw financial support of the United States to the United Nations until such time as they furnish a proportionate number of men and materials to do the fighting in Korea." *Congressional Record*, 82d Cong., 2d sess., April 4, 1952, 98, pt. 3: 3514.

15. For accounts of this crisis, see John G. Stoessinger and Associates, *Financing the United Nations System* (Brookings, 1964), 106–24; Ernest W. Lefever, *Crisis in the Congo: A United Nations Force in Action* (Brookings, 1965); and Susan R. Mills, "The Financing of United Nations Peacekeeping Operations: The Need for a Sound Financial Base," Occasional Paper on Peacekeeping (New York: International Peace Academy, 1989).

16. *Congressional Record*, 87th Cong., 2d sess., April 2, 1962, 108, pt. 4: 5639–40.

17. Richard N. Gardner, "The Article 19 Crisis—A White Paper," 4. This unpublished account of this crisis period is cited with the permission of its author, who served as deputy assistant secretary of state for international organization affairs during these years.

18. For an account of the different strands in the World Court Advisory Opinion, see Stoessinger and Associates, *Financing the United Nations System*, 140–56.

19. United Nations General Assembly Resolution 1739, Dec. 20, 1961. See Mills, "The Financing of United Nations Peacekeeping Operations," 11; and Stoessinger and Associates, *Financing the United Nations System*, 124–33.

20. House Document 321, reprinted in Senate Committee on Foreign Relations, *Purchase of United Nations Bonds (S. 2768)*, Hearings, Feb. 6, 7, 9, 19, 1962, 87th Cong., 2d sess. (Government Printing Office, 1962), 2.

21. *Congressional Record*, 87th Cong., 2d sess., April 2, 1962, 108, pt. 4: 5645. Other Democrats who supported dues payments for peacekeeping operations included senators Stephen M. Young, Ohio, Ibid., 5674; and Albert Gore, Tenn., Senate Committee on Foreign Relations, *Purchase of United Nations Bonds*, p. 85.

22. See, for example, the statement of Senator Frank J. Lausche, D-Ohio, Senate Committee on Foreign Relations, *Purchase of United Nations Bonds*, 44.

23. *Congressional Record*, 87th Cong., 2d sess., April 2, 1962, 108, pt. 4: 5675. For statements of other Republicans concerned about the bonds, see senators Bourke B. Hickenlooper, Iowa, and George D. Aiken, Vt., Senate Committee on Foreign Relations, *Purchase of United Nations Bonds*, 197–98, and 255; and Representative Edgar W. Heistand, Calif., *Congressional Record*, 87th Cong., 2d sess., Jan. 23, 1962, 108, pt. 1: 791–92.

24. Senate Committee on Foreign Relations, *Purchase of United Nations Bonds*, 39 (Capehart), 206 (Hickenlooper), and 207 (Aiken); *Congressional Record*, 87th Cong., 2d sess., Jan. 18, 1962, 108, pt. 1: 552 (Baldwin); *Congressional Record*, 87th Cong., 2d sess., July 1, 1962, 108, pt. 9: 15115 (Pelly).

25. *Congressional Record,* 87th Cong., 2d sess., April 2, 1962, 108, pt.4: 5673.

26. Ibid., 5665, 5666.

27. *Congressional Record,* 88th Cong., 2d sess., March 26, 1964, 110, pt. 5: 6482–883 (Foreman); *Congressional Record,* 88th Cong., 2d sess., June 10, 1964, 110, pt. 10: 13242 (Bennett); *Congressional Record,* 88th Cong., 2d sess., Aug. 10, 1964, 110, pt. 14: 18819, 18823–24 (Miller and Fulbright). Speaking against the Bennett amendment in the House, Thomas E. Morgan, D-Pa., said that it "would put the United States in the same position as the Soviet Union and its satellites who in effect are doing exactly what the amendment proposes." *Congressional Record,* 88th Cong., 2d sess., June 10, 1964, 110, pt. 10: 13242.

28. *Congressional Record,* 88th Cong., 2d sess., Aug. 17, 1964, 110, pt. 15: 19884, 19885 (Ford, Kelly, Mailliard, Fascell).

29. Ibid., 19885, 19886 (Conte, Edmondson, Duncan).

30. "U.N. Sources Say K. Threatens Bolt Over Dues," *Washington Post,* Aug. 2, 1964.

31. Thomas J. Hamilton, "Plan in U.N. Would Allow Some in Arrears to Vote," *New York Times,* July 6, 1964.

32. Editorial, "To Save the U.N.," *New York Times,* Aug. 3, 1964.

33. An analysis along these general lines is presented in Gardner, "The Article 19 Crisis."

34. An account of this meeting of November 20, 1964, is given in ibid., 24.

35. For a brief account of these procedures, see Ruth B. Russell, *The United Nations and United States Security Policy* (Brookings, 1968), 202–03.

36. United Nations General Assembly, Document A/5916, Aug. 31, 1965, Annex No. 21, 85. For summary records, see document A/5916/Add.1, Aug. 31, 1965, Annex 21, 86–92.

37. United Nations General Assembly, Special Committee on Peace-keeping Operations, A/AC.121/PV.15, Aug. 16, 1965, 6, 7, 8–10, 12.

38. Russell, *The United Nations and United States Security Policy,* 202.

39. As Thomas M. Franck phrased it, the United States "had learned that, often, the nation's adherence to U.N. principles and to the international perspective had endured only as long as those happened to coincide with our national self-interest. In this we were being neither more or less parochial than any other member. It had just taken us a little longer to awaken to reality." Thomas M. Franck, *Nation Against Nation: What Happened to the U.N. Dream and What the U.S. Can Do About It* (Oxford University Press, 1985), 86.

40. U.S. General Accounting Office, *United Nations Financial Issues and U.S. Arrears,* GAO/NSIAD-98-201BR, June 18, 1998, http://www.globalpolicy.org/finance/docs/gao.htm, p. 21.

41. Gardner, "The Article 19 Crisis," 22. In his words, "there was almost universal condemnation of the United States for its handling of the issue. On the one side, supporters of the United States position complained at the U.S. backdown. On the other side, opponents blamed the U.S. for immobilizing the General Assembly at a time of crisis. And it must be admitted that both were right." (p. 30)

42. Quoted in the *Congressional Record*, 92d Cong., 1st sess., Oct. 27, 1971, 117, pt. 29: 37821.

43. In her original amendment, Kassebaum had included a second condition as well: the UN and its agencies would also have to reduce secretariat compensation levels to those of the U.S. civil service. *Congressional Record*, 99th Cong., 1st sess., June 7, 1985, 131, pt. 11: 14937. With a longstanding interest in the problems of Africa, she was particularly miffed at the Assembly's decision to build a $73 million conference center in Addis Ababa during a severe famine. Representative Solomon's original amendment was related to the second purpose: to cut 15 percent of the U.S. payment for its assessment in fiscal 1987 because, in his view, the UN secretariat was compensated by at least that amount more than the U.S. civil service. His amendment passed the House by voice vote, without any member expressing reservations on the floor. *Congressional Record*, 99th Cong., 1st sess., May 8, 1985, 131, pt. 8: 11096–98.

44. *Congressional Record*, 99th Cong., 1st sess., June 7, 1985, 131, pt. 11: 14938. Senators Charles Mathias, R-Md., and Claiborne Pell, D-R.I., argued against the measure, but to little avail. Ibid, 14938–39.

45. Joanne Omang, "U.S. Plans to Restore U.N. Funds: Steps Toward Reform Deemed Satisfactory," *Washington Post*, March 20, 1987.

46. Alan L. Keyes, statement before the House Subcommittee on Appropriations for Commerce, Justice, State, the Judiciary and Related Agencies, *Contributions to International Organizations*, Hearing, April 1, 1987, 100th Cong., 1st sess. (Government Printing Office, 1987), 783.

47. Alan L. Keyes, "Why Imperil U.N. Reform?" *New York Times*, Sept. 25, 1986.

48. Omang, "U.S. Plans to Restore U.N. Funds."

49. Ibid.

50. Department of State, *United States Participation in the United Nations, Report by the President to the Congress for the Year 1988* (Government Printing Office, 1989).

51. United Nations Association of the USA (UNA-USA), *Washington Weekly Report* 14-30, Sept. 16, 1988, 2.

52. See, for example, comments by Senator Claiborne Pell, R.I., *Congressional Record*, 100th Cong., 2d sess., Sept. 13, 1988, 134, no. 125: S12436; and by Representative Theodore S. Weiss, N.Y., *Congressional Record*, 100th Cong., 2d sess., Sept. 14, 1988, 134, no. 126: H7548.

53. Richard N. Gardner, "There's More Than Politics at Stake in Unpaid U.N. Dues," *Los Angeles Times*, March 4, 1998.

54. John R. Bolton, "U.S. Isn't Legally Obligated to Pay the U.N.," *Wall Street Journal*, Nov. 17, 1997.

55. Gardner, "There's More Than Politics at Stake in Unpaid U.N. Dues."

56. *Congressional Record*, 105th Cong., 2d sess., March 25, 1998, 144, no. 35: S2552.

57. Gardner, "There's More Than Politics at Stake in Unpaid U.N. Dues."

58. *Congressional Record*, 105th Cong., 2d sess., March 25, 1998, 144, no. 35: E467.

59. Senate Subcommittee on Terrorism, Narcotics and International Operations, *Fiscal Year 1994 Foreign Relations Authorization Act: Budget Requests,* Hearings, May 12, June 9 and 17, 1993, 103d Cong., 1st sess. (Government Printing Office, 1994), 162, 163.

60. Ibid., 101–08. As Christopher J. Dodd, D-Conn., phrased it, "if it is $300 million or thereabouts in arrearages, then our credibility at that table, much as a debtor would be, is de minimus in that debate." Ibid., 104. Paul J. Sarbanes, D-Md., who had been a member of the U.S. delegation to the UN, observed that "my perception is that our ability to exert influence there and provide strong collective leadership is, to some extent, being undercut by the extraordinary deficiencies in the U.S. meeting its obligations at the United Nations." Ibid., 101.

61. See, for example, statements by Senator Olympia J. Snowe, R-Me., a moderate, Senate Subcommittee on International Operations, Committee on Foreign Relations, *United Nations Reform,* Hearings, Sept. 11, 1996, 104th Cong., 2d sess. (Government Printing Office, 1996), 52–53; and by Representative Vincent Snowbarger, R-Ill., a persistent UN critic. *Congressional Record,* 105th Cong., 1st sess., Sept. 25, 1997, 143, no. 130: H7903.

62. Ibid., H7901.

63. Rod Grams, remarks to Hearst Newspaper editors and publishers, New York, Oct. 20, 1997, http://www.usia.gov/topical/pol/usandun/grams.htm.

64. *Congressional Record,* 105th Cong., 1st sess., Sept. 25, 1997, 143, no. 130: H7901.

65. Among House Democrats see, for example, the statements by Tony Hall, Ohio; Esteban Torres, Calif.; Nita Lowey, N.Y.; Eliot L. Engel, N.Y.; Danny K. Davis, Ill.; and David E. Skagg, Colo. *Congressional Record,* 105th Cong., 2d sess., March 26, 1998, 144, no. 136: H1582, H1591, H1593, H1594, H1598, and H1599.

66. Senate Subcommittee on International Operations, *United Nations Reform,* 55–56.

67. Ibid., 10.

68. William F. Buckley Jr., "Let's Change the Way We Play the U.N. Game," *Washington Star,* reproduced in the *Congressional Record,* 92d Cong., 1st sess., Nov. 2, 1971, 117, pt. 30: H38703.

69. Senate Subcommittee on International Operations, *United Nations Reform,* 2.

70. *Congressional Record,* 105th Cong., 2d sess., March 26, 1998, 144, no. 36: H1588.

71. For example, Brett D. Schaefer of the Heritage Foundation argues both that "the U.N. has always possessed the option of tightening its belt, but it has refused to do so" and that "this strategy [of withholding and setting benchmarks] worked before, and it will work again." See "Cash on Delivery: Congress Should Pay U.N. Past Dues After Reforms," Heritage Foundation Executive Memorandum 468, Feb. 24, 1997, 2.

72. Javier Pérez de Cuéllar, *Pilgrimage for Peace: A Secretary-General's Memoir* (St. Martin's Press, 1997), 12.

73. Based on reports from the Kyodo News Agency and the Associated Press; see "Lawmakers Want to Dock UN Money if Japan Not Given Council Seat," *Indian Express,* March 29, 1999, http://www.expressindia.com/news/08802699.htm.

74. Persistent financial concerns have also intruded on the amount of time and attention in the U.S.-UN relationship available for focusing on substantive issues of con-

cern to both sides. In his memoirs, for example, Pérez de Cuéllar complains that "it remains for me a matter of great regret that I had to devote precious time in almost every conversation I had with Presidents Reagan and Bush to dunning the United States to pay its bills." Pérez de Cuéllar, *Pilgrimage for Peace,* 12.

75. Madeleine K. Albright, "Remarks and Q&A Session at the Center for National Policy," Department of State, Office of Spokesman, Jan. 21, 1999, http://secretary.state.gov./www/statements/1999/990121.html, p. 11.

76. U.S. General Accounting Office, *United Nations Financial Issues and U.S. Arrears,* appendix 4, comments from the Department of State.

77. *Congressional Record,* 105th Cong., 2d sess., March 26, 1998, 144, no. 36: H1589 (emphasis added).

78. Christopher S. Wren, "Unpaid Dues at the U.N. Could Cost U.S. Its Vote," *New York Times,* June 28, 1998.

79. Jesse Helms, "Saving the U.N.: A Challenge to the Next Secretary-General," *Foreign Affairs* 74 (Sept.–Oct. 1996): 5–6, 7.

80. Senate Subcommittee on International Operations, *United Nations Reform,* 41.

81. Ibid., 18, 24.

82. At the time of the article 19 crisis, U.S. officials were convinced that voluntary funding would not provide a feasible option for meeting the costs of the Congo and Middle East missions. According to Richard Gardner, "it is a political fact of UN life that many members which will respond to a legal assessment will not respond to a voluntary appeal for funds." Gardner, "The Article 19 Crisis," 10.

83. Senate Subcommittee of the Committee on Appropriations, *Foreign Assistance and Related Programs Appropriations for Fiscal Year 1989,* Hearing, April 14, 1988, 100th Cong., 2d sess. (Government Printing Office, 1988), 164, 165.

84. Senate Subcommittee on International Operations, *United Nations Reform,* 24.

85. Alan L. Keyes, "America's U.N. Policy: Lapse or Collapse?" *Washington Post,* Jan. 21, 1988. Noting the "sad irony in the scenario created by Mr. Keyes," Representative Lawrence J. Smith, D-Fla., contended that "the State Department, the U.S. agency with the greatest interest in maintaining a strong American presence at the U.N., may end up being responsible for the demise of that presence and for engendering ill will toward the U.N. on Capitol Hill." *Congressional Record,* 100th Cong., 2d sess., Feb. 3, 1988, 134, no. 7: E124.

86. Senate Subcommittee of the Committee on Appropriations, *Foreign Assistance Appropriations for Fiscal Year 1989,* 165.

87. Senate Subcommittee on Terrorism, *FY 1994 Foreign Relations Authorization Act,* 69.

88. Senate Subcommittee on International Operations, *United Nations Reform,* 14.

89. Ibid., 2. Helms has also accused the administration of having "intentionally hidden from the American taxpayers" the costs of U.S. military support for UN peace operations. *Congressional Record,* 105th Cong., 2d sess., March 25, 1998, 144, no. 35: S2544. Along the same lines, Representative Roscoe Bartlett, R-Md., declared that he was "not willing to let the State Department be the arbiter of whether or not we are owed by the

U.N. the $4.7 billion [in peacekeeping support] or, as they say, that we do not owe them anything." *Congressional Record,* 105th Cong., 1st sess., Sept. 25, 1997, 143, no. 130: H7900. Likewise, Harold Rogers asserted that arrears payments should be "at the level set by Congress, not by the U.N. or by the State Department" and that reform was "now being advocated by the United States representative largely at the urging of this Congress." Ibid., H7901.

90. Bill Richardson, remarks to U.N. General Assembly's Fifth Committee (Budget and Finance), Oct. 20, 1997, 1, http://www.usia.gov/topical/pol/usandun/richard2.htm.

91. Judy Keen, "U.S. Warns U.N. on Dues Cut, Lower Payment or Risk 'Damage' to Relationship," *USA Today,* Oct. 21, 1997.

92. United Nations General Assembly Resolution 52/215, Scale of Assessments for the Apportionment of the Expenses of the United Nations, Dec. 22, 1997. The resolution was adopted without a vote.

93. Department of State, *United States Participation in the United Nations: Report by the President to the Congress for the Year 1997* (Government Printing Office, July 1998), 75.

94. The floor was lowered from 0.04 percent to 0.02 percent in 1973 and then to 0.01 percent in 1978. Margaret E. Galey, "Reforming the Regime for Financing the United Nations," *Howard Law Journal* 31 (4, 1988): 546.

Chapter 10

The Wilson quote is from a speech in Los Angeles on Sept. 20, 1919, *Public Papers of Woodrow Wilson, War and Peace, Presidential Messages, Addresses, and Public Papers (1917–1924),* ed. Ray Stannard Baker and William E. Dodd (Harper and Brothers, 1927), 2: 324; the Fulbright quote is from the *Congressional Record,* 70th Cong., 1st sess., July 23, 1945, 91, pt. 6: 7962; the George quote is from the *Congressional Record,* 80th Cong., 2d sess., June 14, 1948, 94, pt. 6: 8044.

1. Philip C. Jessup, *International Security: The American Role in Collective Action for Peace* (New York: Council on Foreign Relations, 1935), 10–11.

2. Ibid., 33.

3. *Congressional Record,* 70th Cong., 1st sess., July 28, 1945, 91 pt. 6: 8178 (Ellender); July 25, 1945, 91, pt. 6: 8019 (Lucas); July 24, 1945, 91, pt. 6: 7988 (Pepper).

4. Several individuals who opposed the UN, each given five minutes to testify before the Senate Foreign Relations Committee during the ratification hearings, voiced this complaint. Some of these speakers represented such extreme views that their inclusion may have been designed to discredit the opposition to the charter and the new organization. See Senate, Committee on Foreign Relations, *The Charter of the United Nations,* Hearings, Parts 1–5, July 9–13, 1945, 79th Cong., 1st sess. (Government Printing Office, 1945).

5. Thomas M. Franck, *Nation Against Nation: What Happened to the U.N. Dream and What the U.S. Can Do About It* (Oxford University Press, 1985), 7.

6. *Congressional Record,* 70th Cong., 1st sess., July 24, 1945, 91, pt. 6: 7986, 7988, 7989.

7. Ibid., 8019 (July 25, 1945).

8. Ibid., 8082, 8083 (July 26, 1945).

9. Ibid., 7966, 7969 (July 24, 1945).

10. Ibid., 7962 (July 23, 1945).

11. Ibid., 8105 (July 27, 1945).

12. Yet, according to Gary Ostrower, "The Truman Library contains a surprising number of angry letters by Americans who were as opposed to the UN as to the old League." *The United Nations and the United States: 1945–1995* (New York: Twayne Publishers, 1998).

13. *Congressional Record,* 70th Cong., 1st sess., July 27, 1945, 91, pt. 6: 8121. The Senate vote for ratification, cast July 28, 1945, was 89 in favor, 2 opposed, and 5 not voting. In addition to Shipstead, Senator William Langer, R-N. Dak., voted against the charter. Ibid., 8190 (July 28, 1945).

14. Dean Acheson, *Present at the Creation: My Years in the State Department* (New York: W. W. Norton, 1969), 111. See also 6–7 and 11–12; and James Chace, *The Secretary of State Who Created the American World* (Simon & Schuster, 1998), 107–08.

15. *Congressional Record,* 70th Cong., 1st sess., July 27, 1945, 91, pt. 6: 8122.

16. CNN/*USA Today* Poll (Princeton, N.J.: Gallup Organization, Nov. 21, 1997).

17. Steven Kull, I. M. Destler, and Clay Ramsay, *The Foreign Policy Gap: How Policymakers Misread the Public* (College Park, Md.: University of Maryland, Center for International and Security Studies, Oct. 1997), 7.

18. The Pew Research Center for the People and the Press, *America's Place in the World II* (Washington, D.C.: Oct. 1997), 15.

19. John E. Reilly, "The Public Mood at Mid-Decade," *Foreign Policy* 98 (spring, 1995): 76–93; Chicago Council on Foreign Relations, *American Public Opinion and U.S. Foreign Policy 1995* (Chicago, 1995); John E. Reilly, "Americans and the World: A Survey at Century's End," *Foreign Policy* 114 (spring, 1999): 97–114; and Chicago Council on Foreign Relations, *American Public Opinion and U.S. Foreign Policy 1999* (Chicago, 1999).

20. Twelve percent mentioned UNICEF and 10 percent humanitarian aid. Commissioned by the Office of Secretary-General under Kofi Annan, summaries of the results can be found in a Zogby International Press Release, Jan. 4, 1999, http://www.zogby.com/news/home.htm. and in UN Press Release, SG/2050, Jan. 4, 1999.

21. Gallup Organization, *The Gallup Poll Monthly* (Princeton, N. J., Oct. 1990), 15–16.

22. Cited in remarks made by George Gallup Jr. at the Woodrow Wilson International Center for Scholars, Smithsonian Institution Building, Washington, D.C., Sept. 11, 1985.

23. Kull, Destler, and Ramsay, *The Foreign Policy Gap,* 55.

24. The rise was not as steep as the "good job-bad job" table might suggest, however, because Gallup ceased to include a "fair" category with the 1967 polls.

25. American Institute of Public Opinion, "Changing Opinions: A 50-Year Retrospective," *Index to International Public Opinion, 1992–1993* (New York: Greenwood Press, 1994), 705.

26. Ibid., 706.

27. H. Schuyler Foster, *Activism Replaces Isolationism: U.S. Public Attitudes, 1940–1975* (Washington, D.C.: Foxhall Press, 1983), 81.

28. William A. Scott and Steven B. Withey, *The United States and the United Nations: The Public View, 1945–1955* (New York: Manhattan Publishing Co. for the Carnegie Endowment for International Peace, 1958), 270.

29. In fact, the December 1998–January 1999 Zogby International survey replicates the results of the 1997 Pew poll in almost all respects.

30. African Americans gave modestly positive marks to UN performance in a 1989 Roper Poll and then reversed their view in a 1992 Roper Poll, both conducted for the United Nations Association. As noted in chapter 6, the image of a militarily potent UN, as in Desert Storm in 1991, may have been attractive to traditional UN skeptics (men, conservatives, Republicans) but disconcerting to historic supporters (women, liberals, Democrats, minorities). The demographic shifts between the 1989 and 1992 Roper polls suggest this was so. See Jeffrey Laurenti, *Directions and Dilemmas in Collective Security: Reflections from a Global Roundtable* (New York: United Nations Association of the USA, 1992), 18–19.

31. For example, see a statement supporting payment of U.S. arrears to the UN signed by a group of eleven prominent Republicans who had served in the Reagan and Bush administrations. Emergency Coalition for U.S. Financial Support of the United Nations, "Republican Statesmen Call for U.S. Payment of U.N. Obligations," Press release, Sept. 30, 1998. Asserting that "Republicans stand for responsibility—at home and abroad," the group declared that "throughout the United Nations' 50 year history, Republicans have recognized and supported this unique world body."

32. Steven Kull and I. M. Destler, *Misreading the Public: The Myth of a New Iso-lationism* (Brookings, 1999), 59.

33. Kull, Destler, and Ramsay, *The Foreign Policy Gap*, 46, 57.

34. Concerned about the gap between public and congressional attitudes, the new private United Nations Foundation, funded by Ted Turner and led by former senator Timothy Wirth, has sponsored, in cooperation with its sister organization, the Better World Fund, a major campaign to build a politically effective bridge between public sentiment and congressional action.

35. Eric Schmitt, "Aid Dresses Up in a Uniform," *New York Times*, May 10, 1998.

36. Reilly, "The Public Mood," 82, 83.

37. Pew Research Center, *America's Place*, 70, 97.

38. The results of the August 1998 survey conducted by Wirthlin Worldwide can be found at www.unausa.org/programs/topline.

39. Gallup Organization, *The Gallup Poll Monthly* (Princeton, N. J., Oct. 1990), 16.

40. Kull, Destler, and Ramsay, *The Foreign Policy Gap*, 59.

41. Ibid.

42. Ibid., 58.

43. *Time*/CNN Poll (Norwalk, Conn.: Yankelovich Partners, Inc., Feb. 10, 1997).

44. CNN/*USA Today* Poll (Princeton, N. J.: Gallup Organization, Nov. 23, 1997).

45. See, for example, the 1998–99 Zogby International poll, the June 1996 PIPA survey, an April 1996 Wirthlin poll for the United Nations Association, and an April 1998 PIPA survey. The latter can be found in Steven Kull, "Americans on UN Dues and IMF Funding: A Study of US Public Attitudes," University of Maryland, Program on International Policy Attitudes (PIPA), April 24, 1998.

46. An August 1998 Wirthlin survey for UNA-USA asked a variant on this question—adding that the United States would lose its vote in the General Assembly if the dues were not paid—and found even greater support for congressional candidates favoring paying U.S. dues to the UN. Because of the change in the wording of the question since 1995, however, the results are not comparable.

47. For example, see the results of the 1987, 1990, and 1994 Chicago Council on Foreign Relations polls.

48. Philip Shenon, "U.N. Envoy Likely to Get Energy Post," *New York Times*, May 9, 1998.

49. Lizette Alvarez, "For New Jersey Lawmaker, a Victory on Abortion," *New York Times*, Nov. 25, 1997.

50. Christopher H. Smith, "Foreign-aid Impasse? It's Clinton's Fault," *Trenton Times*, March 5, 1998.

51. Eric Schmitt, "Senate Acts to Pay U.N. Dues, But Clinton Veto Is Expected," *New York Times*, April 29, 1998. Clinton's remarks to the 53d Session of the UN General Assembly can be found in USUN Press Release 154 (98), Sept. 21, 1998. On the day Clinton addressed the General Assembly, Helms in a *New York Times* op-ed piece reiterated that the bill was awaiting the president's signature and pointed out that the antiabortion language had twice been watered down in an effort to reach a compromise. Jesse Helms, "A Day to Pay Old Debts," *New York Times*, Sept. 21, 1998. Also see Joseph R. Biden Jr., "Our Money Could Talk at the U.N.," *Washington Post*, Nov. 2, 1998.

52. United Nations Association of the USA (UNA-USA), *Washington Weekly Report* 20-11, April 29, 1994, 4.

53. Wilson speech of Sept. 23, 1919, *Public Papers*, 2: 345.

54. For all of his tactical errors, Wilson should not bear all of the blame for the course of events. Senator Lodge, who had supported the agenda of the League to Enforce Peace before the cause became heavily identified with President Wilson, at times seemed to be moved by personal animus as much as by principle.

55. Harold Evans, *The American Century* (Alfred A. Knopf, 1998), 172.

Chapter 11

1. David Stout, "Clinton Vetoes Measure to Pay $1 Billion in Late U.N. Dues," *New York Times*, Oct. 21, 1998.

2. According to John R. Bolton, assistant secretary of state for international organization affairs in the Bush administration, "many Republicans in Congress—and per-

haps a majority—not only do not care about losing the General Assembly vote but actually see it as a 'make my day' outcome." Bolton, "U.S. Money and a U.N. Vote," *Washington Times,* Oct. 16, 1998.

3. In early 1999 the United Nations Foundation, funded by Ted Turner, launched a $12 million campaign to bring public opinion to bear on Congress on the question of paying U.S. arrears to the UN. See Nicole Winfield, "Turner Earmarks $12 Million for Campaign to Pay U.S. Dues," *Boston Globe,* March 8, 1999.

4. At times, high-level officials of the Clinton administration have implied that UN opponents are extremists by focusing on the delusions of the more paranoid fringe elements. For example, in an April 1998 speech Secretary of State Madeleine Albright said that "I know there are some who believe the UN is a sinister organization. They suspect that it operates a fleet of black helicopters, which may, at any moment, swoop down into our backyards and steal our lawn furniture. They say it is bent on world domination, which is absurd, and that we cannot trust it because it is full of foreigners—which, frankly, we can't help." Address to the American Association of Newspaper Editors, April 2, 1998, Office of the Spokesman, U.S. Department of State, http://secretary.state.gov/www/ statements/1998/980402.html, p. 5. A similar reference to black helicopters and lawn furniture was made by Richard Clarke, a National Security Council official, in September 1996. See Warren P. Strobel, "Clinton Says Most Americans Support U.N.; Tells Assembly U.S. Will Pay Debt 'Soon,'" *Washington Times,* Sept. 25, 1996.

5. For a harsh critique of "liberal" foreign policy's dependence on internationalism, legalism, and humanitarianism, see Charles Krauthammer, "A World Imagined," *New Republic,* March 15, 1999.

6. As this author has discussed elsewhere, in this age of single-interest groups and constituencies identifying overarching interests that most of the country shares can be difficult. See Luck, "The United Nations, Multilateralism, and U.S. Interests," in *U.S. Foreign Policy and the United Nations System,* ed. Charles William Maynes and Richard S. Williamson (W. W. Norton for the American Assembly, 1996), 27–53.

7. A hesitant step in this direction was undertaken by the United States Commission on Improving the Effectiveness of the United Nations, whose bipartisan study was authorized in December 1987 by P.L. 100-204 and whose members were appointed by the president and by leaders of Congress. Although the group focused on reforming the UN, not U.S. policies toward the UN, it could not reach agreement on several key points. See its final report, *Defining Purpose: The U.N. and the Health of Nations* (Washington, D.C., 1993).

8. See United Nations, General Assembly, Report of the Secretary-General, *Renewing the United Nations: A Programme for Reform,* A/51/950, July 14, 1997, para. 44, p. 19; Note by the Secretary-General, *United Nations Reform: Measures and Proposals—Time Limits of New Initiatives ("sunset provisions"),* A/52/81, March 31, 1998; and General Assembly Decision: *United Nations Reform: Measures and Proposals (E),* A/52/L.73/Rev. 2, May 5, 1998.

9. John M. Goshko, "Annan Says Iraq Will Never Be Fully Disarmed; More Flexibility with Baghdad May Be Needed, U.N. Chief Notes," *Washington Post*, Oct. 17, 1998.

10. On the former issue, see Betsy Pisik, "U.N. Budget Plan Angers U.S.," *Washington Times*, Dec. 29, 1998. Also see USUN Press Release 240 (98), Dec. 21, 1998, for related U.S. statement in the General Assembly. On the latter, see "Fifth Committee Recommends Costa Rica, Pakistan, India, United Kingdom, Italy and Japan for Election to ACABQ," UN Press Release GA/AB/3257, Nov. 6, 1998.

11. State Department, Bureau of International Organization Affairs, *Voting Practices in the United Nations 1996* (Government Printing Office, 1997), 1.

12. State Department, Bureau of International Organization Affairs, *Voting Practices in the United Nations 1998* (Government Printing Office, 1999), 2.

13. "Pope Kofi's Unruly Flock," *Economist*, Aug. 8, 1998, U.S. Edition.

14. See "Drifting to a New Iraq Policy," a *New York Times* editorial of Aug. 12, 1998, that criticized the secretary-general's "equivocating performance" and suggested that his "resolve seems in doubt." The editorial also accused the Clinton administration of a "disquieting retreat" from principles.

15. Barton Gellman, "Annan Suspicious of UNSCOM Role," *Washington Post*, Jan. 6, 1999. For a similar story that did not refer to purported views of the secretary-general, see Colum Lynch, "US and UN to Spy on Iraq, Aides Say; Focus on Hussein Seen," *Boston Globe*, Jan. 6, 1999.

16. Office of the Spokesman for the Secretary-General, "Highlights of the Noon Briefing, UN Headquarters," Jan. 6, 1999, http://www.unorg/news/ossg/hilites.htm.

17. Editorial, "Back-Stabbing at the U.N.," *Washington Post*, Jan. 7, 1999.

18. Frank H. Murkowski, "Our Toothless Policy on Iraq," *Washington Post*, Jan. 25, 1999.

19. On appeasement issue, see, for example, A.M. Rosenthal, "The Carpet of Contempt," *New York Times*, Jan. 8, 1999. *The New York Post*, not known for its admiration of the UN, was even less temperate in a Jan. 8, 1999, editorial entitled "Kofi Annan, Disgrace": "Annan is an embarrassment at best and a disgrace at worst. Once again, he has reminded the world of the well-intentioned evil that an institution like the United Nations can do." The Annan quote is from his op-ed piece, "Walking the International Tightrope," *New York Times*, Jan. 19, 1999.

20. According to a *New York Times* article, "the United Nations seems to be basking in the glow of a celebrity secretary-general." Barbara Crossette, "Annan's Stratospheric Profile Gives U.N. a New Cause Célèbre," *New York Times*, June 14, 1998.

21. *Congressional Record*, 105th Cong., 2d sess., March 26, 1998, 144, no. 36: H1581.

22. "Statement on the UN and US Policy by Senator John Ashcroft," March 9, 1998, http://www.globalpolicy.org/security/issues/ashcroft.htm.

23. John Gerard Ruggie, currently an aide to the secretary-general, reiterated this point in an op-ed seeking to explain Annan's thinking on Iraq; see Ruggie, "Kofi Annan's Goals on Iraq," *Washington Post*, Jan. 18, 1999.

24. For a thoughtful commentary on this legal dilemma, as seen in the Iraq case, and its implications for the role of the secretary-general, see Ruth Wedgwood, "The Enforcement of Security Council Resolution 687: The Threat of Force Against Iraq's Weapons of Mass Destruction," *American Journal of International Law* 92 (Oct. 1998): 724–28.

25. See, in particular, Annan's speech to the UN Human Rights Commission, in which he argued that "if we allow the United Nations to become the refuge of [an] 'ethnic cleanser' or mass murderer, we will betray the very ideals that inspired the founding of the United Nations." UN Press Release SG/SM/6848, HR/CN/8998, April 7, 1999.

26. United Nations, Department of Public Information, "UN Daily Highlights," March 24, 1999, 2.

27. Judith Miller, "Crisis in the Balkans: United Nations; Security Council Backs Peace Plan and a NATO-Led Force," *New York Times,* June 11, 1999.

28. A vocal advocate of the proposed International Criminal Court and of preventive action in cases of pending genocide, such as Rwanda, Secretary-General Annan told the Human Rights Commission in April 1999 that "we should leave no one in doubt that for the mass murderers, the 'ethnic cleansers,' those guilty of gross and shocking violations of human rights, impunity is not acceptable." See UN Press Release SG/SM/6848, HR/CN/898, April 7, 1999.

29. Thirty years ago, 377 NGOs had consultative status with the Economic and Social Council and another 200 were associated with the Department of Public Information. Today, these numbers have grown to more than 1,350 and 1,550, respectively. United Nations, Report of the Secretary-General, *Arrangements and Practices for the Interaction of Non-Governmental Organizations in All Activities of the United Nations System,* A/53/170, July 10, 1998, p. 2, para. 2.

30. See, for example, the secretary-general's addresses to the World Economic Forum in Davos, United Nations, Press Release SG/SM/99/25, Feb. 1, 1999, and to the U.S. Chamber of Commerce, in which he appealed for its help in lobbying Congress for payment of U.S. arrears, United Nations, Press Release SG/SM/7022, June 8, 1999.

31. There is a large and growing literature on the place of nonstate actors in international affairs and the role of NGOs in the UN system, but core questions of their relationship to global governance are little understood and only rarely addressed. For two articles representing contrasting positions about the extent to which nonstate actors are infringing on roles traditionally reserved for governments, see Jessica T. Mathews, "Power Shift," *Foreign Affairs* 76 (Jan.–Feb. 1997): 50–66; and Anne-Marie Slaughter, "The Real New World Order," *Foreign Affairs* 76 (Sept.–Oct. 1997): 183–97. For a more detailed model that attempts a synthesis of these perspectives, see Wolfgang H. Reinicke, *Global Public Policy: Governing without Government?* (Brookings, 1998). Other relevant works include Steve Charnovitz, "Two Centuries of Participation: NGOs and International Governance," *Michigan Journal of International Law* 18 (winter 1997); Tom Farer, "New Players in the Old Game," *American Behavioral Scientist* 38 (May 1995); P. J. Simmons, "Learning to Live with NGOs, *Foreign Policy* 112 (fall 1998); Thomas G. Weiss,

Beyond UN Subcontracting: Task-Sharing with Regional Security Arrangements and Service-Providing NGOs (St. Martin's Press, 1998); Thomas G. Weiss and Leon Gordenker, eds., *NGOs, the UN and Global Governance* (Boulder, Colo.: Lynne Rienner, 1996); and Peter Willetts, ed., *"The Conscience of the World:" The Influence of Non-Governmental Organizations in the U.N. System* (Brookings, 1996). The Stanley Foundation of Muscatine, Iowa, has published several conference reports dealing with UN-NGO relationships; see, in particular, *The UN System and NGOs: New Relationship for a New Era?* (1994) and *The United Nations and Civil Society: The Role of NGOs* (1999).

32. Perversely, as noted in chapter 8, the architects of the UN system sought to distance its functional activities from its political ones, making it that much harder for success in the former to rub off on the latter. For the views of the most influential functionalist, see David Mitrany, "The Functional Approach to International Organization," *International Affairs* 24 (July 1948): 350–63, and Mitrany, *The Progress of International Government* (Yale University Press, 1933).

33. Department of State, *The United States and the United Nations, Report by the President to the Congress for the Year 1946* (Government Printing Office, 1947), iii.

Index